Storytelling
Folklore
Sourcebook

STORYTELLING FOLKLORE SOURCEBOOK

NORMA J. LIVO
University of Colorado at Denver

SANDRA A. RIETZ
Eastern Montana College

LIBRARIES UNLIMITED, INC.
Englewood, Colorado
1991

LIBRARIES UNLIMITED, INC.
P.O. Box 6633
Englewood, CO 80155-6633

Library of Congress Cataloging-in-Publication Data

Livo, Norma J., 1929-
    Storytelling folklore sourcebook / Norma J. Livo, Sandra A. Rietz.
    xiv, 384 p. 22x28 cm.
    Includes bibliographical references (p. 337) and index.
    ISBN 0-87287-601-2
    1. Storytelling. 2. Tales. 3. Folklore.   I. Rietz, Sandra A.
II. Title.
LB1042.L545   1991
808.5'43--dc20   90-19946
                                                         CIP

TO GEORGE, WHO KNOWS WHERE THE WEST WINDS BEGIN!

N. J. L.

UP ALL NITEY, WRITEY HASH;

PRINT-UM, STICK-UM IN THE TRASH.

ROOTIN' TOOTIN', SOME COMPUTIN',

ED-IT, LOCK-IT, SAVE-IT, KNOCK-IT;

WHERE-DI-GO? WHERE-DI-GO? WHERE-DI-GO?

CRASH!

FIX-IT.....FIX-IT----DENNIS.

THIS BOOK'S FOR YOU.

Y--O--U!

S. R.

Contents

Part 3
Story Artifacts

Part 4
Story Activities

Part 5
The Devices of Memory
in the Oral Narrative

Introduction

Storytelling Folklore Sourcebook presents bits and pieces of many categories of folklore to trigger their possible inclusion in stories we tell, write, and read, but especially tell. All themes and characters we encounter in stories belong to one big interrelated family. We are always being reminded of other stories as we experience story. In addition, we are always unconsciously involved with the quest of human beings to discover themselves, what they believe, and their places in society. The use of motifs, archetypes, and formula heroes aid in this discovery. The values of our world view are part of our stories. As Muriel Rukeyser stated: "The universe is made of stories, not atoms." The more we can understand the significance of words and phrases, the better we can grasp the deeper meanings of stories. We cannot fully understand other peoples unless we are aware of their world view. The broader the recognition of folklore elements in a story, the more meaning it will have for us.

Ernest Boyer, president of the Carnegie Foundation for the Advancement of Teaching said, "To sustain a culture, you need points of common memory, tradition and experience." We have these common points but we have long since lost their meaning. Students at all levels today are reading material which has been homogenized so that the content avoids controversy. Publishers see controversy as costing them sales. This educational homogenization was responsible for basal readers. Diane Ravitch observes, "The denigration of literature and history came with the rise of Dick and Jane."

The widespread cries of alarm that Americans have evolved into a land of cultural illiterates spread by books such as Allan Bloom's *The Closing of the American Mind* and E. D. Hirsch Jr.'s *Cultural Literacy: What Every American Needs to Know*, speak to education as gathering discrete facts. Hirsch's 4,500 item list of words, phrases, names, and dates representing the common vocabulary of the culturally literate is the educational equivalent of Dick and Jane style education. Philosopher Mortimer Adler put it well when he stated, "What facts a student should know is the least important part about an education. A student can cram in information, but unless he really understands it, it's easily forgotten." Plato's *Republic* contains the parable of the cave—humans live in a cave looking at shadows on the wall which contain a little reflection of the truth. Education represents turning from the shadows to the source of light. Plato said we don't know the sources of all things, but we know some things.

Storytelling Folklore Sourcebook aims to bring understanding to how folklore of ancient times still influences us in our speech and actions today. It is by no means comprehensive but it contains information and folklore material that can make us all more multiculturally literate. It could spark an interest that might cause us to explore folklore on our own. That is the true expressions of education—we are never finished and we assume responsibility for our own education.

Material in *Storytelling Folklore Sourcebook* is rich with beginnings and pointers to other sources to explore. Part 1 states the importance of knowing about the folklore of other cultures to add authenticity to stories. Suggested categories are given for collecting folklore.

Part 2 samples the variety of formula heroes from diverse folk cultures as depicted in their folk narratives.

Part 3 looks at artifacts that have special cultural significances which lend meaning to the story itself. Knowing cultural significances and symbolic contents of artifacts and their activities can help the teller know how to invent within the constraints provided by the culture and recognize the boundaries beyond which an invented story violates a culture's memories.

Part 4 explores calendar customs, prognostication practices, and games as reenactments of ritual, of work, of daily living, of war, of politics, of historical events, and of religious mysteries. Also included are magical devices which have the power to entrance, transform, transport and transcend. These include folklore beliefs and superstitions. Even in today's high technology societies, some of these ancient vestiges of beliefs are still part of our lives and we aren't even aware of it.

Part 5 involves devices of memory in the oral narrative and refers to thoughts which are cast in regular, predictable, highly conventional language—prescriptive formulae. These formulae encode important, lasting thoughts. Contrivances such as rhyme, meter, alliteration, synecdoche, metaphor, simile, metonymy, onomatopoeia, chant and rhythm, proverb, allegory, riddle, joke, epithet, and other formula sayings provide internal narrative coherence. The more fluent a person is with a language, the better is the understanding of nuances and humor.

Storytelling Folklore Sourcebook is unique in its presentation of material. It is intended for use by storytellers, teachers, writers, and the curious reader. Storytellers can either use particular material from the book in their stories or be motivated to collect material themselves. Writers can certainly make use of some of the background of ideas we hold today. They too can become interested in collecting similar material. And of course, the curious reader can browse in the materials and enrich the association they bring to other reading. This is a book for all levels of education to use. After all, we are all citizens and users of the land of folklore. Above all, enjoy!

1

Story Voice, Research, and the Storyteller

Brunvand (1978a) identifies three classifications of folk invention: oral, customary, and material. Much of the content of oral folklore is storied—myth, legend, folktale, ballad. The remaining subcategories (folk speech, naming, proverbs and proverbial lore, riddles, verbal puzzles, rhymes, folk poetry, folk song, and folk music) collect wit and wisdom that often appear in stories and lend stories a measure of their meaning in the culture. The customary folklore, superstitions, practices, and festivals are often the subject of stories, or, along with dances, dramas, gestures, and games, figure as principal in-story references. The material folk traditions of architecture, crafts and art, costume, and food provide story detail and imagery. Together, these accumulations of sagacity, comedy, and habit represent the substance of stories.

This book's very limited collection of extra-story material is designed to provide the storyteller with a means of initiating investigations into the conventional folk meanings of stories. References made herein to "knowledge," to "study," and to "knowing" are deliberate invocations of the methods of both orality and of literacy; such knowledge requires experience in the content and language of the folklore, and examination of it. The literate, revivalist storyteller who is obliged to work backward, so to speak, from the mentality of literacy to that of orality can be helped through knowing folklore in both ways. The revivalist teller must learn to think in traditional oral frames of reference, but can be aided—though the paradox is clear—by using the more familiar habits of literacy to achieve a more genuinely oral mentality. Correct and honest interpretations of stories, especially if story materials must be converted from print back to orally composed text, require that the teller make every attempt to become steeped in the folkloric traditions supporting the material.

In order to provide the storyteller with a folkloric resource to support a more powerful and informed storytelling, the authors have selected four general categories of folkloric content for treatment: voice, story characters, story artifacts and activities, and the devices of memory in the oral narrative. The storyteller is encouraged to use this necessarily limited collection to find specific material for story development and enrichment, to find materials for story invention, to learn more about the content, sensibility, and coherence of folklore, to know the folkloric experience through immersion in it, to make pleasing discoveries, to find delight and joy, to find emotion, and to rekindle passion.

Bakhtin (1981) suggests that both "centrifugal" and "centripetal" forces are at work during the making of language (a story). *Centripetal* forces (cultural requirements) pull the storyteller toward the center, the norm of the story, its rules, conventions, and etiquettes. *Centrifugal* forces (acts of individual creativity) pull the storyteller away from the story's norm. Without adequate background about the folk contents of a story, the teller may not be able to move appropriately toward story norms when delivering the story, or know what kind of creative latitude, linguistic and otherwise, is available. The teller who becomes a student of the folkloric substance of the story can better balance story requirements (norms) and invention, and can support a more penetrating delivery. Maintaining a balance between story requirements (form) and invention during story delivery is the responsibility of the storyteller; it always has been. To tell a story well, with power and with honesty, one must know more than just the story, and must achieve a necessary intimacy with its "life world" (Egan 1987, 459). With this requirement in mind, the authors offer the following collection.

1

The Making of Story Voice

FOLKLORE

[... they kis]sed her feet,
[saying: "The creatress of mankind] we call thee;
[The mistr]ess of all the gods be thy name!"
[They went] to the House of Fate,
[Nin]igiku [and] the wise Mama.
[Fourteen mother]-wombs were assembled
To tread upon the clay before her.
[...] Ea says, as he recites the incantation.
Sitting before her, Ea causes her to recite the incantation.
[Mama reci]ted the incantation; when she completed her incantation,
[...] she drew upon her clay.
[Fourteen pie]ces she pinched off; seven pieces she placed on the right.
[Seven pie]ces she placed on the left; between them she placed a brick.
[Ea] was kneeling on the matting; he opened its navel;
[... he c]alled the wise wives.
Of the [seven] and seven mother-wombs, seven brought forth males,
[Seven] brought forth females.
The Mother-Womb, the creatress of destiny,
In pairs she completed them,
In pairs she completed before her.
The forms of the people Mami forms.
In the house of the bearing woman in travail,
    Seven days shall the brick lie.
... from the house of Mah, the wise Mami.
The vexed one shall rejoice in the house of the one in travail.
As the Bearing One gives birth,
May the mother of the child bring forth by [her]self.
(Babylonian childbirth incantation of Aruru-Ishtar as potter and creatress [Pritchard 1950, 99; Neumann 1972, 135-36].)

I ween that I hung / on the windy tree,
    Hung there for nights full nine;
With the spear I was wounded, / and offered I was
    To Odin, myself to myself,
On the tree that none / may never know
    What root beneath it runs.
(Odin hanging on Yggdrasil, the Tree of Fate [Bellows 1923, 60; Neumann 1963, 252].)

These two ancient extracts remind us that birth and death are two of the great mysteries through which the human consciousness is refined and elevated. Both are "Participatory Mystiques" (Neumann 1972), that is, riddles of creation and transformation in the life world which must be directly and personally experienced in order to be *known*. Genuine enlightenment and wisdom are only gained when one lives at the unconscious center of the question, becoming its principal participant. The "mystery," the "something puzzling, [the] something that the human consciousness cannot apprehend, [that] moves the whole man to his depths" (Neumann 1972, 136) is known to the conscious mind and spirit through the agency of the unconscious encounter and the physical ordeal. Rational, dispassionate, scientific (literate) activity, which is characterized by reflection (Egan 1987), provides the outside-in understanding of life's circumstances—an explanation or authoritative discourse (Bakhtin 1981). The logic of reflective examination by displacement is the dissertation (knowledge *about*).

Knowing about a phenomenon is one kind of truth or reality. Knowledge gained through participation in a secret provides an entirely different kind of realization. Participation is charged with emotion and gives rise to a knowledge born of passion, a higher form of spiritual enlightenment than that afforded by analysis. The rational thinker would be inclined to view with suspicion and a sense of illegitimacy the insights derived from passionate personal engagement with one of life's mysteries. Still, participation (magical and mystical experience) as a way of finding truth is a reliable and more ancient means of understanding elemental forces in the cosmos than is displaced scientific study. From the point of view of the knowledge gained through participation, the explanations of reason represent "failed magic" (Adler 1986).

Folklore is the personal, emotional, inside-out content of life encounter, distilled to universal principles, smoothed and rounded into formulae by the efforts of the human mind to *remember*. It is both magical and practical. It is what people know, do, think, and make, primarily as a result of participation in and direct engagement with their worlds. As a symbolic and metaphoric product, it exists as one vehicle by which unconscious being is reflected for purposes of conscious recognition (Neumann 1972). It is also the ritual means by which people can initiate the participation mystique.

Folklore, the principal vehicle of human memory in the primary oral culture, encodes a body of knowledge built up through the passionate experiences of a people living in a universe. It is a legitimate compendium of observations and truths that represent collective wisdom. Folklore is not some frivolous drivel of the primitive (read *savage*) mind, nor unscientific misunderstandings and concoctions that reduce the quality of life. Folklore, the result of a different, but equally legitimate, kind of inquiry, understands the universe through the devices of metaphor and emotion. It is not bad science; it is simply not *about* science. Its principal mode of investigation operates by direct human participation in the great mysteries of the cosmos. Its purpose is to provide human communities with ways of living *in* nature, not of controlling it. Folklore is the "personal persuasive discourse" (Bakhtin 1981) of culture, the "voice" of a people in response to their direct encounters with the riddles and secrets that drive the cycle of life.

MYSTERY

Mystery—enigma—is the essence of human experience. Even as science pursues causative principles, we live in wonder and awe made, if anything, all the more intense, exquisite, and terrible by the explanations afforded us by those who study the natural world. Who cannot marvel at rainbows, despite our understanding of the principle of light refraction? Who cannot sense the power made explicit by the germination of a simple seed, without ever doubting the botanical information provided in textbooks? Knowing how and why something happens does not diminish its mystery or its secret power. Mystery has its own special energy or life force. To know mystery, we must enter into and live it rather than participate in dispassionate, disengaged examination of it. Mystery is in *being* in a riddle, not in explaining it. Science and mystery are not about the same kind of knowledge. Mystery is not bad science; mystery transcends science.

Mystery is at the center of folklore. All folklores, (informal) folk religions, (formal) canonical religions, and cultural cosmogonies admit to the existence of mysteries, great cosmic secrets. Mysteries are connected to magic; experiences which seem to be supernatural, for which causation cannot be explained, or which are so profound that scientific explanations cannot account for the effect these experiences have on human life and thought. Universal mysteries, explained and unexplained, include such wonders as conception, birth, death, spiritual ecstasies, dreams, healing experiences, the powers of prayer, and other encounters such as out-of-the-body experiences, déja-vu, visions of supernatural beings, hearing of disembodied voices, altered states of consciousness, memories of other lives, and reincarnation. The seasonal cycle (birth and death), the regeneration of life in the spring, the magical fertility of the soil, the fecundity of plants and animals, and the wheelings of sun, moon, planets, and stars are as amazing today, even in literate, scientific societies, as they have ever been. Folklore (and scientific lore) is what people know, have said, have made, and have done in light of these mysteries.

The heart of mystery is *transformation*—explained or unexplained alterations of states or conditions of being—the secret alchemy of change. Early, primary oral (preliterate) societies often thought that direct human intervention and participation was necessary to bring about change, such as ritual to bring the rainy season, to cause the germination of seed, to ensure the harvest, or to call the sun back on the shortest day of the year. Much folklore is associated with peoples' beliefs and habits in relation to mysterious transformations which took place around them and in them, and upon which they depended for survival. Some folklore, for instance, knowing that the thickness of an onion's skin at harvest is a good indicator of the severity of the coming winter, is no more than good observation. It is, however, no less a wonder even when we can explain it. Folklore conserves and preserves such information in the forms of stories, sayings, riddles, rhymes, and formulaic language. Peoples who know their environments, and who are able to save that knowledge for future generations, are better equipped to survive.

Some folklore casts mysteries in the form of extended metaphors. The Hidatsa Sioux say that the great Wakantanka heard the prayers of the summer flowers (annuals) when the flowers were about to die. Wakantanka created the rainbow from their petals, making for them a new, transformed life. In the rainbow, the summer flowers find regeneration and rebirth. The summer flower rainbow is not bad science; it is a way of engaging a mystery. Even simple riddles and jokes touch upon the profound: "What goes first on four legs, then on two legs, then on three legs?" [Man.] Some lore provides support for individuals who must personally enter into a mystery and suffer the ordeal of change, such as a woman in childbirth or the hero of a sacrifice.

Contemporary (literate, reflective, scientific) societies have no less reason to marvel at the phenomena of natural change than did their ancestral cultures. The powerful transformations that drive and define our lives do not go away because of scientific inquiry, nor does our awe of them. The lore of the ancients, folk observation and metaphor, is as fresh and useful (and necessary) a way of knowing and engaging the great and lesser mysteries today as it was before the advent of literacy and the development of rational (disengaged-from-the-living-experience) thinking.

In every culture, whether ancient or modern, scientifically sophisticated or not, mysteries are regarded as sacrosanct. The greater the mystery (life, death, rebirth/regeneration/reincarnation, conception/initiation, and seasonal mysteries), the more likely it is to be "protected" by ritual and protocol. Joseph Campbell (1988) suggests that practices attending mysteries give evidence of beliefs in the existence of covenants made between humans and gods, and that continued human survival depends upon direct and correct human intervention in natural transformative processes.

Some mysteries are of such critical importance that they must be engaged only by specially sanctioned individuals (guides) who know the proper procedures, incantations, and rites. The more powerful the mystery (transformation), the more control that must be exercised in its invocation. Select individuals are prepared for and initiated (or called) into certain mysteries, usually after a prescribed period of apprenticeship. Such initiates are, in a generic sense and sometimes by definition, priests and priestesses, invested with the power to call the mystery down upon the people. They are able to animate the mystery, to live it, and to bring that heightened inside-the-enigma level of awareness and emotion to the uninitiated. Privileged, secret information possessed by initiates and the resulting *sight* that is ordinarily forbidden imposes burdens of responsibility. The initiate is not personally powerful but is a servant of a greater power. In ancient practices, initiates sometimes faced personal death in order to invoke a sacred experience. Often, the initiate was the one who had to enter the mystery first and be transformed in order for others to be able to follow. To open the mystery, the initiate was often required to fast, pray, or otherwise prepare before inducing an extraordinary experience. Such preparatory ritual itself commonly resulted in an altered state of consciousness, a different kind of attention and awareness.

STORY AS MYSTERY

Story is a reference to orally composed text—to the practices, tactics/strategies, and effects of *orality*. It is creation of the primary oral art form out of in-mind memory for the devices and contents of oral discourse, without recourse to written language. Story is one of the greater mysteries. Its existence as archetype in human memory is a marvel, as are all the phenomena associated with storytelling. No one knows where story comes from, though there is good reason to believe that it is an artifact of the nature and operation of mind. Even if story evolved as a result of accretion of and organization of memory-schema and knowledge structures, one can better apprehend its remarkable achievement by remembering metaphorical references to gods and gifts. The human ability to story both preserves information and transforms it. Storying is, by itself, a participation mystique in which one *makes* knowledge and begets change by imposing "formal coherence on a virtual chaos of human events, a primary and irreducible form of human comprehension, and *the* central instance or function of human mind" (Rosen 1986). Story is a primary act of mind (Hardy 1968). It is the principal organizational frame for folklore, and is the foundation for all other human activity.

The mystery of story, like all mysteries, is the force which lies under and animates the form (Derrida 1978). Story is animate, possessed of its own "living energy" (Rosen 1986), having its own characteristic set of emotions and meanings, and creating its own psychological reality. It is a cognitive process, a way of knowing and thinking which is good and positive, but which is different from the nature and effect of written language. Story causes interior transformations of consciousness (Ong 1982); it is a way of thinking that is a legitimate state of awareness (Egan 1987). From the point of view of the literate individual, trained to the distant and disengaged (critical/reflective) habit of written language, the nature of *story consciousness* appears to be an altered state—trancelike. Story holds both teller and audience in *thrall* (enthrall), in *chant* (enchant), in an emotional state of awareness which is a different reality—story reality. Story consciousness is participatory rather than reflective, drawing teller and audience into themselves—their life energy—through the various devices of oral composition: rhyme, meter, alliteration, synecdoche, metaphor and metonymy, onomatopoeia, parallel and repeat structure, chant, movement, rhythm, vision, and participation. Lord (1964) suggests that the power of story to entrance resides in its ability to take physical control of the body through the effects of sound — the music of voice — creating a "somatic rhythm." The life force of the story directs the pulses of the mind by synchronizing with those of the body. Teller and listener know the story not as an object for reflection and critical analysis, but through the intensity of emotion and existence; that is, through immersion.

> The audience does not so much listen to it [a story] ... as live it. ... [R]epetitive meter, rhythmic body movements, ... the pattern of formulae, and the story ... set up conditions of enchantment that impress the message on the minds of the hearers. The techniques of the skilled performer generate a relaxed, half-hypnotized pleasure in the audience (Egan 1987, 453).

Story is a seduction. It creates a receptive (collective unconscious) state "in which audiences receive the fundamental messages of their cultures" (Egan 1987, 453). "[M]yths operate in men's minds without their being aware of the fact" (Levi-Strauss 1969, 12). When story is treated as mystery and engaged under the proper ritual conditions, the storytelling itself becomes a situation "characterized by heightened emotion" (Egan 1987, 453). "What they [the participants] hear in it awakens a whole gamut of harmonics" (Levy-Bruhl 1910/1985, 369). The teller and the audience go together into the heart of the mystery — into the living substance of the story.

The genuine magic of storytelling happens when teller and listeners *become* the story. This insideness or story-state-of-being is the essence of the mystery. It cannot be captured, only experienced. The messages of the culture are bound in memory by the emotional state of the telling, by the devices of orality, and by the touch of mystery and magic. Story is a very powerful teacher. Study of a literature — knowledge of story and message gained through critical analysis — touches only the dead skin, the dried bones (Rosen 1986). Examination and explication are the tactics of literacy, or written language, which work from the outside and which result in loss of the living essence of the story. If story comes first in the development of literature and language, then the altered state of consciousness is the derived or "second" state — literacy is the consciousness of reflective scholarship, a state in which the magic fails.

Comprehension of oral text occurs when the listener enters into it, experiencing an emotional and even physical being in the story such that story reality becomes the world all around. Orality, the medium of the oral literature and of the special mystery of story, works through passionate, personal engagement in experience — entrancing or causing enchantment (enthralling, ensorcelling, spellbinding, bewitching). The magic and mystery operate at a level of knowing that is accessed directly, through immediate participation, *Knowing* in the story is not a function of the workings of reflective and analytic schema. The devices of literacy, on the other hand, are those of reflective thinking, displacement of reader from text, and disengagement of perspective from the internal, subjective experience. The rational mind works by analysis, which, in turn, places the reader outside the story as a nonparticipant.

The force driving the mystery of story is the energy of *making*, of transformation. Not only can the devices of story (orality) cause transformations of human consciousness and bring people into its mystery, story is the principal tool for gaining access to the other great mysteries of life and living. "Most of the world's cultures and its great religions have at their sacred core a story" (Egan 1987, 456). Because of its power to make truths and realities, story is a vehicle which allows people to enter into the living energies of other phenomena: life, death, birth, rebirth, and regeneration. The logic of myth (story) is tied to the principle of metaphor. "[M]etaphor is not a later embellishment of language but is one of its fundamental modes — a primary form of discursive thought" (Levi-Strauss 1962, 102). It is "one of the foundations of all [our] mental activity"

(Egan 1987, 456), a way of organizing memory, thinking, and knowing. Through metaphor, and story as the archetypal metaphor, we are able to achieve the consciousness needed to know mystery. Story, then, is a maker of mystery, a conjurer, a magician, "an immediate, living, active agent" (Peabody 1975, 1-2), which takes us into the realities of the mysteries, great and small, through the power of the living word.

Story reiterates the greatest magic of all. A story is, during the telling, living proof of regeneration. Every time a story is told, it is reborn, and we enter again into its secrets. It is not so surprising, then, that listeners will ask for retellings of familiar stories. The listener is not expressing a dispassionate need to review the facts, but rather a quite passionate need to live within the story consciousness again and to be drawn into its special emotional way of knowing.

STORYTELLER AS INITIATE INTO MYSTERY

The storyteller lets loose the story force, the living energy that is the story, using the devices of orality—language, voice, and music. The story is an animate thing. The storyteller quite literally breathes the story to give it life, to reanimate it. But story is a mystery, and anyone who would animate a mystery must also do its purpose and work its will. Such is the nature of mystery; its magic cannot and should not be bent to the service of the deliberate, personal schemes of any individual. The storyteller becomes the tool of the story, the channel for the life energy of the thing. Tellers are filled up by the essence of the story, and deliver it by allowing themselves to be taken by it and belong to it. The storyteller lives the consciousness of the story by transcending self and circumstance during the telling and, by doing so, takes the listeners into the mystery.

One would think that to be a storyteller, all one must do is learn a story, then let the story take over. It sounds so simple. Perhaps it is a necessary paradox having to do with things of power, that at the same time a story takes control of the teller, the teller must be under control. The tellers must hold themselves open, acquiescing to the story, purging personal obstructions, maintaining the perfect concentration in order to let the story consciousness come in. Storytelling is a form of controlled possession: the story takes the teller; therefore, the teller must be ready. Practice helps to clear the way. Knowledge of the story and considerations relative to elements of language and paralanguage, audience, and delivery help remove impediments of personality and improve real ability. But storytellers, most importantly, must tell their stories with concentration, imagination, honesty, and wisdom, out of the real learning of their own lives (Hymes 1982). The storyteller, in other words, must assume that level of discipline with regard to stories and their meanings that provides a rich and diverse background in the lore of the culture in order to tell a powerful, emotionally compelling story. To learn and retell a story, while at the same time refusing to become a student of the story itself, disempowers the story. Such storytelling is retailing, not telling (Hymes 1982).

It is not at all unreasonable to think of the storyteller as priest or priestess. In ancient (and contemporary preliterate) societies, the teller of a story relinquishes his or her personal identity to become the teller, the old or ancient one. Long and rigorous apprenticeships commonly attend becoming the storyteller. Customs regulate the telling of stories, each mystery to its proper time in the greater cycles. Stories and their artifacts are often subjected to specific ritual before and after use and are considered sacred. The storyteller is a medium for direct communication between people and their gods, a transformative tool in the mystery.

THE POWER OF LORE IN STORY—
STORY VOICE

The life force of the told story resides in its *voice*. Voice is not the simple matter of sound making or talking to tell a story. Voice is the living power of the story or *the word* (meaning "event" [Ong 1982]) which initiates and maintains the heightened emotion of the mystery it engages. The word happens when a story takes the storyteller.

The storyteller is a better servant to the story, and is better able to give it voice, if the teller knows the story in a passionate way. The common images associated with passion have to do with desire, infatuation, and perhaps vehemence, and are judged by the rational, reflective mind to be inappropriate. However, passion in composition of the oral art form means *with fire* or *with power*, and is a reference to calling the mystery. The passionate storyteller is moved by the story because he or she has the sight of the initiated into its profound meaning.

Passion begins with concentration, study, rigorous preparation, knowledge, and wisdom. The storyteller engages the mystery of the story by knowing the story and understanding its references, its content, its place in the cultural cosmogony, and its lore. Story lore includes the organization or pattern of the story, its motif and archetypal contents, its language, its poetic devices, and also its references to the folklore. Not only is the story a part of a larger body of folklore, it organizes folkloric elements according to cultural convention, and thus teaches the comprehensive cosmogony of the community. The storyteller must know story meaning, through knowledge of its content, in order to give the story its voice. Authentic (passionate) storytelling requires that the teller know a story from the inside, as real and genuine personal experience, thereby "turning [the story] into internal persuasive discourse." Without such passionate, personal, "life-world" (Ong 1982) knowledge, the storyteller is reduced to a mere reciter, an "inflexible mimic" (Rosen 1986). Inside knowledge of a story is gained by knowing its place in the folklore and what it and its contents mean.

2

Research and the Storyteller

INTRODUCTION

The storyteller who can tell a story's meaning such that its mysteries are revealed is also a student of folklore. The story finds its voice in the teller turned student/researcher; the teller provides the story with greater knowledge and wisdom, and becomes a clearer vehicle. The informed storyteller empowers the story and renders an honest telling.

Many worthwhile resources are available for teller research, including motif indexes, archetype studies, examinations of folk wisdom, discussions of superstititon and the supernatural, collections of folk remedies, dictionaries of folk language and expressions, encyclopedias of folklore, and collections of stories, riddles, rhymes, jokes, and the like. Substantial background can be found accompanying story collections themselves. The serious storyteller will eventually need to look beyond the text of the story to learn to tell the story well. The more the teller is able to learn about the many elements of a particular story, the clearer the voice of the story will be. One common obstruction to the telling of a powerful story is a lack of knowledge in the teller.

Rather than describing the process of doing research in depth (that is for other volumes), the authors prefer to provide the reader with an in-depth example of what one would collect when telling a story. This sample of research from many sources provides just a glimpse of Finnish legends, proverbs, and folklore.

SAMPLE FINNISH FOLKLORE

- Finns are wizards and witches who control wind, rain, and frost, according to their neighbors.

- People in the Middle Ages spoke of Finns carrying the wind around in a bag or bringing a storm under control by tying three knots in a rope.

- A dominant motif in Finnish weather lore is fear of frost, the sudden freeze that can destroy a year's work. (During the famine of 1696, early frost ruined most of the crops, and a third of the population died.)

- Frost is the son of the North Wind. He dwells in Pohja, somewhere beyond Lapland.

- Frost bites the leaves off the trees and the grass off the meadows. Frost freezes stones or peels the bark off the birch trees in the north. He comes roaring south with such power that he can freeze the milk in the ewe, the foal in the mare, the housewife's hand in the bread dough.

- October 18 is the day the fox pisses on the birch trees (the day the leaves turn yellow in the autumn).

- The smooth days of January will be paid for in February and March.

- The sun at Christmas could mean frost at harvesttime.

- The colder the winter, the warmer the summer.

- If one cuts firewood without a hat in April, he will work the fields in a fur coat in May.

- The Finnish year has eight seasons, beginning with spring, spring/summer, summer, summer/autumn, and autumn, and winter has tree stages: autumn/winter (November and December), high winter (January and February), and winter/spring (March and April).

- May is "seed time," July is "hay time," October is "mud time," November is "dead time."

- May 18, the day of Eric: Cold Eric is a good sign; warm Eric, a bad one. Rain on Eric's day means a good year for hay. If you cannot hear the cuckoo on Eric's day, you will not find merry harvesters in the fall. Eric's day is the day to let the cattle out from their long winter in the cowshed.

- Rain on Easter Sunday brings a chilly summer. A sunny Easter means a good crop in the fall. For berry pickers, rain at Easter is good luck.

- If a cat sits looking out the window, it means rain is coming.

- Young cattle are nervous before bad weather.

- When you slaughter a pig and find it has a long spleen, the winter will be long too.

- If a cow's droppings are frozen in September, they will thaw in October.

- If the lanes are full of snow on February 2, so the bins will be full of corn in the autumn.

- If March does not show the ground, then neither will April.

- There will be as much rain in the summer as there is foggy weather in March.

- If a dog pulls its feet up high while walking, a change in the weather is coming.

- Pigs carry straw into their sleeping places before cold weather comes. When warm weather comes, they carry the straw back out.

- If the magpie, the crow, and the hawk are quarreling, rainy weather is coming.

- When flies are eager to bite people, rain is coming.

- If waterfalls are roaring loudly, bad weather is coming.

- When smoke goes from the roof straight to the ground, bad weather is coming.

- When bubbles are rising on the surface of the coffee and they hold together, good weather is coming. If the bubbles break up, weather you do not need is coming.

- In frosty weather, horses are lazy and just lie in their stalls.

- If the pig wallows in a puddle before the first of May, the summer will be cold.

- When goats come home from the field in the middle of the day, then rain is coming.

- If soot on the bottom of the pot burns, snowfall will come.

- When an old cow raises her head high and sniffs the air, soon a change to nasty weather will come.

- When the cows come home with hay pieces dropping out of their mouths, then rain will come.
- If it is raining on New Year's Day, it will rain when it is cutting and haymaking season.
- If a horse yawns, rain is coming.
- When one's ears are tickling, rain will come.
- If the cock is busy singing in the evening, it will rain the next day.
- Frogs croaking on dry ground means rain.
- If a cat sleeps with her head upside down, bad weather is coming.
- If fish are jumping high, a drizzle is coming.
- In Finland, taking it easy is a hard job.
- In wartime Finns said, "They ran out of intelligence so they handed out morale."
- Men search through the wisdom of the past to find justification for their present foolishness.
- Stubbornness is a virtue if one is not stubborn about it.
- Ukko is the god of thunder.
- Ikonsaari (old man's island) is the island of the thundergod.
- The Northern Lights are reflections off the shields of the Valkyries who escort fallen warriors to Valhalla.
- The rainbow is the sickle or bow of the thunder god, whose arrow is lightning.
- Ukko dressed in blue and pursued evil spirits and shot arrows at his enemies. These arrows fell to earth in the form of stones and anyone who possessed these stones was especially protected.

Creation

There was water everywhere, and an eagle flew over it looking for a dry place to lay her eggs. Seeing the knee of the sorcerer Vainamoinen, the eagle laid her egg on the knee, taking it for solid ground. As the magician Vainamoinen wakened and moved, the half-hatched egg fell into the water and the yolk separated, forming the moon and the sun. The crusted shell made the firm earth and stars.

- The universe was plunged in darkness when a hero, usually a small person, came to deliver the sun, moon, and stars from the monster who had concealed them in his body. The hero then freed himself from the monster by various magic devices.
- The universe was held up by a *simsi*, a column or tree of life.
- Pygmies live on the far horizon where the sky meets the earth. These pygmies hunt birds with bow and arrows.
- *Manala*, meaning land beneath the earth, was identified with *tuonela* or land of death.
- *Pohjala* is the north land or Lapland.
- The Great Oak is a favorite subject of ballads.
- The cuckoo is regarded as a bird of good humor.

- Ilmarinen forged a woman in gold but was disappointed when he laid her on his couch, only to find that she was cold and lifeless.

- Vainamoinen fashioned the *kantele* from the giant mandible of a fish, stringing Aino-maiden's hair across the distant ends to make the five strings of the instrument. He played his ballads on it and as he played, animals became tame, harmony ruled over the countryside, and even the weather changed for the better.

The Woodpecker

When the great god Ukko went wandering among the katas in Lapland, he saw an old woman busy with her baking. Because he was hungry, he asked for a loaf of bread.

She kneaded a roll and baked it and was about to give it to him, but then she glanced at it and said, "No, that's much too big for the likes of you! I can't spoil beggars who come a-knocking at my door, so I'll make you another roll half the size."

So she kneaded a second loaf and baked it. Again when she gave it a look, she cried, "Why waste flour on a mere vagabond? One half the size will fill *your* stomach just as well."

These remarks made Ukko angry. Then and there he turned her into a woodpecker who pecks and pecks, yet never finds enough to eat.
(Sperry 1971.)

The Kalevala

The national folk epic of Finland, *The Kalevala* ("land of heroes"), is lyrical, yet full of tall-tale extravagance and homey realism. It was composed over the centuries by Finnish and Karelian folk singers and passed on in the oral tradition. *The Kalevala* is the longest epic in the world, with 22,975 lines. One could say it became "frozen" in print in 1835, when the "Old Kalevala" (Lonnrot 1835) was published, followed by an 1849 edition (Lonnrot 1849) with additional material. As for so much of our oral literature, print has been both a blessing and a curse—good news, bad news. The blessing, of course, is that the material is available to read and study; there is no need for a teller who remembers and can tell it. The curse is that no further embellishments and variations will be added. The story has come to an end. Even native Finnish speakers are losing many of the meanings for rich, obsolete idioms and losing contact with the older culture. *The Kalevala* has become history and has also lost touch with today's Finnish culture.

The folk traits discovered by analyzing *The Kalevala* include some basic human values. The hero Vainamoinen, singer of the magic songs, is respected for his wisdom. He is referred to as the eternal sage, yet he is also recognized for his pranks. His brother Ilmarinen is appreciated for his craftsmanship and ingenuity. He discovers bog iron and is called upon to forge the magic Sampo, which grinds out things to eat, money, and things to sell. He is a perfectionist. Present-day Finns alluded to this discovery and refinement of iron when they nicknamed one of their recent Olympic winners "The Ironman."

Then there is Lemminkainen, the boastful, reckless one. He is full of thoughts of pretty girls and claims a bride for whom he must perform incredible tasks. While off to perform one of these tasks, he is "hacked into five pieces and hewed into eight fragments," which are sent floating down the river of hell. Lemminkainen's old mother knows there is something wrong and finds out from the sun what happened. She orders Ilmarinen to forge a rake for her with which she will rake the river. Piece by piece she rakes up all that is left of her son, fits the pieces together, knits the veins, and binds them using skill, prayer, and magic spells. She then calls upon the bird of honey, the bee, to bring her honey from the pots of Ukko the Creator. She annoints her son's body with the honey and restores him to life.

In Lemminkainen's mother we discover the persistence, wisdom, and powers the women of *The Kalevala* possess. The Finnish tradition assumes that females can accomplish and succeed as well as males. In fact, to illustrate the Finnish regard for the equal state of men and women, there are no pronouns in the Finnish language for "he" and "she." There are only words such as *han* and *se*, which translate for either sex according to usage.

The Kalevala contains jousts of wisdom, monsters, magic, and a great variety of charms. There are charms for bewitching, for ransom, against disease, to prevent misadventure, and for banishment. There is also a story of the creation of the world and the origin of snakes and bears. Throughout this epic, we can discover peasant beliefs and images of domestic life along with the intellectual sorcery. All through the narrative, a love of nature is clearly evident. There is a poetic, lyrical mood. This is because the stories were originally passed on orally by folk singers, accompanied by a *kantele* (a type of harp).

Traditionally two singers would sit facing each other on a bench, with their right hands clasped together. The first singer would tell one of the stories, and when he was finished he would lean back and the other singer would retell the same story. The second singer would try to outdo the first teller by inventing his own descriptions and incorporating lyrical rhymes, proverbs, and magical charms. It was a poetic duel. In this way the stories were preserved and traveled across Finland.

The Kalevala has influenced not only Finnish art and music (Sibelius based his music on *The Kalevala*) but also American literature as well. Longfellow used the meter of the Finnish epic in *Hiawatha*. Many Finns settled in the North Woods area of the United States, and Paul Bunyan's Babe the Blue Ox might be a variation of Vainamoinen's huge blue elk and Ilmarinen's giant ox. It appears that *The Kalevala* has had bits and pieces transported to America; maybe we can put the pieces together as Lemminkainen's mother did.

Epics provide continuing material for the storyteller to choose from, and allow the teller to close each telling with a "teaser" for the next session—for example, "Next time, you will hear about how Vainamoinen searches for his lost harp made from a pikebone and finds a solution while having a conversation with a birch tree." Many epic stories do not have a particular order, so the storyteller is free to pick and choose. Using epic material is helpful for maintaining continuity in telling stories to the same group.

WEAVING FOLKLORE FRAGMENTS INTO A STORY

As the storyteller bathes in the culture of the Finns, a certain authenticity and a sense of confidence begins to emerge. Using this background, a tale also begins to emerge. Our example here is one of the "Magic Tales," or *Taiga Tarinoita*. This folk story of the old woman selfishly hoarding bread is one of the basic lessons in Finnish literature. The Finns are gracious hosts and hostesses, sometimes to the point of pushing food (and coffee) on unwilling guests. Using this sense of the culture, the tale's outline forms easily.

Magic Tales or *Taiga Tarinoita*

The venerable old storyteller (*sadunkertoja*) Eric sat on a glacier-smoothed rock with the people of the village gathered around him. His grey beard wiggled as he talked. The long summer day was clear and bright.

"We Finns know that taking it easy is a hard job.

"We Finns are wizards and witches who control the wind, rain, and frost. We carry the wind around in a bag and we can stop a storm by tying three knots in a rope.

"We Finns know there was once water everywhere and that the eagle was looking for a dry place to lay her eggs. She was flying far and fast in her search when she suddenly saw the knee of the old, wise sorcerer Vainamoinen sticking out of the primordial sea. Eagle thought she had found solid ground, so she laid her egg on the top of the knee.

"After a long time, Vainamoinen started to stretch and move as he awakened. As he moved, the half-hatched egg fell into the water. The yolk separated, forming the moon and the sun. The crushed shell became the firm earth and the stars in the sky.

"That is how the world began.

"We Finns also know that Ukko, the god of thunder, lives over there on Ukonsaari, the old man's island. That is Ukko's island. When we see a rainbow, we are seeing Ukko's bow and his arrows are lightning. He pursues evil spirits and shoots his lightning bolt arrows at his enemies. His arrows fall to earth in the form of meteorites, and anyone who finds these stones is especially protected.

"We Finns tell the story of the day the great god Ukko, all dressed in blue, went wandering among the *kataja*, or juniper, in Pohjala or Lapland. He had been working hard chasing the evil spirits when he came upon an old woman baking bread. It smelled soooo good.

"Even mighty Ukko gets hungry, so he asked the old woman for a loaf of bread.

"She set about to knead the dough, shape it into a roll, and bake it. The whole time her mouth puckered up into a point. Her eyebrows were in a frown.

"When she was about to give the bread roll to Ukko, she glanced at it and snatched it back. 'No! That is much too big for the likes of you. If I give you such a big roll you will tell others and then every beggar that comes a-knocking at my oak door will expect the same. No, I'll bake you another roll half the size of this one.'

"So, she kneaded a second loaf and baked it. Her mouth puckered into a sharper point and she looked troubled. Once more she gave this bread a long look and cried, 'Why waste good flour on such a vagabond! One half this size will surely fill *your* stomach just as well.'

"All of this made Ukko as angry as a steam kettle just before it blows. Right then and there he turned her into a woodpecker who spends its lifetime pecking, pecking, and pecking and yet never finding enough to eat.

"With that Ukko sat on the ground with his back nestled against the mighty oak tree, and watched the Northern Lights, which are really reflections off the shields of the Valkyries as they escort fallen warriors to Valhalla.

"Ukko muttered as he watched, 'In wartime they run out of intelligence so they hand out morale.'"

Eric the sadunkertoja continued, "We Finns are wizards and witches who control the wind, rain, and frost. The frog is croaking on dry ground. The fish are jumping high. I see a horse yawn. I see a dog pulling his feet up high as he walks. The magpie, crow, and hawk are quarreling. The cows are coming home with pieces of hay dropping out of their mouths. Go home because, as we Finns know, surely the rains will follow."

2

Story Characters

The characters who populate stories are a significant part of a culture's folklore. They are not ourselves, certainly, though they represent the essences of human nature, nor are they portrayals of specific, random individuals displaying the idiosyncratic habits of real persons. Story characters are universals. When we find bits of ourselves in their behaviors, we are lifted up out of the mundane and take a step towards immortality.

Because the characters have the profiles of archetypes, they can seem unreal when compared to the people with whom we associate daily. But they are real. They inhabit an alternative world, a different universe, their own "real life" world, in which reality is defined by universals. When we enter their worlds, we live their lives. We learn their lessons, make their mistakes, and are glorified by their achievements. We engage their experiences through the vehicle of the story, then disengage ourselves from their circumstances, while retaining perhaps a greater clarity and perspective with regard to our own. They are our power and our weakness. They exaggerate every human potential, good and bad, that we possess. When they act on those potentials in stories, we act with them, but we are not obliged to suffer the consequences of their actions.

Story characters are patterns or mental models—formulaic constructions having psychic reality for individuals and for cultural communities. They interact in stories according to cultural convention and make their appearances in keeping with prescription. They are a substantial part of story memory. The storyteller composes or constructs the story using the distinct schemata which define characters in the story. Meeting these individuals outside the contexts of the stories in which we typically find them can help us to better understand how they work to make story meaning. Characters have significances—dynamics, sensibilities, and symbolisms—for specific cultures which can escape the uninitiated storyteller, and which can, once known, contribute to the effectiveness of a storytelling. The good storyteller knows and understands the characters of the story beyond the limits of the single narrative, and thus is able to infuse them with an authenticity that brings them to the audience.

The story characters presented in the following chapters have been researched for symbolic and folkloric significance. In these character categories are culture bringers/tricksters, the people of faerie, and some tall tale characters. The information is intended to help the storyteller with character development and interpretation, so that story characters may retain their cultural definition.

3

Culture Bringers/Tricksters

INTRODUCTION

The *culture hero* (transformer/trickster/creator) is the culture bringer, usually an animal character living in a mythical age (perhaps what the Australian aborigines would call "the dream time") and who is capable of doing supernatural and magical deeds. The culture hero gives foods; teaches hunting, gathering, arts, and crafts; demonstrates humor and morality; and originates ceremony, taboo, and general behavior. Some culture heroes also give literature: folk stories, songs, and dances. While cycles of culture-hero stories exist to elaborate their character, the culture hero is often said to be responsible for winning all of the other stories that ever were away from their original owners—who were hoarding them—in order to give them to the people.

Skiriki

```
HE--E--E--E--E--E--E
YO-E-YO HA
E-YU  E-YU  E-YO  E-RO
HE--E--E--E--E--E--E
AH!  TIRUS TAKAWAHA
      TIRATPARI--HO!
E-RO  HE--E--E--E--E
      TATARA KITA-WIRA
HAWA RE-RAWIRA
HE--E--E--E--E--E  YO!*
```

*["O great expanse of blue sky, see me roaming here, again on the warpath, lonely; I trust in you to protect me!"]

("Coyote Warrior Song," Chawi Pawnee [Curtis 1987, 111-12, 129].)

```
I HAVE MADE THE MOON!
I HAVE MADE THE MOON!
HURLING IT HIGH
IN THE FOUR DIRECTIONS.
TO THE EAST I THREW IT
TO RUN ITS APPOINTED COURSE.
```

I HAVE MADE THE STARS!
I HAVE MADE THE STARS!
ABOVE THE EARTH I THREW THEM.
ALL THINGS ABOVE I'VE MADE
AND PLACED THEM TO ILLUMINE.

(Coyote's song crediting himself with making of the moon and stars. Pima. Dobie, Boatright, and Ransom 1965, 73.)

According to Navaho and Cochiti traditions, Coyote is responsible for scattering the stars; their random placement is because of his mischief making and typical clumsiness. The Navajo say that after the old men had made the sun and moon and sewn them in place, they laid out all the stars and began to stitch them up as well. Coyote ran into the workshop, where he deliberately kicked the pile of stars. The stars scattered across the heavens and remained, just as they are today. The Cochiti say that the jar in which the stars were kept while they were being hung in the sky was entrusted to Coyote's care. Only the Shield Stars (dipper), the Pot Rest Stars (three stars), and the Siwasila (morning star) had been properly placed when Coyote dropped the jar, spilling the stars across the heavens.

(Dobie, Boatright, and Ransom 1938.)

The time of the culture hero precedes that of humankind. (Some culture heroes are credited with the creation of the people.) In that time, animals are able to talk, the world is often cold and dark, monsters inhabit seas, caves, and mountain tops, and food is scarce. The culture hero steals the sun and moon out of captivity to bring light and warmth, destroys the monsters, finds and releases game animals, locates medicinal and food plants, and makes bargains and does tricks in order to secure those things that are needed for living. Some culture heroes then bring mankind to earth. When their work is done, most culture heroes, with few exceptions (Sen'deh of the Kiowa), retire from active involvement in men's affairs. They wait "above" until they will be needed again, perhaps at the end of the world.

The culture hero is clearly not the omnipotent creator of all things. Creation seems to have occurred before his arrival. He is more the reshaper of things. Because he finds a world which is hostile to life, particularly human life, he rearranges it and transforms it. Some of his transformations are done deliberately—stealing the summer so that the world may have warmth—while others occur because he makes mistakes or behaves foolishly. On these occasions, he is portrayed as a somewhat human figure who has flaws and weaknesses. In yet other cases, he initiates a change in the status of a thing, but does not determine what its final disposition shall be. Instead, he may oversee a casting of lots among the animals or allow the animals to debate or to bargain with one another. When Coyote steals summer and daylight, for instance, the animals decide how long summer will stay and how long the day will be. Though the animals may argue selfishly, the resulting arrangement always benefits everyone. The culture hero has the power to regulate forces which already exist and to determine the natures, cycles, and seasons of those forces. He is able to allow human beings to decide their fates on occasion, and is supposed to have given the first human couple a choice between life with and life without death. Because they chose life with death, human beings die.

The culture hero both is and is not a god. He does not make the world, but he does possess the power to transmute it. He is more of a broker, a go-between, an intermediary, who stands partway between heaven and earth. He has access to both gods and humans, but generally acts as a human benefactor, working changes to suit their specific needs. (When the gods selfishly hoard their creations, he often tricks or bargains these things away from them, or will do heroic deeds to earn one of their prized possessions, which he then bestows upon humankind.) The world existed before his coming, but the world is as we know it to be because of his deliberate or accidental activity.

The presumption that the culture hero came upon a world already made has interesting implications for stories and storytelling. In the Yoruba tradition, the stories existed in the beginning, but were originally in the possession of Nyame, the Sky God. Anansi wagers for and wins them by performing three feats of prowess. His success is not ensured by the use of any kind of supernatural power. He secures the stories because he is clever, and because he victimizes through trickery. When he releases the stories, they go all over the world. This story suggests that the stories were not created by human beings, but by some greater power, that the stories were whole when we got them, and that they are supernatural—that they are not of this earth. Stories about how the people got stories imply that the stories are magical, and appropriate rites often attend storytellings to remind people of their mystery.

Stories about the exploits of a culture hero are usually not stories of an original creation, but of a second creation. Because his hand is in the final arrangements of things, he figures prominently in stories which explain how animals came to have specific features, how certain landmarks came to look as they do, and why the forces of nature behave as they do. He is often characterized as a lazy, self-interested creature, who is capable of premeditated good behavior, but who most often works by accident. His activity benefits others, more because his self-serving plans go wrong, than because he is responding to concerns other than his own. He is an enigmatic figure: subject to the forces of nature, yet able to control them; vulnerable, yet able to work magic; above the world and also in it; omnipotent and frail; careless of and caring about the needs of others. He is the archetypal clown—unwittingly foolish, deliberately humorous, sometimes lewd and obscene, and the quintessence of practical jokers. When he intends to harm others, he harms himself. When he intends to serve himself, he serves others. He is the first storyteller, the first shaman, the first dancer, the first inventor, and the first teacher.

The culture hero might be thought of as the alter ego of a culture. He is very human. His powers are those of mankind and include those which humans suspect exist just out of reach of conscious control. (His ability to change from animal to human form and back is reminiscent of that of the witch.) People also deliberately and accidentally transform the physical world. The antics of the culture hero help to regulate the nature of that activity by illustrating foolish and wise use of the power to cause change. He represents both the godlike and the base qualities of man. He is our folly, our wit, and our potential for both good and evil. He is the ungodly god. If his place in the universe is halfway to heaven, then so is ours.

CULTURE HEROES OF VARIOUS TRADITIONS

Culture heroes emerge and develop in a manner that is consonant with human needs, and they have predictably specific utilities. Figures such as Paul Bunyan, Pecos Bill, Joe Magarak, and Old Stormalong, even the pernicious rapscallion Judge Roy Bean are more recent inventions which share at least some of the essential characteristics of the comic, creator, culture hero.

Like more traditional culture heroes, these newer examples belong to that not-quite-human species which tames the universe by transforming it, and which wrests accommodations from a usually unforgiving and often inhospitable world. The prospect of living is less terrifying because of the antics and activity of the culture hero. Individual and cultural survival is not easy. (If Mother Nature is a friend, who needs enemies?) The seemingly universal invention of the archetypal mediator/helper, the culture hero, who intervenes on behalf of the race, typifies the human inclination to account for and to chuckle at circumstance.

Anansi. Anansi the Spider is the trickster/hero of many African tales. He was imported to the West as Miss Nancy (Georgia Sea Islands), Aunt Nancy (Gullah, Jamaica), 'Nanci (Curaçao), and 'Ti-Malice (Haiti), and is known as Gizo, Anansi, and Kwaku Anansi in various African traditions: Gold Coast, Ivory Coast, Sierra Leone, Liberia, Togo, Hause, Yoruba, Congo, Angola, and others. He is traditionally responsible for much of what is in the world. He gets along principally by his wits, and is often involved in schemes and plots that backfire. He is a clown, a shaman, a judge, an inventor, a thief, a friend, and an enemy. He is a parallel to, if not a prototype for, the character of Brer Rabbit.

Beaver. Beaver-husband and beaver-wife tales are told among the Ojibwa and other Algonquin groups in the United States. Beaver often travels with Porcupine, his companion and sometimes his victim.

Bluejay. Bluejay is the culture hero parallel of Raven. The Native Americans living along the west coast in Oregon and Washington attribute to Bluejay many of the characteristics and deeds that tribes farther to the north attach to Raven. He is the central figure in several epic cycles of stories. For the Jicarilla Apache, Bluejay has the power to control the circumstances of all birds and animals. He is, in both of these parts of the United States, the archetypal trickster.

Bochica. Bochica, the culture hero of the Chibcha Indians of Colombia, is less the clown/troublemaker and more the serious giver of culture. He came to the people disguised as an old, bearded man in order to give them their moral principles, their arts, and their crafts. He occupies a place which is closer to heaven than that of many other culture heroes.

Brer Rabbit. Brer Rabbit (Compère Lapin/comrade rabbit) is the product of the rabbit and spider trickster traditions of African cultures and, perhaps, of an additional infusion of stories surrounding the Hlakanyana of South Africa and the Chevrotain (Cunnie Rabbit) of Liberia. The rabbit is a clever-witted rogue in many northern and western European stories, and is a more godlike creature in Buddhist and Algonquin Indian literatures. The rabbit is often associated with magic, with the working of charms, with good and bad luck, and with escaping, otherwise outdoing, or turning the tables on other less nimble animals. In some Native American traditions, he is a sun bringer and general benefactor. The rabbit's foot was originally used as a countercharm against witchcraft.
Whether the character of the rabbit trickster originated with Africans imported to the Americas or with Native American groups in the southern United States is unclear. However, the fact that both groups of people employed the character suggests that both cultures had traditions which could readily ascribe the attributes of culture hero to the rabbit.
Brer Rabbit is the perfect clown, rogue, and perverse innocent. Like the spider, his size cannot be taken as a measure of his powers, as many of his animal companions repeatedly and painfully discover. He is the proof of the belief in brains over brawn, and he acts to equalize the relationship between the powerful and the powerless in human relationships.

Cadmus. Cadmus is a more serious, less capricious character of ancient Greek tradition. He represents that class of human heroes whose feats of prowess became myth. Cadmus is credited with introducing the Phoenician alphabet into Greece, with the invention of agriculture, and with the initiation of bronze working. It was Cadmus who sowed the ground with dragon's teeth, thereby producing a crop of fully armed warriors.

The stories of Cadmus's quests and adventures constitute an epic cycle. He was changed to a serpent and taken to Elysium by Zeus, and was thereafter worshipped in some parts of Greece as a minor diety. His role as a giver of culture is connected to his heroic adventures; he is not a rogue or trickster.

Cagn. Cagn, the culture hero of the Bushmen of South Africa, appears in the form of a mantis (*!kaggen*) or as a caterpillar (*ngo*). Bushmen will kill neither animal. Cagn is the giver of digging sticks and roots, but he is also the supreme creator.

Caragabi. Caragabi is a god of the Choco Indians of Colombia. He is an original creator, but was himself created by another god. Caragabi created the people, taught them taboo, and gave them food plants, the sun, moon, and stars.

Chameleon. In West Africa, Chameleon is credited with bringing fire to mankind. In East Africa, Chameleon is a champion of mankind, who tried but failed to prevent men from having to die. People in Mozambique tell the story of Chameleon's discovery and care of the first human couple. Though he sponsored them on the earth, they proved to be dangerous to other forms of life, and so destructive and cruel that they drove the gods into the sky. In Nyasaland, people kill chameleons, because it was Chameleon who brought death without hope of resurrection to mankind.

Child-of-the-Water. The Apache and Navaho peoples remember Child-of-the-Water as a slayer of mythological beasts and monsters. His adventures made the earth into a safer place for men. In some Apache tales, Child-of-the-Water kills Metal Old Man, a dangerous and destructive monster who inhabited the mountains.

Cin-an-ev. Cin-an-ev is the Wolf culture hero/trickster of the Ute peoples.

Cirape. In the Coyote trickster tradition of the Crow peoples of south central Montana, Cirape is brother to Old Man Coyote and is his sometime adventuring companion.

Coyote. The character of Coyote as trickster/creator/culture hero is as widely known in the plains, Rocky Mountains, and southwestern United States as is Anansi in Africa. Like Anansi, Coyote lives by his wits. While he does work as a benefactor to mankind, he usually does so accidentally. His motives are often less than lofty and his methods less than honest. He is so clever at deception that he commonly deceives himself. His self-serving habits, his general disregard for and disrespect for others, and the regular backfiring of his greedy schemes serve as reverse lessons in proper behavior.

Coyote, Old Man Coyote, Old Man, and Our Mother's Brother stories abound. In many of these, Coyote is accompanied by other animals common to the region; his favorite traveling companion is Wolf. In some of the more lewd and erotic stories, Coyote becomes a licentious plotter. In other stories, he is unable to believe the truth when he hears it, because he is himself so very dishonest that he cannot trust anyone. He makes trouble for himself because he cannot follow directions, because he bends the rules, or because he is not true to himself (tries to be what he is not). One strong theme in many Coyote stories has to do with *gifts*—strengths given to different animals by the gods. Either Coyote gets no gift, because he tries to get the best or biggest, or he tries to imitate the capabilities of another animal, with amusingly painful results.

Coyote's character has a split personality. He is both the giver and the deceiver/fool. The Navaho call the former aspect "Coyote as Holy Being" and the latter "Trotting Coyote." This apparent discrepancy, viewed as problematic by some, and in need of explaining, might be understood in terms of the utility of the character. In fact, the Chinook peoples of the northwest have two characters: Bluejay is the trickster/deceiver; Coyote—*Italpas*—is the serious and holy giver and teacher/creator. The Blackfeet of Montana also make a clearer separation between the two contradictory natures of Coyote. The culture hero/creator/helper is Napi or Old Man Napi, whose human characteristics are stressed more in those stories in which he acts the role of the holy being. In the trickster tales, Napi becomes identified with Coyote. Many Salish coyote stories also make these distinctions.

Hence, Coyote, like Anansi, Raven, Bluejay, and Brer Rabbit, serves several purposes in some cultures. He manages to bring something of use to mankind in all of them, no matter how decently or how crudely he behaves.

Crane. The crane figures as a culture hero in a number of traditions, but he is not as elaborately articulated as such characters as Spider or Coyote. The attribute associated with Crane in Russia, Sicily, India, and parts of North America is slyness. Crane, like both Fox and Wolf, carries small animals across water only to eat them. Crane is sometimes the animal guide and an aid in escape from pursuit.

Crow. Crow is a Raven-like trickster, whose personality is that of the greedy, stingy opportunist. He is also, however, a mythical figure (Iroquoian) credited with bringing the first corn kernel to earth, and with aiding in its cultivation. He is therefore allowed the first share at harvest.

Fox. Fox is a well-known trickster worldwide. Oriental, European, and North American peoples tell Fox tales and maintain cycles of Fox stories. In some of these, notably the stories of eastern Europe, Fox is the archetypal trickster/deceiver. He is a parallel to Coyote (a companion in North America) and Anansi. He has some sinister qualities which seem lacking in these others, however, and in some parts of the world he is also dangerous to man. He is a shape-changer who can assume human form to deceive, to cause human suffering, or to steal the vitality of other persons. His malevolence implies witchery and is not paralleled in some of the other culture heroes. The Fox who studies scripture (China) will appear in human form as the teacher/scholar and do good works.

Perhaps the most familiar Fox is the rapacious and dishonest trickster/fool who punishes his tail by giving it to the dogs, only to find that it is attached to him; whose greed rewards him with a sack that contains a large dog; and who dupes Bear into going ice fishing with his tail.

Also see the cycle of Reynard the Fox, the trickster hero of the medieval beast epic *Roman de Renart*. Reynard the Fox is not a particularly sterling character. He is clever, immoral, rebellious, a coward, a liar, a seducer, and a traitor.

Glooscap. Glooscap (Gluskabe) is the human mythical hero of Native American groups from the northern woodland areas. Glooscap is the true adventuring hero, not the bumbling fool/ deceiver like the culture heroes of some other cultures. His collected escapades constitute an epic cycle of the quality and kind of *Gilgamesh*. He performs the role of culture hero as he encounters beasts, monsters, and hardships, and makes the world more habitable for humankind.

Grandfather. In Brazil, the Cariri Indians maintain stories of a god of intermediate status who brought the people tobacco, and who also provided the men with women. In this last interesting tale, there are many men in the world, all obliged to share one woman. They beg Grandfather to make more women. He complies by cutting the one woman into many small pieces, hanging one piece each in the lodges of each of the men, and bringing these pieces to life. When the men return from hunting, they discover that they each have a woman waiting in the house, happily cooking.

Hayk. Hayk, the mythical epic hero of Armenia, is, like Glooscap, a legendary man of supernatural capabilities, a giant who keeps his people from harm and guides them in battle.

Hodja. Hodja stories are the ever-popular Turkish "noodle" tales (tales of a supposed nitwit or "noodlehead") about the teacher/scholar/priest/trickster who usually outwits everybody, even himself. The Hodja is the epitome of the wise rustic. His clever antics generally harm no one, are very funny, and teach powerful lessons. The Hodja is the one who buys his own donkey back after selling it at the bazaar, because it looks better when it belongs to someone else than when it belonged to him. He is the one who wiggles out of preparing a worship sermon for three successive Fridays by asking the people if they know what he is about to tell them. When they say no, he tells them that he cannot waste his time with people who will have no idea what he is saying. When they say yes, he tells them that since they already know, he has no need to tell them. When they say yes and no, he tells the ones who know to tell the ones who do not know. The Hodja is the one who proves that he knows more than the wisest of the Magi, when pitted against three of them in a contest of wits.

The Hodja is a popular culture hero precisely because he is so very common. He reminds the plainest of people that worth is not measured by beauty, money, or station. The cycle of Hodja stories brings self-respect to the common people.

Ibeorgun. This culture bringer of the Cuna Indians of Panama is credited with giving the people food, cooking, shelter, liquor, certain crafts, and rites of passage.

Jack. Jack, of the Jack Tales, embodies some of the common characteristics of culture hero. He is a third son—the magic number. He is the honest, straightforward, guileless one who never suspects the tricks and deceptions of others. He is the western European hero who lacks all sophistication but is exceptionally clever. The deliberation and premeditation of Coyote, Fox, or Brer Rabbit are absent in Jack—his uninformed state is not feigned—but his quick wit is legend. Unlike some other culture heroes, Jack is the fool who always bumbles his way to success.

In some Jack story cycles, Jack is the son of a bear. His name is given, then, as Juan el Oso, or Ivanko, the Bear's Son. The Thompson River Indians, who have heard these European stories, remember that Jack was also a bear.

Jackal. In the animal tales of the Near, Middle, and Far East, Jackal is a parallel to the familiar Fox as trickster/buffoon. Jackal figures in Turkish and Armenian stories are similar to those found in Fox and Brer Rabbit traditions; for instance, in the common motif of sharecropping, in which the trickster "shares" the crop by making a bargain to divide it into tops and bottoms. The trickster claims bottoms, then plants beets or potatoes. Jackal also serves the role of trickster for the Hottentot peoples of Africa.

John. John (Old John), from the southern United States, is a human Brer Rabbit-like character, a slave who matches wits with the archetypal "massa" and generally wins. Old John comes out on top because he uses his head to evade punishments and other forms of control imposed by white slave holders. He is an illustration of the oppressed controlling the oppressor through justifiable trickery and deception. Old John stories, like Jack Tales and Clever Elsie collections, are noodle stories, in which Old John and "massa" meet in a comic battle of wits, and in which John, while playing the fool, wiggles to freedom time and again. While Jack might qualify as a culture hero, because he rids the world of loathsome giants, Old John brings perspective and a message about dignity.

Juskaha. Juskaha (Sapling) is the human culture hero of Seneca mythology who increases the size of the land, controls harmful creatures, and does good works on behalf of mankind.

Kaleva. Kaleva is the national epic hero of Finland and Estonia. He is the most ancient of heroes in Finnish and Estonian traditions, the bringer of cultivation. His name means "hero," and may have its origins in related words referring to strength and "strong man." Though Kaleva may have once lived, and been a flesh-and-blood individual at an earlier time, and though place names in the region are related, *Kaleva* is now legendary and a generic for "hero." *Kalevala* means the home or land of Kaleva. Taken literally, Finland is, by definition, a land of heroes and exceptionally strong people.

Kalevipoeg. Kalevipoeg, son of the most prominent hero in Lithuanian tradition, is a giant, strong, and a protector of mankind. His history is largely the creation of a known author, who applied material from generic hero tales.

Kleing. Kleing (Indonesia) is the indigenous human/transformer culture hero of Borneo. His stories are the adventures and exploits of the mythical warrior/hero.

Kresnik. Kresnik, the national hero of the Slovenes, is a mythological person of great strength, who slew monsters and worked magic. He is associated with spring, crops, and cattle, and eventually became syncretic with St. George the dragon slayer.

Kwati. The transformer/culture hero/trickster of the Macah people of the Puget Sound area in the state of Washington is the mink—clever, sly, slippery. He is a parallel to Raven and other culture heroes of the Pacific Northwest, and enjoys his own cycle of trickster stories. Mink is different from many culture heroes in that he is depicted as a great lover. His amorous escapades help to develop the comic aspects of his character. His powers reside more in his ability to transform than in his use of cunning and wit. He prepared the earth for the coming of humankind by making mountains, streams, and springs, by killing monsters, by stealing the sun, and by changing many plants and animals for the benefit of humans.

Legba. Legba, the youngest son of the creator god, is the trickster of the Dahomean people of Africa. He is the god of crossroads and entrances, and, imported to the New World, appears in voodoo ceremonies in a manner that is not inconsistent with his original identity. Missionaries, evidently in an attempt to convert native peoples to Christianity, equated Legba with Satan, an association that still exists, but this equation is not supported by Dahomean tradition.

Loki. Loki is the trickster god of Teutonic myth. He is the personification of destructive fire, and some of his deeds have the spreading and engulfing habit of fire. The pre-Christian Loki, though not entirely harmless, was more the prankster and did not use his capacity to transform for working evil. He was perverse, but not wicked. He was somewhat like the character of Till Eulenspiegel: impish and devilish, irrepressible and unrepentant, yet forgiveable. The later Loki developed an unredeeming meanness of character and behavior that placed him in parallel to the Christian devil. The eventual "fall" of Loki to the status of trickster-as-personification-of-evil may have been engineered by early Christian missionaries in their attempts to cast pagan gods and practices in an undesirable light.

Lone Man. Lone Man (Mandan Indian) or Only Man (Hidatsa Sioux) is one of two equally endowed original creators. Lone Man created all the low lands and low places. His handiwork was separated from that of his co-creator, First Creator, by the Missouri River. Later, Lone Man (Mandan tradition), returned to earth as a man by begetting himself through the vehicle of a virgin birth. In this human form, he gave the people rites and customs, law, and control of the river, and he worked many miracles that equal those worked by Christ.

Maira-monan. Maira-monan is the creator/transformer/culture hero of the Tupinamba Indians of South America. Maira-monan was the law giver, and brought agriculture and taboos to the people. He often transformed himself into a small child to go among the people.

Marunogere. Both god and culture hero, Marunogere is the bringer of the coconut tree, the pig, and of shelter and ceremony to the people of Kiwai Papua society. Though he gave human-kind many good things, he could also bring trouble, in the form of two ferocious dogs which sometimes came forth to raid villages.

Masewi. The people of the Keresan tradition, a linguistically related group of pueblo cultures of the southwestern United States, believe that Masewi led them up from Shipap at the time of emergence. He told them where to go and what to name their pueblos. He also placed the sun in the sky to bring light. He is most prominent in the mythology of the Cochiti people of central New Mexico.

Maui. Maui is a common trickster/culture hero among Pacific Island peoples. He appears in mythologies from Melanesia and New Zealand to Hawaii, where he is the protector and friend of mankind. He fished the land up from the sea, gave fire, slowed the sun in its course, raised the sky, trapped the winds, and invented the kite, barbed spear, eel pot, and navigation. He personifies the abandoned-child-who-reclaims-his-birthright motif. His devotion to mankind was so profound that he died in an attempt to obtain immortality for humans.

Monkey. Monkey tales in Japan, India, the Middle East, and parts of Africa portray the Monkey as a clever trickster who outwits other animals to his own benefit, and who, in typical prankster fashion, is sometimes ensnared by his own plots.

Mountain Lion. Mountain Lion is a trickster companion, Coyote's brother or friend (and occasionally dupe), among the Native American peoples of Utah, Nevada, and eastern California.

Mrikanda. The Koshti, a caste of weavers (India), revere Mrikanda as the inventor of the loom, slayer of giants, and protector from tigers.

Mudjikiwis. Mudjikiwis is the hero of the Plains and Swampy Cree, the Ojibwa and Plains Ojibwa people. In Longfellow's *Hiawatha*, "Mudjekeewis" (Hiawatha's father) kills the Great Bear.

Nanabozho. Nanabozho (Manabozho/Nanabush, Wisakedjak/Wisaka/Whiskey Jack) is a major figure in the mythologies of Central Woodland Indian cultures, principally among speakers of various dialects of Algonquin. The character, sometimes the wolverine, is central to many creator/trickster/transformer story cycles, and has a number of adventures in the form of a wolf. He is not the single-dimensioned Glooscap, with whom he is sometimes confused, but more a parallel to Coyote. He has the usual dual personality—the creator/giver/helper and the trickster/deceiver/buffoon.

Ninhasan. Ninhasan is the trickster/buffoon of the Arapaho. Ninhasan figures exclusively in stories in which he behaves foolishly or obscenely. Though the original meaning of the word is "spider," and Unktomi (Dakota) is the spider trickster among the Santee, no association with a spider trickster is attached to the Arapaho character. Rather, *ninhasan* has come to mean "white man," and the stories reflect the Arapaho view of his behavior.

Old Woman Advisor. A ubiquitous character in many Native American mythologies, the Old Woman Advisor, sometimes in the form of an animal, gives aid and advice to heroes.

Pariaca. Pariaca is the human culture hero of the Huarochiri Indians. He transformed the landscape, gave irrigation canals, and was able to change people into other objects.

Porcupine. Porcupine, along with Beaver, is a companion trickster figure in Coyote tales. While he is not as quick as Coyote, and sometimes is in danger of playing the dupe, he seems to be able to protect himself. He is endowed with the power to control cold.

Possum. Possum is the trickster in the story cycles of the mestizos and the Amazonian Indians. In the southern United States, Possum is more often portrayed as a kind-hearted dupe who will, for instance, put a rattlesnake in his pocket even though he knows his peril.

Quikinna'qu. Quikinna'qu (Kutkinn-a'ku, Big Raven, Big Grandfather) is the mythic creator of the Koryak and Chukchee peoples of the Pacific Northwest. He is transformed from supreme creator to Big Raven by putting on his raven coat. He is also shaman, first man, and culture hero. As culture hero, he displays that baser nature which is found in many such figures. He appears in stories which are comic and obscene, and becomes involved in the exchanging of many practical jokes.

Raccoon. Among Native American peoples of the eastern woodlands, Raccoon is a minor trickster character who lacks many of the attributes of other tricksters. He is neither creator, benefactor of mankind, nor transformer, and he is rarely duped or trapped by his own chicanery.

Raven. The raven is a familiar character in many mythologies worldwide. The bird was considered to be unclean (that is, unfit to eat) in ancient times, and has borne, then and now, the burden of being an omen of bad luck and calamity. In many European traditions, the raven is a bird of battle, and is spared from hunting in some parts of England owing to the Cornish belief that King Arthur lives on in its form. In Russia, the raven represents the enemy; in German and other indigenous folk cultures, the raven is the form of choice for the transformation of evil from human to animal. The raven is the devil's messenger and transporter of the souls of the dead. In addition, the bird is believed to have great supernatural powers.

Among Native American peoples of the Pacific Northwest, Raven is the trickster/transformer/culture hero, but the Jicarilla and Lipan Apache claim that men die because Raven so willed it. They name Raven as a source of evil and as magician.

Sen'deh. Sen'deh (Sen'deh Old Man, Seh'nedeh) is the Kiowan culture hero/transformer. The Kiowa feature Sen'deh as a trickster; however, he is not Coyote, nor any other animal. Though he can transform himself into any animal form at need, his character is more human. His purposes seem to be much more centered about good works and the role of giver, and he is less likely to appear in the lewd type of trickster tale common to other cultures.

Sitkonsky. Sitkonsky is the trickster of the Assiniboin peoples of North America.

Spider. Spider, Spider Man, Spider Woman, and Unktomi are names for the very potent creator/culture hero/trickster of many western and southwestern Native American cultures. While the division of the character between trickster and creator varies, Spider is a powerful benefactor of mankind, who brings the sun down, kills enemies and monsters, saves the people from monster rocks, and gives custom, arts, and crafts. Spider Man and Spider Woman taught the Navaho to weave; Spider Man is a good medicine man and Spider Woman a helper for many pueblo peoples. The Hopi revere Spider Woman by maintaining a cycle of stories devoted to telling her works.

Sunawavi. The Utes of southwestern Colorado present Sunawavi as Coyote's brother, or sometimes as shaman and chief. He is a companion creator/trickster.

Tchue. Tchue is the culture hero/transformer/creator of Bushman folklore. Tchue works to the benefit of man by transforming himself into those things which men might find useful, thereby creating them. Among the many things that Tchue brought was fire. One difference that seems to exist between Tchue and many other creator/culture heroes is the manner of creation. While other culture heroes create one thing out of something else, acting only as a catalytic agent, Tchue appears to create by making things out of his own substance. According to tradition, Tchue dies with each creative act, then is resurrected afterward, leaving behind the object of his effort.

Tcikapis. Tcikapis is a human creator/culture hero in the traditions of the Montagnais-Naskapi Indians of the northeastern North America. Tcikapis does not play the fool. He displays a sincere concern for the welfare of mankind and uses his considerable conjuring capability to improve their condition. The Tcikapis tales cycle is also told by the neighboring Cree, Algonquin, and Ojibwa.

Uazale. Uazale, a hairy, bat-like creature, discovered manioc and brought tobacco and cotton to the Paressi Indians of Matto Grosso.

Yankee. The Yankee trickster is an American Colonial development, a generic character given to lying (bellybending), story swapping, practical joking, and general chicanery. The character seems to be based in traditions of Yankee shrewdness in business, ability in manufacture, and irrepressible enterprising spirit. Often, the Yankee trickster is the rustic, backwoods sage, who looks the fool but can outwit any clever townie or city slicker. The Yankee trickster can also surface in the person of the common peddler who is a sharp horsetrader and a skilled hoodwinker, and who knows how to ensnare the unwary with his guileless tactics.

CHAPTER

4

The People of Faerie

Do you believe in fairies?
If you believe, clap your hands!
— James Barrie, *Peter Pan*

INTRODUCTION

Once upon a time, a long time ago, the fringes of the mortal world included delightful and not-so-delightful creatures. For instance, there were elves, considered to be nature spirits, Mother Nature's offspring. As the natural world was tamed, the little people retreated.

The words for *fairy* in Italy and Spain were *fata* and *fada*, which probably were derived from the Latin *fatum*. *Fatum* ("fate") acknowledges attributes of the fairies in predicting and controlling human destiny or fate. The French term means to enchant, which probably refers to the reputed ability of the fairies to cast a spell over human vision. The term *elf* comes from the Scandinavian *alfar*, which was connected with the earth. *Fee*, or fairy, is also thought to be from the last syllable of *nympha*. Another plausible derivation for the word *fairy* comes from the Persian *peri*. Because Arabic has no hard *p* sound, and substitutes an *f*, *peri*, in this theory, became *feri*.

The word *fairy* is used in four different senses. The first is the sense of illusion and enchantment. The second is the abode or country that these enchanting folk inhabit. The third use of the term indicates the inhabitants themselves—a group terminology. Finally, the fourth usage signifies individuals of fairyland.

Nancy Arrowsmith, in her book *A Field Guide to the Little People*, identifies three groups of elves. The Light Elves are air dwellers and are capable of shape-changing. They are good-natured. The Dark Elves make their homes underground and prefer dark corners. They appear at noon or late at night. The Dusky Elves are tied to their environment and are easily recognized by humans. They stay near their tree, brook, mound, pond, or glade. In general, elves are venerable and conservative (Arrowsmith 1977).

Keightley distinguishes between beings of the human race who are endowed with powers beyond those usually possessed by people, and the little beings of northern mythology—the elves or popular fairies (Keightley 1968; 1978).

FAERIE FOLK OF VARIOUS TRADITIONS

Without getting into the intricacies of theories of fairy relationships, and their inheritance from past religions and mythologies, here is a brief description of some cultures' fairies.

Abbey Lubbers. At a time when monks were considered worldly and lazy, the Abbey Lubbers were said to feast in the cellars and kitchens of the monasteries and tempt the monks to all kinds of evil.

Alven. These Dutch elves live in ponds in which there are no fish. They travel with the wind and through water inside air bubbles or broken eggshells. They are shape-changers and are strongest at night. They are very attached to the night wort and elf-leaf, and are capable of strong mischief.

Apple-Tree Man. The oldest apple tree in the orchard of Somerset was the "Apple-Tree Man." The spirit of the orchard was believed to live in it.

Asrai. Shy Asrai come to the surface of the water to look at the full moon. They are many hundreds of years old, can only grow in the moonlight, and can only surface once every century. They die immediately if the sun touches them. They are always female, two to four feet high, with long green hair and webbed feet. They are English and cannot live on land.

Bagan. The Bagan are only visible on Holy Thursday and on Easter Sunday. They are the protectors of all farm animals. When choosing farm animals, pick their colors according to the Bagan's preference: A piece of cake should be wrapped in a rag at Easter and hung in the stable for six weeks. On inspection, the color of the maggots on it will show what color the Bagan prefer.

Bannik. These are the folk that live inside the bath house and do not like to be disturbed.

Banshee. The Celtic prophet of death is the Banshee. She wails before the death of any of her family. Once a beautiful maiden, she died before her time. A Banshee has long streaming hair and eyes that are fiery red from weeping. Her green dress is covered by a grey cloak. If you have a Banshee in your family, it is a point of pride, because it shows that you belong to one of the old families of Ireland. The Scottish Banshees are Bean-Nighe, which means "the little washer by the ford." Down by the riverside, the Bean-Nighe wash the funeral clothes of those who are about to die. There is much keening and wailing as they wash the clothes.

Barabao. The Barabao are particularly fond of bosoms and teasing. Usually, they are two to three feet high and are shape-shifters. They like to wear red caps and elegant red clothes. Also, they are quite fat. The Barabao live only in Venice.

Black Dogs. As a rule, the Black Dogs have fiery eyes and are large and shaggy. In some places they are supposed to be the form taken by the ghost of a human. More recently, there are stories in which the Black Dogs guard and protect people.

Blue Caps. These were mine goblins, but they were the friendly, helpful type. They worked in coal mines of northern England pushing the filled tubs of coal. These Brownies accepted pay for their work—no more and no less than ordinary wages. Generally, they were not seen, but one could see a blue light shining on a coal tub.

Blue Men of the Minch. They haunted the straits between two islands. If the ship captain could talk to the Blue Men in rhyme and get the last word, they would not wreck his ship. They were tattooed blue and, when captured, they broke all the ropes that bound them and escaped back to the sea.

Bogies. There are many names for them, such as Bug-a-Boos, and Bogey-Beasts. Their great delight is to torment humans. They have been known to travel in hordes and can be easily tricked.

Brownies. Brownies crave sweets and can be invaluable helpers if treated correctly. In Scotland, each home used to have its own Brownie who helped brew the beer. They are twenty inches high and often invisible. It is rude of people to leave a suit of clothes for the naked Brownie.

Bucca or **Bucca-Boo**. Cornish fishermen used to leave a fish out for Bucca and leave ale on the ground so Bucca would give them a good catch. He degenerated from a kind of fertility god into a threat to frighten children.

Bwciod. This is the Welsh relative of the Brownie. They only frequent houses where they are well fed and well treated. One thing they despise is a teetotaller.

Callicantzaroi. In Greece, they appear during the twelve days of Christmas and take part in the long processions in the hills. Many of them are blind. They have large heads and small bodies; their tongues always hang out of their mouths and there are big humps on their chests. The genitals of the Callicantzaroi are always visible. The Greeks use fire and torches against them. Their feet are horses' or asses' feet. They rape and are dangerous, so a sieve and a broom should be laid by the door. Pork bones hung in the chimney and incense burned at night also keeps them away. They hate the stench of old shoes burned in the fireplace.

Changelings. Changelings are left in place of women or children. To identify them, look for an outrageous appetite and a nasty temper, along with fits of squalling and howling. They also have wrinkled skin and swollen heads with bright eyes. To get rid of Changelings, make them reveal their age. Quiet Folk Changelings live in Germany, Holland, Poland, Czechoslovakia, Romania, and parts of England.

Crodn Mara. From the Highlands and the Isle of Man, these wild fairy cattle are welcome additions to any herd.

Dames Vertes. These invisible forest elves live in thickly wooded areas of eastern France. Dames Vertes prefer forest caves, waterfalls, springs, meadows, and slopes near fishponds. They can tease travellers, but they are the life-giving, greening force that melts the winter's snows.

Daoine Sidhe. Once tall and beautiful, the regular fairy people of Ireland have gradually dwindled and are now called the "Little People" or the "Wee Folk." It is unlucky to call them by their real name, and people fear them.

Domoviye. They are the most important Slavic house elf. Treat them well and they will make a household run smoothly. They like to live behind the stove in the corner of the house. The Domoviye can foretell the future, warn of disasters, and sound the alarm in case of fire or robbery. Throughout the year, give them gifts. You will recognize them by their dark hair from head to foot. They can fit behind the stove and can be seen only at night. All of them grumble, quarrel, and swear.

Drakes. Many times Drakes are confused with fire spirits. They are house spirits who travel like fiery streaks in the air. They are hard workers and only take on the characteristics of fire when they hurry to bring milk and crops to their masters; then they look like egg-shaped flaming balls and can travel amazing distances with incredible speed. They leave behind them the smell of burning sulphur. They live in England, Scandinavia, Germany, and France.

Duende. They cling to their chosen homes and have no fear of priests or holy water. These night elves play pranks and cause many sleepless nights for people. A favorite game is *Nip the Napper*, in which they dream up new ways to wake sleepers. They have also been reported to move furniture, throw stones at roofs, toss plates out the windows, and carry on other rattling, singing, and dancing activities. On the other hand, for a bowl of milk they will do all sorts of work during the night. They are about two feet high and can make themselves invisible or change their shape. They are universal spirits in Spain and Portugal, and prefer to live indoors.

Duergar. Always full of malice towards people, these black dwarfs of northern England seek to destroy.

Dwarfs. The Dwarfs are most common in Germany, Switzerland, and the Isle of Rugen. There are industrious Dwarfs who live in cottages, and quarry jewels and gold in the mines (like the ones who befriended Snow White). They are related to the Cornish Tommyknockers.

Ellefolk. Ellefolk are often classed as Trolls. They travel with great ease through fire, air, wood, water, and stone. Females like to ride sunbeams through keyholes. They foretell the future and are the guardians of ancient secrets. Watch for them dancing on moonlit nights. The magic of their dance is the most dangerous temptation for humans. Their homes (next to rivers, under hills, in marshes) can be seen only once by humans, and then they vanish never to be seen again.

English Fairies. These less powerful, modern fairies are the offspring of powerful majestic fairies who intermarried with humans and other elvish races. They love to dance in the meadows on moonlit nights, particularly in May. They are transformed from their night-time beauty to ugly, wrinkled dwarfs during the day, so they usually assume the form of birds, cats, toads, butterflies, or flowers during the day. Ivy on walls drives them away, as do misers, salt, iron, rowan, and St. John's wort. Cakes should be marked with a cross before baking; if they are not, they get tiny holes which some say are made by the fairies who dance on them with high-heeled shoes.

Erdluitle. They are extremely reluctant to show their feet to humans. They have great control over the weather and knowledge of the secret powers of nature. Erdluitle are the size of a seven-year-old-child. Some of them have goose feet and animal ears. These Dwarfs are from Switzerland and northern Italy. Their homes are in dark caves or under standing stones.

Fankenmannikin. They live in eastern Switzerland and northern Tirol. Even though they are naked, hairy, and rough-looking, they are gentle. Fankenmannikin can change leaves into gold and can be very helpful. They avoid the hot, dry mountain wind called Fohn.

Fauni and **Silvani**. Many consider them the oldest Italian wood spirits. The Fauni mated with the Faunae and gave birth to the Incubi. The Silvani mated with Wood Women and the Folletti were born.

Fees. Originally they were nature and fertility spirits who were quite old and had great power. Fees are widespread. Some live in the woods, the plains, the mountains, and underground. The field Fees can be recognized by their long breasts which they throw over their shoulders for the children on their backs to suckle. They brought fertility to the land. The Fees differ widely in shape and form. Duck feet, a snake's tail, and hairy body should make them easily distinguishable, but they have the power of invisibility.

Fir Bolg. Generally Fir Bolg are three feet high, shape-changers, and stout of build. They are mortal and are substituted for upper-world creatures when they grow old.

Folletti. They are known throughout Italy, but are most numerous in Sicily and travel in twirls of wind. Farmers know to chew as much garlic as they can if the wind begins to blow on a saint's feast day. Folletti are the offspring of Silvani and Wood Women. Folletti have the form and mentality of small children, but are extremely interested in sex and have magical powers. There is an almost endless number of names for them, and there are many very exact ways by which to exorcise them. It was believed in Sardinia that all unbaptized children became Fuglietti when they died. They are between one and three feet tall, have curly hair, bright eyes, and love to wear red. Their magic red hoods give them the power of invisibility.

Fylgiar. A child born in Iceland with a caul (*fylgia*), or membrane over his head, is considered very lucky. Lucky attendant spirits are called Fylgiar. They shadow their masters and can be seen only by their masters on the point of death or through the gift of second sight.

Gabriel Hounds. In the old days, people believed that the sounds made by migrating birds were the noises of ghostly hounds with human heads. They thought these hounds flew high up in the sky, hunting unrepentant sinners to capture their souls. Among the hounds' other names are Devil's Dandy Dogs, the Sky-Yelpers, and Cwn Annwn (Wales—the Dogs of Hell).

Giane. The first Giane were wood spirits and lived in caves in the hills. They could foretell the future and knew where treasures were buried. These tall, beautiful women with long breasts were industrious in their spinning and embroidery. They had trouble finding men so they turned into bloodsucking predators. The Giane of today are small, wear furs, and are not bloodthirsty. They are fantastic weavers and can make white veils that cover entire valleys. They live in caves in the cliffs, forests, and hills of Sardinia.

Green Children. These are fairy children who were found near Wolf-pits in Suffolk at the beginning of the twelfth century. It was said they came from St. Martin's Land where there was no sun or moon but only a continuous twilight. All creatures and people there were green.

Gwagged Annwn. Tall, proud, blonde, and immortal, these lake maidens are the most beautiful Welsh fairy folk. They dance in the meadows from a minute before midnight until the first cock crows in the morning. Many times only their heads can be seen bobbing up and down in a field of silver mist. Their beauty is irresistible and sometimes they marry human men. Their children have magic powers. They inhabit Wales, Brittany, England, Scandinavia, France, and Germany.

Habetrot. These were the patron fairies of spinners. Habetrot did people favors.

Hedley Kow. They were mischievous practical jokers. These bogey-beasts haunted the village of Hedley. As shape-changers, they could have lots of fun with people.

Hey-Hey Men. This group of forest spirits ranges from southern Germany and Czechoslovakia, Poland, Hungary, and Romania. They are often heard calling out and travellers should beware. Hey-Hey Men lead people astray and also start storms, make people's ears grow, give girls beards, and make straw into horses. They take on many disguises and change shapes often. Originally they lived in deep forests, but have had to resort to other locales such as swamps, grain fields, and deserted millstreams.

Hobgoblins. These are the most populous of the house elves. There are numerous Welsh, Scottish, and English sprites. They prefer to stay warm and cozy in the house next to the hob (projecting ledge at the back or side of the fireplace). Tom Tit Tot and others are individual hobgoblins. They are usually one or two feet tall with dark skin, and can either be naked or dressed in tattered clothes.

Imps (or Impets). *Imp* meant a cutting or an offshoot. The *ympe* tree was an apple tree grown from a cutting or grafted onto a tree that was already rooted. There was thought to be something magical about the Imp. Goblins and bogies are sometimes called Imps.

Klabautermannikin. This was the name given to the spirits in carved figureheads on ships. Tree spirits stayed in their trees even after the trees were cut down and carved. The most treasured wood for figureheads was trees which had the souls of dead children living in them. Guardian trees were planted at the birth of a child and the tree's fate was connected with that of the child; if the child died, his or her spirit lived in that tree. Klabautermannikins took over the duties of the ship's spirit and cared for it. Some have moved to the land where they have become corrupted by the easy life. Gifts of clothes or curses will drive them away. Their red jackets are always too small for them. They love to smoke.

Knockers. They make their homes inside mines and quarries and are extremely helpful fairies. Since they know the location of rich ore veins, they knock and tell friendly folk where it is. They also warn miners when disaster is about to strike. Food offerings are the polite, thoughtful thing for miners to give them. Cornish Tommyknockers can be recognized by arms that are so long they drag on the ground, beards, and wet boots.

Kobolde. At one time Kobolde were quite common in northern Europe. They are the oldest and most famous of the home sprites, though they used to live inside trees. The tree sprite remains in the carved figure of the Klabautermannikin. Originally the Kobolde were carved from mandrake roots or boxwood and enclosed in glass or wooden containers. The Kobolde could not leave unless sold to a new master for less than the original price. Only the master could open the box holding the Kobolde, otherwise the Kobolde would escape and cause endless damage. Jack-in-the-boxes were created to teach children never to open the Kobolde's box. The Kobolde of today are elves who once lived inside figurines.

Korred. These are the Old Ones who brought the massive standing stones into Brittany, Cornwall, and Iberia. Korrs or Korred have bright red eyes that are set far back into their heads, and dark skin. They are prophets and magicians and know the secrets of all hidden treasures. At night, usually on a Wednesday, they dance with vigor. The Cornish Korred are called Spriggans. They guard underground treasures and control the wind. Their bodies are hunched, up to three feet in height. They have cats' claws or goats' hooves instead of feet. They always live below sea level.

Korrigans. The Korrigans and female Lamignak are the special guardians of springs and fountains. They live in underground caverns and rarely awaken before sundown. At night, the moonlight transforms them and they sing old songs, brush and comb their long hair, and bathe in cool water. They sing so sweetly the night stops to listen to them. If a human man catches the Korrigan bathing, he must pay with his body. He is bound to marry her within three days or else die. The Korrigans are probably descendants of the Korred. The Korrigans say everything in reverse—if they say the weather will be good, it will be bad. They are two feet tall with long blonde hair. These shape-changers are from Brittany and the Basque Pyrenees.

Kyrkogrims. Swedish Kyrkogrims, or Church Grims, are said to be the souls of animals sacrificed by early Christians at the building of each new church. They are most common in Denmark, Sweden, Finland, and Yorkshire.

Lauru. These home sprites are the most handsome of the Italian Folletto. The Lauru wears only the finest of clothes, loves women, and always tries to seduce them. If a woman rejects him he gives her nightmares. To get rid of him, the woman must hang a pair of bull or ram horns over the door or else yield to his advances.

Leprechauns. The Irish Leprechaun is the faeries' shoemaker. His two great loves are tobacco and whiskey. They are between six and twenty-four inches tall with light grey skin, old wrinkled faces, and bright red noses (from the whiskey?). Leprechauns wear three-cornered hats, and like shiny buttons, leather aprons, and high-heeled shoes with large silver buckles. They make their homes under the roots of a tree or in ruined castles.

Leshiye. The sounds heard inside a forest are the Leshiye trying to gain control of people and lead them into the dark woods where they are at the Leshiye's mercy. People have been reported tickled to death by them. The Leshiye cradle themselves in the branches of a tree and make all kinds of noises. They vary wildly in size—from a leaf to a tall tree. Their height changes with the seasons. They have goat feet and horns, only one eye, claws, green hair, and grey skin. Czechoslovakia and European Russia are home to them. They hibernate in the winter.

Linchetto. This Tuscan spirit causes nightmares, and is classified as a night elf and as a Folletto. He only appears at night, but is usually invisible. He is two feet tall and has pointed ears.

Lutins. They are irrepressible and full of mischief, along with being very helpful. One Lutin, the Cula, is a master of shape-changing. Lutins seem to prefer stagnant waters, caves, moors, seashores, and fields, and lurk near standing stones. They are familiar in France and parts of Switzerland.

Mer-Men. The elves who live in fresh water love to seduce mortals. They generally are handsome young men who play the fiddle or harp. The salt-water spirits have long hair and beards and live to a great old age. They control the weather at sea and take those who drown to their homes on the ocean floor. It was assumed that only sea captains who were on good terms with Mer-Men had safe passage in the seas. Mer-Men are shape-shifters, and usually have green or fish-like teeth. Water horses or Kelpies are Mer-Men who adopt the shape of a horse. In the Mediterranean they take the combined body of man and fish.

Mer-Women. Another name for them is Sea-Women. They are the mistresses of the oceans and herd and protect sea animals. They also collect gems and gold from the ocean floor. Their marriages are usually May-December ones and are not successful. They follow ships with handsome crewmen and sing sweet songs to entice them. When a Mer-Woman finds a man she wants, she will wheedle, cajole, sing, call, and follow the ship for hundreds of miles. If the sailor does not respond to her advances, she either has him washed overboard or has the ship wrecked. After she rescues him, she will either let him go after a while or keep him a prisoner. Mer-Women have long breasts that they throw over their shoulders. In the sun, their hair is brilliant yellow, but it is dark green when they are in the water. They are best known in northern Europe, but are also known as Sirens in southern European countries, and there are many other names for them as well.

Moerae. In ancient Greece, the three Fates, or Moerae, determined the destiny of every newborn child. One of the Fates spun the thread of life, one wound it, and one cut it short. They personify change and appear at the three most important moments in people's lives: birth, marriage, and death. The third night after a baby is born, they come to foretell the future, give advice, and favor the child with birthmarks. Moerae live in caves, and young girls and women about to give birth make pilgrimages to them with offerings. They are also invited to weddings. When a person dies, the Moerae appear to usher him or her out of the world. These spinning women are from three to five feet tall. Generally, they are extremely old, ugly, and disfigured. In Italy, the Befana is a descendant of the Moerae, who brings sweets for good children and coal for the bad ones at the Epiphany in January.

Monacielli. They dress like monks and tease, pinch, and torment. They will only stay still if a sieve is placed next to them. It takes them hours to count all the holes and keeps them from trouble. Known as "little friars," they are the guardians of underground treasures. They all wear red hoods. If you catch hold of one of their hoods, there is a chance you can win a treasure. These spirits are native to southern Italy, but some have been sighted in Sardinia and Greece.

Moss People. Moss Maidens will help if no one peels the bark off a tree, bakes caraway seeds inside bread, or tells their dreams. They are very industrious, have secret healing knowledge, and can turn leaves into gold. Moss Maidens make the crops grow better by dancing in the fields. They spin and weave all the moss in the forest and are clothed in moss. They live in virgin forests of central Europe.

Mound Folk. These tall, thin elves are quite old and clever. They are the master smiths and clever mechanics and know the secrets of old runes. They maintain a village life inside mounds. They are between four and six feet tall, and love to dance on warm summer nights or when the moon is full. It is said they know the secret of the Elf King's Tune. Unless they come into contact with the sunlight, their skin is a pale blue translucent color. If sunlight hits them, they darken or turn to stone. They are shape-shifters. Subgroups of the Mound Folk are the Norwegian Thusser, the Finnish Maanvaki, the Norwegian and Faroe Island Hulde Folk, and the Swedish Pysslinger-Folk. They inhabit Iceland, Norway, Finland, Sweden, Denmark, and the Faroe Islands. The mounds of the Icelandic Mount Folk can be seen, raised on high red pillars, on New Year's Eve and on other full-moon nights.

Muryans. The Cornish word for *ant* is *muryan*. Once the Cornish people believed fairies were the souls of the heathen who were not bad enought for hell and not good enough for heaven. They had to stay on earth, and every time they changed themselves, they got smaller and smaller until they were the size of ants. Cornishmen believed they had to be very careful about killing ants in case they destroyed a human soul.

Nereides. Nereides are most dangerous at noon and midnight. Life is meaningless for the female Nereid without her white shawl, and many young men try to get them as wives by capturing their shawls. Nereides often travel in whirlwinds and are always beautiful. They are not immortal. At one time they were called Nymphs, and were known throughout Greece, Alvania, and Crete.

Night-Elves. Nightmares are caused by elves who ride their victims like mares. Since the Middle Ages, various plants have been used to keep Night-Elves away. Amulets of diamonds, coral, jet, jasper, or special hide were also used for prevention. Current preventatives include a knife, horseshoe, or cross hung over the door, or one can throw flax before the door. Mistletoe or a blessed olive or vine leaf can also be hung over the bed. There are other preventatives, such as shoes kept with the toes pointing away from the bed. All these remedies vary from place to place. Night-Elves have many names and forms, as these shape-changers are quite common throughout Europe.

Nissen (Tomtra, Nis, Tomte). A happy home spirit is responsible for the well-being of the entire house. These sprites work hard but will not accept regular wages. They do insist that people keep the house and grounds neat and clean all the time or they will leave and take all the good luck with them. They love to dance on full-moon nights and skate on frozen lakes and rivers in the moonlight. The Finnish home sprites are called Tontuu and Para. There are also many other names for them. They have large heads, long arms, bright eyes, and old faces. Nissen are strong and very old. Previously they lived in ash, linden, or elm trees. Now, dark corners of the house, barn, or woodpile are their homes.

Norggen. They are small descendants of the large and malevolent giants, Orchi, who have been known to eat children. Usually, they are about three feet high and have blazing red eyes. They can be capricious or helpful. These wood sprites steal everything.

Orculli. Here we have the master shape-changers, who can be recognized by their stinky smell. The Orculli live in northern Italy. They prefer valley or mountain caves, but have been known to visit houses and mines. Although they have relatively pleasant dispositions, they are quite capricious at times.

Pamarindo. These Folletto of northern Italy are particularly nasty, lazy, obese, and cruel. They lure animals over a cliff to their deaths. There, these two-foot-tall, fat creatures gorge themselves. They have pointed copper shoes and copper hats. Their clothes are red.

Peg O'Nell. She is supposed to claim a life every seventh year. As the evil spirit of the Ribble River, Peg O'Nell demands a cat or dog by drowning, or else she then claims a person.

People of Peace or **Sith**. These little people of Scotland are proud and independent. They are descendants of the Irish Sidhe and the Scandinavian Trolls. The Sith are three to four feet high, blond or red-haired, wear green, and have pointed hats. They speak old Gaelic. During the full moon, their green hill homes can be seen raised on pillars. Most often, they are seen in May. Another name for them is Trows.

Phouka. This is a great Irish jokester who will do a good turn for people if they can tolerate his pranks.

Pixies. According to popular beliefs, Pixies are the last survivors of the original red-headed inhabitants of Cornwall. The children of these first settlers, along with unbaptized children, turn into Pixies after death. Currently they are naked, hairy, tiny field sprites. They dance to the music of crickets, frogs, and grasshoppers. Their dance circles are found in Devon, Somerset, and Cornwall. They are only nine to twelve inches high now, although they were once the size of people. Their pointed ears, turned-up noses, and red hair identify them. In west Somerset they are known as Grigs. Their homes are under rocks, in caves, trees, or meadows, and sometimes inside houses.

Poleviki. Humans are allowed to harvest crops only if they know how to do it properly. These field elves are fiercely protective of their domain. The Noon Woman stops women she meets in the fields at noon and questions them about growing and spinning flax. If they give the wrong answers, they have to pay with their lives. The Russian Poleviki change their size according to the field they live in. Their territory includes eastern and northern Europe and Russia.

Poltersprites. These Kobolde descendants make knocking or poltering sounds. They are shape-changers who help with the housework and delight in making noises. They are free to travel as they wish and have red or grey caps which give them the power of invisibility. They are known in most of Europe, and some of them have migrated to the United States.

Portunes. They have been extinct now for several centuries. The Portunes were remarkable mainly for their size. They were even shorter than the Thumblings of fairy tales—one inch high. They invade deserted farmhouses in the night in France and England. In spite of their mischievous nature, they were welcomed because they were good workers and brought luck with them.

Puck. In pictures, Puck often has goat's legs and feet and little horns on his head. He is a prankster who is always ready for a joke but does not take them to the extreme. Shakespeare used Puck in his stories. The Irish Puck is the Phouka.

Quiet Folk. Their wealth is staggering because they know all the hiding places of all ores and precious stones. They are extremely generous and very slow to anger. However, when angry they are impossible to calm. Quiet Folk are not as boisterous as their Erdluitle relatives. Like the Erdluitle, they have goose feet. These dwarfs are one-and-a-half to two-and-a-half feet high. They live in Denmark, northern and eastern Germany, and along the Baltic coast, and are strictly subterranean. Treat them kindly.

Red Caps. These lowland castle spirits are some of the most bloodthirsty Scottish elves. They dye their caps red with human blood, which they get by hitting travellers with boulders. Crosses, cross-handled swords, and words from the Bible are the only things that discourage them.

River Men. The Elf King's Tune, played by the River Men (or Nixen) on harps and fiddles of gold, lead men to their land. These moody water spirits can be helpful at times by warning of drownings. However, if they teach a man the Elf King's Tune, the man will not be able to stop fiddling until he plays the tune backwards, note for note, or until someone cuts the strings of his fiddle from behind. They do not like steel. The verse, "Neck, neck, needle thief, you are in the water, but I am on land. / Neck, neck, needle thief, you are on land, but I am in the water," will render them powerless. Their teeth are green or like fish teeth. They always have wet tips on their shirts or aprons. River Men (or Stromkarl, Fossegrim, Nixen, Seemannlein, Hakelmanner, Nickelmanner, Soetrolde, and Manx Nikkisen) live near waterfalls and have their homes in streams or under bridges.

River Women. The main occupations of the River Women are singing, hair-combing, dancing, and shape-changing. Their dispositions reflect the waters they haunt. River Women have a turbulent, youthful beauty. They are about four feet tall, fair-skinned, golden-haired, green-eyed, and dressed in white, and have long breasts that they throw over their shoulders. Their homes are in river banks, under tree roots, or in crystal underwater palaces. Among the River Women are the Genetten, Dracae, Nixies, Kallraden, Nereides, and the Rusalky.

Rusalky. They can be seen in the water combing their green hair only on Holy Thursday. Rusalky move into the trees in the sixth week after Easter. Walking on their laundry can cause the unwary person to lose either their strength or coordination. On the seventh week, on Sunday, the Rusalky walk for the first time in the grain fields and make the grain wave. On June 29, they dance each night by the light of the moon and snare men. They vanish when the first snow falls. The Vodyaniye are extremely jealous of the Rusalky. The Rusalky tickle to death those who cannot answer their riddles. They cannot live if their hair dries out, so they always carry combs with them. They can cause a flood when they pull the combs through their hair.

Salvani and **Aguane**. They are married and protect the lower Alps. They keep the meadows fruitful, the water clean and pure, and the trees and forests safe. Their clothes are of bear, wolf, or wild bull skins. They are human size, hairy, and strong. The Aguane have drooping breasts and goat-hoof-like feet, but are shape-changers, often taking the form of ugly old women. They can be found in Italy, Austria, Yugoslavia, the French Pyrenees, and Spain.

Seal People (Sea Trows, Selkies). In order to travel through the water, the Seal People must put on a seal or fish skin. On full-moon nights they dance on the shore of rocky beaches. Trows have been reported to marry a man who steals their skin in order to get it back. In human form, Seal Women have a slight web between their fingers, rough palms, and slow breathing. They love swimming and diving, can foretell the future, and have knowledge of medicine and midwifery. They never lose their love for the sea and return to it after regaining their skins. Seal People are found in Scotland, Orkney, Shetland, and Ireland.

Seligen. Seligen are extremely benevolent female elves who care for the woods and animals. They protect chamois and deer from hunters and milk them in underground stalls. They can heal, spin, weave, and make crops grow faster. If their hair is touched by a man, if anyone curses, if they are hit in anger, if they are called by their proper names, or if they are given gifts of clothing, they will leave. They love bells and dancing. Their homes are in Germany and Austria.

Servan. These home spirits run away with useful objects and hide them. They are full or pranks but can be very helpful. A bowl of soup or cream left on the roof every night is payment for their help. They are one to two feet high, are shape-changers, dress in red, and have a loud, hearty laugh; they live in the Swiss Alps and Basque Pyrenees.

Sidhe (pronounced "shee"). Sidhe are descendants of the original Irish little people. They are the aristocrats of faerie. Sidhe have great powers, make beautiful music, and are domestic. Maeve is their queen. It is important not to anger them because they can change humans completely. Sidhe despise slovenly people and appreciate offerings of food and water.

Sirens. They are similar to the Mermaids and enchant men with their sweet songs, especially on moonlit nights. They lure ships onto reefs and rocks. Ancient Greek stories tell of the three Siren sisters who were punished first by being changed into bird-women, then into fish-women. They were fated to die if they let a single sailor pass them unharmed. They killed themselves when they were tricked by Odysseus. They are shape-changers and are rarely seen in the open sea. River mouths or along coasts are their preferred places.

Skogsra or **Wood Trolls**. Great care should be taken in dealing with the Skogsra. These Swedish elves are wood and forest sprites. They cannot travel far from the forest and their lives are tied to their own trees. They gain control over people and lead them astray. Never answer "yes" to any sounds heard in the forest. Garlic and steel are effective against the Skogsra. They fear thunder and wolves, and can be wounded with one of their own hairs fired from a shotgun. They are shape-shifters, but their true form is that of an old man with a wide hat. When in human form, they have a long cow tail which they try to hide behind themselves. They live in trees and prefer to remain invisible to people.

Sleigh Beggey. The original inhabitants of Man have the entrances to their world near their dancing circles, under stones, on open moors, behind caves, under river banks, or in ruined castles. The only time a human will want to visit the Sleigh Beggey world is on May Day. Otherwise, humans are not permitted to leave and must stay for a great length of time. Sleigh Beggey react best to flattery. However, they are horse stealers. Sleigh Beggey will travel only on specific paths and will not let a human cross their path when they are on it. They do not like salt, artificial light, horseshoes, silver, and most yellow flowers.

Tom Tit Tot (also his relatives **Rumpelstiltskin** and **Whuppity Stoorie**). Tom Tit Tot is an imp or little devil. He is full of malice and drives hard bargains. Foul-Weather is the name of the Cornish Tom Tit Tot.

Tree Elves. Each elf is born directly from a tree and takes on the characteristics of the particular tree it came from. The elder tree has the highest elf population. People are expected to ask permission before cutting a branch or picking fruit from a tree. Tree spirits are known throughout the world.

Tylwyth Teg. These small (two to three feet tall) folk lived in Wales. They were fond of stealing blond human children, and their offspring are the modern lake maidens. To protect blond babies, baptize them early and always protect them with iron and rowan crosses.

Vazila. Since the Vazila take care of the horses, it is probably only natural that they themselves should have horses' ears and hooves.

Vily. They are malicious, jealous, and wicked. The Greek Nereides are their relatives. They are exclusively female, and live in mountain forests and on craggy peaks. They protect and care for springs, streams, trees, plants, and animals in their domains. It is said that the Vily are only born during a fine rain on summer days when the sunlight makes tiny rainbows on tree branches. They have reddish-brown, curly hair that falls to their feet. Sometimes they have invisible wings and fly through the air. People born on Tuesday or Sunday can see Vily with ease. Vily live in trees, and if their host tree is cut down they will die.

Vodyaniye. This bloodthirsty heathen spirit of the water is ugly, fat, and bloated. Young girls who drown or commit suicide can choose to be companions of the Vodyaniye, and are called Rusalky. Vodyaniye live under waterwheels, in millstreams, rivers, springs, pools, or lakes. Trying to rescue a drowning person offends the Vodyaniye mightily, but he is appeased by offerings. He is a shape-changer, but can be identified by the small puddle of water he leaves whenever he sits down.

White Ladies. They are from northern Europe (Germany, Austria, Holland, and parts of Denmark), and are associated with the old pagan priestesses. White Ladies are helpful to humans and serve fertility functions.

Wichteln. These domesticated house spirits are from southern Germany and Austria. Wichteln have tireless energy and are full of mischievous tricks. Otherwise, they are hard workers and accept no pay, only gifts that are left quietly in their favorite spots. Their bodies are hairy and only three feet tall. They have spindly legs, long silver beards, large heads, deep-set eyes, and big bellies.

Will-o'-the-Wisps. They take a variety of forms. Stillborn, unbaptised Russian children are stolen after their deaths to live in underwater homes. Spunkies of England and Scotland are also the souls of unbaptized children. Will-o'-the-Wisps can be seen at sea or on land. They prefer to live in damp places or in the vicinity of graveyards. Other names for them are St. Elmo's Fire, the Northern Lights, Merry Dancers, Elf Fire, Kit-with-the-Canstick, Jack o' Lanthorn, and Chevres Dansantes.

3

Story Artifacts

Stories commonly make references to special things—artifacts—which turn up for specific purposes in context. The artifacts included in the story are neither incidental nor purely utilitarian. They have special cultural significances which lend meaning to the stories themselves. The kind of tree under which a protagonist sits might signify clues, portents, and meanings that would be revealed only to someone who knew the hidden implications of the reference. That a story makes use of eggs, butter, cheese, and bread is also not arbitrary. Substitutions of more contemporary, and hence more recognizable, artifacts in story contexts might seriously harm story integrity and meaning, and might deprive today's generally uninformed, literate audience of some aspect of the folkloric content of their collective human inheritance. Folkloric backgrounds for stars, gems, rocks, minerals and stones, trees, plants, and flowers are collected in chapters 5-8. The nature of the folklore surrounding each can enlighten the storyteller with regard to liberties which can and cannot be taken with the stories, and can help the teller to enrich a story and bring the content of the folklore to the audience.

The storyteller works as conservator of the memories of primary oral cultures, as these come to us in both oral and printed form. Knowing cultural significances and symbolic contents of such story aspects as artifacts and activities (see part 4) can help the teller know how to invent within the constraints provided by the culture, and recognize the boundaries beyond which a culture's memories are distorted or abandoned (the occurrence of intrusion errors) and a story is violated.

CHAPTER

5

Stars

Star light,
Star bright,
First star I've seen tonight,
I wish I may,
I wish I might,
Have the wish I wish tonight.
— Traditional

INTRODUCTION

Consider the sky and its constellations of stars as the first picture book, illustrating the stories explaining their symbols and meanings. A great tragedy of modern times is that so many people spend almost their entire lives in the glare of city lights. Never to experience the great vault of the night sky, with stars so near they can almost be touched, is a distinct pity.

The stars were used by ancients for timing the planting of crops and the observation of festivals. Such events were planned in accordance with the rising of certain stars. Very early on, the stars served to record the passage of time and as a guide for early navigators.

The wonder and mystery of the stars not only inspired utilitarian uses but led to their becoming objects of idolatry. The heavenly bodies were consulted before courses were pursued or actions taken. Stars became the earliest form of religion. Many traditions have emerged from the mists that shroud the origin of the constellations.

Immediate descendants of Adam studied the stars. Seth and Enoch inscribed the names, meanings, secret virtues, and the science of the stars on two pillars. One pillar was made of brick and the other of stone. These two pillars are part of a symbol that is well-recognized by everyone today. Examine the symbol " $." The history of the two mysterious pillars entwined with a serpent, which was the symbol of revolution, can be traced through the ages from remote antiquity until it becomes our dollar sign.

Early in the world's history, astronomy and astrology flourished in China, India, Arabia, and Egypt. The Chinese were called "Celestials" because their empire was divided after the celestial spaces. Early astronomical annals of the Chinese reveal that, before the year 2357 BC, the Emperor Yao had divided the twelve zodiacal signs by the twenty-eight mansions of the moon.

Astronomy runs like a golden thread through history and binds together all tribes and peoples of the earth. Some of the conceptions about the stars that were popular in ancient times include:

- The Persians are said to have considered, over 3,000 years ago, that the heavens were divided up into four great districts. "Royal Stars" (Aldebaran, Antares, Regulus, and Fomalhaut) watched over each of these districts.

- The Assyrians looked upon the stars as divinities, endowed with beneficial or evil powers.

- The Chaldeans regarded the sky as a boat shaped like a basket. The space below was the earth, which was flat and surrounded by water.

- The Egyptians worshipped Osiris and Isis as ancestors and even showed Plutarch their graves, as well as the stars they had changed into.

- The Peruvians thought that there was not a beast or bird on earth whose shape or image did not appear in the sky. They considered stars to be guardian divinities and worshipped them.

- The Hebrews believed that the sun, moon, and stars danced before Adam in Paradise.

- The African Bushmen saw the more conspicuous stars as men, lions, tortoises, etc. They also believed that the sun, moon, and stars were once mortals on earth.

- In New Zealand, heroes were thought to become stars of greater or lesser brightness according to the number of their victims slain in battle.

- Native Americans believed that many of the stars were living creatures, such as Ursa Major (the Bear).

- The Tannese Islanders divided the heavens into constellations, with definite traditions to account for the canoes, ducks, and children they saw in the skies.

- The South Pacific Island people considered that dying people would become stars. When near death, they could even indicate where in the sky their stars would be located.

- The Eskimos felt that some of the stars had been men and others were different sorts of animals and fish.

- Slavonic mythology regarded the stars as living in habitual relationships with men and their affairs.

- Anaximenes thought that the stars were fixed in the dome of heaven like nails.

One ancient legend tells us that there were no stars until the giants of old threw stones at the sun. These stones pierced holes in the sky and let the light of that orb shine through — we call these holes stars. Native Americans say that, "As our last breath of life leaves us, our spirit climbs aboard a little cloud formed by this breath. This cloud carries us up to live among the cloud people where we reside for a period of time, until next we are stars in the sky. The stars keep track of our people."

Bless my stars!

Thank your lucky stars!

Star-crossed

These are some of the expressions related to stars which are part of our language. We still use them even though their history is ancient and tied to folklore. We also refer to specially prominent film and stage actors as stars. In ecclesiastical art, a number of saints may be recognized by the stars depicted on them or around them. A star of some form constitutes part of the insignia of every order of knighthood. The Star Chamber was a court of civil and criminal jurisdiction at Westminster, England. It was abolished in 1641, but is still notorious for its arbitrary proceedings. It was called Star Chamber either because the ceiling or roof was decorated with gilt stars, or because it was the chamber where the "stars" or Jewish documents were kept. We also refer to star witnesses. Obviously, stars and their lore make good material for storytelling.

THE NORTH STAR, POLE STAR, OR POLARIS

Specific stars have cultural significance in our star lore. Take for instance, the North Star or Pole Star, or Polaris.

In their legends, the Norse believed the gods ground the universe out of the bodies of their defeated enemies, the ancient race of giants. The gods then drove a huge spike into the center of the universe and around this spike they made the heavens revolve. The end of the spike is fastened to the outer rim of the universe by means of a jeweled nailhead—the North Star.

The Greeks called the North Star Cynosura, meaning the "tail of the dog." Even today the word *cynosure* means the center of attraction. The Mongols called the Pole Star the Golden Peg, and like the Norsemen they thought it was a stake that held the whirling heavens together. In India, the North Star is called the Pivot of the Planets, and in China it is the Emperor of Heaven. These indicate the recognition of the constant position of the North Star as well as its importance.

The Chinese believe that Shang Ti, the supreme ruler of heaven and earth, lives in the Pole Star. He has two ministers of state to help him administer all the complicated organization of the sky above and the Middle Kingdom below. (See the following material on Ursa Major, or the Big Bear constellation, p. 48.)

Chinese stories also relate that there is a goddess of the North Star. Taoists especially worship her. Her name is Tou Mu. Once she lived on earth, where she was so virtuous that she attained a deep knowledge of celestial mysteries and came to possess supernatural power. She was able to cross the seas at will without wetting her feet as she skimmed the waves. She saved many sailors from shipwreck in this way. Her reputation grew until the ruler of a kingdom in North China sent for her and married her. After a long life span on earth, when she was ready to die, the Lord of Heaven himself came to earth and invited Tou Mu and her husband and nine sons to heaven. There they still dwell in the palace of the Pole. Tou Mu is now a goddess seated on a throne of lotus, who holds the books of life and death in her eighteen hands. It is believed that if you pray to her with sufficient faith, she has the power of prolonging life.

The Egyptians considered Polaris an evil star. It is associated with death and the coffin of Osiris. The coffin was made of fragrant wood, fashioned by Osiris' brother Set, and is the constellation known as Ursa Major.

Arabs also referred to the constellation Ursa Major as a great coffin with mourners. They thought the Pole Star was the biggest villain in the skies: he was the one who killed the warrior now lying in the huge coffin. This dead warrior was the hero for whom all the stars mourned as they moved in their slow funeral procession through the night. For this murder, the Pole Star was ostracized by all his brethren, and he alone must remain fixed in his place. He remains imprisoned in the cold and unfriendly north sky, while his angry fellow stars look at him with scorn and circle around him, keeping a considerable distance from him.

URSA MAJOR

The stars in the constellation Ursa Major were commonly identified with the bear in India, Greece, and North America. In fact, it is said that when the first European explorers came to the North American continent, and had learned to speak the language of the natives, they pointed up north one evening and said, "See those seven stars? They are stars we call the Bear." The Native Americans agreed that those were their bear stars too.

A modern Greek legend relates that originally the sky was supposed to be made of glass which touched the earth on both sides. It was soft and then someone nailed a bearskin on it. The nails became stars, and the tail of the bear is represented by the three bright stars which are also known as the handle of the Big Dipper. The Big Dipper is contained within the Ursa Major, or Big Bear, constellation.

A source of particular wonder to the Greeks was the apparent reluctance of the Bear to wet his feet in the waters that girdled the earth—or so it must have appeared, because of the constellation's position high above the horizon. The Greeks observed that all the other stars rose from the sea and set there again when their night's journey was done. The story of Callisto explained this peculiarity.

Callisto, a nymph, was beloved by Jupiter. As usual, Juno was jealous of the beauty of the nymph and Jupiter's interest in her. In revenge, she transformed Callisto into a bear and left her in that form to wander, disconsolate and helpless, in the forests near her home in Arcadia. Callisto's son Arcas was out hunting when he came upon this bear, and would have killed his own mother without recognizing her in her beast form had Jupiter not intervened. Jupiter seized both bear and hunter, first Callisto and then Arcas, and swung them up to the skies. Callisto became the Great Bear and Arcas the Little Bear.

Juno was not satisfied with her revenge, because her rival was shining gloriously in the sky, alight with brilliant stars and even more lovely than she had been on earth. Jupiter watched her every night as she danced gracefully around the Pole. Juno went to Neptune and secured a promise from him that neither of the Bears would ever enter his deep, green kingdom of the sea, to rest, bathe, or even drink from the rim of the ocean. Consequently, the Bears spend eternity circling far above the north horizon. Every time they come down close to the water, as they pass under the Pole, Neptune drives them away.

The most ancient of temples, the Tower of Babel, was called the Temple of the Seven Lights or the Celestial Earth. It embodied the astronomical kingdoms of antiquity. The seven lights were supposedly the seven stars of the Great Dipper.

The sacredness of the number seven originated in the Euphrates Valley. Some possible explanations for the attribution of great mystic power to the number seven include the sun and moon and five planets, the Pleiades, the Bear stars, the division of the twenty-eight days of the month by four (which has given us our week), or some other high magic. The stars of the Great Bear were a symbol of this special virtue. The nightly appearance of the Great Bear was an omen that all was well in the land above.

Ursa Major was always a constellation of great importance in the religions of the Far East. Its seven stars were sometimes embroidered on the robes of emperors. The seven stars are still one of the most common symbols in Chinese design, and are often seen in paintings, on coins, on mirrors, and in stone carvings. The sun, the moon, and the seven stars are together known as the nine lights of heaven. Chinese astronomers imagined that the circular motion of Ursa Major was responsible for the seasons. They believed that the destiny of man was controlled by some force that lay in the heart of the constellation, which was called the Palace of the Fates.

The Chinese people considered the Dipper a sign of fate. They called the constellation the Bushel or Measure because of its shape. They likened it to the container in which they weighed out rice and other grain. Being a staple, the measure of grain was also the measure of life. Therefore, it seemed appropriate that the gods of fate who determined man's fortune and length of life lived in that constellation.

A Chinese legend tells of the supreme ruler of heaven and earth who lives in the Pole Star, Shang Ti. His two ministers are the Spirit of the Great Bear, who rules the lands of heaven, and the Spirit of T'ai Shan, the sacred mountain, who rules China. They are called "the stars that assist." The Bear constellation has therefore long been associated in the minds of the Chinese with T'ai Shan, the highest peak of a mountain range in Shantung. A number of shrines and temples to its stars are to be found along the pilgrim path leading to the summit. This is a most holy mountain and the pilgrim path is well worn. Since the first records of Chinese history, pilgrims have come from all parts of the country to climb the six thousand steps to the summit. A square altar, dedicated to the seven stars of the Bear, stands there.

King Arthur of the Round Table is also interwoven with the history of the Great Bear. Arthur's name supposedly came from the Welsh words for bear, *arth*, and wonderful, *Uthyr*. The Bear stars were his special symbol, and some of his followers claimed that he was actually an incarnation of the spirit of the constellation. The shape of the famous Round Table might also have come from the conspicuous circle made by the swinging of the Bear's tail and the great arc it made.

> Arthur once fell asleep on the seashore and in his sleep a spirit came to him. The spirit guided him far north to where the stars of the Bear are bright. There Arthur found the knights of heaven seated at a great circular table, resplendent as the shining stars. The knights of heaven told Arthur that he would be king, and that he must pattern his life and rule on that of the kingdom of heaven. When Arthur died, his soul traveled once again among the stars to the shining Septentriones. It is said he will eventually return to rule over the people of England.

The American Indians recognized a bear in the Bear stars, but they were too familiar with the anatomy of that animal to believe that the three curving stars in the handle of our Dipper could be its tail. The earthly bear had no such tail to speak of. They believed the tail stars were three hunters, hot on the trail of the great beast.

The Bear is a Great Spirit and one of the immortals. He lives in the far frozen north where no one has ever ventured. Since bears sleep throughout the winter, the Bear is hibernating in his den, that half-circle of stars we call Corona Borealis. In the spring he rouses himself and appears in the east. He lumbers around the polar skies silently stalking the three hunters behind him. The first hunter has a bow and arrow, the second carries a pot — the faint little star Alcor — in which to cook the meat of the Bear. The third hunter gathers stars along the way to build a fire under the pot. However, the Bear swings from one side of the Pole Star to the other in dizzy circles. The Bear weakens and is shot by one of the enchanted arrows. In the autumn, the leaves of the maple and sycamore and other trees turn red, because the blood of the old celestial Bear is dripping on them from the sky. The blood soaks into the veins of the leaves until they take on the color of blood. They mourn the passing of the Great Spirit as, one by one, leaf by leaf, they fall sadly from their branches. Winter blows down from the north. The Bear is dying and the year is at an end.

Meanwhile, the wounded Bear crawls into his den and dies. The hunters carry away his body, boil it in their pot, and feast on it. The soul of the Bear cannot die, since he is a Great Spirit, so it enters another body. All through the long winter, this new Bear sleeps in his den. Like the earth, he awakens refreshed in the spring and the whole cycle of nature begins again. This story is found in the legends of the Iroquois, Algonquin, Cherokee, and many other tribes.

The Blackfeet tribe explains Ursa Major differently.

A small Blackfeet camp had a family of a father, a mother, seven brothers, and two sisters. Six of the brothers and one sister were grown up. The other girl and boy were still children. The six older brothers were on a hunting expedition when the elder sister fell in love with and married a grizzly bear. The girl's father called all the men of the tribe together when he heard of this. They attacked and killed the bear. Since the bear had strong magical powers, something of the creature entered into his wife, and she herself took the form of a bear whenever she pleased. In this form, she avenged her husband's death by killing her father and mother. Returning to her human form, she began to plot the death of the two children remaining at home.

The boy Okinai and the girl Sinopa were alarmed at the behavior of their sister. They realized she meant to do away with them. Sinopa went down to the river one day to get water and while she was there she met her six older brothers, who had returned from the hunt. She told them what happened and they promised her that they would all be safe. They helped her collect a great number of prickly pears, which she scattered everywhere in front of the tent when she got home. She left only a very narrow path along which she could find her way out of the tent. That night, she awakened her brother Okinai and took him to where the six brothers were waiting.

Their sister, the bear-woman, heard them and chased them. She got caught among the prickly pears. Roaring with pain, she transformed herself into a grizzly bear and rushed after them. Little Okinai also had certain unusual magical powers. He shot an arrow, which put them all as far ahead of the chasing bear as the arrow had flown, but the bear kept gaining on them. Okinai waved a feather and thick tangled bushes sprang up behind them; the bear's magic cleared a path through the tangle. Okinai waved his hand and a huge tree shot up into the air beside them. The eight terrified brothers and sister climbed into the branches of the tree. The bear caught up with them and climbed into the tree herself. She dragged four of them down and was just reaching for the fifth when Okinai called on his strongest magic. One by one he shot eight arrows into the sky, and with each shot one of the children soared up to heaven. As they reached the sky, they turned into stars and there they may still be seen in Ursa Major. The four together in the bowl of the Dipper are those who had already been pulled out of the tree. The three in the handle are those who were still high up in the tree branches. The tiny companion star of one of these, Alcor, is the frightened Sinopa huddling close to one of her brothers.

CASSIOPEIA, CEPHEUS, ANDROMEDA, PERSEUS, AND PEGASUS

That starred Ethiop queen that strove
To set her beauty's praise above
The sea-nymphs and their powers offended.
—Milton, *Il Penseroso*

Cassiopeia, the Lady in the Chair, is one of the oldest and most popular of the constellations. The arrangement of stars that constitute this constellation easily resembles a chair. This constellation revolves around the pole. When it is below the pole, it is a slightly distorted capital "M." This is reversed when Cassiopeia is above the pole, making it a celestial "W."

Cassiopeia belonged to the so-called "Royal Family" of starland. In Greek mythology, Cassiopeia was the wife of Cepheus, the King of Ethiopia and the mother of Andromeda.

Cassiopeia was a woman of great beauty, but unfortunately she was as proud as she was lovely, and she made a habit of boasting of her beauty. At first she boasted that she was the most beautiful creature in Ethiopia; then she included the world; last, she claimed she was the most beautiful either on earth or among the gods.

One day, she insulted the water nymphs who lived in the seashore and cool waters of bubbling streams. Further, she stated that she, Cassiopeia, was far more lovely than any nymph that ever lived. At this, the nymphs complained to Poseidon, their father.

Neptune emerged from the sea and plunged his trident deep into the waters. He created a monster unlike any that had ever been known on earth or in the sea. This evil and ferocious creature, Cetus, was sent off to lay waste to the country and strike terror into the hearts of its inhabitants. Cetus did his assigned job well. Ethiopians fled from the coast in terror and begged Cepheus, the king, to save them. Cepheus consulted an oracle and was told that the only possible way to appease the wrath of Neptune would be to offer his daughter Andromeda as a sacrifice for the ferocious, ravenous monster. Even though the king loved his daughter, he had no choice. Andromeda was led to the edge of the sea, chained to a rock, and left there as an offering to Cetus.

Perseus, the hero son of Zeus and Danae, had been given the almost hopeless task of obtaining the head of Medusa, which turned all who looked on it to stone. With the help of the gods, he was successful. Perseus had managed to slay Medusa using Minerva's shield, Mercury's winged shoes, and Pluto's helmet of invisibility. Using these gifts, he hovered above Medusa while she slept by means of the magic shoes. He guided himself by the reflection in the shield, cut off Medusa's head, and flew away across the sea with it. Some drops of blood from Medusa's head fell into the water. Nepture felt these drops and, overcome with grief (he had once loved Medusa), he lifted up the drops of blood, mixed them with white sand from the beaches and foam from the waves, and created Pegasus, the winged horse.

There are several versions of what happened next. Some say Perseus mounted Pegasus and flew over the coast of Ethopia. Others have him still flying with the winged shoes of Mercury. At any rate, he saw Andromeda chained to a rock in the sea, as the hungry Cetus was also approaching the rock. Perseus fell on the monster and plunged his sword so deeply into the neck of Cetus that the blood spouted up and soaked the winged sandals. They became so wet and heavy that Perseus could no longer fly, and had to balance himself on a rock for the final blow. In the end, he simply held up the head of Medusa in front of the monster and Cetus was turned to stone. Of course, Andromeda and Perseus were then married.

All of the characters in these adventures were transformed into constellations, and they continue their story in the sky. Neptune saw to it that Cassiopeia the vain was given a seat in heaven placed so that she would swing completely upside down as she revolved around the Pole Star. There she is, still in her chair, spending half of every night hanging with her head down. Certainly the position is uncomfortable as well as humiliating.

DRACO THE DRAGON

Here the vast Dragon twines
Between the Bears and like a river winds.
—Warton's *Virgil*

The serpent is historically very interesting. It is referred to in myth and legend more often than any other creature. It is connected with the story of the Garden of Eden. Some Asian cultures believe the snake grows up to become a dragon.

Even though the dragon was abhorred by men of all ages, it assumes a prominent place in the heavens. The dragon surrounds the Pole Star and winds around the pole of the world and guards it. The dragon is also one of the twelve signs of the Chinese zodiac, and, as Scorpio, of the western one as well. The Egyptian hieroglyph for the heavens was a serpent whose scales denoted stars.

Babylonians regarded Draco as a monster who personified primeval chaos. Other stories consider the serpent to be the guardian of the stars (the golden apples) which hang from the Pole tree in the Garden of Darkness near Mount Atlas in Africa. Since this constellation never sets in north temperate latitudes, the Greeks saw it as an emblem of eternal vigilance. Legends also relate that the dragon was slain by Hercules. Plutarch said that the hippopotamus, or its variant the crocodile, was certainly one of the forms of the dragon. On a wall at Thebes, in Egypt, Horus, the great god and the light of the heavens, is represented as destroying the hippopotamus or crocodile. This is echoed in the legend of St. George and the dragon.

There were gods in Greece long before Zeus and his followers. Earth-gods and sky-gods and primeval forces were the heritage of earlier mythologies. The Greek stories tell of Draco fighting on the side of the Titans in the battle against Zeus and his cohorts. As the struggle neared its climax, Athena, the goddess of wisdom, seized the dragon. She flung him with all her strength into the sky overhead. As Draco sailed far up into the highest heaven, his body kept spinning around and around so that he was coiled in a twisting and knotted circle. He struck the arch of the sky at the very spot around which the firmament itself revolved. Before he could even uncurl, he was caught in the axis of heaven, where he remains today, his snaky coils tangled with the North Pole.

There are many other stories from around the world explaining how the twisted dragon of the north stars got there. Regardless of the origin of these stories, there he is. There seems to have been some effort to symbolize the presence of the Evil One in a star group—ever watchful and ever vigilant.

TAURUS THE BULL

Our vernal signs the RAM begins,
Then comes the BULL in May the TWINS;
The CRAB in June, next LEO shines,
And VIRGO ends the northern signs.

The balance LIBRA brings autumnal fruits,
The SCORPION stings, the ARCHER shoots;
December's GOAT brings wintery blast,
AQUARIUS rain, the FISH come last.

—E.C.B.

The zodiac is an imaginary belt in the heavens, extending for about eight degrees on either side of the apparent path of the sun, and including the paths of the moon and the principal planets. It is divided into twelve equal parts, or signs, each named for a different constellation.

Some feel the constellation Taurus was one of the first to be invented. Over four thousand years ago, the Bull marked the vernal equinox. Taurus was the prince and leader of the celestial hosts. In a sepulchre excavated at Thebes, Taurus is shown as the first of the zodiacal signs. Taurus, to the Egyptians, was the emblem of a perpetual return to life. They identified it with Osiris, the bull-god, the god of the Nile, and worshipped it by the name "Apis." The divine Osiris was thought to be incarnated in this living animal. The bull was kept in surroundings of luxury in Memphis. Sacrifice and offerings were brought to his shrine. He was sought out as an oracle. When one bull died, it was thought that his spirit passed from his body into another, which had to be a black bull with a white square on his forehead and a second white mark in the shape of an eagle on his back. Under his tongue was a lump similar in form to the sacred scarab beetle. He also had double hairs in his tail. When an Apis bull died, all of Egypt mourned.

The spring equinox was New Year's Day. It was the most important date in the year, for that was the time for plowing and planting. It was a time of joy as well, for the unfriendly hours of darkness and winter were at an end. There was new life, warmth, and light. This made the Bull the first and most powerful of the zodiacal constellations.

There is also a suggestion that Taurus may have been the ancestor of the unicorn. This comes from stylized bas-relief and carvings in which only a single horn was shown in profile.

Ancient Chinese knew Taurus as "the White Tiger" and later as "the Golden Ox." In the Amazon country of South America, natives called this star group "the Ox." The Druids worshipped the Bull at their Tauric festival; the May Day festival is a survivor of this great celebration. It has been claimed that the tors of England were the old sites of the Tauric worship, and our hot cross buns are the present representatives of the early bull cakes. The old English morris dance is a remnant of this festival time when the sun enters into the constellation Taurus. The Masonic Tau Cross is another expressive symbol of the vernal equinox and of immortality.

Taurus contains the greatest number of stars of any constellation (141 in all), exclusive of the Pleiades.

THE PLEIADES

One of those forms that flit by us, when we
Are young, and fix our eyes on every face; ...
Whose course and home we know not, nor shall know
Like the lost Pleiad seen no more below.

—Byron, *Beppo*, xiv.

In all ages of the world's history, the Pleiades have been admired and critically observed. Their misty lights have appealed to the imagination. Minstrels and poets sang of their bewitchment and beauty. Homer, the author of the Book of Job, and Tennyson have each celebrated their mystery with lyrical charm. They have been compared to a rosette of diamonds, a swarm of fireflies or bees, and shining drops of dew. Others have seen them as a hen surrounded by her chicks, and some have thought they represented the seven virgins. The "Seven Stars" appears in the New Testament. In Revelation, St. John the Apostle wrote, "The Seven Stars are of the angels of the seven churches, and the seven candlesticks are the seven churches."

The Pleiades appear in the constellation Taurus, perched on the shoulder of that great beast. They were worshipped in Egypt, where they were identified with the goddess Nit, one of the principal divinities of Lower Egypt. The seven chambers of the Great Pyramid are said by some to commemorate these famous stars.

Young Chinese women worshipped these stars as the Seven Sisters of Industry. It has also been suggested that the "tors" and Arthur's Seat (names given to British hilltops) may be connected to the worship of the Pleiades. The Arabians called them "the little ones." The Hindus pictured these stars as a flame, and there may be a connection between the Hindu title "Flame" and the great Feast of Lamps of the western Hindus held in the Pleiad season.

The Aztecs sacrificed humans in the month of November, when the Pleiades would culminate at midnight. Their ceremonies were similar to those of the Druids. Both groups tried to extinguish every fire the length and breadth of the country, so the souls of all who had died during the year could pass over the water to the west in the darkness. The Japanese, even today, celebrate the Feast of Lanterns at this same season of the year. Some great calamity is supposed to have overwhelmed the race of man in the far distant past when these seven little stars were prominent in the sky. The Talmud associates the Pleiades with an all-destroying flood. The ancient Druids celebrated the first of November as a night full of mystery, during which the world was reconstructed. Remains of their celebration can be found in today's All Saints Day on November 1, All Hallows Eve on the last day of October, and All Souls Day, celebrated on the second of November.

In the symbols of Masonry, the Pleiades play a prominent part. The emblem of the Seven Stars alludes to this star group as emblematic of the vernal equinox and a symbol of immortality.

There are many fables and stories surrounding the Pleiades. The Hottentots regarded them as wives who shut their husbands out because they missed their game while hunting. The Pleiades were a favored constellation for the Iroquois nation. In all of their religious festivals, the sacred pipe was presented toward these stars and prayers for happiness were addressed to them. The Iroquois also believed that the Pleiades represented seven young people who guarded the holy seed during the night.

> Another legend relates that seven brothers took to the warpath and discovered a beautiful maiden living all alone. They adopted her as their sister. One day they all went hunting and left the youngest to guard his sister. This youngest brother was distracted by some game and left his sister unprotected. A powerful buffalo came to her lodge and carried her away. When the brothers returned, they went in pursuit of her. They discovered she was being held in a lodge in the very center of a great herd of fierce buffalo. The youngest brother tunnelled beneath them and rescued his sister. The brothers then built a high iron fence around her lodge. This enraged the buffalo. They attacked and battered the fence only to find that the maiden and her brothers had been carried upward to the sky, out of their reach, where they may be seen as the Pleiades cluster.

According to Greek mythology, the Pleiades were the seven daughters of Atlas and Pleione. They were transformed into stars because they grieved so inconsolably over the fate of their father, who was punished for rebelling against Zeus by being made to bear the weight of heaven on his shoulders. One of these daughters, Electra, is invisible. Some say this is because of shame, since she was the only sister married to a human being. Others tell that Electra hides herself from grief for the destruction of the city and the royal race of Troy. She is known as the lost Pleiad. Another myth has it that the Pleiades were so beautiful that Orion pursued them unceasingly. They appealed to Jupiter for help and he changed them into doves. Then they flew into the sky and found refuge among the stars.

The Mongols say the seven stars of Ursa Major are seven robbers and that they stole one of the stars of the Pleiades, which has remained with them ever since.

ORION

Begirt with many a blazing star
Stood the great giant Algebar
Orion, hunter of the beast,
His sword hung gleaming by his side.

— Longfellow

Along with Ursa Major and the Pleiades, Orion is replete with historical and mythological interest. It is beyond question the most brilliant of the constellations, as well as probably the best known. It is visible from every part of the globe. There are arguments about the name *Orion*. Some say it is from *Uru-anna*, meaning the "light of heaven," and that the title originated in the Euphrates Valley. Another explanation is that it is derived from *Kesil*, a Hebrew word that signifies a fool, meaning a godless and impious person.

The figure of Orion represents a mighty giant trampling on a timid hare and pursuing a flock of defenseless doves. According to Greek legend, Orion pursued the Pleiades, who were considered doves or virgins, and was confronted by Taurus the Bull. The figure of the hare has always been associated in folklore with the moon. Since Orion is identified with the sun, there is a symbolic representation of the perpetual strife between the powers of light and darkness.

Orion is connected with the constellation of the scorpion. It is told that Orion boasted that there was no animal on earth which he could not conquer. To punish this vanity, a scorpion sprang out of the earth and stung his foot, causing his death. At the request of Diana, Orion was placed among the stars opposite his slayer.

The Hindus regard Orion as a stag. They say the lord of created beings fell in love with Orion's daughter, who took the form of a dove and fled. The lord changed himself into a stag and chased her. Sirius was selected by the indignant gods to kill him, and he did.

Another legend has Orion as the lover of Merope, the daughter of the king of Chios. Since Merope's father did not favor his advances, Orion attempted to elope with Merope. The king discovered his plan, drugged Orion, put out his eyes, and left him alone on the seashore. Orion followed the sound of a hammer from the forge of Vulcan. He asked for assistance. Vulcan placed him on the shoulders of a cyclops who carried him to the top of a mountain. There, facing the rising sun, he regained his sight.

Among the many stories about Orion is the one in which he was born like Athena, without a mother. He became a famous iron worker and joined Vulcan in building a palace under the sea.

Most legends attribute a stormy character to Orion. In Egypt, the soul of Osiris was said to rest in the constellation Orion. Some say that Egyptians represented Orion as Horus, the young or rising sun, in a boat surrounded by stars. Orion was extremely important in Egyptian folklore, since the constellation preceded and announced the approaching rise of Sirius, the Dog Star, which in turn heralded the inundation of the Nile.

The Hebrews knew Orion as the Giant, bound to the sky for rebellion against Jehovah. The Chinese called Orion *Tsan*, which signifies "three," and corresponds to the "Three Kings," a title sometimes given to the three prominent stars in the belt of Orion. Eskimos called Orion's belt "Tua Tsan," a title that is quite similar to the Chinese one. They thought Orion represented a party of bear-hunters, with their sledge, and the bear they were chasing, transported to the sky, Early inhabitants of Ireland called Orion "the armed King." The Maya knew the constellation as a warrior.

The constellation, as stated earlier, is visible from every part of the globe. It contains two stars of the first magnitude and four of the second. With all its brilliance and beauty, it is not surprising that Orion is one of the most familiar and admired of all the constellations. Its arrival is an announcement that the outdoor season is past and that the nights will become more and more brittle with frost and cold. Interestingly, stars visible in winter are much more brilliant than the summer stars. Some consider Orion to be the masterpiece of the stars.

THE MILKY WAY

A broad and ample road whose dust is gold
And pavement stars as stars to thee appear
Seen in the Galaxy, that Milky Way
Which nightly as a circling zone thou seest
Powdered with stars.

—Milton, *Paradise Lost*

No look at the stars would be complete without some mention of the Milky Way, that mysterious cloud that crosses the sky like a river of mist. The romance of it does not dim even when one realizes that this veil across the heavens is woven of a myriad of close-set suns. During all historic time it was regarded as the "River of Heaven."

Asians fancied a river of shining silver, whose fish were frightened by the new moon, which they imagined to be a hook. It has also been described as a serpent. Ancients also saw it as the road to heaven travelled by the souls of the dead. According to a French tale, the stars in the Milky Way are lights held by angels to show mortals the way to heaven. The Greeks saw this road to heaven as having palaces of illustrious gods along the road. The Algonquin Indians believed that this was the Path of Souls leading to the villages in the sun. As the spirits travel along the pathway, their blazing campfires are seen as bright stars. Norsemen and Scandanavians knew our Milky Way as the path to Valhalla which was travelled by the souls of heroes who fell in battle.

Swedish legend tells of two mortals on earth who loved each other. When they died they were doomed to dwell on different stars far apart, so they bridged the distance between them with a bridge of light. This story is very similar to the Japanese one. They believe that on the seventh day of the seventh month, the shepherd boy-star, Altair, and the Spinning Maiden, Vega, cross the Milky Way on a bridge to meet each other. This happens only if the weather is clear, so that is why the Japanese hope for clear weather on the seventh of July, when the meeting of the Star Lovers is made a gala day throughout Japan.

The Danes regarded the moon as a cheese formed by the milk that has run out of the Milky Way. Greek mythology attributed the Milky Way to the milk dropped from Juno's breasts while she was suckling Hercules. In Germany, the Saxon god Irmin was said to possess a wondrous chariot which he rode across the sky along a path called "Irmin's Way."

Far removed from people who lived in cold climates, the African Bushmen thought the Milky Way was composed of wood ashes thrown up into the sky by a girl, so that people might see their way home at night. Australians call it "the fire smoke of an ancient race." The Masai named it "the road across the sky." Peruvians and the Incas knew it as the "dust of stars." In the Punjab, it was "the Path of Noah's Ark." Ottawa Indians believed it was the muddy water stirred up by a turtle swimming along the bottom of the sky. Other North American Indians regarded the galaxy as the pathway of the ghosts to the land of the hereafter.

A familiar concept in many parts of the world is that the Milky Way represents a serpent with its tail in its mouth. It is a natural symbol for all that is round and closed and endless. The Mongols saw the Milky Way as the Heavenly Seam, and thought it was the line where the two parts of heaven were sewn together. In sacred Mongol and Tibetan books, it is written that there is a great sea that completely encircles the earth. In that sea, there is an elephant. The elephant lies deep in the water, with only his head above water. He breathes very heavily. The steam from his breath rises to the cold air of heaven where the outer winds blow. There, it becomes the Milky Way. In Thailand, they call the Milky Way the "Road of the White Elephant." The white elephant is sacred in Thailand. It is taught that the white elephant must not be worked—just prized. (That is why useless gifts are called *white elephants*; in olden times in Thailand, to give a white elephant might doom the new owner to poverty, since the animal had to be cared for but not worked.)

The Pawnee Indians thought of the Milky Way as a cloud of dust kicked up by a buffalo and a horse racing across the sky. The Finns and Lithuanians knew it as the "Bird's Way," believing that spirits take wing and fly along it to a far, happy land. Germans call the Milky Way "Jacob's Road" and identify it with the ladder which Jacob saw reaching up to heaven in his dream.

Over the ages, people have seen the Milky Way as a river or road or bridge to a place of immortality and a promise of peace and happiness. Everyone hopes for a better world after life on this earth is over. If we are going to such a place, what better way to get there than on the Milky Way?

SUMMARY

This sampling of star folklore is just that—a sample. The world's first picture book is filled with stories and symbols demonstrating humans' fascination with the stars. It is almost as if each constellation is an installment in a serial story. Imaginations created related stories worldwide. Stars are part and parcel of religions and ceremonies. Many of these rituals are still celebrated today, though without the understanding of why we are doing them. We are tied by tender threads to the ancients.

6

Gems, Rocks, Minerals, and Stones

GEMS AND PRECIOUS METALS

"All that glitters is not gold."

Our speech is filled with idioms relating to the wealth of minerals and gems. For instance, "Thar's gold in them thar hills," "Diamonds are a girl's best friend," "The streets are paved with gold," "fools' gold," and of course, "He has the Midas touch."

The ancients thought gems had all manners of supernatural powers. Scientists later came to the understanding of the powers of geology and the earth's caldron in the formation of these treasures. Only when certain elements of the earth's molten inner magma have combined under enormous pressure in precise proportions, and then cooled and solidified at a specific rate, are rare crystals with fire and radiance found. Gold panners today still wash sand and pebbles in streams looking for the gold nuggets and gold dust they know are there.

During the Middle Ages, during the Black Death, people draped themselves in gems in the belief that the purity of the crystals would save them. This same belief in the purity and power of crystals is currently contributing to an increasingly popular fashion look. People throughout the ages have judged wealth by the jewels and minerals owned. Here are some of the legendary attributions and beliefs related to gems that make gems important story artifacts.

Agate. Agate was considered to be a remedy against poisonous wounds.

Amber. A yellow, translucent, fossilized vegetable resin. Legend has it that amber is the tears of birds who were the sisters of Meleager, and who never ceased to weep because of the death of their brother. Amber has been sold as a cure for croup, asthma, and whooping cough.

Amethyst. The Greeks thought a goblet made of amethyst could ward off drunkenness. Roman women thought the amethyst would preserve the affections of their husbands. Along with sobriety and faithfulness, the amethyst was considered to be an antidote for snakebite (when used in a pendant suspended on a dog-hair cord).

Carnelian. Carnelian had the power to restrain anger.

Crysolite. Clear crysolite brought joy as well as calming the eyes and heart.

Crystals. Historically, crystals have been used as spiritual and healing tools by American Indians and Far Eastern cultures. Currently, believers in crystal stones swear they contain and emit energy that supports us in harmonizing our thoughts, emotions, and consciousness with the energies of the universe.

Different crystals have different properties attributed to them:

- *Adventurine* is supposed to give courage in social and group situations, adventures in love and life, and luck where perception is required.

- *Amber calcite* is said to stimulate memory, instill greater intellectual capacities, open the doors of creativity, and aid the digestive and reproductive organs.

- *Amethyst* (*purple*) is believed to protect, provide spiritual attunement, give visions and open spiritual and psychic centers, reduce mental tension, induce dreams, and encourage transformation.

- *Aquamarine* is suggested to provide direction in life and spiritual visions, lift one's spirits, and calm the nerves.

- *Azurite/malachite* is believed to cleanse the subconscious, revealing a clearer mental state.

- *Carnelian* is said to firmly anchor ideas and inspirations, alleviate absent-mindedness and mental confusion, aid in circulation and rheumatism, and strengthen the reproductive organs.

- *Citrine* is regarded as an antidepressant, with the ability to strengthen self-confidence, will, and creative power.

- *Fluorite* is considered to still the mind and allow one to experience inner knowing, to keep the mind clear when under pressure, and to aid mental achievement connecting to higher self.

- *Hematite* is believed to ground and balance the energy patterns between the mental, physical, and spiritual bodies, and to stimulate a weak sex drive.

- *Malachite* (*green*) draws out pain and is considered to be an all-purpose healing stone. Also, it is thought to clear repressed emotions and stimulate thought.

- *Onyx* (*black*) is said to ground spirit forces in the body and gain ability to work lovingly on physical pain.

- *Quartz* (*rose*) is felt to be the heart healer and good for emotional wounds such as grief, as well as promoting love of oneself.

- *Rhodochrosite* is thought to clear the solar plexus, integrate physical and spiritual energy, heal emotional trauma, help in manifesting vision, and restore poor eyesight.

- *Sodalite* is believed to awaken the third eye and mind to inner sight and intuitive knowledge, and is good for rational and logical thinking.

- *Tourmaline* (*black*) is felt to deflect negative energy and instill self-control and discipline.

Diamond. Diamonds are the symbol of love, hope, and purity. Diamond engagement rings testify to these attributes.

Emerald. Emeralds increased riches and brought tranquillity. To strengthen the eyes, do not resort to carrots, but wear an emerald instead.

Garnet. The name is derived from the Latin word for *pomegranate* because of the resemblance between this gem and the seeds of that fruit. Garnet is the birthstone for the month of January. Legends say the garnet will protect its wearer from accidents during travel. It was also felt that the garnet had a curative power against melancholy.

Garnet bullets were employed against the British in 1892 in the war in Kashmir.

Gold. Many stories are intertwined about gold. One of the most familiar is that of King Midas and the golden touch. King Midas was granted the golden touch and, when he found out it was not all he thought it would be, he overcame the curse by bathing in the Pactolus River. Midas ruled in what is now central Turkey from 738 BC until 696 BC. The legend of the golden touch was probably inspired by Midas's great wealth.

The Pactolus River in Lydia, Asia Minor, where Midas was told to bathe to rid himself of the golden touch, was long famous for its gold. The Midas legend was used to explain the presence of gold in the river. This is tied in with the Greek story of the quest for the Golden Fleece and Jason's celebrated Argonautic expedition. It had been the custom to gather gold from gold-rich streams by placing the fleece of a sheep in the rapids of the water. Since gold is heavy, gold dust and small nuggets settled in the fleece. The skin could then be taken from the water and the gold shaken out of it. This custom could have been the inspiration for Chrysomallus, the winged ram which had a golden fleece. The ram's fleece was hung on a sacred oak after its sacrifice to Zeus. This was the fleece that Jason sought.

Gold was used as a treatment for sties. An eye with a sty was rubbed with a golden ring to cure it.

Jasper. Jasper was believed to stanch the blood and bring rain.

Lapis Lazuli. Legend says that lapis lazuli encourages the speaking of truth, as well as relieving throat congestion, swelling, and nervousness.

Moonstone. If you had consumption, it was believed the moonstone would help.

Opal. Opal has long been considered to bring bad luck. Alphonso XII of Spain (1874-85) is said to have had one that seemed to be fatal. On his wedding day, he presented it to his wife in a ring, and her death occurred soon afterwards. Before the funeral, Alphonso gave the ring to his sister, who died a few days later. He then presented it to his sister-in-law, and she died within three months. He decided to wear the ring himself, and in a very short time he too was dead.

In spite of all of this bad luck, black opals are thought to bring good fortune.

Quartz crystal. Ancients believed that the quartz crystal was water permanently frozen into rock. Beliefs about clear quartz crystal include that it promotes healing on all levels and is the mirror of the soul. It is also believed to enhance intuitive abilities and expression through all aspects of being.

Ruby. The Burmese believed that a ruby sewn into the flesh would make a warrior invulnerable. The ruby was a remedy for spleen and liver disorders. It was referred to as the blood stone. The ruby in Buddha's forehead was the third eye (of knowledge).

Sapphire. Roman Catholic cardinals wear blue sapphires in their rings. It was believed that the sapphire imparted purity. Sapphires were also thought to be a cure for eye disease.

Staurlite. These twinned crystals, resembling a cross, were worn as an amulet around the neck. Staurlite became a Christian symbol.

Star sapphire. In Sri Lanka, star sapphires are believed to be effective amulets against witchcraft. Also called the Star of Bethlehem.

Tiger's eye. The tiger's eye is considered to separate our false desires from what is truly needed, and also to be a blood purifier.

Topaz. The topaz is thought to make its wearer beloved and to cure madness, as well as to increase wisdom.

MAGICAL ROCKS AND MINERALS

Blarney Stone. A stone in Blarney Castle in the county of Cork, Ireland, is said to impart skill in speech and a glib tongue to those who kiss it.

Granite. Granite denotes strength.

Lava. Lava was thought to be the rock from hell.

Lodestone. The lodestone (magnetite) was the mariner's first compass.

Stone of King Arthur. Arthur pulled the sword Excalibur from the stone in a churchyard beside the fortress. No one else was able to take the sword from the rock.

Stone of Scone. This is the coronation stone on which the kings and queens of Great Britain are crowned. It lies beneath a special coronation chair in Westminster Abbey. It is also called the Stone of Destiny. King Edward I took the stone from Scotland and brought it to England in 1296. Before that, for hundreds of years, the kings of Scotland had been crowned on it.

Stonehenge. Stonehenge is a circular arrangement of prehistoric monoliths on Salisbury Plain, England. Probably set up in the neolithic period, these stones were used in religious ceremonies.

Sulphur. Sulphur was believed to be the devil's rock. The expression "fire and brimstone" also refers to the devil's territory.

7

Plants and Flowers

A flower of grass hath made me gay:
It saith, I shall find mercy mild.
It measures in the self-same way
I have seen practiced as a child.
Come look and listen if she really does:
She does, does not, she does, does not, she does.
Each time I try, the end so augureth.
That comforts me—'tis right that we have faith.

— Walther von der Vogelweide (1170-1230 AD)

INTRODUCTION

Throughout history, flowers and greenery have played a myriad of roles: sacred, ceremonial, superstitious (such as in use as love charms and witchery), medicinal, legendary, and prognosticatory (as in weather forecasting). An old proverb claims that a bit of fragrance always clings to the hand that gives roses. Yet another alludes to the fact that awareness of good deeds precedes the doer like the fragrance of flowers on a gentle breeze.

Along with secret meanings from mythology, other mystical meanings were attached to flowers, plants, and trees. The Druids of Britain gave the oak a supernatural significance, and the old Scots cherished the rowan (which is related to our mountain ash). Greeks and Romans garlanded their victorious athletes. Laurel leaves were used by the ancient Greeks to crown victors in the Pythian games; hence, one crowned with (or as with) a laurel wreath for excellence or achievement is known as a *laureate*. Palms also have been a sign of triumph. The Orient is rich with the language of flowers.

One of the best known references to plants is from Matthew in the New Testament. In this reference the Three Wise Men took gold, frankincense, and myrrh to the baby Jesus. Frankincense is a tree that grows in the Himalayas on the Tibet-India border and in areas of the northern Arabian peninsula. Its leaves look somewhat like those of the mountain ash, and it bears pink flowers that have a center of yellow shaped like a five-rayed star. The preparation of the incense is a long and expensive process. In February, a thin layer of bark is peeled. A month or so later, the same step is repeated, and this time resinous sap flows out. The juice is collected and allowed to harden. The end result is a shiny, brittle material that is bitter to the taste but a marvel as an incense.

The plant that produces myrrh is tortured-looking. It is a small tree or a large bush. The trunk is short and heavy, with gnarled branches and tough-looking thorns. Leaves are in small clusters, and the outermost bark is thin and easy to break. The bark is cut or pierced to allow viscous white gum to ooze out. Once in the air, the gum turns reddish, hardens, and can be gathered to be sold as spice or for medicinal purposes. Back in biblical days, the tree grew along the coastal areas of the Red Sea. Myrrh was not only present as an unguent at the birth of Christ, but was also brought by Nicodemus on the night of His crucifixion to be used with linens in wrapping the body. It is thought that the Old Testament refers to a different plant as the producer of myrrh, however. This plant grows all over, on mountain sides as well as on the plains along the Arabian deserts. It is called the rock rose because of its profusion of pink flowers which resemble those of a wild rose. This plant exudes a sweet-smelling resin that is gathered today just as it was many centuries ago. The resin is pressed into gum cakes and is used as a base for perfume.

Another plant associated with Christmas is the poinsettia. One legend tells the story about a little girl in Mexico. She stood at the door of an adobe hut, weeping as though her heart would break, because she was poor and had no gift for the Christ child. It was the custom for the people to come to the nearby church on Christmas Eve with flowers to place around the crib. An angel came to her and told her to gather an armful of the weeds by the roadside and place them by the crib. That night, she picked as many as she could carry, and made her way to the crib, where she placed the weeds among the flowers. The next morning, the people in church were amazed, for the weeds she had placed at the crib had become a most beautiful scarlet flower.

The legendary attributes and medicinal uses of plants and flowers are often intertwined. For example, mistletoe was regarded by the Druids as a heal-all. Even later, this plant was said to be "good for the grief of the sinew, itch, toothache, biting of mad dogs and venomous beasts." In France, amulets of mistletoe were popular to prevent sickness, and the Swedes made finger rings of it for the same reason. One legend has it that the cross of the crucifixion was made of mistletoe and that ever since the plant has been a parasite growing on other woody plants. Mistletoe also figured in Norse mythology. Balder the Beautiful had become invulnerable because of the powerful conjurations of his mother, the goddess Friga. An enemy of Balder discovered that Friga had forgotten to cast a spell protecting Balder from the mistletoe. He gave the blind god Heder a piece of mistletoe and told him to throw the branch at Balder. Even though he was blind, Heder hit his mark and Balder fell dead—an invulnerable man killed by mistletoe thrown by a blind man.

In this chapter you will find many legends, traditions, and uses for flowers and plants, all of which can enrich the background and meaning of stories which include them.

FLOWER-NAMING STORIES

The names of many flowers come from Greek mythology or from Latin. Some come from a variety of sources, including Roman mythology, and the Old English or Old Italian languages. Of course, botanists and naturalists have added to plant names as they collected data on flowers, but the names and meanings of flowers can and have become stories in themselves.

Anemone. Also known as windflower. It was believed that wind made the blossoms open. Another legend says it grew for the gods on Mount Olympus where prevailing winds blew. It got its name from the Greek god of the winds, Anemos.

Aster. Means *star* in Greek. Legend says that the aster was created from star dust when Virgo looked down from the heavens and wept.

Bird-of-Paradise. Named after actual birds. They are considered to be the most beautiful birds in the world, with brightly colored plumage and fanlike tails, which these flowers resemble.

Chrysanthemum. Comes from a Greek word meaning "gold flower." In the language of flowers, red shades speak of love, white of truth, and yellow of slighted love.

Cinquefoil. Named from the French for its five leaves, the cinquefoil is the symbol of the beloved daughter because, when it rains, the leaves bend over the flower to cover it, as a mother would protect a beloved daughter. One superstition has it that if a pregnant woman drank a tea made from the white blossoms, she would have a baby girl. If she drank the tea made from the yellow blossoms, she would have a baby boy.

Columbine. From the Latin for "dove." To some, the spurs look like dove heads in a circle. It is also possible to see the shape of inverted spurs like the talons of a bird of prey. Its formal name, from the Latin *aquila*, means "eagle." Chaucer also mentions the columbine.

Cornflower. The cornflower was named after a melancholy youth, Cyanus, who loved flowers so much that he passed all his time in making wreaths of them. He especially admired the cornflower. One day Cyanus was found dead in a field among the flowers he had gathered. Flora, the Roman goddess of flowers, transformed him into a cornflower, the cyanus.

Daffodil. Also called narcissus. In Greek mythology, Narcissus lay down to rest from the midday heat by a pool whose waters had never been disturbed. Leaning over to drink from it, he saw his own face and was transfixed in adoration. Cupid, the god of love, anxious for revenge, mockingly decorated the face of Narcissus and preened his hair, then abandoned him to the delirium of self-love. Echo alone saw his pain and heard his moans. Narcissus fell into the pool, and died still groping along the bottom of the water for the idol-image. The nymphs prepared a funeral pyre for Narcissus, but his body was suddenly changed into the pale and melancholy flower, the daffodil.

Daisy. From the Old English phrase "day's eye," as some varieties of daisies open in the morning, revealing the center disc, and close again each night. The disc is made up of hundreds of tiny flowers. Daisies are thought to protect homes from thunderstorms.

Dandelion. Its French name means "the tooth of the lion," and refers to the sharp, tooth-like leaf edges.

Forget-me-not. A German folktale explains that this beautiful blue flower led a man down through the mountains to a cave full of treasures. A lovely lady appeared to the man and said, "Forget not the best." The man did not listen to her note of warning and took only gold and jewels, leaving the little blue flower behind. As he left the cave, a rock slide from high on the mountain came crashing down, killing the man and closing the cave forever. Another legend tells of two lovers on the eve of their marriage, walking along the banks of the Danube. She saw a beautiful blue flower and asked for it. As he reached for it, the man slipped and fell into the river. As he went under, he threw the flower to the lady and cried, "Love me, forget me not." Yet a third legend has it that when God was naming all the plants, the blue flower with the yellow eye could not remember its name. God finally whispered to it, "Forget me not—that is your name."

Foxglove. Some people believed the little people or fairies gave these blossoms to foxes to wear as gloves so the foxes would not be caught raiding the chicken coop.

Gentian. Named for the king of Illyris, Gentius. A Hungarian folktale tells of a terrible plague epidemic. King Ladislas shot an arrow into the air while begging God to let it fall on a plant that would help his people. The arrow landed on a gentian, which was used with miraculous success to stop the plague.

Ginseng. The Cherokee name for it is "plant of life." *Ginseng* is a corruption of the Chinese word *jin-chen*, which means "manlike" or "trouser-shaped."

Gladiolus. Derived from a Latin word meaning "little sword."

Goldenrod. The symbol for treasure and good fortune. An ugly old woman was tired and footsore after walking in the woods. She asked the trees for a walking stick to help her, but all the trees refused. Finally, an old broken stick offered her help. The old woman turned into a beautiful fairy and turned the stick into a lovely flower with gold dust sprinkled over it.

Indian paintbrush. One legend tells that a brave who was painting a picture of the sunset with his warpaints was frustrated because he could not capture the vibrant colors. He asked the Great Spirit for help. The Great Spirit gave him paintbrushes dripping with the colors of the sunset. The brave used them and then threw them away. Wherever these brushes landed the plant now grows.

Another Indian paintbrush legend was told at the Wind River Reservation in Wyoming. A powerful medicine man, called White Buffalo, was asked by a young maiden in the village, Running Deer, to make a love charm for her. She had fallen deeply in love with He Who Walks Tall. White Buffalo gathered the paintbrush, ground them up with a flat stone, and placed them in a medicine bag. Over this powder, he chanted and sang incantations. He told Running Deer that she must sprinkle the contents of the bag upon her loved one that night—then his love would be hers forever. That night, the two of them crept to where He Who Walks Tall slept and sprinkled the crushed paintbrush upon him. Within a month He Who Walks Tall brought a dowry of several ponies to the lodge of Running Deer's parents. That first summer together was good. The charm was extremely good medicine. When the golden aspen leaves began to fall, the encampment moved to get closer to their food supply of buffalo, deer, and elk. Now that she was with child, Running Deer made a ceremonial robe for White Buffalo. The inside was covered with drawings of battles he had fought. She used porcupine quills and the juice of berries and paintbrush for color. Her child was born as winter was slowly replaced by the green of spring. It was a boy, called Grey Wolf. One hot summer day, the men of the village decided to raid another village to steal ponies. On the eighth day after the young men of the village left for the raid, a band of marauders attacked the village which had mainly women, children, and old people left in it. People were indiscriminately cut down. The evil tribe stole everything and then set fire to the village. When He Who Walks Tall and the other braves returned, all that they saw left in the camp was a howling camp dog. Bodies were thrown about like broken dolls. Amidst the scene of destruction, He Who Walks Tall detected broken grass which led up the river. He searched and later found Running Deer huddled under a ledge on the river's bank. She was barely alive and moaned at his touch. She died in his arms but the child she had protected under her body lived. Crazed with grief, He Who Walks Tall swore vengeance. He and the other men tracked the marauding band and killed them all, but He Who Walks Tall was mortally wounded in the battle. He and his beloved Running Deer were buried together. The following spring, in the shadow of the ledge where they last met, the fire of the paintbrush glowed, preserving forever the love of a couple in the flower's fiery beauty.

Iris. In Greek mythology, Iris was the goddess of the rainbow. The Greeks so named this genus because it has flowers in almost all hues of the rainbow. The name *iris* is translated as "eye of heaven," which is the name for both the center of the eye and the rainbow. Louis VII called the flower *fleur-de-lis*, and the iris was later included in the French banner.

Lupine. It was thought that the lupine robbed the soil of its richness just as wolves (lupus) robbed the shepherds.

Marsh marigold. Also known as the king's cup, buttercup, or cowslip. The plant may have been named in honor of the Virgin Mary. However, *cowslip* comes from the French *cuslyppe*, meaning "cow dung."

Phlox. Greek for "flame."

Queen Anne's Lace. A member of the parsley family. Crowns of parsley were worn by the victors of the Grecian games. An old legend has it that parsley takes a long time to germinate because it goes to the devil nine times before appearing above ground. If you planted it on Good Friday you could raise it in a hurry. When put on a plate, it was a token of trust. Its name comes from the story that a queen was making lace and pricked her finger. The center purple floret of the flower represents the drop of blood from the queen's finger.

Snapdragons. So named because of their snoutlike blossoms. A light pressure on either side of a single blossom will make the "jaws of the dragon" snap open.

Sunflower. Also known as a helianthus, its name is directly translated from two Greek words, *helios* (sun) and *anthos* (flower). The Inca Indians of Peru worshipped the sunflower as a symbol of the sun. The sun temple priestesses wore necklaces of sunflowers made from gold.

Teasel. Was brought from Europe by wool manufacturers. The dried seed head was used for carding wool, and, when fastened to a spindle, was used to "tease" or comb the nap of woolen cloth. It is also called the gypsy comb.

Trailing arbutus. One story says that after the Pilgrims came to America, and after they had survived a long and cold winter, this was the first flower they found in the woods. It had fragrant pinkish flowers. They named the flower after the ship that had brought them here.

FLOWER AND PLANT LEGENDS
AND LORE

Buttercup. A Libyan boy who could sing very beautifully always wore green and gold silk. One day, while he was singing in the woods, the wood nymphs heard him. They turned him into the green and gold flower so that they could have some peace and quiet.

Clover. A symbol of fertility and domestic virtue, the clover is considered a good-luck gift to a woman. It is also considered a symbol of the Trinity. A superstition says that if a girl finds a four-leafed clover and puts it in her shoe, she will marry the first man she sees. A second superstition is that if a girl swallows a four-leafed clover, she will marry the first man she shakes hands with.

Geranium. Considered descendants of the mallow. Legend has it that once the prophet Mohammed washed his shirt in a stream and laid it on a bed of mallow to dry. The flowers blushed deep pink at their distinction.

Hawthorn. In the Middle Ages, on May Day everyone went a-maying, and brought back branches of flowering hawthorn.

Lily. Throughout the ages, the lily has stood for purity and sweetness, modesty, whiteness, and fragility. Various species are widely referenced in Greek mythology.

Lily of the valley. The lily of May. The lily of the valley seduces the nightingale who pipes his own version of the return of happiness to all who listen.

Mayapple. An old mountain superstition says that a girl who pulls up the root of the mayapple will soon become pregnant.

Rose. According to ancient legend, the Greek god of silence, Harpocrates, stumbled upon Venus, the goddess of love, in the course of one of her amorous adventures. Cupid, Venus's son, happened along at an opportune moment and, by making a gift of a rose to Harpocrates, bought his pledge of secrecy.
Since that time, the white rose has been the symbol of silence. Whenever a white rose was hung above the banquet table, no secrets were ever to be repeated. During the Renaissance, and later during the reigns of the pre-revolutionary kings of France, the rose was a favorite architectural motif and often was sculpted on ceilings of rooms where diplomats gathered. The obvious implication was that matters discussed under the rose (*sub rosa*) were considered to be confidential. A phrase for diplomatic meetings, "Sub vino sub rosa est" ("What one says under the influence of wine is secret"), ruled international negotiations. The symbol of the rose was placed over confessionals in 1526.
The Romans believed red roses grew where the tears of Venus fell as she mourned the loss of her beloved Adonis. Her son Cupid, stung by a bee, shot arrows into the rose garden. The "sting"

of the arrows became thorns. Venus pricked her foot on a thorn and the droplets of blood dyed the formerly white roses red.

Medieval legend asserts that the first roses appeared miraculously at Bethlehem as the result of the prayers of a "fayre mayden" who had been falsely accused and was sentenced to death by burning.

In heraldry, the rose is the mark of cadency for a seventh son.

In Christian symbolism, the rose is an emblem of someone without peer. One of the titles for the Virgin Mary is "The Mystical Rose."

In the language of roses:

- A burgundy rose signifies simplicity and beauty.

- A China rose represents grace or beauty ever fresh.

- A daily rose is a smile.

- A dog rose conveys pleasure mixed with pain.

- A faded rose signifies that beauty is fleeting.

- A Japan rose denotes that beauty is one's sole attraction.

- A moss rose communicates voluptuous love.

- A musk rose means capricious beauty.

- A Provence rose denotes a heart in flames.

- A white rose bud indicates someone too young to love.

- A white rose branch full of buds conveys secrecy.

- A wealth of roses represents beauty and virtue rewarded.

- A yellow rose declares infidelity.

Shamrock. When St. Patrick was a missionary, he had trouble explaining the doctrine of the Trinity. The tribal chief asked how one could be three, whereupon St. Patrick picked a shamrock and said, "Here in this leaf, three in one, is a symbol of my faith. Three Gods in One."

Thistle. The Scottish national emblem. When the Danes invaded Scotland, they tried to sneak up on the Scots. They took off their boots and were creeping through the fields when a soldier stepped on a thistle and yelled out. The Scots, thus alerted, were able to defend themselves and their country. The superstition that whoever wears the thistle is safe from harm came from this.

Trillium. There is an old Indian story of a beautiful young girl who wanted the chief's son for her husband. She boiled the root of the trillium to put in his food. On the way, she tripped, and the root fell into the food of an ugly old man who ate it. He followed the poor girl around for months begging her to marry him. An old mountain superstition has it that if you pick the trillium, it will rain.

Violet. Legend says that the nymph Io was loved by Zeus, who changed her to a white heifer to hide her from his jealous wife, Hera. Io began to cry because of the rough grass she had to eat, so Zeus changed her tears into violets.

FLOWER AND PLANT ORACLES, FORMULAS, AND PORTENTS

Flower petals or plant twigs are often used as counting-type oracles or in question-and-answer forecasting and games. For example, select a common daisy or black-eyed susan, a bloom with one single circle of ray flowers (petals). Frame a question, then chant a formula sequence of possible answers, pulling one ray flower from the head per alternative. Continue in this fashion until all of the petals are gone but one. The last petal will answer the question. Perhaps the most common question is: "Am I loved by _____?" The most common answer ritual is: "He (she) loves me; he loves me not; he loves me; he loves me not." If the last petal is "he loves me," then that is the answer. Another common answer formula is: "Yes, no, maybe so." Still another is: "Hate her, have her, this year, next year, sometime, never" or "He loves me, he don't; he'll have me, he won't; he would if he could, but he can't, so he don't" (Baring-Gould and Baring-Gould 1962). This procedure can also be done with the buttons of one's coat, the plaits in a braid, etc. The outcome is, however, vulnerable to human tampering!

Other Questions and Answers

Will we get married? (Yes, no, maybe so.)
Will we have children? (Yes, no, maybe so.)
How many children will we have? (1, 2, 3, 4 ...)
When will we be married? (This year, next year, I don't know.)
                  (This year, next year, sometime, never.)
                  (January, February, March ...)
                  (The first, the second, the third ...)
                  (Sunday, Monday, Tuesday ...)
Have I already met him? (Yes, no, maybe so.)
What is his first initial? (A, B, C, D, E, F ...)
How will we get to the wedding? (Coach, wagon, wheelbarrow ...)
Where will the wedding be? (Church, cathedral, chapel ...)
What will he be? (Rich man, poor man ...)
(See "Gypsy, Gypsy" in Jumprope Prognostications, p. 147.)

In Switzerland, the leaves are plucked from the stem of a daisy or a marguerite (a "love's measure"). Girls ask about their adult state and chant: "Single, marry, go to the cloister." Boys ask about their future fortunes and say: "Rich, poor, moderate." Both ask about afterlife, for which the formula is: "Heaven, hell, purgatory, paradise" or "Paradise, purgatory, cauldron."

In France, children chant: "Je t'aime, un, peu, beaucoup, / Tendrement, pas, du tout."

Italian children find a tree leaf of the sort that has leaflets along either side of a central stem, such as an ash, or a twig of leaves. They pluck the leaves, chanting: "This year, next year, sometime, never" or "He loves me, longs for me, desires me, wishes me well."

During the Middle Ages, grass stems or stalks of straw of varying lengths were drawn to find an answer, with each length denoting a possible alternative: short was "yes"; long was "no"; middling was "maybe."

In the Middle Ages, the qualities of flowers and flower proprieties were of great significance. One gave flowers with the correct implicit characteristics, sometimes to make a proposition or to set a charm for which the bloom itself was the symbol. The use of dandelion garlands and chains is ancient. The dandelion—chain or ring flower—is perhaps the most important flower of spring, and has religious and symbolic meaning. Its power is the power of light, as reflected in its brilliance. It has healing virtues, can remedy eye troubles, and bring happiness to lovers. If you hold a dandelion blossom up underneath your chin, the sunlight will shine there.

The dandelion seedhead—clock—is used as an oracle. Ask the question, then blow the seeds or parachutes from the head. If all the seeds can be blown away in three attempts, the answer is favorable: for example, successful love, or marriage within the year.

The apple seed oracle uses a divided apple, its seeds removed and used to answer a question. The seeds are counted out to one of the following rhymes:

One, I love,
Two, I love,
Three, I love, I say,
Four, I love with all my heart,
And five, I cast away.
Six, he loves.
Seven, she loves,
Eight, they both love;
Nine, he comes,
Ten, he tarries,
Eleven, he courts,
Twelve, he marries;
Thirteen, wishes;
Fourteen, kisses,
All the rest, little witches
(Newell 1963).

One, my love loves me.
Two, he loves me not.
Three, we shall agree.
Four, I am forgot.
Five, is coming bliss.
Six, love will not tarry.
Seven, a faithful kiss.
Eight, we're sure to marry
(Daniels and Stevans 1971).

One, I love,
Two, I love,
Three, I love, I say.
Four, I love with all my heart.
Five I'll cast away.
Six, he loves,
Seven, she loves,
Eight, they both love.
Nine, he comes,
Ten, he tarries,
Eleven, he courts,
Twelve, he marries
(Knapp and Knapp 1976).

One I love, two I love,
Three I love, I say,
Four I love with all my heart,
Five I cast away;
Six he loves, seven she loves,
Eight, both love,
Nine he comes, ten he tarries,
Eleven he courts, twelve he marries.
Thirteen they quarrel,
Fourteen they part,
Fifteen, he dies of a broken heart
(Baring-Gould and Baring-Gould 1962).

On Halloween, shoot the seeds of an apple, using thumb and forefinger (like marbles), up and forward at friends standing around you in a ring. While doing this, chant:

Kernel, come kernel, hop over my thumb,
And tell me which way my lover will come.
East, West, North, South;
Kernel come jump in my lover's mouth (Daniels and Stevans 1971).

The kernel will go into the mouth of the right person.

Eat an apple immediately upon awakening on Easter morning. While eating, say:

> As Eve in her thirst for knowledge ate,
> So I too thirst to know my fate (Daniels and Stevans 1971).

Then count the apple seeds. An even number means that your lover will be true; an odd number means that he will be false.

Twist an apple's stem while chanting the letters of the alphabet, one letter per twist. The stem will come loose at the letter which is the initial of the first name of one's lover or husband-to-be.

Peel an apple carefully so that the peel comes off in one long, twisted length. Throw the peel over your shoulder. The shape of the peel can be interpreted. If the peel assumes the form of a letter, or an approximation of a letter, that letter is the first initial of your future lover or husband.

Pluck a sprig of yarrow at the time of the new moon; place it under your pillow. Wish that the man whom you love will come to claim it. Say:

> Good night, fair yarrow,
> Thrice goodnight to thee;
> I hope before tomorrow's dawn
> My true love I shall see (Baring-Gould and Baring-Gould 1962).

Cut a melon into seven pieces. Distribute the pieces by lot to seven people. Each counts the seeds in his or her piece. The last seed tells one's fortune:

> One will be wealthy,
> Two will be healthy,
> Three will seek fortune and fame;
> Four will be stingy,
> Five will look dingy,
> Six will secure a great name;
> Seven, for me, my best friend shall be (Daniels and Stevans 1971).

Sprinkle a sprig of rosemary and one of thyme three times each with water. Then place one in your left shoe and the other in the right shoe. Put one shoe on either side of the bed, and say:

> St. Valentine, that's to lovers kind,
> Come ease the trouble of my mind.
> And send the man that loves me true
> To take these sprigs out of my shoe (Baring-Gould and Baring-Gould 1962).

Clover is lucky

> Find a two, put it in your shoe;
> Find a three, let it be;
> Find a four, put it over the door;
> Find a five, let it thrive.

For a four-leaf clover, say:

> One leaf for fame, one leaf for wealth,
> One for a faithful lover,
> And one leaf to bring to glorious health,
> Are all in a four-leaf clover (Baring-Gould and Baring-Gould 1962).

Find an ash leaf with an even number of leaflets on it. You will see your love before the day is done.

> The even-ash leaf in my hand,
> The first I meet shall be my man.
> The even-ash leaf in my glove,
> The first I meet shall be my love.
> The even-ash leaf in my bosom,
> The first I meet shall be my husband.
> The even ash I double in three,
> The first I meet my true love shall be;
> If he be married, let him pass by,
> But if he be single, let him draw nigh (Baring-Gould and Baring-Gould 1962).

> An apple a day
> Sends the doctor away.
> Apple in the morning,
> Doctor's warning.
> Roast apple at night,
> Starves the doctor outright.
> Eat an apple going to bed,
> Knock the doctor on the head.
> Three each day, seven days a week,
> Ruddy apple, ruddy cheek (Baring-Gould and Baring-Gould 1962).

> Onion's skin very thin,
> Mild winter coming in.
> Onion's skin thick and tough,
> Coming winter cold and rough (Baring-Gould and Baring-Gould 1962).

Representative Flower Portents and Superstitions

- If you accidentally cut an apple seed in two while dividing an apple, your love affairs will go badly; if you cut two seeds, you will soon be a widow.

- If you wear a flower to a funeral, you will bring yourself trouble.

- Burning faded flowers signifies approaching sorrow.

- Touching a flower used at a funeral could bring bad luck or death (United States black).

- A hedge bearing yellow flowers brings good luck to whatever it surrounds.

- It is very lucky to wear a flower that has been presented to a god (Hindu).

- The bright reflection of the buttercup, when held up under one's chin, reveals a fondness for butter.

- Take a blue flower from your mother's grave at midnight to protect yourself from all misfortune.

- You will have good luck if you leave the first spring flower that you see, and say: "Increase and grow, and so also my luck."

- It is very unlucky to present someone with a flower stem first.

- Flowers worn with the stems pointing upward signifies being in love.

- Preserved funeral flowers are unlucky, especially skeleton leaves.

- If you pull flowers to pieces, you will die of consumption.

- If you smell flowers gathered in cemeteries, you will lose your sense of smell.

- Having flowers wilt quickly in your hand is a sign of ill health.

- If you receive a flower, you will be successful in business.

- Wearing flowers that have been on a coffin is a sign of great misfortune.

- If someone gives you a yellow flower, it is a sign that you will have money.

- Cross-shaped flowers (*cruciferae*) are good omens, since they have been marked with the sign of the cross.

- Flowers which fade or die suddenly signify coming poverty (China).

- If you keep a scarlet geranium in the house all year round, someone will die.

- Purple flowers signify tears and coming troubles.

- It is unlucky to gather flowers out of season.

- If you are wearing flowers that wither suddenly, someone is deeply in love with you.

- The first flowers found in spring:

    On Monday—good luck all year

    On Tuesday—successful undertakings

    On Wednesday—a wedding

    On Thursday—hard work, little profit

    On Friday—unexpected wealth

    On Saturday—misfortunes

    On Sunday—the best of all.

- If you give flowers to a man, you will have a new lover.
  If you give flowers to a lady, you will have love quarrels.
  If you receive flowers from a man, you will hear of a marriage.
  If you receive flowers from a lady, you will hear of a childbirth.

- For good luck, wear snowdrops if you were born in January, primroses for February, violets for March, daisies for April, hawthorn for May, honeysuckle for June, waterlily for July, poppy for August, morning glory for September, hops for October, chrysanthemum for November, and holly for December.

• Many plants, flowers, and fruits carry traditional significances:

Almonds—success in business	Leeks—hard labor
Apples—disappointment	Lettuce—poverty, many ups and downs
Apricots—health	Nuts—gratified ambition
Artichokes—embarrassment	Onions—dispute with an inferior
Asparagus—profit, success, pleasure	Oranges—approaching marriage
Beans—considerable losses	Peaches—pleasure, contentment
Cabbage—health, long life	Pears—tidings of death
Cauliflower—sickness, infidelity	Peas—troubles and misfortune
Cherries—deception by a woman	Raisins—infidelity
Cucumbers—serious indisposition	Roses—a happy omen
Cypress—a precious object	Strawberries—unexpected good fortune
Flowers—happiness	Thistles—folly, approaching dispute
Garlic—woman's deception	Turnips—annoyance
Grapes—great gains	Vegetables—toil and trouble
Herbs—prosperity, success, happiness	Violets—success in all undertakings.
Laurels—gain of great honors	

MUSHROOMS

As Millicent Selsam said, "There is something mysterious and ghostlike about a plant that is not green, has no leaves or roots, and springs up suddenly after rainstorms" (Selsam 1986). For thousands of years people have made up stories about mushrooms and looked for answers to questions. Did lightning that hit the ground make mushrooms? Did toads really sit on these plants? Did fairies dance on their caps or use them as umbrellas? What are the "fairy rings"?

Some types of mushrooms contain chemicals that make people act in wild ways. Certain Native American groups use mushrooms as a religious object. Are these plants enchanted? Are the visions and dreams induced by ingesting mushrooms magical? In ancient times in Mexico, Central America, Egypt, Greece, Rome, France, England, and the Orient, mushrooms were used as foods, medicine, superstition, religious ceremonies, and folklore. Mushrooms have been carved in stone sculptures, recorded in Egyptian tombs, and painted and written about since before Christ.

Investigate these plants and some of the folklore connected with them. They are also rich in potential for jokes. One of the latest jokes about the conditions necessary to develop good administrators is that they must be treated like mushrooms: they must be kept in the dark; they must be fertilized with raw manure; and they must be canned.

FOLK MEDICINE

A word of caution throughout about the following folk remedy considerations! Not all remedies are effective. Nature can be a dangerous drugstore. Even the good herbs can be toxic if abused. Beginners should never pick wild plants without expert guidance. Check wild samples with a botanist before using them. You can easily get a look-alike wrong plant.

The plant kingdom is a virtual gold mine of new chemical compounds waiting to be discovered. Many of them have potential for future benefits to mankind. That is one of the concerns with the rapid disappearance of rain forests—plants may be eliminated before they are ever discovered and analyzed for medicinal possibilities.

Folklorists and researchers agree that cod liver oil is good for arthritis. Folklorists have long believed that cod liver oil works by "oiling" the joints. Now researchers agree that fatty fish (salmon, mackerel, herring) and cod and shark-liver oils contain beneficial fatty acids—omega three acids—that appear to slow the body's production of inflammatory agents linked to arthritis. There is also evidence that these fatty acids help protect against heart disease and psoriasis. Aunt Minnie's instructions to take one tablespoon of cod liver oil along with two tablespoons of vinegar every morning may not be too bad.

Researchers are also indicating that you can fleaproof yourself with brewer's yeast. Humans produce a flea-repelling odor when yeast is metabolized through the sweat glands. Since dogs' sweat glands are limited to their noses and pads, yeast unfortunately does not work for them (fleas do not show up there anyway).

What about snoring? When you sleep on your back, the tongue drifts backward, partially blocking the air passage into the throat. When you lie on your stomach, gravity pulls the tongue forward and down, making room for air to pass through without a snore. Therefore, to cure a snore, roll over or raise the head of the bed by putting a pillow under the mattress.

For heartburn (the discomfort you feel when acid stomach contents back up into the esophagus), use something alkaline to neutralize the acid and wash it back down into the stomach. Seltzer and club soda works.

These are a few examples of the concurrence of modern medicinal practice and traditional, folkloric remedies and beliefs. The uses of plants and flowers may be part of common lore, or may be known only to a culture's healers. All peoples have discovered remedies for health disorders; sometimes these beliefs and practices are part of religion. Some cultures have healers who have learned to heal either from special initiations, dream experiences, ordeals, or as an apprentice to an older healer. Some healers have symbolic objects for their power, such as rattles, drums, masks, and fetishes. In the southwest, Hispanic folk seek the advice of a *curandero* (healer). They believe that healing derives from God, and the curanderos rely only on religious paraphernalia such as crosses, pictures of saints, and holy water. However, they also are adept at herbal healing.

Some of the herbs used by curanderos in their healing include:

- *Ajo* (garlic)—one crushed button, pressed against the gum, lessens toothaches. It is also good for stomach trouble and gets rid of gas after being throughly chewed and swallowed with cold water.

- *Alhucema* (lavender) — good for phlegm, colic, headaches, and stomach trouble.

- *Anis* (anise) — a good stomach remedy to overcome gas, nausea, and colic when used as tea. Also good for coughs. When the seeds are ground up, toasted, and mixed with whiskey and rubbed on painful shoulders and chests, the discomfort will go away.

- *Chamiso* (sage) — well known as a seasoning for meats, it is also a remedy for stomach troubles, nervous troubles, and fevers. It will stop bleeding wounds. A wash with sage tea will help wounds of any kind heal rapidly.

- *Manzanilla* (chamomile) — good for a weak stomach, colds, fever, bronchitis, and kidneys when used in a tea. It is also a good rinse for hair and good for earaches.

- *Oregano* — use as a tea for colds (drink it while hot). Ground powder can be rubbed on the head for headache or on the body for fevers. For a sore throat, drink it as a tea and wear some around your neck in a bag.

- *Poleo* (peppermint) — makes a good tea for reducing fever, chills, colic, dizziness, and stomach ailments. It strengthens the heart muscle. Take in place of aspirin. It is also good as a body bath.

- *Raiz de osha del monte* (root of osha of the mountain) — used by sheepherders to draw out poison from snakebites and to ward off reptiles. It can be ground and used for stomach trouble (gas), and made as a tea for colds, pneumonia, and headaches.

- *Romero* (rosemary) — good for colds, colic, nervous conditions; strengthens the eyes. It can also be used as a mouthwash for mouth, gums, halitosis, and sore throat. The oil can be used as perfume in ointments, liniments, and shampoos.

- *Yerba buena* (spearmint) — good for indigestion, hangovers, and diarrhea, and as a wash for wounds and sores.

Sample Herbal and Folk Remedies

These general herbal and folk remedies have been collected from many cultures, and are, of course, only a small sample of the plant and herbal lore connected with healing and remedies. Nevertheless, herbal healing and plant magic are recurrent themes and artifacts in stories throughout the world, and the storyteller's knowledge of this background enriches and verifies the story details.

Beets. Are said to help prevent kidney stones.

Bitterroot. Peel the bark off and boil, bake, or grate it. Add to flour or meal. This was considered a great delicacy by pioneers and American Indians.

Blackberry juice. Boiled with four tablespoons of honey and a pinch of clove or allspice, was administered at half a glassful every one or two hours for diarrhea.

Bluebell. The Indians boiled bluebell and made a tea to cure intestinal worms.

Boxwood juice. Cures nosebleeds.

Burdock. At one time, the seed pods were eaten to help things stick in the mind. Pioneers made tea from the roots to help purify the blood. A poultice made from boiling the leaves in salt water was said to be good for bruises and swelling.

Cattail. The root was often given to women and animals in labor, and when boiled in milk was effective against diarrhea. Cattail tea was drunk to help stop hemorrhaging.

Chickweed. Used for predicting weather. If the chickweed blooms fully and boldly, there will be no rain for at least four hours. If the blossoms shut, get out your umbrella.

Chicory. Chicory coffee is said to be good for liver and gall bladder ailments. Pliny and Homer also mentioned its medicinal value.

Cinquefoil. A tea made from the leaves was used as a gargle and mouthwash, and was said to cure inflammation of the mouth and gums. Witches of earlier ages used cinquefoil as a drug, rubbing it over their bodies to produce a trancelike state. Cinquefoil was also used as protection against witches.

Clover blossoms. Used as a cough medicine. Made in a tea, it improves the texture of finger and toe nails. The tea also thins and purifies the blood.

Columbine. The juice of a fresh plant was used to cure jaundice or abdominal pains or to reduce swelling of the liver. It also was supposedly a cure for measles and smallpox.

Corn (parched, cracked), brown corn meal. Mix with skim milk and drink for diarrhea. Corn meal is also good for sties.

Cowpeas. Thrown onto the road, ensure fertility.

Daisy fleabane. An old superstition said that if a pregnant woman wanted to know the sex of her baby, she should plant a seed of fleabane. If the flowers were tinged with pink, she would have a girl; if blue, a boy.

Dandelion. Contains high amounts of vitamins A and C and is used as a general antidote. An old mountain superstition says if you drink a cup of dandelion tea every morning and every evening, you will never have rheumatism. A Dutch legend says if you eat dandelion salad on Monday and Thursday, you will always stay healthy.

Dwarf crested iris. American Indians used it to treat sores on legs. The roots were cleaned and boiled and mashed into a poultice that was applied to the affected area. These Indians also used it as a carthartic.

Field mustard. A powder made from the seeds was eaten to improve the appetite and promote digestion.

Fireweed. For asthma and whooping cough, boil the young shoots and eat like asparagus.

Flax seed. This or a bread poultice is often effective for abscesses.

Forget-me-not. Boiled in wine, they were said to be an effective antidote for the bite of an adder. Egyptians believed if you put the leaves over your eyes during the month of Thoth, you would have visions.

Gentian. North American Indians used it to ease back pains. Pioneers added a little bit of gentian to gin or brandy to stimulate the appetite and aid in digestion.

Geranium. Boiled root concoction was used to treat sore throats and mouth ulcers. Native Americans used it as a tonic and as an astringent. Northern tribes also used the powdered root when they were wounded to help coagulate the blood.

Ginseng. In China, it was used as a heart stimulant as well as an aphrodisiac. Native Americans used ginseng to treat coughs, headaches, and fevers.

Goldenrod. American Indians used the goldenrod as a component in steam baths used to steam pain out of an ailing person.

Hepatica. Thought to cure lung diseases.

Horseradish. Rub warts every day with horseradish. A spoonful of crushed horseradish and honey, taken three times per day, promotes kidney action.

Indian paintbrush. Used to soothe burned skin and to ease the burning sting of the centipede. Indian women drank a concoction made from the roots to dry up menstrual flow.

Jack-in-the-pulpit. American Indians used the powdered root in making flour. The pulp was applied to the forehead in an attempt to cure headaches.

Jimsonweed. Native Americans would heat the leaves and apply them directly to a burned area to soothe the burned skin. American pioneers smoked the leaves like tobacco to relieve labored breathing.

Marsh mallow. Pliny suggested that one tablespoon of the mallows daily would keep one free of disease. It was especially good for cramps and convulsions, bee stings, dandruff, and loss of hair.

Mayapple. Shawnee tribe used the boiled root as a very strong laxative.

Milkweed. The Quebec Indians used the roots as a contraceptive. The Shawnee tribe used the white sap to remove warts.

Morning glory. Drop a handful of leaves into boiling water and drink a quarter of an hour before breakfast as a gentle laxative.

Moss. In the Okefenokee swamp, in Georgia, a love potion is produced from the white moss from the skull of a murdered man. This practice comes from the belief that the body of one whose life was prematurely terminated retains an unexhausted quantity of life force that can be drawn upon for therapeutic purposes or for love magic.

Mustard flour, crushed mustard seed. Mix with cold water or vinegar to make a paste for arthritic and gout conditions.

Parsley and **linden flowers**. The Czechs treat sluggishness with tea brewed from these.

Phlox. An extract made from the leaves was used as a laxative.

Pickle. Placed in the mouth of a newborn baby, prevents colic.

Pine rosin and sugar. Apply and change each day for abscesses.

Pokeweed. An old mountain recipe says to wash and cook the stems and leaves together and to boil and drain them several times. Eaten in the spring, it is said to revive the blood. The Algonquin tribe called the plant *puccoon*, which means "plant used for staining or dyeing."

Pumpkin, crushed pumpkin seed tea. Effective for kidney and bladder ailments.

Queen Anne's lace. Had a reputation for curing internal parasites such as worms. Eating the center purple floret was once thought to cure epilepsy.

Sheep sorrel. Chop up the leaves and eat with a cup of wine to soothe a queasy stomach.

Skunk cabbage. Once sought after as a contraceptive. It was thought that one tablespoon three times a day for three weeks would cause permanent sterility in men or women. Native Americans smelled the crushed leaves for headaches. Boiled root was used as a cough syrup.

Snakeroot (powdered). Prescribed for headaches.

Snapdragon. Choctaws applied them directly to the head to relieve a headache. The smoked leaves were used for respiratory ailments. Native Americans also boiled the leaves and applied them to body joints to relieve the aches of rheumatism.

Soapwort. Found to be useful in cleaning and lightly bleaching fabric. It was also quite effective in restoring the color and sheen to old china and glass.

Tansy. It was believed that a leaf on the naval of a pregnant woman would induce childbirth. A powder made from the leaves was used to kill fleas and lice.

Turpentine and sweet oil. Rub sore back with mixture of one part turpentine and two parts sweet oil.

Vinegar and brown paper bandage. Soak brown paper in vinegar and apply to sprains and strains. This old remedy is mentioned in the Mother Goose rhyme "Jack and Jill."

Violet. The leaves are high in vitamins A and C, and can be eaten raw in salads or cooked like greens. Made into a tea, violets help get rid of a headache. A poultice of violets is useful in curing ulcers and bedsores.

Watercress. Used in salads and as garnishes. Romans used it to quiet deranged minds.

White oak bark, calcium, myrrh. The Amish use these for circulation problems.

Wild lupine. In the thirteenth century, lupine was used in healing the spot left after an infant's umbilical cord was cut.

Wild onion. The Winnebago and Dakota tribes used the onion for treating bee and wasp stings. The eastern tribes would slice an onion, wrap it in cloth, and tie it around their wrists when they were ill. They believed it drew out fever from the body. If you wore one around your neck, it would prevent diseases from entering your body.

Yams, beans. The Yoruba people of western Nigeria have the highest rate of fraternal twinning in the world. It is believed to be due to their diet of yams and beans. Twins are said to be a blessing reserved only for the poor and kind-hearted. Twins are given to the poor to make them rich. They bring good luck.

Yarrow. The most frequent use of yarrow was to staunch the flow of blood from a wound. The leaves were ground up, boiled, and made into a salve which was applied to wounds. According to legend, Achilles always carried the plant with him to treat wounded soldiers during the Trojan Wars. American Indians soothed bruises and burns with it.

Aphrodisiacs

Practically every fruit, vegetable, meat, fish, fowl, root, oil, herb, and spice has been considered an aphrodisiac by someone at some point in history:

- Egyptians favored radishes.
- Greeks and Romans believed in onions and garlic.
- The Old Testament mentions mandrake.
- Marilyn Monroe swore by raw eggs.
- Oyster references are heard everywhere.
- Legendary aphrodisiacs were made from the powder of ground horns of rhinoceros and young Noble Spotted Deer.
- Spanish fly and p'ang chiang are made from ground insects and are widely used.
- South American curanderos supply damiana, which is known as "Indian lover herb"; they also prescribe basil and rosemary.
- Sarsaparilla has long been used in Mexico as an aid for machismo.
- Royal jelly, the food given the hive's queen bee, and ginseng are Chinese recommendations.
- Ancient Romans prized truffles.
- The Marquise de Pompadour was supplied with vanilla and celery to keep in shape for her lover, Louis XV.
- Sushi and rice are listed as a likely source of sexual stamina.

8

Trees

INTRODUCTION

The idea that the tree is more ancient than humankind exists in most folk traditions. "It is perhaps correct to say that in the whole range of symbolism, no emblem is more widespread or has exerted greater influence on the institutions of mankind than the tree" (Orlinsky 1970, 27). Ancient, primitive peoples were undoubtedly impressed by the size, strength, and longevity of trees, and must have been awed by their various voices as they responded to breezes. People were also dependent upon the materials and foods produced by trees, naturally associating trees with life giving and sustenance. The tree was, even in early times, identified with both male and female aspects of fertility: the womb and the phallus.

Even today, trees have haunting and magical qualities about them. If the midday twilight of a grove of ancient trees produces auras, shadows, presences, and mysteries that can force reverie upon the hardened twentieth century soul, what effect did it have upon our distant ancestors?

Down yonder green ash grove,
Where streamlets meander,
Where twilight is fading,
I pensively roam.

Or at the bright noontide,
In solitude wander,
Amid the dark shades
Of the lonely ash grove.

'Tis there that the blackbird
Is cheerfully singing;
Each warbler enchants
With his notes from the tree.

Oh then little think I
Of sorrow or sadness.
The ash grove entrancing
Spells beauty for me.
(Traditional.)

Initially, the tree was a manifestation of the Archetypal Feminine as the Great Mother, the "goddess of the tree that confers nourishment on souls" (Neumann 1963, 241). The Great Mother Tree is the container or vessel in which all major transformative processes take place; it is the source of life, the provider, and the grave. All life generates from the great world tree. In many mythologies, the goddess as tree gives birth to the sun (god/hero). "Hathor, the sycamore goddess, who is the 'house of Horus' and as such gives birth to Horus, bears the sun on her head; the top of the tree is the place of the sun's birth" (Neumann 1963, 214). The tree as universal womb and the giver of life is represented by the crib and cradle; as bringer of death, by the sarcophagus, the devourer of flesh (Neumann 1963). Numerous wooden vessels and containers, including ships, are symbols for the Mother, whose law is the cycle of life: birth, life, death, regeneration, and rebirth. All things generate from, are suckled and sustained by, and return to the Mother. The Mother tree is the source of Mana: life, food, wisdom, spirit, and soul. Wood itself, and all trees, remind us of these associations.

Because the goddess-as-tree gives birth to the sun (sun god/sacrifice hero), the tree is also a focus in seasonal sacrifice rites and rituals. The sun emerges (is born) from the great womb tree in the morning and returns to it (dies) again at night, descending into and making its way through the darkness or underworld. The sun also dies yearly at the time of the winter solstice.

The sun god is the sacrificial sun hero who shows the way. In numerous myth cycles, he is hung on the tree, where his blood is spilled on the earth (the altar). Hence, the tree is also a gallows upon which the sacrificial victim is hung. In Old Norse, *drasil* meant "gallows tree," while *Yggr* was another name for Odin as Lord of Death (Walker 1983, 412). *Yggdrasil* is translated as "Odin's Gallows Tree," the place of hanging and sacrifice of the sun god at the appointed time of his death. "Scandinavian sacred kings were identified with Odin and suffered the same kind of holy death, probably followed by apotheosis as was usual for sacrificial victims" (Walker 1963, 734). The earth was reddened with their blood, a reenactment of the fecundating of the Mother with the water of life of the male principle. Gallows tree sacrifices were common worldwide; sometimes the tree became a pole or cross connected to the sun hero/savior's giving of himself for the well-being of all. The uprightness of the trunk, therefore, came to represent his ability to impregnate, and also the reason for his death.

"The obelisk, Maypole, pillar, sacred tree trunk, upright cross, [and] other male divinity symbols" (Walker 1983, 799) were worshipped as representative of the Father principle. (The sun hero/savior is the goddess's son, who later fecundates her with his blood, dies, and is resurrected or reborn. He is, thus, his own father.) These symbols were deliberately phallic, and were often "blooded," that is, rubbed with the blood of the sacrifice hero, representing the belief that both male blood and semen were necessary ingredients in ensuring fertility. Blooding the pillar was the later version of hanging the sacrifice hero on the tree. Such pillars stood at the entrances to temples, at the centers of sacred groves, and next to or under altars. The pillar or post standing at the threshold, or "the Holy Door of the Goddess" (Walker 1983, 799), signified the strength of the male principle. The pillars in front of Solomon's temple, named *Boaz* and *Jachin* ("Strength" and "God Makes Him Firm") (1 Kings 7: 19-20) represented phalli (Walker 1983, 799). The sacred pillar within the temple represented the holy union of goddess and god, or the sacrifice of the hero to ensure the fertility of the earth. The blood or fertilizing essence of the sacrifice hero was often dripped upon the altar (a womb symbol).

The great cosmic tree is described as having its roots in the depths (of the primitive collective unconscious) of the void and chaos of the beginning, and its branches in the heavens (Neumann 1963). It holds the universe together. At its foot flows the spring of the water of Life (female blood), while its fruits represent Mana, the many physical and spiritual gifts of creation. Next to the spring, the Norns (Scandinavian Fates) spin, twist, and cut the golden threads of life. The tree stands, in Paradise, at the very center of the earth. When the tree (the Mother) dies, all time will end. In its phallic aspect, the tree is also the *axis mundi*, or great pole, which pierces the earth (Mother/womb).

In the Orient, the World Tree or Tree of Life and Immortality was the (feminine) rose tree. Central Asians called her "Woman, Wellspring, Milk, Animals, Fruits" (Walker 1983, 867). Mongols named her *Zambu*. The Tree of Life referenced in Ezekiel—"whose leaf shall not fade, neither shall its fruit be consumed" (Ezek. 47: 12)—is very like Yggdrasil, which grew in Asgard. Later patriarchal religions associated this same tree exclusively with male genitalia.

All trees are known to have been objects of worship in ancient Semitic cultures. The Egyptian mother goddess Nut, the keeper of the heavenly waters of life, was also the great tree of the sky. The ancient Hebrews believed that the oak was the divine presence; oaks were therefore sacred. Numerous Old Testament references to trees reveal that trees played a significant religious role. Groves of trees were regarded as sanctuaries, as places of worship, and as focal points for the activities of special cults. The tree was a divine oracle, a source of The Word and divine wisdom and enlightenment. Modern-day Arabs "call sacred trees 'manahil' [Mana] and look upon them as places where the angels play about and sing. All men are advised to treat them with the utmost reverence and to hang beads upon them" (Orlinski 1970, 30). In Babylon and Persia, trees were believed to have curative powers. People hung articles of clothing and other personal belongings on tree limbs as acts of personal sacrifice, supplication, and respect. Assyrian and Babylonian reliefs depict kings prostrated before trees.

We still worship in association with symbols of the great cosmic tree representing both male and female principles of fertility. The symbolism of the phallic pole is transferred to the columns of the cathedral; that of the trees spreading their branches overhead appears in the more regular designs of the arch of ceiling and window. The great height and sweep of the church vault, imitated almost universally, contains both altars (female) and representations of the original idea of the gallows tree (male). Great stone altars in British churches, which were disturbed during World War II, were discovered to contain phallic idols (Walker 1983). The temples of Babylonia and Assyria were constructed from sacred cedar trees, ceremonially cut, blessed, and built into churches in such a way that the dead wood imitated the arching, lofty habit of the living.

Tree worship was universally practiced among all European peoples. The Druid word for "sanctuary" derives from the Latin *nemus*, meaning "grove or woodland glade" (Frazer 1922, 127). The old Teutonic word for "temple" suggests association with the sacred grove of trees built into a manmade construction using the natural woods of those trees. The skins of sacrificial victims were hung in sacred trees; trees could not be cut or otherwise harmed. Under the old laws in Germany, the penalty for peeling the bark from a tree was a most painful execution, in which the culprit was disemboweled while alive by cutting out and nailing his navel to the trunk of the tree, then winding him around the trunk repeatedly until all of his bowel was pulled from his abdomen to swath the damage that he had done. (Woodcutters still beg the forgiveness of a tree that they must fell, lest its spirit remain to haunt them.) Many folk stories portray the tree as sentient, or at least as inhabited by its own guardian spirits.

Tree oracles abounded in the ancient world. In many oracular groves, priests hung ornaments and people suspended tokens of their faith from the branches. In some groves, every tree was regarded as specially divine, although all trees were considered animate, possessed of living souls and inhabited by their own individual gods.

Despite the efforts of Christianity to root out pagan practice and its objects and symbols, the church has often been obliged to graft a Christian frame of reference onto the vigorous and unremitting vestiges of older forms of worship. The continued widespread observance of May customs is an ancient habit which calls forth the spirits of vegetation. It is the rebirth of the great tree, enacted with the living materials serving as symbols. The people of Upper Bavaria bring in a living fir tree and hang it with wreaths, flags, and inscriptions (Frazer 1922). The winter solstice practice of worshipping the seasonal tree of birth (the fir) is far more ancient than modern Christmas custom, and if one of these habits amounts to the borrowing of another, the decorated tree in the house in December is more than likely an echo of the old habit of celebrating the renewed promise of life by worshipping a tree than it is an invention of the "new" religion. The Christmas tree is a custom descended from the ancient Norse belief in Yggdrasil, the world tree, an immense ash. Its roots were in Hel, the kingdom of death, its branches in heaven. The stars hung in its crown. At the base of the tree, around the sacred well, were the three Nornir, or fates, who decided the course of human events. The Druids (ca. 200 BC) put evergreen branches on their altars to give the elves a place to live while the other trees were bare. The Mayday and Midsummer habit of dancing and chanting, in mind-numbing and exhausting repetitions of footwork and rhyme, still has the effect of producing altered states of consciousness, though the purposes for conjuring these have been forgotten. In the Highlands of Scotland, St. Brigid, who is clearly the old Celtic fertility goddess, the goddess of fire and crops, comes asking to be taken in. Many customs require the choosing of a bride and, perhaps, a bridegroom, both of whom must be pure. These two are garlanded and perform rituals whose specific purposes are lost, but appear to be somewhat sacrificial. Often, these two must go from door to door, begging for eggs. They will be given eggs, butter, bread, milk, and candles. In parts of Russia, the bride or bridegroom is ceremonially awakened, a sign of the quickening of life (Frazer 1922). Many people still go outside at the Yuletide to pour libations of wine on the trees, and they remember and sing the tree-wassailing songs which predate the coming of Christianity.

Everywhere, and in all religious practice, the tree holds a special meaning. In Europe, where the motions and words at least have not been forgotten, the echoes of earlier practices ring through the attempts of the newer religion to reorganize and tame them. Folklore remains to testify to the significances of the trees, both as legend and in common superstititon.

TREE LORE

Alder.

The alder (Greece and old Britain) was one of the three trees of resurrection.

Norse mythology claims that the first man and woman were made from the wood of ash and alder.

Because it "bleeds" when cut, and perhaps because of its role in divination practices, the cutting of alder trees was a punishable offense in old Ireland, and is still avoided there today. German folklore demonstrates the pagan belief in the sensitivity of trees. It holds that alders will begin to weep if one even talks of cutting them down.

The alder was used in ancient times to diagnose diseases, and is still recommended to cure certain infirmities. An infusion of alder buds will help with itch and rheumatism, and its bark is one of the ingredients in a salve for the soothing and healing of burns.

Almond.

To climb to the top of an almond tree signifies success in business.

Because it is the very first to leaf and bear flowers—in January in Palestine—the tree is the "waker" or the "watcher."

Aaron's rod was an almond staff.

In Phrygia, the almond was thought of as the father of all things.

It serves as a divining rod in Tuscany, and is assigned to the Virgin by the Christian Church.

In Islam, the tree is called the hope of heaven.

The fruit of the almond has often been prescribed for various ills. Pliny wrote that if you ate five almonds, you would be able to drink alcohol without experiencing any of the usual effects. In the sixteenth century, almonds were used to make pills for travelers to carry for food. More recently, Edgar Cayce (the "Sleeping Prophet") recommended three almonds daily as a cancer preventative.

Apple.

An apple eaten on New Year's Day will produce an abcess.

If you find an apple on your own tree which is one color on one side and another on the other, there will be a division in your family. If you send an apple to the one that you love, it will induce that person to also love you.

If the peels of winter apples are very thick when they are harvested, the upcoming winter will be severe.

Finding a large, thin seed in an apple is a sign of the arrival of a letter.

If you eat an apple that has only one seed, you will have exceptionally good fortune: a legacy or marriage.

It is good luck to find a worm in the first eating apple of the season.

If you slip on an apple peel, things which begin with difficulty will end well.

If an apple falls from a tree and strikes you on the right shoulder, you will have good luck; if it strikes you on the left shoulder, bad luck.

If a bloom appears on an apple tree when the apples are ripe, someone is going to die.

You can win the good will of the fairies if you leave a few apples on the tree at harvest.

Cut an apple, and place one half in your bosom and the other behind the door. The first man to walk through the door will be your future husband.

In England, the boys go out at New Year's, encircle the trees, and sing a charm to ensure a good crop that year.

> Stand fast root, bear well top,
> Pray God send us a howling crop.
> Every twig, apple big,
> Every bough, apples enough.
> Hats full, caps full,
> Great quarter sacks full (Daniels and Stevans 1971).

In Devonshire, the women carry wassail into the apple orchards, where they sprinkle a few drops on each tree to ensure its fruitfulness. In Somersetshire, the apple trees must be wassailed in order to guarantee a good crop.

> Old apple tree, we'll wassail thee,
> And hoping thou wilt bear.
> The Lord doth known where we shall be
> To be merry another year.
> To bear well and to blow well,
> And so merry let us be.
> Let every one drink up his cup,
> And here's health to the old apple tree (Traditional).

If you share an apple with another, and you split a seed between you, the one with the larger part of the seed will have troubles.

If you gather apples under a shrinking moon, they will not rot in storage as readily as when they are harvested under a waxing moon.

In Scandinavian mythology, the Iduna was the goddess who had charge of the tree upon which the apples of immortality grew. The gods ate these to stay young and strong. On one occasion Loki stole both Iduna and the tree and hid them where they could not be found. The gods, the world, and Asgard itself began to age. Finally the gods collectively overpowered Loki, reclaimed the tree and set things to rights.

The apple, though reputed to be the forbidden fruit of Eden, probably was not. Apples are not mentioned in the Bible in connection with Adam and Eve, but oranges and apricots are.

The apple is prominent in many folk motifs: the poisoned apple; the golden apple; the apple thrown down to provide a distraction; the apple as a fertility symbol; the apple as giver of immortality; the apple as a love charm, as a means of divination, as a test of chastity, as a magic object; the apple that, when eaten, causes pregnancy; the quest for the apple.

Apples drop in on people's heads regularly, with different results. William Tell's son's experience was not the same as that of Newton.

The apple is the great cosmic tree—the center of heaven—for the Iroquois, and provides shade in heaven in Wyandot myth.

Apple-shaped birthmarks can be removed by rubbing them with apples and by going on an apple diet.

In Denmark, lovers give apples as tokens of fidelity. If your lover's apple gift fades, he or she has been unfaithful.

Bobbing for apples or trying to bite into an apple on a string is a remnant of an old Druidic divination practice.

Arbutus.

The arbutus was sacred to the Romans; the goddess Cardea used it to drive away witches and to protect small children.

Snakes fed on a diet of arbutus berries cease to be poisonous.

The coming of leaves to the arbutus is the marker of spring for the Algonquin. They believe that every year the winter manitou, Peboan, becomes old and weak from hunger. When he calls for help, Segun, the summer manitou, appears. Segun turns the old man's teepee into a tree, takes some of these leaves, places them on the ground, and breathes them to life.

Ash.

Yggdrasil, the world tree of Scandinavian myth, is an ash.

The first man was made from an ash which was ripped from the earth.

The Irish believe that the shadow of an ash will blast crops and grass; therefore, they do not plant ash where they do not wish its shadow to fall.

If you pass a child through a cleft in an ash tree, he or she will be cured of ruptures or rickets. The astringent sap of the ash is given to children in Scotland as a protection against witchcraft. If you have warts, you can lose them by rubbing them with a piece of bacon, then sticking the bacon under the bark of an ash tree. You can also cure warts by sticking a pin into an ash tree, then into the warts, then into the tree again. If you leave the affected pin in the tree, the ash will take the warts. Be sure to say:

> Ashen tree, ashen tree,
> Pray, buy these warts of me.

Pliny wrote that a snake will not crawl over a barrier made of the leaves of the ash. A circle drawn around a snake with an ash stick will cause it to die of starvation. Snakes will avoid the shadow of the ash tree (England and United States). One blow from a stick of ash will kill any snake. Hang a circlet of ash twigs around the neck to cure snakebite.

Ashen rods can be used to cure some diseases of cows, horses, and sheep (England).

If you bore a hole in an ash, insert a live shrew, then plug the hole, you can cure certain cramps and lameness in cattle. The diseases will be given to the tree. Suspend the branch of an ash over the stall of a sick cow to effect its cure. Tie mountain ash to the horns and tails of cattle to protect them.

It is lucky to have axles made of ash under your wagon (Germany).

If a boat is constructed with one ashen timber, it will never capsize, nor will anyone drown from it for at least one year.

If the ash fails to seed, the royal family will have a death.

The child Jesus was first washed and dressed next to an ashwood fire.

The ash and the juniper are enemies. If you bring both into the house at the same time, the house will burn down. If you plant a third kind of tree in the ground between an ash and a juniper, the opposing forces of these last two will cause the other to split apart (Iceland).

A garter made of the green bark of the mountain ash will protect against all evil from witches, conjurers, and sorcerers.

If a twig of ash is placed in the cockfight ring, no one will be able to work a spell in order to affect the outcome of the fight.

Old bards worked a charm by carving their initials in the bark of the mountain ash.

Aspen.

The leaf of the aspen trembles, because Christ's cross was made of aspen wood (Brittany).

The aspen trembles, because it witnessed Christ's agony in the Garden at Gethsemane.

The aspen trembles, because Judas Iscariot hanged himself from the limb of an aspen tree.

The aspen trembles because it, of all the trees and plants, committed the sin of arrogance and pride by refusing to weep at the Crucifixion. It must tremble, now, until Judgment Day.

The aspen trembles because it, of all the trees, stood on the hill at Calgary and witnessed the Crucifixion.

Aswattha.

In India, the aswattha tree will bring misfortune if it is touched on any day but a Sunday.

Bamboo.

The flowering of the bamboo is an omen of famine.

Bamboo will bring good fortune in the future (Japan).

Because bamboo dies when it seeds, planting it next to a house is unlucky.

If you cut bamboo by the dark of the moon, it will last for years. If you cut bamboo by a full moon, it will not last out the month.

To tell fortunes, a Chinese priest will throw bits of bamboo at the supplicant, then interpret the patterns in which they fall.

Bamboo is the symbol of friendship and of sacred fire (India).

In India, people believe that jungle fires are caused by the rubbing together of sticks of the bamboo.

Bamboo crosses placed in the fields will aid the growth of the crops (Philippines).

Banana.

If you slip on a banana peel, you know that your life will be a busy one, but that you will get nowhere.

It is bad luck to cut a banana open. Always break it.

Plentiful bananas means healthy weather (Philippines).

The bride who is married under the banana tree will be lucky (Philippines).

It was the banana, not the apple, which was the legendary forbidden fruit. The first woman clothed herself in banana leaves (Philippines).

Banyan.

If you walk under a banyan tree in the dark, it will reach out its limbs and strangle you (India).

In Polynesian mythology, the shadows on the moon are the branches of a giant banyan tree, from which the goddess Hina takes bark to make clothing for the gods. The banyan tree was brought to earth by accident when Hina broke a branch that then tumbled to earth and took root. Another story says that the banyan tree was seeded on earth by Hina's companion, the little red parrot, who ate the figs and scattered the seeds.

The Hindus believe that if they desire revenge against an enemy, they can call upon the banyan, which they call "the breaker."

Vishnu was born under the banyan.

The banyan represents the god Siva. Anyone who cuts down a banyan will suffer the annihilation of his entire family.

The banyan tree is the Tree of Knowledge, therefore also the tree of ascetics and seers (India).

Baobab.

The baobab tree of South Africa brings bad omens and bad news. When its branches sway in the wind, the evil spirits are cursing and threatening the people.

Bay.

The bay tree is a protection against witches, the devil, thunder, and lightning.

If you wear an amulet made of a bay leaf wrapped around a wolf's tooth, no one will ever speak an angry word to you.

Apollo always wore a garland or wreath of bay leaves in memory of Daphne, who was changed into the bay tree by her father in order to help her escape Apollo's amorous advances.

Victory garlands and wreaths are made of bay leaves.

If you put bay leaves under your pillow, you will have good luck. If, when you burn bay leaves, they crack and snap noisily, you will have good luck. A quiet burning does not bode well.

Because a withered bay will revive at the roots, the bay tree is a symbol of resurrection (England).

Beech.

The time of the flowering of the beech is the time of lunatic behavior.

The bark of the beech is deadly to snakes. They will die if they touch it.

The oracle of Zeus at Dodona was a grove of beech and oak trees.

Bacchus drank wine from beechwood bowls.

Jason's ship *Argo* was made of beech.

Beechwood in the house will cause hard labors during childbirth and miserable deaths.

Beech leaves are good for chapped lips, sore gums, and blisters.

Beechbark tea will cure a weak back.

Water taken from a place of decaying beeches will cure certain diseases of the skin.

Beech tea mixed with lard will aid rheumatism.

Bela.

The ghosts that dwell in the bela tree must have a yearly offering (Hindu).

Bili.

The *bili* were the sacred trees of the ancient Celts, who first believed that elemental spirits or gods inhabited the trees. Later, the Celts associated the trees with their understanding of the divine right of kings and of the divinity of their rulers.

The *bile* (singular) was the Celtic "king's tree," from which the king's scepter was made. The Celts believed in the separability of souls; their king's soul lived in the tree. This belief is reflected in folktales in which a monster must be slain, but in order to kill him, the hero must go on a quest to find the hiding place of the monster's soul. The monster himself is safe from harm as long as his soul remains hidden and unharmed. The utility of this idea is readily apparent. The Celtic kings were immortal and physically invulnerable, because their bodies were not also receptacles for their souls. They could undertake any mission without fear of death. They could be killed only if the soul tree was chopped down. Cutting a bile tree, or taking its leaves or branches, was sacrilegious, since the soul of the king was bound up in the tree. To kill the tree was also to kill the king.

In Ireland, today, an ancient or oddly shaped tree is considered sacred and called a *bile*. Such trees are considered good luck to pray under, and are still given offerings.

Birch.

In folk medicine, birch is a protection against wounds, gout, barrenness, the evil eye, caterpillars, and lightning.

If a birch tree near your house withers and dies, you will die.

If you stand under a birch tree during a storm, you will be safe from lightning.

The dwarf birch is stunted because it supplied the rods which were used to scourge Christ.

Boil yellow birch buds to a syrup, add sulphur, and apply to ringworm or open sores. Put cod liver oil on the inside surface of birchbark and apply to frostbite. Take juice from or make a distillation of birch leaves. Use this mixture to wash sores and to break kidney stones. Birch branch steam baths are curative. A cordial of birch sap will help cure consumption.

The birch tree, which is consecrated to Thor, is the symbol of the return of spring.

Birch will make good torches.

Birch oil is an effective lubricant for cart wheels.

It is unlucky to make birch-bark brooms in May; they will sweep one's family away (Newfoundland).

The birch arose from a maiden's tear (Finland).

The birch is used to beat the evil spirits out of lunatics.

Birch brooms (besom brooms) can be used to drive out witches.

Bog Myrtle.

The bog myrtle, or yellow willow, is the source of the Palm Sunday palms carried in parts of Ireland.

One must never make a cattle switch of the bog myrtle; it was the tree from which the scourges used on Christ were cut.

Boiling the tips of the branches of the bog myrtle will produce a fine yellow dye which can also be used in tanning.

Botrad.

The *botrad* is the lime or elm tree growing next to the house in Sweden. It is the "abode tree," the home of the guardian spirit of the family. It is never abused or cut, but is prayed and sacrificed to regularly.

The pregnant woman who embraces the botrad will have an easy delivery.

Bo-Tree.

The Bo-Tree is the Tree of Knowledge.

It is good luck to see or to sit under a bo-tree (Hindu).

Happiness is given to those who are married under the bo-tree. They shall have its wisdom.

The Gautama Buddha sat under the bo-tree until he attained perfect knowledge and the perfect state of being. This Buddha tree has been sacred and an object of pilgrimages for over 2,400 years. It is said that the tree was twice cut down and twice restored itself.

A bo-tree in Ceylon is believed by local Buddhists to be the parable tree of the universe. Its roots and branches represent man's striving for perfection, while its trunk represents the connection between the visible and invisible universes.

Box.

The box, a low-growing evergreen which can attain great age, was prized in the ancient world for the quality of musical instruments which could be made from its wood.

In the north of England, one funeral custom involves the dropping of box sprigs onto the coffin after it is lowered into the grave.

In France, boxwood wreaths made for Palm Sunday are kept and dried. They are later burned in the stalls of ailing animals to drive out diseases.

In Breton mythology, a hidden boxwood is the receptacle for the separable soul of a particular giant. He cannot be slain unless the box tree is felled at the root with one blow of an axe.

In Japan, one runs one's fingers over the teeth of a boxwood comb to invite the gods to speak. In order for this method of divination to work, one must be able properly to interpret the sounds made by the comb.

Breadfruit.

Cutting a breadfruit tree is a sign of death (Polynesia).

Calabash.

If you drive an old bolt or spike of iron into a calabash, the fruit will stay on the tree until it is ripe.

Hawaiian sorcerers confine the wandering souls of the living, when they are able to capture these, in the dried fruits of the calabash.

If the calabash is planted on St. John's Day (June 24), the fruit will not fall from the tree before it is ripe. If the calabash tree fails to bear fruit, it must be beaten on St. John's Day.

Camphor.

Camphor crystals are popular in China, where they are used for embalming the dead, for incense, and in certain medicinal preparations. Because the crystals are rare, a special kind of witchcraft attends their gathering. The spirit of the tree must be propitiated by speaking the "camphor language" and observing the proper rituals; then the crystal gatherers will have good luck.

The spirit of the tree is named *Bisan* ("woman"). She rests near the tree at night. When the cicadas are singing, it is really Bisan. Her singing is a signal that camphor can be found.

Cassia.

The cassia is the great tree of life, or world tree, which grows to a remarkable height in Paradise, over the Hoang Ho River. The mortal fortunate enough to eat of its fruit will live forever (China).

Cedar.

It is bad luck to transplant a cedar tree. If you transplant a red cedar which subsequently dies, your own death will follow shortly.

Cedar trees and poverty are companions. Do not keep cedar trees in your yard. However, if a cedar tree comes up on your land by itself, don't cut it. It will bring good luck to you and your family.

The Dakota Indians believe that the white cedar can ward off evil.

It is very unlucky to burn cedar wood. Cedar, according to some reports, was the wood from which Christ's cross was constructed.

The Arabs believe that the cedars of Lebanon are saints. Persons who injure them invite evil into their lives.

Cherry.

St. James's night is generally unlucky, but is made double so if you climb a cherry tree. You will be exposed to great danger, and could fall and break your neck.

Two people eating a double cherry together will both have their wishes, if they wish together.

A bit of wild cherry in your pocket will make you immune to poison ivy.

If you want to know how many years you are given to live on this earth, run round a ripe cherry tree, then shake it. The number of cherries which fall to the ground will tell you.

If blossoms and ripe cherries are found together on the same tree, a child's death is imminent.

A cherry tree will sprout in the stomach of a child who swallows a cherry stone.

A lock of an asthmatic child's hair is sometimes put into the bark of a cherry tree in order to effect a cure.

The cherry tree bowed down for Mary, when a jealous Joseph refused to gather cherries for her. It was by this sign that he knew that her child had been begotten of God.

Chestnut.

A thick burr coat and long spines mean that the coming winter will be long and cold.

A horse-chestnut in the pocket brings good luck. Three horse-chestnuts in the pocket will relieve giddiness. A borrowed or begged-for chestnut in the pocket has great curative powers.

Dried chestnuts are emblems of success, victory, and conquest (Japan).

A stale joke or tale is a "chestnut" ("Oh, *that* old chestnut!").

It is very lucky (Japan) to possess a chestnut from the "tooth marked" chestnut tree of Oki. According to legend, the sick daughter of an emperor bit into a chestnut, then discarded it. The tree which grew from the discarded chestnut produces chestnuts which bear the markings of her little teeth.

Chestnut leaves boiled in water will relieve complaints of asthma and chest pains.

On All Soul's Eve, one must remember to leave some chestnuts on the table for the souls of the dead.

Coconut.

For best results, plant coconuts under a full moon.

The coconut needs to hear the sound of the human voice to thrive.

The coconut is a treasure (Hindu). A concoction of powdered nut, mixed with coral, placed in a porphyry vase, then mingled with wine, will bring good luck to the wedding couple who drink it.

South Sea island peoples believe that the coconut is a gift from the gods. They use it as medicine for all diseases.

The Celanese legend says that the coconut originated because the king's astrologer forecast a particular day that would be so propitious for growing plants that anything planted on that day would grow. The king planted the astrologer's head at the right time, and from it grew the coconut tree.

On Figi, the shaman spins a coconut to determine whether or not a sick person will die. If the coconut falls to the west, death is the diagnosis.

In Senegal, the people claim that coconuts fall only on those who have displeased the gods.

On Mindoro, you must make coconut oil at high tide to get the best yield from the coconuts. People also say that if you watch your coconut grow, or look up at it, it will get very tall. If you comb your hair instead, it will get many nuts.

Coffee.

The Tete of Africa believe that it is very unlucky to plant coffee. The Portuguese of South Africa harbor similar suspicions.

Cottonwood.

The cottonwood, like the quaking aspen, will always turn its leaves up before the rain.

Cypress.

"Plant not a cypress vine, lest it bring death to thine."

A mallet made of cypress wood could impart the power to discover thieves (Germany).

Cypress is the immortal wood. Cypress mummy cases have lasted to the present time. The cypress doors of St. Peter's Basilica are said to be 1,100 years old.

Cypress trees are the transformed daughters of Eteocles. These virgin women, the Graces, were changed to trees in order to save them from an untimely end. Another Greek legend holds that the cypress is the pet stag of Apollo, changed to a tree when the god accidentally slew him.

Other stories of the origin of the cypress say that Zoroaster brought the first seedlings from heaven to plant at the door of the temple. The cypress was one of the three seeds given to Seth by an angel; he was to plant these seeds under Adam's tongue when Adam died.

Bad luck would visit the pagan who forgot to throw a sprig of cypress into the grave at a burial.

The Chinese revere the cypress because its roots grow in the shape of a seated man.

The fruit of the cypress will maintain strength, health, and youth; will cure dysentary, diarrhea, blood spitting, and bleeding gums; and will tighten loose teeth.

Date.

Saving or planting a date stone will breed discontent.

You will have bad luck if you pick wind-blown dates from the ground.

Bad luck attends the one who cuts down a date.

For the ancient Egyptians, the Sumerians, and contemporary Taoists, the date was and is considered the great tree of life. All parts of the date palm serve the needs of man: it gives timber for building, fruit to eat, leaves for the making of utensils, juice for wine, and seeds for oil. It is the archetypal and ancient tree of life.

In one story, Mary gave birth to Jesus under a date palm.

A new mother must eat three dates.

Boiled date root mixed with flour makes a good poultice for swellings and will regulate the bowels.

Djambu Baros.

Djambu Baros is the tree of life in Sumatra, and grows far into the heavens. On each leaf of the tree are inscriptions such as "wealth" or "fruitfulness." Since these inscriptions are formulae for earthly lives, each new soul, before it can depart for the earth to be born, must obtain one of these inscriptions.

Ebony.

It is dangerous to stand under an ebony tree during a storm.

The ebony, a token of strength, value, and beauty, was a gift from the gods (ancient Ephesia).

Elder.

You will not "lose leather in riding" if you carry a bit of elder in your pants pocket.

Never make household furniture of elderwood, especially a child's cradle. Harm will come to those who use such furniture. If you put a child in a cradle made of elder wood, the fairies will take him.

Expectant mothers should kiss the elder tree for good fortune in their child (Sweden).

Witches lurk under elder trees after dark. Keep away.

No evil force can withstand the elder tree.

Having an elder tree near to one's house is a sign of prosperity.

Burning elder wood is unlucky.

Elder trees can move about, and will peep in windows at night (Denmark).

The elder can protect against charms and witches. An elder planted at the stable door will protect cattle from sorcery.

If you fall asleep beneath an elder tree, you will never awaken (Germany).

The elder is inhabited by an imprisoned soul. When you cut it, it weeps and speaks.

One may stand under the elder for safety during a storm, as lightning will not touch the wood from which Christ's cross was made.

If an elder bush trimmed into the shape of a cross and set on a new grave blossoms, the deceased has gone to paradise.

The Hyldemor (Elder-mother) is a spirit which dwells in the elder tree. She will avenge all injuries done to the tree (Denmark).

It is not safe to move articles of furniture made of elder wood (Denmark).

If you must cut branches from an elder, say, "Elder, Elder, May I cut thy branches?" If you are not rebuked, you must spit three times, then you may proceed (Denmark).

If you bring elder branches into the house, ghosts will come in with them. If you hang elder branches over the doors and windows outside of the house, witches and spirits will stay away.

If you burn elder branches, you will reveal all of the witches and sorcerers in the neighborhood. If you cut an elder stick on St. John's Eve, you will be able to detect witches and witchcraft.

Elder is believed to be a general cure-all. In particular, warts and diseases can be got rid of by rubbing them onto elder sticks, then burying the sticks in the ground. Other remedies—salves and concoctions—have a more direct application.

Elderberry.

Elderberry picked on St. John's Eve will prevent possession from witchcraft and bestow magical powers.

In some North American Indian traditions, Elderberry is responsible for causing the early deaths of mankind. Because she made the decision to give birth before Stone, men die. This is why elderberries grow on graves.

Elm.

Elm leaves which fall out of season signify murrain among cattle.

According to Teutonic myth, the elm was the first woman, Embla.

In Finno-Urgic lore, elms were the mothers of *Ut*, the goddess of fire.

In England, the elm (*elven*) was associated with elves. It was the custom to decorate the churches with boughs of the elm tree on Ascension Day.

Barley should be planted when the elm leaves are as big as a mouse ear.

Lightning will never strike an elm tree.

Elm leaves, boiled, will make a very effective poultice for swelling.

Fig.

Athletes in the ancient world were fed dried figs.

An evil spirit lives in each and every fig leaf (Italy).

If you eat figs out of season, you will have great sorrow.

A gift of figs signifies a future legacy.

Bury the first fig of the season under the fig tree to achieve one's wishes.

The fig tree gave knowledge of evil. Those who ate of it had children with an inclination toward evil.

If you write your name on a fig leaf, and it quickly curls and dies, you will have a short life (Brittany).

If you tie elm branches around the trunk of the fig, the fruits will not fall until they are ripe (Sicily).

In ancient times, the fig leaf was worn as a sign of justice and law. The fig was also a phallic symbol in the ancient world.

The expression "a fig to you" and the accompanying hand sign—thumb stuck between and through the fore and middle fingers—has its origins in the Milanese revolt against Frederick Barbarossa. The Milanese placed his wife, the Empress, backwards on a mule and expelled her from the city. Barbarossa, in a rage, retook the town, then forced everyone that he captured—on pain of death—to take a fig from the rear compartments of a mule with his teeth. The hand sign and saying thus came to be. Both are used derisively.

Some folktales, principally Estonian, employ the motif of the Magic Fig, which causes sleep, and which can cause horns to grow on one's head. Still other stories use the fig for the motif of food (figs) raining from heaven—usually in a noodle story.

Fir.

Fir plants are lucky (Japan).

Carry a piece of torch fir for good luck (Scotland).

Fir and hazel tied together into a horse's mane will keep it from running away.

The fir is a charm which will protect a house (Germany).

A fir branch on a sickbed will help the sick and ward off illness (Germany).

Solomon's temple had a roof made of silver fir. The Trojan horse may have been constructed of silver fir.

The silver fir is as ancient a tree in legend as the palm, especially in northern Europe.

In pagan Europe, the fir was the tree of birth (sister to the yew, the tree of death), was female, and was dedicated to the first day of the new year, the first day of the winter solstice. The use of the fir tree at Christmas is very likely related to the association of the tree with the old solstice customs.

For the Votjaks of Finland, the fir is sacred. Certain branches are family gods and must receive proper sacrifices of foodstuffs. When a new house is being built, a small fir is set up beneath it. Sacrifices are offered on a cloth which is spread out under the tree.

Furze.

Plant a hedge of prickly furze to keep fairies out.

Furze is almost always in bloom in Scotland, where custom holds that if the gorse is out of bloom, kissing is out of season.

On May Day Eve and Midsummer's Eve, the Irish burn furze bushes to protect cattle and crops.

"Blessed furze," a hill variety, is worn in order to help a person locate lost objects and keep from stumbling.

Gingko.

The gingko was saved from extinction because the Chinese considered it to be sacred.

Hazel.

If you can drive three pins of hazel wood into a house, it is a sign that the house will not catch fire.

A sprig of hazel will keep you safe from lightning.

Break a hazel nut in one stroke. If it separates into three pieces, you will soon be married.

Cut a twig of hazel on Good Friday, and you will have the magical ability to strike someone who is at some distance from you.

It is ominous to cut down either hazel or oak.

Hazel nuts can make you invisible (Sweden).

A great crop of hazel nuts means a great crop of illegitimate children (Bohemia). The large crop of babies that comes with a large crop of hazel nuts is composed mostly of boys.

A plentiful harvest of hazel nuts:

> Many nits (nuts),
> Many graves (pits).

If you rub the ashes of hazel nuts on the back of an infant's head, the irises of its eyes will turn black.

Hickory.

When the hickory leaves turn bright yellow in the autumn, the following year's harvest will be a rich one.

Holly.

A piece of holly will prevent lightning strikes.

Holly flowers were once thought to have the power to freeze water and tame animals.

If holly bark water is thrown in the faces of newborn children, they will have power over the evil one (Parsee).

A branch of holly in the house brings good luck. That luck is diminished with every berry that falls from the branch before the new year.

Holly and mistletoe will gain the favor of the fairies (Ireland).

Holly is an ancient pagan symbol of life. It was brought into the temples in the wintertime to soothe the sylvan spirits.

Judas Tree.

The Judas tree is a favorite witch haunt. Never go near a Judas tree after dark.

The Judas tree (redbud) blooms red because Judas Iscariot hanged himself from this type of tree.

Jujuba.

The jujuba, in legend, can cause forgetfulness. It may have been the lotus tree of Greek epic which was eaten by Ulysses and his men, and caused them to lose all memory and to desire nothing but dreamy forgetfulness.

The jujuba is the *Sidrat*, or tree of paradise, of the Koran. It grows at the highest point in the seventh heaven, to the immediate right of the throne of God. Every leaf of the Sidrat is inscribed with the name of a living human being. Once yearly, on the fifteenth day of Ramadan, the tree is shaken. All of the leaves which fall from the tree are those who will die in the upcoming year.

Juniper.

Burning juniper in the house will bring good fortune.

A sprig of juniper pinned to the clothing will bring protection from accidents.

One who cuts a juniper will die within the year (Wales).

Branches of the juniper will protect a stable from demons and lightning, and burning juniper in a stable will purge it.

In Newfoundland, the larch (called the juniper) always points its leaves to the east (toward Christ), so it always gives hunters their directions. It is said, too, that one can always find water under the juniper.

The Juniper Tree is a European folktale with many variants, which uses the cruel-stepmother and abuse-of-stepchildren motifs.

Kankantri.

Taki-taki, the silk cotton tree, or "god tree," is sacred to the Earth Mother (Gro/Gro Mama) of Surinam. Every plot of ground, however small, has its obigatory silk cotton tree which is propitiated according to custom.

Larch.

A popular superstition asserts that larch wood cannot be burned.

In the Americas there is, supposedly, a larch that has the power to make those who sleep under it temporarily delirious and crazy.

Laurel.

Laurel leaves which crackle when burned foretell a good harvest. Leaves which burn silently are a bad omen.

Laurel bark, leaf, and berry will cure wasp stings.

Carry the wood of the laurel on your head during thunderstorms to protect against lightning.

Wear a bay leaf under your chin as a charm against thunder (Norway). In England and Scotland, wear it around the neck.

If a man gives his sweetheart a bay leaf, he pledges that nothing but death will change his love.

No evil or sickness can infest the place where stands the bay tree (Sweden).

A bay leaf carried in the mouth will ward off evil and bad luck. Never leave home without one.

If you are not carrying or wearing the leaf of the laurel, and a dog or weasel crosses your path, you can only avert the evil thus forecast by casting three stones at the offending animal.

The laurel planted on the capitol grounds was said to wither when the emperor was about to die (ancient Rome).

The ancients believed that laurel embodied the spirit of prophecy and poetry. Poets, actors, and actresses were, appropriately, crowned with laurel wreaths. The contemporary custom of naming a writer as "poet laureate" is thus derived.

If you sleep with laurel leaves under your pillow, you will be inspired.

In Japan, the bronze laurel is a tree of good omen. Its old leaves do not fall until the new ones that will replace them are also full grown. The tree represents the hopes of fathers — that the son will attain his majority before the death of the father.

Lemon.

Lemon juice will encourage long life (France).

To ensure the lasting friendship of a visitor, put a slice of lemon under his chair.

If you write the name of an intended victim on a slip of paper, then stick pins through it into a lemon, you will cause the named individual pain and even death. This form of witchcraft was indigenous to England, Italy, and Sicily.

Because the lemon is such a bitter fruit, it has become the metaphor for "loser," "worst of the lot," "something that is useless, because it won't work as it should."

Preparations of lemon have found wide medicinal use: skin, hair, stomach, problems of the teeth, constipation, upset stomach, sore throat, congestion, contraception, epilepsy, fever, malaria, measles, dizziness, and seasickness.

Linden.

The linden or lime tree is planted at the front of a new house to keep witches out (Germany, Hungary).

The linden tree is possessed of many magical qualities.

The bark of the linden can help to prevent intoxication (ancient Rome).

In Scythia, soothsayers turned to the linden and wound its leaves around their fingers when they spoke.

In central Europe, the linden is the tree of immortality.

Women in Europe, especially in Germany and the former Balkan states, made sacrifices to the linden. It was, in many respects, a woman's tree. Men made their sacrifices to the oak.

The linden tree is the haunt of dwarves and dragons (Germany, the Tyrol).

The linden tree is the tree of justice. Magistrates often sat underneath it to hear cases and to pass judgments.

The tree must not be harmed; it is the home of domestic spirits (Sweden).

In legend as well as in practice, the linden and the oak are related. When Hermes and Zeus were forced to seek shelter in the home of a humble old couple, they showed their gratitude by changing the woman into a linden, the man into an oak.

The linden tree of Germanic legend, the *Susterheistede*, withered when the Dithmarschen lost their freedom, and will not live again until they are freed. A magpie will serve as the portent of their return. (This legend has been borrowed into the high fantasy of contemporary written literature. Tolkein describes a very linden-like tree that must stand dead in the courtyard of the castle of the high king. It comes into flower again, after centuries of dormancy, when the high king returns [Tolkein 1986].)

The dried flowers of the linden are used to make tea for headache, debility, insomnia, nerves, and purity of blood. Its sap is fermented to wine; its seeds are made into a confection. Linden oil is used in Russia for toothache, the inner bark by Native Americans for poultices. Native American peoples also found use for the fibers that can be pulled from the bark. These were used for the making of ropes and household utensils. Indians called the linden "string tree."

Magnolia.

If you sleep under a magnolia tree when it is in full bloom, it could cause your death (Native American).

Maple.

If the first maple sap from the tap is not sweet, the sugar season will be long. If it is sweet, however, the season will be very short.

Many maple tree customs are similar to those involving the ash. If you pass a child through its branches, the child will be assured long life.

Maple wood is good for making divining rods for locating water.

Maple was once the emblem of reserve.

Once the first peepers are heard in the spring woods, the maple sap will stop running.

One story from Algonquin tradition tells of how a woman who was too lazy to go for cooking water tapped a maple tree instead, poured the sap into her stew and thereby invented maple syrup. She fled in terror when her moose meat thickened into a sticky mass of maple syrup, but her husband supposedly enjoyed the meal.

Moon Tree.

The moon tree is an oriental variety of laurel or bay tree. In Japanese folklore, the tree grows on the moon, where the changing color of its leaves also changes the color of the moon.

In China, the moon tree is associated with the cassia or tree of immortality, which also grows on the moon.

In India, in ancient times, there stood two oracular trees, one male and one female, the sun tree and the moon tree. These trees were able to provide answers for a questioner, provided that that person observed the preliminary rites of purification. When Alexander was in India, he determined that he would speak to the trees. The trees, one of which spoke Greek, the other an Indian tongue (Parsee?), told him that he would never return home, that he would die in Babylon, and that he would be poisoned. Marco Polo also reported seeing these trees.

Mulberry.

The mulberry is the sacred tree of Burma.

In China, the mulberry, because of its traditional association with the production of silk, is the emblem of industry. The Chinese propitiate San Ku Fu Jen, the goddess protector of multerry trees.

In China one must never plant a mulberry in front of a house; it will bring sorrow.

If you carry a staff of mulberry, you signal that you are in mourning for your mother (China).

Oak.

You must look for grass at the top of the oak tree.

Good crops are to be expected, if the oaks bend in January.

Spread oak boughs over casks of beer for good luck.

It is an old custom to tell the nearest oak of a death in the family.

If oak and walnut stand together, one will die.

If you plant an acorn by moonlight, you will receive money.

An acorn around a child's neck is a charm for good luck.

If the acorns are plentiful, the bacon will be bad (Yorkshire).

Oak leaves which change from their natural color foretell catastrophe.

Fairies haunt oak trees.

A grove of oak at Loch Saint, Isle of Skye, is still held to be so sacred that no one would dare risk harming the trees in any way.

The Celts would not touch even the falling leaves of the sacred oak.

If an oak were to be felled and burned, and the ashes carried away, a dog would appear to compel the people to return the ashes to the site where the tree had stood.

Felling an oak is fatal.

Holes in oak trees are fairy pathways (Germany). Holes in oak trees are the doorways for the spirits who inhabit the trees. If you put your hands over these holes, you will be cured of affliction (India).

Oak wood has great spiritual powers and can overcome evil.

In the village of Shookhoot in Russia, there is an ancient oak in which an angel regularly sits. People take their problems to the tree, but pass it with great care, reverence, and respect.

The oak is a prominent figure in ancient Hebrew scripture. The oak has been sacred to most major godheads of recorded history. It was the principal tree of the Druids. Many major decisions have been made under the oak, law is given there, and a substantial number of well-known historical figures have been buried at the root of an oak tree.

If you place an acorn in your window, you will be protected against lightning.

A blasted oak is usually a portent of disaster.

The acorn is a phallic symbol and a sign of fecundity.

The last leaf never falls from an oak.

Two acorns which float close together in a bowl of water mean love. If they drift apart, there will be no wedding.

Olive.

The wearer of wild olive will have good luck.

If you wear at your breast a leaf from one of the seven sacred olives of the garden of Gethsemane, no harm can ever come to you.

If an olive is planted by a virgin, it will thrive. If planted by a woman who is unchaste, it will die.

Pick an olive leaf while standing with your back to an olive tree's trunk. Make a wish; throw the leaf over your right shoulder. Say:

> Go forth little message,
> Like Noah's faithful dove.
> And bring me an olive leaf of love.

If the leaf falls to the ground, you will be unlucky in love, but if it floats down, you will be happily married within one year.

The olive is the emblem of peace, chastity, fecundity, and prosperity.

The olive tree was sacred to both Athena and Apollo; olive wreaths were worn by heads of state in both Greece and Rome, as well as by returning heroes and conquerors.

In China, the olive wreath is given for literary merit.

Olive branches over the door could keep witches and demons from entering a house (Italy).

The dead were often laid out on or covered with olive branches before being placed in a coffin.

A magic olive branch could both ensure a husband's fidelity and make a woman master at home (Spain).

The fruitfulness of olive trees could be increased by having young, innocent children tend to them.

Peepul.

The *peepul* or pagoda tree is venerated by Hindus because Visnu was born under a pagoda tree. Breaking branches or otherwise harming the tree is a sacrilege.

Yet another variety of pagoda tree, the devil's fig, provides shelter for evil spirits.

Pine.

Pine wood will never soak up water if it is cut by moonlight.

Pine trees moan, because they contain the imprisoned spirits of all the winds.

Put a branch of pine wood over the door to ensure continual happiness (Japan).

The hand of Jesus can be seen in the pine cone.

If a drop of rain falls on you from a small pool of water trapped in the branches of a pine, you will have a nightmare that night.

If you eat pine kernels from the topmost cone, you will be invulnerable to gunshot. Thieves and robbers believe that if you gather pine cones on St. John's Day, then faithfully eat one seed daily, you will become immune to gunshot.

The pines of the Figi Islands are haunted with ghosts and spirits.

The pine is a symbol of unflinching purpose and vigorous old age, and possesses the power to drive out demons (Japan).

The pine is the sacred tree of life in ancient Semitic cultures.

In China and Japan, the pine also represents longevity and immortality. Pine juice, taken regularly, can lengthen life.

The pine is revered in Europe for its qualities in ship construction.

In the Tyrol, the pine is planted as a marriage tree.

Native Americans use the pine to treat colds and wounds, and to conduct ceremonials for the deceased.

Plum.

If the plum crop is heavy, there will be cholera, but little lightning.

If you eat plums given to you by a stranger, you will be overtaken by feelings of shame and/or disgrace.

If a plum blossoms in December, there will be a death in the family.

The Chinese believe that the plum tree sprang up from the blood of a dragon whose ears had been cut off.

The plum signifies long life and immortality, and is the seasonal symbol for winter (China).

Carry a plum pit around in your mouth and you will avoid sunstroke and overeating (Texas). Carry a plum pit around in your mouth and you will probably be able to avoid saying things that you might later regret.

The metaphoric use of *plum* (as in "that was a 'plum' of a job") most probably derives from the common reference to the sum of £ 1,000,000 that was slang in the late fifteenth and early sixteenth centuries. Courtiers were rewarded with sums of money which totalled to exactly one "plum." Henry VIII was reputed to have paid "plums" to some of the loyal nobles who helped him confiscate and liquidate many church holdings. When Jack Horner reached in his thumb, the "plum" he pulled out was a sum of money, with which Jack purchased land and built a manor that still remains in the family.

Pomegranate.

The pomegranate is lucky. Make a wish before eating pomegranate and the wish will come true.

The pomegranate tree is the discoverer of concealed wealth (Sicily).

To prevent eye trouble, eat three small pomegranate flowers daily.

If you want to foretell the number of children that you will have, throw a pomegranate to the ground, then count the number of spattered seeds (Turkey).

The pomegranate has long been a symbol of fertility and fecundity in many cultures.

The pomegranate is the symbol of wealth.

The pomegranate is said, by some, to have been the forbidden fruit of the Garden of Eden.

Because she ate six seeds of the pomegranate, Persephone must spend six months out of every year in Hades.

The pomegranate is a Christian symbol of hope.

Zoroaster recommended the use of pomegranate branches against demons and witches.

The wood of the pomegranate makes a good divining rod.

Poplar.

When the leaves of a poplar turn bottom-side up, it will rain within an hour.

Poplar trees near a house are unlucky.

In *The Odyssey*, the poplar was one of three trees which stood at the mouth of Calypso's cave.

The sisters of Phaethon, who wept at the death of Euripides, were transformed into a poplar grove.

Because of Hercules's journey into the underworld, the white poplar has come to signify the promise of life after death. Perhaps in memory of this significance, the Irish still measure out their dead with measuring sticks made of the white poplar.

The white poplar may once have been used as a preventative against leprosy.

The black poplar is associated with the earth mother, and, in divination practices in the ancient world, is an omen of hopelessness.

Some North American Indian groups use boiled scrapings of poplar roots to cure stomach worms.

For the Irish, the poplar is the tree of autumn and of old age.

Ancient Irish warriors carried shields made of poplar.

In Macedonia, people believe that the shade of the poplar is inhabited by haunts and malevolent spirits, and they take care to avoid patches of it.

In medieval France, witches made salves from poplar leaves.

Raintree.

In India, one who drinks the distilled water of the raintree will have good health and happiness.

The New Zealand raintree is a mythical plant created by the leaves which fell from the crown of Hatu-patu, the god of the wind.

In the Andes mountains, the raintree is so called because it drips a sticky residue even under clear skies. The cicadas, which suck the juice from its more tender branches, squirt this substance from their perches in the tree.

Sala.

The mother of Buddha gave birth to him while holding onto a branch of this sacred tree.

Buddha also died under a sala tree. The tree, it is said, bloomed out of season and showered his body with blossoms.

It is lucky to always carry sala blossoms on one's person, especially out of season.

Spindletree.

If you pierce meat with the branch of the spindletree, it will not spoil.

Spruce.

Traditions and lore associated with the spruce are much like those of the fir and pine.

The Navaho make use of spruce branches in their ceremonies.

Penobscot hunters carry a spruce twig next to the skin to prevent pain in the side.

Sumac.

If you burn green sumac in the stove, you will cause the death of a member of the family.

Sycamore.

If the sycamore tree peels white in the fall, the winter will be cold.

Tamarind.

The shadow cast by the tamarind can induce leprosy.

The tamarind is an unlucky tree. It is named for Yamadutaka, the messenger of the god of death and the underworld (India).

Theomat.

The theomat grows in Peru, where its branches are used for divination. If the cut branch of the theomat is placed in the hand of a person who is sick, and if that person immediately shows signs of happiness, he or she will recover. If, however, that individual shows signs of sorrow, he or she will die.

Thornapple.

Eating thornapples will make you behave like an idiot (Ireland).

In earlier times, the thornapple was thought to be a poison. Sorcerers used it to become intoxicated.

Certain tribes of Peruvian Indians believe that they are able to communicate with the dead when they are under the intoxicating influence of the fruits of a particular thornapple tree.

In Arab countries, the thornapple is the devil's apple. If laid on someone's doorstep, the thornapple will cause the inhabitants of the house to be driven out by evil spirits.

The wild, native American thornapple seems to have intoxicated soldiers, making them temporarily unfit for duty.

Turpentine.

The turpentine is yet another of the trees upon which Judas Iscariot is supposed to have hung himself. Like the others, this tree should never be cut down.

Walnut.

If you put the germ or nail of the walnut in your shoe, you will have good luck.

If someone gives you a gift of walnuts, your wishes will come true.

Sleeping under a walnut will bring bad luck. The walnut is the witch's tree. One must never sleep under it.

Wear walnut leaves in the hat to prevent sunstroke and headache.

Empty out several walnut shells, then fasten them back together, so that they look whole. Mix the empty shells with an equal number of full ones. Without looking, select one shell. If you pick a full shell, you will be happily married, or you will get your wish.

Willow.

In India, the species of willow called *saraca indica* is an unlucky plant which drives away feelings of love.

Willow branches are used in China as charms against evil spirits and the diseases they cause.

The weeping willow suffered the agony of the Apostles during the Crucifixion, and has wept ever since.

If you take ninety-nine different leaves from ninety-nine different willow plants, burn them to powder, then ingest the powder, you will gain the power of prophecy.

The willow which makes music has a soul (Ireland).

Never cut down a hollow willow. If you do, the devil who lives in it will exact a revenge.

Burning willows is bad luck.

If you tie knots in willows, you will be able to kill distant enemies (Germany).

If you throw your shoe at a willow on Easter or New Year's Day, and it catches on a branch, you will marry that year. You may have no more than nine tries.

If you have a weeping willow whose branches grow up instead of down, remove it. It is unlucky.

A weeping willow in a yard marks a family with an unhappy life.

Plant a willow in a field at Easter to protect that field from storms.

If a man passes a water willow without touching or smelling it, he will lose his sweetheart.

The soul of the willow dies when the tree is cut down (Bohemia).

The common willow is under the special protection of the devil. If you tie a knot on it, then sit under it and renounce your baptism, the devil will give you supernatural powers.

If you stick needles into a willow, the spirit of the tree will cure your toothache.

When Adam and Eve were banished from the garden, two angels sat on a willow tree and wept for man's misfortune. Their tears ran down the branches, causing them to turn down, and the willow has wept ever since (Italy).

Never buy or rent a house which has a willow tree on its property. You will have great trouble.

Yew.

The yew is distasteful to witches, because it grows on consecrated ground, near churches.

RHYMES CONCERNING TREES

Rhymes of the sort collected here are recipes. Before print was used to save information, people had to depend upon the device of oral language for ensuring that the experiences of one generation were not lost to the next. The wisdom of the folk—when to plant, when to harvest, which plants were of medicinal value, how to cure, store, or prepare foods, how to make and use tools—had to be remembered. This kind of knowledge is base and common, the stuff of daily toil, yet it represents a community effort to improve individual circumstance by conserving the collective experience. The familiar-pattern rhyme provided a structural frame for saving and passing on accumulated knowledge. Little ditties boiled a larger body of data down to essences. Mnemonic devices made memory and retrieval easier.

Much of folklore is not superstition or metaphoric reference, but is a collection of rather utilitarian stuff about the immediate environment and how best to get along living with it and in it. Literary devices which serve to aid memory, such as meter, rhyme, alliteration, and onomatopoeia, may have had their beginnings in such observations of the natural world as are provided in oral traditions. The need to remember required application of the formulae of oral composition to even the mundane, making poetry of the ordinary and the common.

In the following verse, the *bourtree* is the elder; "drawing a stroke" refers to lightning. The rowan or mountain ash is also known as the "witchwood," "quicken," or "whicken-tree" for its powers to hold witches in check, to "gar the witches tyne their speed." A *farden* is a farthing.

Burn ash-wood green,
'Tis a fire for a queen;
Burn ash-wood sere,
'Twill make a man swear.
(Baring-Gould and Baring-Gould 1962.)

Bourtree, bourtree, crooked rung,
Never straight and never strong,
Ever bush and never tree,
Since our Lord was nailed on thee.
(Baring-Gould and Baring-Gould 1962.)

If the oak is out before the ash,
Then we'll only have a splash;
If the ash is out before the oak,
Then we'll surely have a soak.
(Baring-Gould and Baring-Gould 1962.)

Beware of an oak,
It draws the stroke.
Avoid an ash,
It courts the flash.
Creep under the thorn,
It will save you from harm.
(Baring-Gould and Baring-Gould 1962.)

Oak-logs will warm you well,
That are old and dry;
Logs of pine will sweetly smell
But the sparks will fly.

Birch-logs will burn too fast,
Chestnut scarce at all;
Hawthorn-logs are good to last—
Catch them in the fall.

Holly-logs will burn like wax,
You may burn them green;
Elm-logs like to smouldering flax,
No flame to be seen.

Beech-logs for winter time,
Yew logs as well;
Green elder-logs it is a crime
For any man to sell.

Pear-logs and apple-logs,
They will scent your room,
Cherry-logs across the dogs
Smell like the flower of broom.

Ash-logs, smooth and grey,
Burn them green or old,
Buy up all that come your way—
Worth their weight in gold.
(Baring-Gould and Baring-Gould 1962.)

When a fire burns without "blowing"
You'll have company without knowing.
(Baring-Gould and Baring-Gould 1962.)

A cherry year,
A merry year;
A pear year,
A dear year;
A pear year,
A dumb year.
(Baring-Gould and Baring-Gould 1962.)

Rowan-tree and red thread
Gar the witches tyne their speed.
(Baring-Gould and Baring-Gould 1962.)

When elm leaves are as big as a farden,
You MAY plant your kidney beans in
    the garden;
When elm leaves are as big as a shilling,
It's time to plant kidney beans if you're
    willing;
When elm leaves are as big as a penny,
You MUST plant kidney beans—
If you mean to have any!
(Baring-Gould and Baring-Gould 1962.)

Who sets an apple tree,
May live to see its end;
Who sets a pear tree,
May set it for a friend.
(Baring-Gould and Baring-Gould 1962.)

TREE GAMES

Many games make references to trees, and provide some insight into the roles played by trees in earlier cultures. Games particularly remember the function of the sacred grove as a sanctuary. In many forms of tag, there must be a "safety"—the word alone, used in this manner, tells us much about the power that was attributed to the tree.

Of these games, Alice Gomme, a well-known collector of children's lore said:

Children are always mimics, or rather unconscious dramatists of the real events of life; and the action and words of some of these games are so divergent from present-day life, that we must look to the events of earlier periods for an explanation of them. It is impossible that they can have been invented by children by mere effort of the imagination, and there is ample evidence that they have but carried on unchangingly a record of events, some of which belong to the earliest days of the nation (Gomme 1967, 11-12).

Old Roger

Old Roger is a singing and dancing game in which the players act out the event of a funeral. We see in the play the ancient custom of planting trees on the graves of the dead and the belief that the violation of such sacred trees might waken the dead. (Legend tells that when Adam became ill, Seth went to the gate of heaven to beg the angel for a branch from the Great Tree of Life. His request granted, he returned to cure his father, but was too late. He planted the branch on Adam's grave, where it grew to a great tree. It was regarded as sacred and inviolate.) The curious bowing or bobbing which continues throughout, and which is specified expressly in all contemporary references to the game (Gomme 1967; Gomme and Sharp 1976), may be a remnant of a funeral custom.

Old Roger is dead and gone to his grave.
Heigh-ho! Gone to his grave.
They planted an apple tree over his head.
Heigh-ho! Over his head.
The apples were ripe and ready to drop.
Heigh-ho! Ready to drop.
There came an old woman a-pickin' them up.
Heigh-ho! Pickin' them up.
Old Roger jumped up and he gave her a knock.
Heigh-ho! Gave her a knock.
Which made the old woman go hippety hop.
Heigh-ho! Hippety hop.

To play, three children must be chosen to act out the parts of Old Roger, old woman, and apple tree. (In alternate versions, all players act all parts.) These three go to the center of the circle. Old Roger must lie flat on his back; sometimes he has a cloth draped over his face or body. The apple tree and old woman come in on cue and do what the verses tell them to do. Throughout the play, the childen standing in the circle must face the players in the center, keep their hands and arms folded across their chests in the "dead" pose, and bow somewhat stiffly from the waist to the rhythm of the verse.

The Oakum in the Wood

The Oakum in the Wood (*The Green Grass Grew All Around/The Rattlin' Bog*) is a cumulative singing game in which the object is to be able to remember all the lines. Up to tempo, this game also becomes a tongue twister.

There was a little oak grew down in the woods;
Prettiest little oak that you ever did see.
Oh, the oakum in the woods,
And it's all gone away.

And on that oak there was a twig;
Prettiest little twig that you ever did see.
Oh, the twigum on the oakum,
And the oakum in the woods,
And it's all gone away.

And on that twig there was a little nest;
Prettiest little nest that you ever did see.
Oh, the nestum on the twigum,
And the twigum on the oakum,
And the oakum in the woods,
And it's all gone away.

And on that nest there was a little egg ...
And on that egg there was a little bird ...
And on that bird there was a little feather ...
And on that feather there was a little spot ...
(Chase 1972.)

This version is perhaps less well known than the one that follows, but contains some curious features: the specific mention of the oak and the reference to its being gone away. This next verse, aside from being a more common form of the song, incorporates ancient memories of cycle and regeneration.

There was a little hole;
'Twas a hole in the ground.
'Twas the prettiest little hole
That you ever did see.
Pretty little hole,
Hole in the ground,
And the green grass grew all around, all around,
The green grass grew all around.

Now in that hole,
There was a root.
'Twas the prettiest little root
That you ever did see.
Root in the hole,
Hole in the ground,
And the green grass grew all around, all around,
The green grass grew all around.

Now on that root,
There was a trunk.
'Twas the prettiest little trunk
That you ever did see.
Trunk on the root,
Root in the hole,
Hole in the ground,
And the green grass grew all around, all around,
The green grass grew all around.

Now on that trunk there was a limb ...
Now on that limb there was a branch ...
Now on that branch there was a twig ...
Now on that twig there was a leaf ...
Now on that leaf there was a nest ...
Now in that nest there was an egg ...
Now on that egg there was a bird ...
Now on that bird there was a beak ...
Now in that beak there was a seed ...
Now from that seed there grew a tree ...
(Traditional.)

Tag

Ha! Ha! Ha!
Hee! Hee! Hee!
Can't catch me for a bumblebee!

Mardy, mardy mustard,
You can't eat a custard.
Hee! Hee! Hee!
You can't catch me.
(Opie and Opie 1984.)

The game of *Tag* is universal. The person who is "it" in the game has the power to immobilize, stop, take away the freedom of, or eliminate another player. While rules can vary—and sometimes they are concocted on the spot—there are several givens: the transforming power of the "it," the freedom of the others to run away, and, usually, the designation of a "safety."

The safety, often a tree around which the play is conducted, is the place that a player under hot pursuit can run to and touch to get away. Once the player has touched the safety, he or she is immune from the otherwise transforming touch of the it. Players who continually stick too close to the safety will not earn the respect of their peers. They must take risks and demonstrate that they can survive by skill and wit. If the rules allow it, someone who is touching the safety can extend an outstretched hand to other endangered runners, thereby making them safe as well. (If the game includes a jail—some kind of imprisonment—players who are free can tag those who have been caught and imprisoned and free them.)

Baseball uses these ancient principles. The base/bag is the safety. A player can be tagged out (transformed) if he is not touching the base. We realize just how serious the business of being safe (in sanctuary) is when we consider the function of the base umpire. Even the idea of home base incorporates folk tradition. A player who "makes it home" is free, no longer in danger of being tagged out. (From what old memories, one might wonder, came the early version of the base in baseball? It was an upright *pole*.)

The game of *Tag* contains reminiscences of the sacred grove, and perhaps the sacred tree or pole at the altar. We still view the altar as sanctuary, and call that part of the church in which it is housed by that name. In an earlier time, a person who came to the altar for sanctuary could not be taken from it by force by his pursuers; the sacredness of the holy place was not to be desecrated in such a manner. This custom could very well have been in force long before the advent of Christianity in Europe. An individual who ran into a sacred grove for safety might have been irretrievable while in that place. If the gods were believed to punish all but the initiated (priesthood) for setting foot on consecrated ground, the taboo may have been so powerful that persons went into the grove to find sanctuary only when in the gravest danger, perhaps only when in peril of their lives.

One source (Opie and Opie 1984) cites a game of tag called *Tiggy, Tiggy Touchwood* which children in Great Britain still play. Wood is the safety in the game. *Tiggy* or *tig* is synonomous with "tag."

TREE PROGNOSTICATIONS

- A tree will grow well, if, when you plant it, you grasp it firmly with two hands, while a second person helps.

- Old trees crashing down in the mountains signal a coming storm.

- A heavy acorn or beech nut crop portends a severe winter.

- The family living nearest to a withered tree will have sickness.

- If you gather some of the fruit from a tree at its very first bearing, and also leave some behind on the branches, the tree will always bear well.

- If you see a few leaves trembling on a tree, while the others are still, you will have bad luck.

- If you carve your name into any tree, you will have an enemy that will be with you until the tree is cut down or burned. If you cut your name into a tree, it will die when you die.

- A tree which bears leaves in late autumn foretells many deaths in that vicinity.

- If you come upon a tree standing in the middle of a path, always pass it on the right. To do otherwise is unlucky.

- If the tops of your trees wither, the head of your family will die.

- It is very bad luck to cut down a very old tree. The older the tree, the more souls that reside in it (Borneo).

- A tree with a trunk which is twisted in the direction of the setting sun will be easily split, but not so the tree whose trunk twists toward the sunrise.

- It is bad luck to pass a place where a tree is blown down across the road. Remove the tree first.

- If a tree branch grows into your window, you will be successful in those things for which you wish.

- If you unexpectedly kill a tree, expect domestic troubles.

- If you are hit by a falling tree, you will not live out the year.

- If you touch a tree which is inhabited by a tree fairy (dryad), the fairy will injure you in some way (Germany).

- If a tree growing near your house splits in two, you will have bad luck, perhaps the death of someone in the family.

- If you cut a tree under a waning moon, the lumber will shrink and decay.

- If you plant a tree which subsequently grows crookedly, there will be a black sheep in the family.

- Never cut, hurt, or disturb a tree which grows near a sacred well (Ireland).

- You will have bad luck if you cut down a green tree.

- If you cut a tender branch from a tree, your children will die young (Persia).

- It is lucky to plant a shade tree (India).

- It is unlucky to sit on a tree stump.

- You bring poverty if you peel the bark from a tree (Germany).

- If a tree sheds its leaves from the top down in the fall, the winter will be light. Leaves which are shed from the bottom up foretell a hard winter.

- On Orkney, there stood a sacred tree that could not be touched. People believed that if even so much as one leaf were to be removed, they would be conquered by a foreign nation.

- If, immediately after a storm, you dig at the base of a tree which was struck by lightning, you will find the thunderbolt. Thunderbolts are walnut-sized, look like melted glass, and are very lucky. Dig quickly, or a groundhog will eat the prize before you are able to recover it.

- In the spring, go into the forest and locate a healthy tree. Bite into one of its branches. If that branch later withers and dies, you will also die.

- If you ever cut down a lightning-struck tree, cut three crosses into the stump to keep evil from you.

- You will get warts if you touch the wartlike growths on a tree.

- Knocking on wood, a charm to make a dream or wish come true, is a custom which dates to Druidic times. The Druids believed that trees were inhabited by gods. To ask a favor of a god, the Druids would knock on the trunk of the tree, then wait for a favorable reply — a return knocking.

- In Sweden, a mother who draws her sick child through the exposed roots of a tree will effect a cure for the illness, but only if she does it on a Thursday.

- Burning wood from a lightning-struck tree is bad luck.

- Using a few old pieces of wood to construct a new building is good luck.

- California's Maidu Indians believed that the earth was originally a mass of fire. When, eventually, the fire collected in the center of the earth, tree roots became connected to it. Thereafter, the fire could be extracted from the roots of the trees by using special drills.

4

Story Activities

Activity also plays a major role in the unfolding of the story. Like artifacts, activities represent the cultural mind, and appear in stories because of their specific symbolic significances. The nature of the folklore surrounding activities and processes will alert the storyteller to liberties which can and cannot be taken with in-story activities, and can help the teller to enrich a story and bring the content of the folklore to the audience. Calendar customs, holidays, and festivals; divination (forecasting, prognosticating, and counting out); magic and superstition; and games are documented in this part.

The storyteller works as conservator of memories as they come to us in both oral and printed form. Knowing cultural significances and symbolic contents of such story aspects as artifacts (see part 3) and activities helps the teller invent within the constraints of each culture's memories and shared references.

9

Calendar Customs, Holidays, and Festivals

INTRODUCTION

Holidays and festivals of modern times are but remnants and glimpses of the rites and rituals of the ancient mysteries through which humankind became bonded to the earth and discovered its purpose. In literate societies, these shreds of lost practices are tied to the rather dispassionate, disengaged, displaced from experience, nonparticipatory habit of print. Adler (1986) refers to the more cerebral experience of the modern religion as "dead magic." In a very real sense, and because so much modern religious activity is based in print, people spectate rather than enter into the rapture of religious experience. The rites and rituals from which all others descend originated long before the advent of print, long before people could use print as a vehicle for knowing about and studying religious practice. Practice was a communion in which participants were transported and transfigured, in which they gained access to the great mysteries by experiencing them, living in them, being one with them, and knowing an all-consuming rapture and passion (magic). Campbell (1988) claims that people today "underexperience" the mysteries offered them through religious practice, that modern (literate) people no longer know how to become one with the god and become the god.

Stories and storytelling were, in ancient times, one of the means by which people could enter into mystery; hence, many stories served religious purposes. Storytelling was itself associated with religious experience, perhaps because of the power of the story to induce passion, rapture, and those conditions of mind associated with communion. Many stories are holiday stories, their original functions most likely having to do with transporting people into mystical experience. Still other stories contain references to rites and rituals, the manners in which these are conducted, and the natures of the mysteries to which they refer. Ancient (now transcribed and edited) oral religious texts, which often instruct as to the proper way to conduct ceremonies and their symbolic significances, were sung, chanted, and/or danced, more to establish the right frame of mind for entering the mystery than to reflect upon the specific content of the text.

Even today's highly literate individuals, who are steeped in the reflective mentality that is the inevitable outcome of written language technologies, can be brought closer to genuine rapture through stories and other devices of the older oral traditions than through reading religious texts. The story, the psalm, the chant, the hymn, the dance, and the ancient metaphor for the sacrifice can make the most serious student of canon law feel the rise of passion and the imminence of tears. We still hear the rhythms of the earth in what is left to us of those old rites and rituals.

For Sports, for Pagentrie, and Playes,
Thou hast thy Eves, and Holydayes:
On which the young men and maids meet,
To exercise their dancing feet:
Tripping the comely country round,
With Daffadils and Daisies crown'd.
Thy Wakes, thy Quintels, here thou hast,
Thy May-poles too with Garlands grac't:
Thy Morris Dance; thy Whitsun-ale;
Thy Sheering-feast; which never faile.
Thy Harvest home; thy Wassaile Bowle,
That's tost up after Fox i' th' Hole.
Thy Mummeries, thy Twelfe-tide Kings
And Queenes; thy Christmas revellings.
(Robert Herrick, quoted in Briggs 1962.)

SAMAIN — ALL SOULS

Soul! Soul! For a soul-cake!
I pray you, good missus, a soul cake!
An apple, a pear, a plum or a cherry,
Or any good thing to make us all merry.
One for Peter, Two for Paul,
Three for them that made us all.

Soul, soul for an apple or two,
If you've got no apples, pears will do;
If you've got no pears, ha'pennies will do,
If you've got no ha'pennies, then God bless you.
(Opie and Opie 1959.)

Samain (Samhain, Sowain) is the first festival of the Celtic calendar, the new year's celebration, marking the first quarter of the first half of the year.

The souls are about, because the wall between the worlds of the living and the dead is thinnest at this time of year. Cracks open up between the two worlds. The earth is closest to death at this time.

All fires everywhere are extinguished to put out the old year. (*Samain* means "end of summer.")

Sacrificial victims used to be burned in the sacred fire of the new year, from which all new fires were lit.

Families circled the fields sunwise to raise the power of life there. They often carried torches of fir.

Boys, led by hornblowers, went from door to door to beg for provisions for the festivities.

Girls believe that if they observe a proper ritual, such as looking into a mirror at midnight while brushing their hair three times, they will see their future husbands.

The Celts believed that Samhain, a Celtic god, the "Prince of Darkness," brought winter, the season of death, when crops, leaves, and flowers died and everything was cold.

Samhain called together the spirits of the dead on October 31. If a person had been bad during life, he or she would come back in the form of an animal. A really bad person would return as a black cat.

The Celtic people wore costumes made of the skins and heads of animals on the festival day (November 1) to honor the god. The costumes were believed to scare away the evil spirits that Samhain had called from the dead.

The early Romans had a festival on November 1 to honor Pomona, with whom the custom of bobbing for applies is associated. The apple is the sign of the Crone aspect of the Goddess, the Hag of death. To be given an apple is to receive a death wish or a foretelling of one's death. To bob for and catch an apple signifies rebirth. The apple is the repository of the soul; the dead were buried with apples to ensure the safe passage of their souls through the underworld and to rebirth.

The Irish carried a light or lantern carved from a large turnip (a jack o' lantern) on October 31 to keep away evil spirits.

The Irish went from house to house begging for food in the name of Muck Olla, an old Celtic god. They said, "Muck Olla will be good to you if you help us."

In Lithuania, the new year feast was celebrated at Halloween. Domestic animals were sacrificed to Zemiennik, lord of the underworld.

BELTANE—MAY DAY

Round and round the maypole,
Merrily we go,
Tripping, tripping lightly
Singing as we go.

O, the happy pasttime
On the village green,
Dancing in the sunshine—
Hurrah for the queen!

I'm the queen, don't you see,
Just come from the meadow green;
If you wait a little while,
I will dance you the maypole style.

My hair is long, my dress is short,
My shoes are laced with silver,
A red rosette upon my breast
And a guinea gold ring on my finger.

Hop, hop, hop to the butcher's shop,
I dare not stay any longer,
For if I do, my ma will say
You naughty girl to disobey.
(Opie and Opie 1959.)

Beltane (Walpurgisnacht) officially begins at moonrise on May 1. It marks the third quarter and beginning of the second half of the Celtic year.

It is a fertility festival, probably derived from the very ancient custom of turning the flocks out to summer pasture.

May Day was also the marriage rite of the goddess and her king consort. The maypole (the phallus) was planted in the earth, signifying their sacred union.

Witches and fairies are out in great numbers, probably in association with the female fertility cult.

If you get caught by fairies on Beltane Eve, you will be held captive for one year, then released at the next Beltane festival.

The beltane fire is kindled from a spark. People dance sunwise around it, and livestock are driven through it to protect them and to prevent barrenness.

Contact with the fire is synonymous with contact with the sun.

Rowan branches are employed to keep the fire itself from bewitchment.

Originally, Druids kindled the Beltane fires. Today, processions are held which end at the church, where the priest kindles the fire.

King and Queen May symbolize the coming of fertility, and, in Scotland, boys carry pitchfork loads of burning material and spread it across the fields to ensure fertility, all the while exhorting the fire to burn the witches.

The ashes from the fires are good for the crops.

Beltane cakes were given, eaten, and used for divination. Each cake was made of sections, usually four, each dedicated to an animal. A person, upon receiving a Beltane cake, would face the fire, then break off the portions of the cake, one at a time. Each portion would be thrown over a shoulder with a prayer to that animal to spare his livestock or help his crops.

Beltane cakes were rolled downhill to imitate the continuous motion of the sun. If a person's cake broke while rolling, he or she would die within the year. A whole cake, after the ordeal, was a portent of good luck.

Pieces of the Beltane cake were drawn by lot. The person who got the blackened, scorched piece became the Beltane Hag. "She" was thrown into the fire in ritual play, even thrown to the ground and subjected to the mime of being quartered. In some practice, the hag was shunned as if dead for one year. The original hag was female, and was actually given to the flames, usually clothed in greenery.

LAMMAS — FIRST FRUITS

Lammas is the festival which marks the beginning of the fourth quarter of the Celtic pagan year.

Lammas is from the Old English *hlaf*, meaning "loaf," a reference to the breads which were made from the first harvested wheat or winter wheat.

Lammas apples are the first to ripen, and are ready by Lammas.

Lammas was later confused with "lamb-mass," also August 1, the "Feast of St. Peter's chains," when lambs were taken to the church.

Lammas lands were lands, fenced until that day, which then were thrown open to common pasturage.

On Lammas, landlords received the first rents, the first wheat of the harvest.

In the Scottish highlands, people sprinkled the floors of their houses and their cattle with menstrual blood, as it was believed to be a powerful repellant of evil.

THE WINTER SOLSTICE

'The winter solstice festival is the first of the cross-quarter days of the Celtic calendar. The sun is reborn at the winter solstice; it must be called back. The sun is the sun king sacrificed and reborn from the Great Goddess. The Old Saxon term for Christmas Eve, the birth night of the Christ of the Wheel, was *Modranect*, or "Night of the Mother" (Walker 1983, 666). In Egypt, it is the scorpion (Scorpio) who sends the sun god Horus to his death, from whence Isis must revive him.

Fire is used as a sun-charm to engender the return of the sun by sympathetic magic. The Yule log was originally a charm designed to aid the sun in its struggle against expiring, and to show it the way to climb in the heavens.

All of the refuse is carried out, and a new fire is kindled.

Masked festival dancers mimed the victory of the sun over death and exorcised evil spirits.

Sunwise round dances were done to aid in the making of the new fire and to make strength for the waning sun.

Christmas was a very deliberate invention of the church to supersede the old pagan sun birth holiday (Frazier 1922). Many of the old customs of the pagan birthing festival are practiced at Christmas, including the bringing of living evergreen trees indoors.

In the southern hemisphere, the winter solstice is celebrated on June 20.

THE VERNAL EQUINOX

The vernal equinox marks the second cross-quarter day of the Celtic calendar. It has, in large measure, been replaced by Easter, but was itself a resurrection festival.

Some say that the sun "dances" or "shouts" on Easter.

The custom of collecting eggs is retained from old; the egg is a symbol of fertility and new life.

The rabbit is a fertility symbol. The rabbit was the escort of the German goddess Ostara, after whom the festival is named (*ostern*).

The lamb was the preferred sacrificial animal.

It is at this equinox that the sun is resurrected from the darkness, and the days become longer than the nights.

Schmeckostern (Germany and Austria) are beatings that the people administer to each other with newly sprouted branches of willow or cherry to bestow the power of young life. The beatings often take place on Good Friday.

New fires are lit at dawn to celebrate the return of the sun to predominance in the heavens.

The Romans celebrated the resurrection of their "savior god" Attis on March 25. This "Day of Joy" was celebrated like a carnival.

THE SUMMER SOLSTICE— MIDSUMMER DAY

The summer solstice marks the third cross-quarter day of the Celtic calendar.

Summer solstice celebrations in Europe resemble those of Beltane, but acknowledge that the sun now begins its decline in the sky.

The best divining rods are to be cut at this time, and all magical plants have enhanced powers. This is the time to gather herbs to dry for healing and other purposes.

Herbs, especially mistletoe, picked at midsummer are powerful protections against witchcraft, disease and evil.

All magic, good or bad, is especially potent. Witches and demons are abroad.

All natural waters have curative powers on this day. One should bath in a river, lake, or stream to be cured of an affliction.

The sun is at its most powerful, yet begins to relinquish that power.

People rolled burning hoops or wheels down hillsides in imitation of the sun's coming course, and burned effigies of death and bad luck. Ixion, or "Strong Moon Man" of the Lapiths was originally a sacred king sacrificed on the fiery wheel. His name also means "axis" (*axus mundi*). Ixion's death took place at the hub of the world or the world navel. Kris Kringle was also originally a "Christ of the Wheel"; he was born at the winter solstice, the returning sun god (Walker 1983).

Games, mock battles, and dramas played out the battle between summer and winter, good and evil. Tug-of-war is a surviving remnant of those games.

Hearth fires were extinguished, then rekindled from the midsummer fire.

Burning torches were carried through the fields, houses, and barnyards, and amongst the animals, to ward off evil and disease.

People circled houses, fields, and barns with a sunwise rotation.

The summer solstice was also a powerful charm for lovers. If a girl put a bunch of flowers under her pillow, her lover would appear to her. If she set a clean table with bread, cheese, and ale and left the yard gate open, her future husband would come to share the midnight feast.

Ashes from midsummer fires are the best fertilizer and go into the soil.

The midsummer fire is sometimes called the "fire of heaven."

The burning of effigies eventually substituted for the custom of human sacrifice.

St. John's Day (John the Baptist), June 24, is today the common substitute for midsummer, but many of the customs of the earlier festival hold firm.

10

Divination

Eeney, meeney, Chili beanie;
The spirits are about to speak.
—Bullwinkle Moose

INTRODUCTION

Divination is an ancient form of sympathetic magic, generally white or good magic, which allows one to foresee future events or circumstances by making contact with a divine source of knowledge, a supernatural source of knowledge, or by activating the divine harmonies of the universe. Such prognostication is practiced formally and informally by almost all peoples, and usually requires the deliberate or uninvited intervention of some kind of instrumentation. Ceremonial manipulation of traditional tools of divination (casting and reading of bones), the prescriptions associated with the unforeseen accident (splitting a clothespin while hanging wash out to dry), and taboo-like superstitions (bad luck resulting from stepping on cracks in the sidewalk or walking under ladders) are forms of folk knowledge. These notions are not simple, primitive, or "bad" science, but belong, rather, to that other and mystical universe of the folk culture. Divination is a magical folk art which has its own function and its own truth. Like all magical art, it is consensual. People must accept its practices and its results as realities in order to have appropriate expectations for those effects which can be induced through divination.

DIVINATION AS MAGIC

The diviner does not make magic to influence events or to create change, but plays the part of an agent who is specially empowered to act on behalf of the people by using (often sacred) tools or procedures to gain access to the will of the gods. Since divination transcends the ordinary by magical means, the diviner might be called *magician*—one who can contact greater powers. However, the diviner is not a witch or a sorcerer; the act of divination in itself is not witchcraft or sorcery. While witches or sorcerers might be capable of performing specific rites of divination according to custom, they can also use (send or bend) supernatural power in a premeditated fashion. The need to seek divine guidance in a specific matter is the only precondition motivating practices of divination. The result of such activity cannot be designed by any mortal. Sometimes, even this precondition is not necessary; the gods can choose to speak at will and without the aid of an interpreter, through signs and portents. Hence, omens and superstitions are evidences of divine will, and their significances are understood according to custom.

DIVINATION AS A SOCIAL TOOL

Formal rites for discovering divine intent are often performed at times of social crisis and peril, when grave and critical circumstances require a judgment of a higher order, when trouble or violence threatens, or when custom demands that the gods be consulted. The diviner then operates the instruments that allow greater powers to make clear the actions that people must undertake. Omens and portents can serve as initiators, signalling the need for a more deliberate ritual. All cultures have evolved definitive lists of circumstances which require divine intervention: choice of marriage partners, where to build a house, which animal to sacrifice, where to look for food, settling of unresolved conflicts between individuals or families. Divination undertaken in such cases provides prescriptions for mortal activity which can command obedience without complaint. If the decisions made by the gods in such cases were made instead by mere mortals, relationships between individuals, families, and clan groups or tribes (countries) could be severely strained, and the structure of society itself placed in jeopardy. The gods presumably have no conflicts of interest with regard to human affairs (or have different motivations than humans—gods have been known to meddle), and can give impartial decisions which then have the binding force of law. The diviner is a "public conscience" whose role is to remove the "agency and responsibility for a decision" from the individual and "cast it upon the heavens, where it lies beyond cavil and beyond reproach" (Park 1979, 236).

DIVINATION AS FOLK ART

Divination is an ingenious folk invention which helps to provide form and structure for society, and which aids in the governance of human affairs. Divination may not be scientific, but the fact of its not being founded in empirical scientific practice does not make it less true or real. Absence of science implies a different function, and not necessarily hodgepodge, mumbo-jumbo, wrong-headedness, or lack of organization and substance. The purpose of divination is not science, but rather regulation of social intercourse. Science cannot replace social order without becoming a lore in its own right. Thus, the tribal diviner continues to practice in tribal societies whose people watch television, cook with electricity, and hunt on snowmobiles.

Divination in folklore and folk literature is a predictable and reliable form of "procedural intervention" which "has as its regular consequence the elimination of an important source of disorder in social relationships" (Park 1979, 234). In many folk stories, divination acts as a check-and-balance system which protects common folk and regulates the whims and actions of the rich and powerful. It works as "a terrible safeguard of due procedure against the depredations of expedience" (Park 1979, 243). The lore and practices of divination are, therefore, central to the origin of the myth of inviting disaster. Many folk stories and legends share the motif of the gods' approval or disapproval of the enterprises of persons and nations and of the consequences which await those of any station, king or commoner, who disobey commandments writ in heaven. Before attempting something that could bring great benefit or great suffering, we must ask the gods for instruction. If the gods tell us to go ahead with a venture, we can do so with the positive psychology of a people who know that their god is with them. If, on the other hand, the gods tell us to abandon the quest, we proceed at the peril of our lives, because we act without the protection of divine blessing. Our defiance risks the swift and terrible punishment of angry gods. Divination is the mechanism for requesting and obtaining permissions; the diviner is an artist-medium.

DIVINATION AS RANDOMIZING PROCEDURE

Overall, divination is a game of chance in which the diviners manipulate objects, repeat ritual language or movements, or allow themselves to be possessed by supernatural powers. In each case, divination procedures are institutionalized within the folk practices of the culture, and the outcomes are out of the reach of human control. The gods work through a randomizing device to tell the people which course of action is to be taken in a given case. The diviner, like the spinner of a wheel of fate, is not culpable in the making of decisions and cannot play favorites. Divination, unless the diviner is acting dishonestly, is inherently resistant to power plays, political machinations, and deal cutting (Park 1979).

Divination works because people agree to its legitimacy. Like judge and jury, it is a practical device for obtaining consensus and approval for a given course of action. Its built-in randomizing operations, paradoxically, work to stabilize and derandomize a people's behavior and to make individuals' actions more regular and predictable (Park 1979). Divination controls and channels public opinion about the things that other people do. It is this contradiction of modern logic which makes it logical and gives it real social utility.

As with other forms of cultural activity, divination is magic or evil if it is the work of the other guy, the opposing culture, or the enemy religion. It looks quite rational, legitimate, and natural, and probably rather unmagical, if it is a part of one's own heritage. While some ancient writers credit Prometheus with the invention of divination, and others attribute its invention to the Phrygians, the Etrurians, Zoroaster, Ahriman, darkness, evil, or the devil, divination is more surely a folk invention which served, and still does serve, necessary social functions. It translates into the folk literature in the form of games, chants, rhymes, movements, and stories, and serves as the prototype for making random choices by a population.

FORMS OF DIVINATION

Mechanical

Mechanical divination involves the use of physical devices which, when properly manipulated, create a chance pattern that must then be interpreted. The diviner is the person charged with both manipulation and interpretation; therefore, the diviner is a special and magical person. Throwing dice, spinning a wheel or a bottle, casting sticks or bones, tossing a coin, and reading tea leaves are examples of mechanical divination.

Ritual

Ritual divination involves the use of prescribed ritual or formulaic language or actions to determine an outcome. Many children's choosing routines display characteristics of ritual divination. When no one wants to take the blame for choosing or not choosing a particular individual or thing, ritual randomizing procedures are used (e.g., eenie-meenie-minie-mo, numbering for teams). Hands on the handle of a baseball bat determine which team bats first. The hand game of "Rock / Scissors / Paper" employs two randomizing operations to eliminate people or objects: the ritual of making hand signals that match by chance and the ritual of turn taking. "Open the Gates" is a children's singing and dancing game which provides for the random selection of team members. It uses the device of the bridge (two players with hands joined) which closes upon the person who, by chance, is inside the bridge when a certain word is sung. Even "Musical Chairs" is a formulaic means for choosing and eliminating. Ritual divination is a vigorous part of the living oral literature and social custom of child culture, and performs for children the same functions that similar practices perform for adults.

Emotive/Possessive

Emotive or possessive divination requires that the body of the diviner be used by the gods to deliver a message to the people. In the case of emotive divination, the diviner has the power to transcend to another level of awareness or state of consciousness through emotive processes, thereby allowing him or her to "see" or to "know" information that would otherwise be inaccessible. With possessive divination, the gods enter the diviner's body and become incarnate (uncontrolled possession), or the gods tell the diviner what to do or say (controlled possession). The Dinka people (Africa) believe that their diviner is a medium who divines by uncontrolled possession, and who therefore has the supernatural ability to become a god. The Greeks consulted the oracle at Delphi, a virgin who was entranced as a result of breathing the fumes which escaped from a crack in the earth. The Delphic oracle was a case of a chemically induced altered state of consciousness, and only one oracular source of the many which inhabited the ancient world. One presumes that some contemporary fortune tellers and psychics, legitimate and otherwise, fall into this class of diviner.

TYPES OF DIVINATION

Aeromancy — divination by air. Properly schooled diviners were able to "read" weather conditions, winds, winds through tree branches or leaves, movements of strips of cloth tied to sticks, cloud patterns and movements, the directions of rain or snowfall, and other physical phenomena associated with weather. This type of aeromancy was an early form of weather forecasting. Aeromancers were sometimes schooled in the reading of water surfaces, especially those disturbed by wind. Ceremonial aeromancy often involved the interpretations of water surfaces in specially consecrated basins which were uncovered under specified conditions. The Greek oracle of Zeus, the Dodona, was a sacred grove of trees tended by both priests and priestesses (*selli* or *helli*) who knew how to read the breezes moving through the grove and the resulting rustlings of the leaves. Brass ornaments were hung in the tree branches to accentuate these words of the gods. This oracle, the most ancient of all Greek oracles, also provided information from a spring which "spoke" as it issued forth from the roots of a sacred oak. (Many peoples also have traditions of belief in bad air, usually damp or cold night air — malaria — which can bring diseases or steal souls. One should not expose oneself to bad air.)

Alectryomancy—divination using cocks and hens. Draw a circle on the ground. Write the letters of the alphabet in succession around its circumference. Place a grain of corn on each letter. Release a rooster or hen at the center of the circle. Record the succession of letters chosen according to the order in which the bird eats the grains of corn. These letters form patterns, sets, or puzzles (anagrams) that can be interpreted to obtain a reading of the future or an answer to a question. If each letter represents a "point" on the circle, then lines can be drawn from point to point to make a figure, which also would require "reading." (Note: *Corn*, to the ancients and in Europe, did not mean maize, but wheat, oats, or rye.)

To forecast recovery from illness, draw a cross on the ground. Kill a cock, then place the bird at the center of the cross. If the cock dies with its head inclined to the east, the sick individual will recover (Mexico).

Mark a group of cocks with letters or numbers. Draw slips of paper marked with the same numbers, or cast sticks or bones. The bird whose number matches the number drawn or cast will provide the answer. A white cock is lucky, a black one unlucky. Black cocks were often used as sacrifices in devil worship.

Aleuromancy—divination using flour. Write messages on slips of paper. Enclose these in balls of flour paste, one message per ball. Mix up and distribute the balls of flour. The flour balls will be selected at random. The modern-day Chinese fortune cookies are one version of this tradition.

If a person is suspected of a crime, guilt can be determined by giving the individual an ounce of barley bread and cheese. If he or she chokes, the verdict is guilty.

Alomancy—divination using salt. Throw salt into the flames of a fire. The message will be given in the pattern and height of the flames. (Alomancy may be connected to the practice of throwing salt over the left shoulder when a salt shaker is overturned in order to prevent trouble.)

Alphitomancy—divination using barley meal. See *Aleuromancy*.

Amniomancy—divination using afterbirths. The pattern and general condition of an afterbirth is used to predict the future of the newborn. In particular, the caul (membrane sometimes enveloping the head of a child at birth) will tell of the future overall health of the baby.

Anthropomancy—divination using human entrails. The best forecasts could be gotten from reading the entrails of young children or virgins, because these victims were of known purity. Prisoners of war were also sacrificed to determine the outcomes of upcoming battles or the wisdom of certain battle strategies.

Arithmancy—divination using numbers. *Gematria*, the letter/number symbolism of Jewish scholasticism, is the cabalistic, cryptographic method of interpreting Hebrew scripture by substituting numerical values for alphabetic letters in a selected verse. Jewish, and later Christian, scholars were convinced that the Old Testament contained secrets hidden in the text by God. (God spoke to Moses, "These words thou shalt declare and these thou shalt hide" 2 Exodus 14: 5-6 [Seligmann 1948, 243].) These secrets could only be revealed through study and manipulation of scripture using numbers. The text was not to be understood literally; it was nothing more than "a mantle in which are clothed sublime revelations. Woe to him who takes the mantle for the law" (Seligman 1948, 343). Scripture was a riddle and a collection of riddles that had to be deciphered.

One simple operation allowed two words whose sums were identical to be interchanged and the text reread. Or, two words with identical sums could be "melted together" to make anagrams which required further interpretation. The number value of a word might, by itself, show new meaning. "The numerical value of Jehova (Yehova) is 10,5,6,5 or 26" (Seligmann 1948, 347). These numbers were interpreted mystically. The cabalists summed the name of Abraham's majordomus, Eliezer (total of 318), to determine that Abraham rescued Lot (Gen. 14: 14) with the help of only one man, rather than the 318 cited in scripture (Seligmann 1948). Other methods allowed the first and last letters of each word in a passage to be arranged as anagrams and for a single word to be considered as an acronym. *Bereshit* ("at the beginning"), the first word in Genesis, becomes an acronym for "He created the firmament, the earth, the heavens, the sea and the abyss" (Seligmann 1948, 348). Substitutions, transpositions, and permutations of letters permitted the construction of anagrams with hidden meanings. Cabalists thus discovered that the number of heavenly hosts is 301,655,172, and that the most powerful of God's names must contain 72 letters (Seligmann 1948). Formulae for determining the numerical values of words became quite complex, and finding hidden messages involved the operation of very subtle procedures. God's intentions for creation could be foretold using these methods.

Though cabalistic practice peaked in the fourteenth and fifteenth centuries, a cosmogony based upon letters appears in Israel in the second century before Christ. Cabalists, or *mekkubalim*, were consulted during World War II in order to determine whether Hitler's armies in Greece would attack Syria. The mekkubalim studied the word "syria," which, in Hebrew is an anagram for "russia," transposed the letters into "russia," then declared that Syria was in no danger: the Germans would invade Russia. And so they did (Seligmann 1948).

Gematria is founded in the Pythagorean belief in the virtues, harmonies, and powers of certain numbers—"number is all"—and in the more ancient belief in the inherent magical qualities of words—"name is all" and "the word"—hence of the equally potent qualities of letters. ("Letter" in Greek is *gramma*. The English derivative *gramarye* means "magic.") The cabalist believed that the universe was constructed of letters and numbers, an idea that had its roots in the Greek fascination with the proportions of the universe. The neo-Pythagorean belief that numbers and letters were "divine beings endowed with supernatural powers" helped to convince cabalists that scripture was magical and mysterious (Seligmann 1948, 344).

Cabalists used numbers, letters, and scripture to practice magic, to divine, and to prognosticate. Contemporary number divination games, represented in the pseudoscience of numerology, are related to early sacred practices and retain the aura of magic. (See Pseudosciences, p. 160.)

The following example of a numerology table illustrates a number-for-letter substitution method. Number-letter relationships are based upon the Hebrew alphabet, with numbers assigned according to the common ordering of Hebrew letters (Shadowitz and Walsh 1976, 130).

1	2	3	4	5	6	7	8
A	B	C	D		U	O	F
I	K	G	M	H	V	Z	P
Q	R	L	T	N	W		
J		S					
Y							

Letters in chosen words (names) or text are assigned numbers using the table. Numerical values of words are determined by adding the letter values. The meanings of word values are, in turn, discovered according to predetermined formulae. The *Book Yetzirah* sets out the basic principles of cabalistic practice.

Astragalomancy—divination using bones. Small bones, usually vertebrae or finger bones, were lettered, numbered, or otherwise marked, then mixed together to produce a chance effect. If the bones were cast upon the ground, the resulting pattern or patterns required interpretation. If the bones were placed in a bowl, then drawn at random, the letters or numbers were recorded and the resulting puzzle or anagram solved. Bone cylinders, marked cubes, and other similar devices used for gambling may have developed from the practices of astragalomancy.

The Wu priests of China are also readers of ceremonial oracle bones.

Astrology—divination using the situation, appearance, and movements of the stars and planets. (See Pseudosciences, p. 160 and Astrology, p. 181.)

Axinomancy—divination using an axe. A suspended axe will turn or rotate more quickly when the correct name or answer is spoken.

An axe which has been upended on a stake will fall at the mention of the correct name or answer.

Belomancy—divination using marked arrows. Write solutions or answers on slips of paper; fix these, one each, to the shafts of arrows. Shoot all of the arrows in the same general direction. Send an individual to look for the arrows with instructions to return with the first arrow located. The message fixed to that arrow is the answer.

Put many inscriptions on a single arrow. Shoot the arrow, then measure the distance it travels. Distance will determine which of the many inscriptions is correct.

Put a single letter of the alphabet on each of many arrows. Shoot the arrows, then fetch them. Record the order in which the letters are retrieved. This order will provide a pattern, set, puzzle, or anagram which, when properly interpreted, will give the answer.

Mark one arrow, "God wills it me." Mark a second arrow, "God forbids it me." Leave a third arrow unmarked. Shoot all three arrows, then retrieve one of the three. Its marking will give the answer. A time- and energy-saving alternative allows the three arrows to be placed in a quiver. The questioner then draws one arrow at random. If the arrow selected is the unmarked shaft, the procedure must be repeated.

Notch, band, or otherwise mark a set of arrows. Cast the arrows upon the ground. Read the patterns made from the casting. (This practice is believed to be the forerunner of divining sticks, divining cards, and playing cards.)

Shoot a poisoned arrow into an individual or into an animal. If the individual dies, he or she is guilty as charged. If the animal dies, the answer is no.

Bibliomancy—divination using books. Usually the Bible, or another sacred text or verse is used as an oracle. The use of sacred text for divination was based upon the assumption that God could speak to specific problems through the sacred Word. The fact of God acting as a force through the agency of the text apparently made the use of a chance mechanism acceptable. (*The Aeneid* was a popular oracular source in the Middle Ages.)

Open the Bible (or other text) with a golden needle. Note the first line or verse upon which the eye rests. This text, properly interpreted, will give the answer.

Weigh an accused criminal against a Great Bible. A guilty individual will outweigh the book.

Balance a Bible or book on its spine. Allow it to fall open to a page at random. The first passage the eye encounters will be a sign from God. (Opening the Bible to a blank page was a signal of impending disaster in the Middle Ages.)

Allow a book of ceremonies or psalms to fall open under the light of a full moon. Whichever ceremony appears tells the future: marriage means marriage, funeral means death (Sweden).

Tie a large key into a Bible. Suspend the keystring and key over the extended forefingers of two people. Chant the letters of the alphabet or recite names. The key will turn or sway when the correct names or letters are spoken.

The *Tonalamatl* is the "day count" book of the Aztec diviner, who consults the page corresponding to the week of an event to determine signs and omens. The *tonalpohualli* (diviner) can thus advise parents of a newborn as to the auspices connected to the child's birthdate. The book is made from the bark of the wild fig tree and is hand-illuminated.

Botanomancy — divination using leaves or other parts of plants. The Burmese diviner heats thin, green bamboo stems until the wood splits to reveal small hairy fibers. He then "reads" the manner in which the stick is split and in which the fibers protrude from the stick.

"Midsummer men" is an old pagan European practice still in use in some areas. On Midsummer's eve, a man or woman cuts two slips of orpine, a common sedum, then plants these side by side in a pot. One of the slips is designated the representative of the man or woman, the other of his or her lover. If one of the slips withers and dies, trouble, perhaps death, awaits the individual so represented. If both slips remain healthy, root, and grow, both individuals will live in good health. If the two slips also incline toward one another as they grow, marriage is in the future.

The *babawelo*, a cult of Yoruba diviners, manipulate and read combinations and patterns of palm kernels. Their interpretations are given in the form of elaborate recitations of extended verse which, in turn, introduce stories appropriate to the message to be understood. The story is then told and interpreted in light of the verse. The babawelo require years of intensive training. They must commit to memory a voluminous oral literature in verse and story form, and must learn to associate various elements of this literature with the habits of the palm kernels.

Write names or questions and answers on leaves. Expose all to the wind. The leaves which do not blow away will give the needed information.

Reading of tea leaves or coffee grounds might also qualify as botanomancy, and is a modern-day version of the employment of a divining cup. Pour coffee or tea grounds into a (wet) white cup, shaking the cup well to spread the grounds across the cup's inner surface. Overturn the cup to dump out loose material. Study the remaining grounds for shapes and figures.

Capnomancy — divination by examining the movement and density of smoke. Throw seeds of a plant (jasmine or poppy) into a fire. Watch the thickness and movement of the rising smoke. Thin smoke which moves to the right and which spreads over the area (altar) is a good sign.

For other burnings, thin, light smoke ascending straight up portends good fortune.

Capnomancers were also known to inhale smoke to induce trance states from which they were able to make prophesies.

Cartomancy — divination using cards (fortune-telling with Tarot or regular playing cards). The Tarot is a five-suit deck of cards which is the predecessor of the modern card deck. Only the Joker remains from the fifth suit, the Major Arcana (Great Secrets), a picture suit often used to "read" fortunes. The other four suits of the Tarot contained an additional court card, the knight, as well. The Tarot itself has its roots in ancient "books" of picture cards used in the Orient to teach mystical doctrine to those who could not read, thus extending knowledge of the mysteries to all people. The missing cards are pagan in origin and tradition, bearing pictures of symbols of the great pagan mysteries of life and death. Their name (*Tarot*) is probably derived from the ancient name of the goddess—Tara/Terra/Earth/Terra Mater (Walker 1983). One old Tarot game, the Game of Rebirth, is still enjoyed in the Far East; the cards themselves, in divination practice, are related to the rods of the I Ching. The twenty-one cards of the Tarot represented the three trimesters of life: birth "to coming of age at 21; from 21 to middle age at 42; and from 42 to the 'grand climacteric' at 63" (Walker 1983, 982). These trimesters represented birth, life, and death; beginning, middle, and end; and maid, mother, and crone. The pagan system of counting age has been incorporated into common law (e.g., age twenty-one as attainment of majority), and appears in riddles related to the stages in man's life. For purposes of divination, the cards are laid out in circles, representing the wheel of life; in figure eights signifying the sacred union of goddess and god consort; and in the triangle, standing for the feminine principle and fate. Because the goddess in her threefold aspect is Fate, the cards and her mysteries (or law) could be used to reveal her divine will. Each card has a secret sacred meaning, as do specific card pairs and their combined numbers. For instance, the twelfth card is the Hanged Man, recalling "the famous Twelfth Rune sacred to Odin the Hanged God, the rune by which hanged victims could be made to speak, and reveal the mysteries of the death world" (Walker 1983, 984). Because the cards of the Major Arcana clearly had a sacred significance of a non-Christian nature, the church "regarded the Tarot as a Bible of heresy comprehensible to the illiterate" (Walker 1983, 985). Many packs of Tarot cards were confiscated and burned during the Middle Ages, and the church mounted a campaign against the sacred symbolic character of the cards such that their spiritual potency was eliminated. Once people had forgotten the meanings of the pictures and the numbers, the cards were harmless, though playing cards was, and still is, associated with the devil. "'Ludicrous,' in the new interpretation of the old Pagan 'ludi' (sacred games)" (Walker 1983, 985), further debased the sacred nature of such card play.

Catoptromancy—divination using a mirror. If one is very ill and in danger of death, suspend a mirror from a thread into a fountain (a light spray of water). Look into the mirror. If the face in the mirror is misshapen and ghastly, death is near. If the face appears fresh and healthy, recovery awaits. Ancient Greeks used this method at the fountains at shrines of their gods.

If the mirror is used without water, staring into it can produce visions of things to come. The practice is very much like crystal gazing, in which the gazer experiences self-hypnosis, or at the very least a light-headed, disoriented state.

Cephalomancy—divination using heads. Broil the head of an ass on hot coals. The jaws will move to give the name of a guilty person.

Ceromancy—divination using wax. Drop melted wax into cold water. "Read" the figures assumed by the drops of wax.

Chilomancy—divination with keys.

Chiromancy—divination by examination of the hands.

Cledonismancy—divination using words. Cledonism appears to have operated by taboo. Certain words could not be said at certain times without inviting specific kinds of trouble. The Pythagoreans believed that it was unlucky to say the word "incendium" at a meal. The Pythagoreans also warned against naming certain things directly, recommending euphemism instead. "Prison," they suggested, should be called "domicilium," and care should be taken to avoid use of words unpleasing to the gods. Calling the Furies by the name "erinnyes," for instance, would make them furious (Daniels and Stevans 1971).

Interpret the meanings of the first words uttered following the salutation when meeting a friend.

Cleromancy — divination by the casting of lots. *Sordition*, or divination by casting of lots, is an ancient practice which is recorded in scripture. Cleromancy employed dice, knuckle bones, marked stones, and a variety of spinning devices such as bottles and coconuts. Sordition was practiced in ancient Greece as a means of electing representatives to government. Apparently, nomination and election by lot was regarded as a more reliable method of ensuring good government, since the gods were able to choose through such devices, and since candidates were not above illegally influencing popular balloting.

Bones used for cleromancy were "read" from the points and patterns of points which were turned up. Dice and marked stones may have been variations on the use of bone points.

Coscinomancy — divination using a sieve. To obtain the name of a guilty party, hold a sieve between the tips of the forefingers. Chant the names of suspected individuals. The sieve will turn, tremble, or shake when the name of the guilty person is spoken. The sieve can also be suspended by a thread or fixed to the points of a pair of scissors, provided that it has room enough to turn.

Coscinomancy was widely practiced in the ancient world and is still in use in some parts of Great Britain. Coscinomancers claim the ability to discover secrets as well as criminals.

Crystalomancy — divination using crystals; "seeing" the future in the stone while in an altered state of consciousness. A pure maiden or youth will be able to see figures or answers in a crystal, if they hold the stone together while appropriate chants, verse, or prayers are recited.

The fortune teller of common experience often uses a crystal ball.

Dactylomancy — divination using finger rings. Suspend a finger ring on a string over a round table. Divide the surface of the table into twenty-six equal pie-shaped sections, marking these with lines. At the center of each wedge, along the outside rim of the tabletop, print one letter of the alphabet. Record the movements and vibrations of the ring as it swings over various wedges on the tabletop, taking down the letters of the alphabet thus specified and in order. Interpret the resulting puzzle or anagram. For best results, consecrate the ring using mysterious incantations and procedures. Wear white linen clothing, head to foot, or a white linen robe. Shave the entire head. Hold a handful of vervain, and say the proper prayers.

Demonomancy — divination using evil spirits.

Eychnomancy — divination using lamps.

Gastromancy — divination by examining sounds made by the stomach or in the abdominal cavity. Originally, gastromancy may have involved the straightforward interpretation of abdominal noises. It evolved, however, into a practice which used ventriloquism to project voices that were then said to originate in the abdomen.

Gastromancy is also identified with a magic art in which the diviner makes figures appear inside of glasses or other clear, hollow containers. These figures, like those which appear in crystal balls, can tell of future events.

Geomancy — divination by earth. Geomancy was common in the ancient world and is still in practice in China and the Arab nations today.

Arab diviners read points found at random in the sand, read a pattern appearing in such points, interpret pebbles, patterns in pebbles, and patterns of pebbles and grains of sand. These figures eventually were read from points or dots made at random on the surface of a piece of paper.

The Magi of Persia originated the practice of divining from little clefts or chinks made in the earth.

The Greeks cast handfuls of little pebbles, then interpreted the patterns thus created.

In China, geomancy (Feng Shui) replaced turtle-shell oracles as the method for determining auspicious locations for houses, tombs, cities, and other constructions. One Feng Shui school deduces the laws of consonance and dissonance of prospective sites by a method called *pakua*. Pakua uses the five great stars and eight trigrams to locate building projects. The second Feng Shui school studies the features and relationships of existing structures and of landscape to channel the yang influence properly for a new construction.

Gyromancy — divination by rounds and circles. Draw a circle on a board or tabletop. Print the letters of the alphabet around the outside of the circle. Whirl a nicked or marked coin inside the circle of letters, recording the sequence of letters pointed out by the nick or mark on the coin with each fall. Interpret the puzzle or anagram thus constructed.

Horuspication — divination using twisted entrails. Horuspication is related to other forms of divination which use animal sacrifices.

Hydromancy — divination by water. The Lukuman of Surinam in west Africa divine by looking at the surface of a container of water (or a mirror).

Interpret the images which appear in the waters of a fountain.

Fill round bowls with clear water. Set these on the floor in the center of a circle of lighted torches. Employ a pure boy or a pregnant woman to watch for changes in the reflections on the surface of the water. Then invoke a demon to come to answer a given question. The demon will come, then return through the reflections in the water; his passing will change the reflections and give the answer. The bowls used were often referred to as "divining cups" in the Old Testament (ancient Egypt).

Ichthyomancy — divination by fishes.

Idolomancy — divination by consulting idols. The Yukaghir people of the northern Pacific divine through the use of a *Xoil*, a figure of a deceased shaman made and kept by the shaman's sons. The figure, topped by the shaman's skull, is fed and worshipped. Consultation follows a lifting ritual in which the Xoil is laid upon the ground. The question is posed; then the people try to lift the figure. If the people cannot pick the idol up at all, because it is too heavy, the answer is no. If the idol lifts easily three times in succession, the answer is yes, and an undertaking will succeed. If the figure can be lifted once or twice, but not three times, or, if it is lifted three times, but only with extreme difficulty, the success of a specified undertaking is in grave doubt.

Keraunoscopia — divination using thunder.

Libanomancy — divination by the pouring out of liquids.

Licanomancy — divination using a basin of water.

Lithomancy — divination using stones. The *seide* is the sacred luck stone of the Laplander. It is a "found" piece, bearing a resemblance to an animal or a human being, which has special uses in divining and which brings good fortune to the fisherman.

The *anapel* or "Little Grandmother" of the Koryak is a divining stone which can discover the identity of a deceased relative reincarnated into the body of a newborn. Anapel hangs from a suspended stick while names of all the deceased are ritually chanted. The swinging of the stone quickens when the name of the proper soul is recited.

Molybdomancy — divination using lead. Interpret motions and figures in molten lead.

Pour molten lead on the ground. Note its movement and interpret the shapes it assumes when cold.

Myomancy — divination using mice.

Necromancy — divination by communication with the dead. The Zulu diviner, the *Inyana*, makes contact with the *Itongo*, the ancestral spirits, from whom he learns needed information. He transmits messages in the form of incantations of magical verse organized in couplets.

In Surinam, on Africa's west coast, the *Okomfo*, or priest, becomes possessed by the spirit of a deceased diviner. The diviner speaks directly through the medium of the Okomfo.

Ancient Hebrew necromancers employed objects, often mummies or mummified parts of human bodies, which became residences of familiar spirits (*oboth*). The *ob* ("spirit") was either the spirit of the object itself, or the ghost of an ancestor which came into the object when called. Perhaps using ventriloquism, the necromancer was able to call a voice from the object. Some practitioners of the art drew diagrams on the ground, performed at sacred places or at oracles, or conducted ceremonies which allowed the spirit to speak.

In medieval Europe, the skull often replaced other body parts as the object of choice for the practice of necromancy. In the Middle Ages, necromancy was evil, a black magic consisting of any form of communication with the dead or magic performed with or on the dead. Necromancers were sometimes black witches, who robbed graves to obtain the body parts necessary to their craft. They shared a popular belief in the reanimation of corpses and the ability of the dead to locate lost items, find hidden treasure, tell secrets, reveal the future, or prevent disaster. Because the dead were thought to know all, necromancers applied the charms required to persuade the dead to give forbidden information. Since the dead came to command reluctantly, they were dangerous and constituted a threat to the person of the necromancer. The necromancer had to work powerful magic to keep from harm.

One "black book" (*Red Dragon*) sets out a formula for summoning the dead, then warns the practitioner: "Do not forget the slightest detail of the ceremony as it is prescribed. Otherwise you would risk falling into the snares of hell" (Seligmann 1948, 305).

Oneiromancy — divination by the study of dreams. Many diviners heard and interpreted dreams. Many of the ancient prophets interpreted and reported the significances of their own dreams. Scripture is filled with dream references, many of which are formulaic: drowning, flying, the seven fat and seven lean cattle. "Dream books" became popular in the late 1600s. These were generally simple listings of dream circumstances with cryptic interpretations given for each. Yet, beneath the use of dream reading as fashionable play, there lurks the suspicion that dreams are the tangled revanances of the wandering soul which can leave the body and commune with spirits during sleep. Daniels and Stevans list dream contents which signify prosperity, riches, good fortune in business, money, inheritance; good fortune, good luck; success; pleasure, joy, happiness; good health; satisfaction and fulfillment of desires; honors; comfort; discoveries, journeys; visits from or return of friends and family; friends and friendship; good luck and success in love; good luck and success in marriage; children; sickness; death; troubles; quarrels; sorrow; suffering; failure; misfortune and/or ruin; poverty; distress; loss; disappointment; worry; dishonor; slander and enemies; triumph over enemies; danger; scandal and deception; bad luck; loss of money or financial trouble; want; separation; domestic grief; working hard (for others); change in life; lawsuits; anxiety; anger. The additional categories which follow (adapted from Daniels and Stevans 1971) are examples of dream content associated with prediction of the future:

- *Dreams signifying overcoming of difficulties*

    climbing out of a pit

    driving away rats

    killing rats

    walking fast

- *Dreams signifying surprise*

    seeing oneself as young again (agreeable surprise)

    Zodiac (will win a lottery)

    giving birthday presents

    butcher

    large fire (will soon attend a festivity)

    traveler in a carriage (unexpected good fortune)

- *Dreams signifying bad omens*

    ghosts and spirits

    playing any game

    going hunting

    being in a hunting party

    killing a person

    any kind of monster

    moon (Native American)

    ocean (especially swimming in it or walking on it)

    owl

    oysters

    finding a treasure

    window

    women

- *Dreams signifying good omens*
  fire (Japan)
  moon (especially if bright and clear)
  position
  seeing a dream in a great light
  one's own wedding

- *Dreams signifying peace or hope*
  anchor (hope)
  trees (realization of hope)
  valley (peace)
  flight (peace)
  olives (peace)

- *Dreams which signify news*
  angel (good news)
  seeing a burial
  butcher
  dead man or burial (news from afar—Belgium)
  unable to use one's knee (bad news)
  letter (good news)
  letter carrier (important news)
  music (good news from an absent friend)
  seeing white paper (good news)
  eating pies or pastries (good news)
  seeing others running (bad news)
  bright, clear stars (good news)
  stove (good news)
  sunrise (good news)
  sunset (bad news)
  losing a tooth (bad news)
  tombs (good news)
  writing (pleasant news)
  cherries (good news)
  being accused by a woman
  pregnant woman (good news)
  quarrel (bad news)

Onomancy—divination using names. The letters of one's name can be used to foretell good or evil fortune. The practice is related to cabalism, in that onomancers believed in the divine supernatural powers inherent in letters of the alphabet. Names were studied and interpreted according to fixed formulae. For instance, a name with an even number of vowels signalled imperfection in the left side of a person. An odd number of vowels revealed imperfection in the right side. The happiest and most successful people were those whose names summed to the largest numbers (see Numerology, p. 160). People with large number names are "victorious" in their dealings with people with smaller number names.

Roman gentlemen toasted their mistresses the same number of times as the number of letters in the women's names.

Theodotus, king of the Goths, employed an onomancer to determine the outcome of his war with Rome. The onomancer named a number of pigs, some of them with Roman names, some of them with Gothic names. He then shut the pigs into separate little sties, with their names properly recorded. On the given day, he opened the sties to find that the pigs with the Gothic names had died. From this sign, the diviner predicted the defeat of the Goths (Daniels and Stevans 1971).

Onychomancy—divination using fingernails. Cover the fingernails of a pure boy with oil and soot. Read the images revealed when the fingernails are then turned to the sun.

Assign meaning to the spots and ridges on fingernails.

Ooscopy—divination using eggs. In Mexico, the diviner (shaman) rolls or rubs an egg over the body of a sick person, then breaks the egg to determine the nature of the illness and of the cure.

On Mayday, Midsummer's Day morning, Halloween Eve, Christmas Eve, or New Year's Eve, break open a newly laid egg. Carefully separate white from yolk, then drop the white into a glass which is filled half way with water. Allow the mixture to sit undisturbed and uncovered in a dry place. After twenty-four hours, figures will have formed. These can be studied and meaning ascribed to them using the same questions as those given for reading tea leaves.

Ornithomancy—divination by birds. By strict definition, *augury* is the practice of divination by examination of auspices present in birds. (*Avis*—bird—and *specia*—view: the viewing of birds.) In Rome, a powerful class of augurers arose. They were educated shamans who wielded great political influence and were not above abuse of office. Though, by definition, the augurers worked with bird signs and omens, they eventually extended their practice to other forms of divination, especially to weather signs. Some augurers were kept as "watchers" who looked carefully at all aspects of the natural world for signs from the gods.

The augurer read signs implicit in the direction, timing, speed, and height of bird flight, in bird song, and also in movement of the animals under specific ceremonial conditions. Omens could be found in what a bird did when released into flight or startled from a roost. A released bird which took flight to the right signalled bad luck. Flight to the left meant good fortune. Favorite subjects were crows, ravens, hawks, eagles, and owls. The cuckoo is a folk oracle in European countries.

Orphiomancy—divination using serpents. The Delphic oracle, the most famous in ancient Greece, was originally a Great Mother shrine honoring the earth mother goddess. It was guarded by a mythical dragon and populated by a class of priests who divined using snakes. When Apollo slew the dragon and claimed the oracle as his own, orphiomancy was replaced by the intoxicated mutterings of the woman who sat on the tripod. However, the history of the oracle was remembered in her name—Pythia or Pythoness.

Palmistry—divination by study of the lines on the palm of the hand. (See Palmistry, p. 174.)

Palpitim—divination using involuntary muscle movement, trembling, and tremors. In Guatemala, the Chorti diviner rubs saliva from chewed tobacco over the calf of his right leg, then asks questions of the spirit living there. If the muscle twitches, the spirit has answered yes.

Both the Southern Athabaskan and the Jicarilla Apache peoples understand involuntary muscle movements to signal good luck or warn of danger.

The Navaho shaman interprets hand tremblings.

Pedomancy—divination using the feet.

Pharmancy—divination using medicated drugs. Pharmancy was an art (often black magic) that was practiced for many purposes. When it was practiced to learn information, ordeal by poison was a common procedure.

The calabar bean of Africa is used to determine criminal guilt and to settle disputes. The bean, which is highly poisonous, is ingested by the accused, either whole or mixed with water. The innocent person will vomit and survive, or will simply endure the pain caused by the bean. A guilty individual will succumb, giving both judgment and punishment. In a dispute between two individuals, each litigant eats half of a single bean. The decision is rendered in favor of the one who survives or, should both survive, in favor of the one who suffers least.

Psychomancy—divination using souls, minds, and wills. In Surinam in West Africa, the *Lukuman* divines by asking questions of souls of the living. He places a bowl or a cup containing rainwater and an egg either on the subject's head or in his right hand. He then calls the subject's soul into his own body, and, when the soul comes over, questions it. The water in the bowl or cup will spill if the answer to a question is yes. If the water remains still, the answer is no. The Lukuman can also divine through possession. The spirit can speak directly or can answer through manipulation of a fan held by the diviner. If the answer is yes, the fan will unfold.

The Druid priests ate the acorns of the sacred oaks to prepare themselves for prophecy, presumably done in a state of altered consciousness.

Psychomancy is likened to necromancy. However, the psychomancer usually calls the spirits of the living, and, when calling the dead, does not ordinarily use human remains as tools.

Pyromancy—divination using fire. Both Greek and Roman diviners sacrificed human victims for purposes of fortune telling. The manner in which the victim burned, the characteristics of the smoke, and the shape of the construction—wood, victim, stake—as the burning progressed all contributed signs from which the pyromancer was able to determine an answer. A silent, vigorous, smoke-free burning in which the victim was quickly consumed, and a construction which retained a pyramidal shape throughout were good omens.

Pitch, when thrown into flames, should catch fire immediately. This means good fortune.

The shapes of the flames, along with their height, movement, and color, also contained signals for those trained to see them.

The pyromancer could also interpret the crackling sounds made by the burning of laurel leaves.

Rhabdomancy — divination using a staff or rod. See belomancy practices; apply to spears or rods.

Many references to rhabdomancy exist in Old Testament scripture. The people consulted their rods or staffs to gain information by supernatural means. Making arrows bright, or mixing arrows, are references to marking and shuffling arrows for purposes of divination.

Scapulamancy — divining using shoulder bones. In Asia and Central Africa, tribes read the cracks which appear in the dried shoulder bones of sheep.

Sciomancy — divination using shadows. Sciomancy refers to both the use of shadows cast on the ground and the "shadows" or spirits of the dead. In this second sense, the diviner practiced a form of necromancy by calling upon the names and souls of the deceased.

Scyphomancy — divination using oil on water. Fill a bowl with water. Place several drops of oil on the water's surface. Read the images that form and reform as the oil droplets move about.

Sideromancy — divining using straws. Lay a number of straws on a hot iron. Interpret the contortions and shapes of the straws as they brown and burn.

Stareomancy — divination using the elements. The Roman diviners called *Haruspices*, who were not officers of state, read signs and omens in the weather.

Theomancy — divination using scripture.

Theriomancy — divination using lower animals. The Haruspices of Rome divined by examining and reading omens revealed in the entrails of slaughtered animals. A quality divination could be had with the use of a pure animal. Theriomancy was reputed to be a holdover from Etruscan practice, and of lesser worth than augury.

The *asvamedha*, or horse sacrifice (India), was done by rulers in order to determine whether to go to war and with whom. One year before the sacrifice, the chosen horse was released to wander at will. It was closely followed by a retinue of nobles, both to protect it and to record its passing. If the horse wandered into the territories of a neighboring ruler, that individual was informed that his properties were forfeit. He could either submit, becoming a vassal of the first king, or fight, since the horse had, by chance, identified the foe. At the close of the year of wandering, the horse was sacrificed as part of a larger fertility celebration.

Other divination practices involve the hanging of "sex tokens," construction of oracles through magical operations, and ceremonial ordeals. North American Indian peoples customarily hang tiny token implements up where they can be reached by an unseen visitor, bow and arrows for a boy and basket or mortar and pestle for a girl. The token that falls to the ground or that disappears indicates the sex of an expected child. In Mexico, the shaman will throw small balls of copal incense into a bowl of water — sinking balls mean no, floating balls mean yes. Magic was mixed with divination in the Middle Ages, when magicians used magical spells and operations to tell the future. Less a matter of random selection and more one of magic is the creation of the "brazen head," an oracular brass head reputedly fashioned by magic and capable of telling the secrets of past, present, and future.

Divination by a special priest class was systematized, often esoteric, and required special training. Divination in societies with more elaborate social structures often produced a highly educated class of people and a flurry of related scholarly activity. In tribal societies, the diviner, whether chosen for natural ability or by inheritance, still required (sometimes extensive) training. All of the natural world provided signs and portents. Those which remained more abstract, ambiguous, or obscure required specialists for interpretation. Still, many signs could be read easily by the uninitiated, their portents being a part of the oral folk tradition.

DIVINATION IN THE
LORE OF COMMON FOLK

Common-lore significances fall, roughly, into three categories: chance games or rituals, formula prognostications for the chance accident, and taboo-like formulas—if you do or do not X, Y will happen or not happen.

Popular Games and Rituals of Chance

JUMPROPE PROGNOSTICATIONS

Letters

The player jumps to the entire rhyme, then at the end of the rhyme, recites the letters of the alphabet, sometimes with "pepper" (fast). The letter he or she misses on will answer the question asked in the rhyme, usually by giving the intial of a sweetheart-to-be. Sometimes a jumper will do the routine twice in order to learn both first and last initials. Depending upon local custom, a jumper who does not miss through the entire recitation will be an old maid. These routines are not really randomizing; a jumper can miss deliberately on a chosen letter to guarantee that the right sweetheart will be named. Even so, the mystery and power of older superstitions haunt such jumprope play. If a jumper with a boyfriend or girlfriend accidentally misses on the wrong letter, what kind of mischief might be let loose? And, isn't it just a wee bit possible, says a small voice in some hidden recess of memory, that missing on the right letter will make a wish come true?

Red, white, blue,
Stars shining over you.
Red, white, and yellow,
Who is your fellow?
A   B   C   D   E   F   G   H ...

Red, white, blue,
Stars shining over you.
Red, white, and green,
Who is your queen?
A   B   C   D   E   F   G   H ...

Ipsey, pipsey, tell me true,
Who shall I be married to?
A   B   C   D   E   F   G   H ...
(1898)

Apple jelly, my jam tart,
Tell me the name of your sweetheart.

Strawberry shortcake, cream on top,
Tell me the name of your sweetheart.

Ice cream, soda water, ginger ale, pop,
Tell me the initials of your sweetheart.

Ice cream soda and lemonade punch,
Tell me the name of your honeybunch.
(Barbados)

Ice cream soda, Delaware Punch,
Spell the initials of my honeybunch.
A   B   C   D   E   F   G   H ...
Does he love me?
Yes, no, maybe so, certainly;
Yes, no, maybe so, certainly ...

Red, white, and yellow,
Have you got a fellow?
Yes, no, maybe so;
Yes, no, maybe so ...

Bluebells, cockle shells [swaying rope],
Evie, ivy, over [turning rope].
I like coffee, I like tea,
I like the boys and the boys like me.
Yes, no, maybe so;
Yes, no, maybe so ...

Numbers

Fire alarm, false alarm,
_____ fell in _____'s arms.
First comes love and then comes marriage.
Then comes _____ with a baby carriage.
             or
Then comes _____ in a baby carriage
How many babies did she get that year?
1   2   3   4   5   6   7   8 ...

_____ and _____ sitting in a tree,
K-I-S-S-I-N-G.
First comes love, then comes marriage,
Then comes _____ with a baby carriage.
How many babies did she have?
1   2   3   4   5   6   7   8 ...

How many bottles did she have?

How many diapers did she have?

Down in the valley where the green grass grows,
There sat _____ as pretty as a rose,
She sang, and she sang, and she sang so sweet;
Along came _____ and kissed her on the cheek.
How many kisses did she get?
1   2   3   4   5   6   7 ...
First came love, and then came marriage ...

Calendars

All together,
Stormy weather,

What is your month?
January, February, March, April ...

What is the date?
First, second, third, fourth ...

What is your day?
Sunday, Monday, Tuesday, Wednesday ...
(This routine will tell the birthdate of a future mate.)

Fortune Telling

> Gypsy, gypsy,
> Please tell me,
> When I grow up,
> What will I be?
> Army, navy, air force, marine,
> Lady, baby, gypsy, queen.
>
> Gypsy, gypsy,
> Please tell me,
> If my wedding will ever be.
> This year, next year, sometime, never.
> This year, next year, sometime, never ...
>
> Gypsy, gypsy,
> Please tell me,
> When my wedding's going to be.
> [Count out months, dates, and days—a calendar]
>
> Gypsy, gypsy,
> Please tell me.
> Where my wedding's going to be.
> Church, chapel, abbey, temple,
> Cathedral, house, yard, street.
>
> Gypsy, gypsy,
> Please tell me,
> What my husband's going to be. (Who will I marry?)
> Doctor, lawyer, banker, thief,
> Richman, poor man, Indian chief.
> (Adapted from Skolnik 1974; Bley 1957; Opie and Opie 1955.)

CANCELLATIONS AND ELIMINATIONS

L	M	D	H	E
O	A	I	A	N
V	R	V	T	G
E	R	O	E	A
	Y	R		G
		C		E
		E		

Ask a friend to choose a number. Go through the words one by one, crossing out every letter that falls on the chosen number. (If seven is chosen, then every seventh letter in sequence will be crossed out.) Continue to repeat the process, cancelling out every (seventh) letter. If you come to a letter that has already been eliminated, do not count it; go to the next uncancelled letter. The first word to be eliminated will signify the first thing that will happen; the second, the second thing; etc. This routine can also be used with names, dates, and months to answer common questions related to affairs of love and marriage (Knapp and Knapp 1976).

E M I L Y   D Y S O N   —   B O B B Y   W I N G E R

Write the names of a "couple" out as given above. Cancel out all letters which their names have in common (here, E, I, Y, N, O). Then ask a question and find its answer in the letters by counting letters and chanting a formula. (See Flower Oracles, p. 70.) Or, label the remaining letters, one for each alternative answer; then choose a number and count to cancel.

Choose a collection of categories related to the questions you want answered. For example, Who is my sweetheart? Where will we get married? What will he do for a living? What will I do for a living? How many children? Rich or poor? Car? Name alternative answers to these questions; construct a chart:

James	Jeremy	Cooper	Ryan	a stranger
Church	Home	Outdoors	live together	JP
Doctor	Teacher	Stay home	Builder	Mechanic
Teacher	Doctor	Architect	Stay home	Decorator
One	Two	Three	Four	Five

Choose the age at which you will marry; use that number to perform cancellations until only one item is left in each row (Knapp and Knapp 1976).

A "color oracle." Children commonly make a folded-paper, origami-like construction that can be manipulated in several directions. Although it resembles a bird's broad beak when stuck on thumb and forefinger, its interior folds and flaps are numerous. Children in Great Britain call these devices "saltcellars" (Opie and Opie 1959). According to the Knapps (Knapp and Knapp 1976), children responding to their collectings in the United States had no name for them. However, we have known them as "counters," "catchers," or "cootie catchers."

To use the oracle, put it on your hand, keeping it closed, so that the numbers in the center cannot be seen. Present it to a friend, asking him or her to choose a color. Open and close the device, alternating directions, once for each letter of the chosen color. If the color choice is *green*, you open and shut the oracle five times, chanting a letter with each opening. (The idea is to open the device in one direction, to reveal four numbers; then to open it in the other direction, to reveal the remaining four numbers, and continue to alternate in this manner.) On "n," allow the device to remain open. Your friend must then choose a number from the four which are visible. That done, you must repeat the alternate-opening-and-closing routine while counting up to that number, chanting the count as you open and shut the oracle. When the number is reached, keep the figure opened, allowing your friend to select another number. Now unfold the flap on which that number is written to reveal the prophecy written immediately behind it. THIS is your friend's future.

Weather Prediction

- Put a lump of sugar into your morning coffee. If the rising bubbles stay in the center of the cup, the evening weather will be fair. If they drift to the sides, rains will soon come.

- To get the wind to blow, turn a hat in the direction you want it to come from and whistle in the same direction (Estonia).

- To make the wind blow, tie a cord with knots. Untie the first knot to get a breeze, the second for a brisk blow, the third for a heavy wind, etc. (Lapland).

- Killing a daddy longlegs spider brings rain.

  > Step on a beetle; it will rain.
  > Pick it up and bury it; the sun will shine again.
  > (Opie and Opie 1959.)

Chance Accident Formulae

Chance accident formulas specify the fate one automatically assumes when some unexpected event, which is out of one's control, happens. Thousands of such verdicts exist. The following list is intended more as illustration than as a collection selected for special divination purposes.

- If your apron comes untied, someone is speaking of you.

- If a married woman's apron falls off, she will soon be vexed.

- Ashes from the fire which retain their heat for a long time foretell a marriage in the family.

- If a cat enters the room while you are handling the bread dough, the bread will not rise.

- A baking bread which cracks across the top means death.

- If you break a string of beads or pearls, you will have a great illness.

- A slat falling out of a bed means great riches.

- If you hear the side of your bed crack, you will hear of the birth of a child.

- If lumps of feathers are found in a bed, witches have been sitting on it.

- If, while you are in bed, a cat scratches at the door, you will be sick for a long time.

- Finding broken glass in a bedroom is a sign of death.

- If you drop food while handing it to a beggar, he will do you some harm.

- If you break a bell, you will hear of a death.

- If you accidentally ring a bell, it means sudden and happy elevation in life.

- If you hear a bell which rings from swaying in the wind, you will have good luck.

- If the toasting glass breaks during the toast, it is very unlucky for the one being toasted (Norway).

- If you spill beer, it means a christening coming soon.

- If you spill milk on the table, it means that a child will be baptized within the year.

- It is bad luck for milk to boil over and run into the fire.
- If a book falls out of the bookcase, company is coming.
- If a pair of sparrows flies into the house, you will have good luck.
- If a bird leaves its droppings on your window in a rather free and profuse design, great riches are coming.
- A caged bird cleaning its feathers foretells company on the way.
- A caged bird which sits and hangs its head foretells the arrival of a deceitful person.
- If you drop a comb, you will have disappointment.
- If a mirror breaks, the last person to have looked into it will die.
- If a hand mirror breaks, a child will die.
- If an oval cinder jumps out of the fire, a baby is coming.

Body Markings and Characteristics

The types of folk observations below are used to read the characters of individuals. But consider these formulae: they are also the kinds of descriptions found in many folk tales for archetypal characters. Perhaps this kind of divination makes comparisons between persons living and those archetypes buried in the recesses of human memory.

HAIR

- Hairy arms mean a rich and successful business.
- A mustache (man) is associated with pride, self-reliance, manliness, and vanity.
- A raggedy mustache, or one which is unkempt and flies about, means lack of self-control.
- A straight, orderly mustache means presence of self-control.
- A mustache which curls at the outer ends denotes ambition, vanity, and display.
- A curl running up a mustache means geniality and fondness of approbation.
- A curl running down a mustache means sedateness of mind.
- A man who habitually twists his mustache upward is generally good-natured.
- A man who habitually twists his mustache downward is morose, difficult, stubborn, and sometimes perverse.
- If you cut your mustache off, your eyes will weaken.
- A man whose mustache hair sticks straight out will be quarrelsome.
- A man wearing a long, pointed beard which he strokes constantly is generally well respected, but also dangerous and untrustworthy.
- Red beard or red hair are a sign of bad luck:

> Beard of red,
> Of the devil bred.
> (Daniels and Stevans 1971.)

- If a grey-bearded man finds that his beard is turning back to its natural color, he has not much longer to live.

- Losing one's beard or hair is very unlucky and a sign of shame. It may also be a prediction that one will soon be in mourning.

- It is unlucky to make reference to one's own or someone else's beard (Syria).

- A man with a beard will never be a beggar (China).

- A man without a beard is a man without a soul (Russia).

- A man whose beard is cut may never enter heaven (Russia).

- It is unlucky to shave a beard on Sunday, Tuesday, and Saturday.

- A woman with light brown, smooth hair will seldom be lucky.

- A brunette will fare better in life than a blonde, but will stand more danger from infectious diseases.

- Yellow hair is unlucky and an ominous sign.

- The yellow-haired person is cunning, industrious, accumulating, and given to pleasure.

- "Let not the eye of a red-haired woman rest upon you" (Old Irish).

- Red hair signifies the vixen, curly hair the scold.

- If you walk between two red-headed girls, you will someday be very rich.

- If you allow the shadow of a red-headed person to fall upon you, you will have bad luck.

- A man who has a single lock of white hair in the midst of hair of another color brings bad luck to others.

- A young person who gets white hairs will live long (Madagascar).

- If a woman's hair turns grey on only one side of her head, she is soon to be a widow.

- If you have two colors of hair, you will live in two countries.

- A bald-headed man is never a fool.

- A hairy man is a happy man (Turkey).

- A long hair growing on any part of the body is lucky and must not be pulled out (China).

- Never swear at your hair when combing it.

- A man who parts his hair on the left side will never die of drowning.

- A man who parts his hair in the middle will have a brighter future.

- A man who parts his hair on the right side will go to prison or will be very judicial.

- A man who does not part his hair will be fond of music.

> Hair cut Monday—meet an enemy.
> Hair cut Tuesday—go on a long journey.
> Hair cut Wednesday—news of a death.
> Hair cut Thursday—have a lawsuit.
> Hair cut Friday—attend a wedding.
> Hair cut Saturday—have a misunderstanding with a friend.
> Hair cut Sunday—success in all you do.
> (Daniels and Stevans 1971.)

- If you cut your hair on the first Friday before the full moon, you will have good luck.
- Never cut your hair after dark.
- If your hair has never been cut, you will come into a fortune.
- If you tread on someone else's hair clippings, that person will go insane (Poland).
- If you place your hair clippings on the fire, and they fail to kindle to flame, you will die within one year (old Wales).
- Place your hair clippings on the fire. If they smolder slowly, it is a sign of death. If they burn brightly, it is a sign of long life. Brightness of flame is a measure of how long one will live.
- If a man sets his hair on fire, he will go mad (China/Japan).

EARS

- A broad, well-shaped ear means long life.
- A large ear signifies a taste for music, but also indicates coarseness.
- A small ear, together with a small, straight nose, signifies poverty.
- Full, protruding ears mean musical talent.
- If your ears are ringing, repeat the names of your acquaintances. The name upon which the ringing stops identifies a person who is thinking of you. If the ringing is in the left ear, the person is thinking or speaking well of you; if in the right, the opposite.
- Both ears ringing simultaneously means that someone in the spirit world is thinking or talking about you.
- Ringing in the ears means that the dead are asking for food (Eskimo).
- If one of your ears is ringing, ask someone to guess which ear it is. If the person guesses correctly, people are speaking well of you. If he or she chooses the wrong ear, people speak ill of you.
- A small hole behind or in the right ear (and in the right nostril) will bring good luck (India).

EYES

> Black eye, pick-a-pie,
> Turn around and tell a lie.
> Blue eye, beauty,
> Do your mother's duty.
> Green eye, greedy gut,
> Eat all the world up.
> Deep and sly,
> Beware of the eye,
> of grayish dye.
> The brown less shocking,
> Merry and mocking,
> Also pass by.
> Honest and true,
> Seek out the blue.
> (Daniels and Stevans 1971.)

- Husbands: Black-eyed—jealousy and suspicion.
              Gray-eyed—most faithful.
              Brown-eyed—best provider.
              Blue-eyed—most henpecked.

- Blue eyes are luckier than dark eyes.

- Gray-eyed people are the only ones with whom secrets are truly safe.

- Green eyes mean deceit and coquetry.

- Brown eyes mean mischief.

- A man with the "crimson eye" is very dangerous, and meeting him means that you should prepare for danger. This is a very bad sign.

- Yellow or citron-colored eyes are the worst of all eyes. The yellow-eyed person is powerful and very dangerous to those whom he or she ensnares.

- Weakly colored eyes, or eyes with absence of color, denote listlessness, coldness, indolence, and selfishness.

- Bright eyes prove good health and signify quietude and reservation.

- It is good luck for one's eyes to change color.

- A person with an eye that droops cannot be trusted.

- A large eye in a small face means maliciousness.

- Eyes which are close together at the bridge of the nose identify a stingy, untrustworthy person.

- A shifty eye denotes dishonesty.

- Soft, languid eyes betray a voluptuous disposition.

- Fullness beneath the eye means sensuality or power of language.

- A blue tint above the eye is a sign of love.

- Someone who keeps his or her eyes almost closed cannot be trusted with confidences.

- Half-shut eyes mean presence of natural shrewdness and lack of sincerity.

- The red, blotched, or bloodshot eye (evil eye) identifies a person who is in league with the devil (Southern United States black).

- The glance of the squinty eye is unlucky.

- The person who squints, or whose eyes are focussed away from or toward one another, is miserly but honest.

- Oblique eyes signify cunning and deceit.

- Pop-eyes denote a good nature.

- A cross-eyed person is protected by the dark powers and can sometimes bring good luck (Southern United States black).

- If you touch a cross-eyed woman's hand too often, you will ensure a loss of domestic tranquility.

- A person whose eyes are unalike is not a trustworthy friend.

- Wall-eyed people are very lucky.

- A wandering eye means deceit.

- Beware the owner of the usually inquisitive eye which becomes kindly when he or she talks to you.

- Very quiet, reposed eyes which embarrass signify self-command.

- It is a bad omen to speak to someone who avoids looking at your eyes.

- If your right eye twitches, you will have news; the left, misfortune.

- If both eyes twitch together, you will hear from a long-absent friend.

- A cinder in the eye means unexpected pleasure; while traveling, a safe journey.

- If you remove dirt from a woman's eye, you will have your next wish; from a man's, indifferent luck.

- A mist before the eye means the death of a friend or a relative.

- It is unlucky to be looked at by a man wearing glasses (Italy).

- It is unlucky to shade your eyes with your hands (Natal).

- If you lose an eye, or if you lose your eyesight, you will lose a dear friend or suffer the death of a relative or good friend. Losing an eye is bad luck.

- A person with a double pupil in an eye is unlucky. If you meet such a person, beware. He or she has the power to kill you (Ancient Rome).

- Freckles around the eye means death by drowning.

EYEBROWS

- Thick toward nose, tapering to points: Surly, capricious, jealous, fretful, easily provoked to rage, intemperate in love.

- Highly arched: Vivacity, brilliancy.

- Regularly curved: Cheerfulness.

- Square: Deep thought.

- Irregular: Fickleness, versatility, excitability.

- Raised at the inner corners: Melancholy.

- Prominently arched: Great perceptive powers regarding form and color.

- Thick, regular, heavy arched: Sound judgment.

- Black, thickly connected over the nose: Great spiritual/occult power and force, hypnotic. (Stay away from a double dark-browed person.)

- Thin, wide apart: Easily led by others, even from a distance, without will.

- Far apart: Warmth, frankness, impulsiveness.

- Close to the eye on one clear line: Strength, will, power.

- Strongly marked, then ending without sweeping past eyes: Irascability, energy, impatience.

- Meeting over the nose (man): Werewolf (Germany, Denmark, Iceland); vampire (Greece); dishonesty, unsettled mind, deceitful disposition, jealous, born to be hung, will die shortly after father dies.

- Meeting over nose (woman): Will marry someone near home; will never marry.

> If your eyebrows meet across your nose,
> You'll never wear your wedding clothes.

- A formula to determine the number of years you have to live: Elevate your eyebrows as high as is possible. Count the crossfolds in the forehead. Subtract that number from 100. The remainder is the total number of years given to you on this earth.

FINGERNAILS

Extremely long: Delicacy of lungs and throat; wealth and prosperity (China); good luck (Nubia).

- White specks: predict events depending upon location—a gift, a friend, a foe, a lover, a journey.

> A gift on the thumb
> Is sure to come.

- White marks: Unfortunate in love until these go away, fair weather, summer heat, omens of coming evil (China/New England); good luck, good health, and money (Germany); counted to see how many lies you have told (Massachusetts); bad luck (Madagascar); bad fortune (Japan).

- A new white spot: Will get new clothing (Japan).

- Many white marks (girl): Marriage to a man owning many sheep (Turkey).

- Bruised fingernail that comes off: Will hear of bad luck.

- Torn: Disappointment.

- Jagged, ragged, bitten to the quick: Envious, jealous, malicious—beware.

- Fingernail biter (girl): Will suffer great pain when she lives to become a mother (China).

- Ridges: Approaching death.

- Cupped over: Short life.

- Cutting fingernails: Good luck on Friday. Cut on the first Friday of the month, save in a paper wrapping until the end of the month for good luck. Unlucky on any day with an "r" in it (France). Never cut them just before a journey or you will have bad luck or disgrace when you arrive at your distination (Japan).

> Cut on Monday—hear good news.
> Cut on Tuesday—get new shoes.
> Cut on Wednesday—cut for wealth.
> Cut on Thursday—cut for health.
> Cut on Friday—cut for woe.
> Cut on Saturday—journey to go.
> Cut on Sunday—cut for evil;
> All next week you'll catch the devil!
> (Daniels and Stevans 1971.)

- Never walk over or step on someone else's cut fingernails or toenails; you will hurt that person.

ITCHING

- Crown of the head: Advancement in life, good luck, a blow of some kind (woman).

- Eye: Expect a vexation that day, will see strange sights in strange places (both eyes); bad luck (northeastern Scotland); will see something pleasant (right eye), will see something sad (left eye).

- Eyelid: A stranger will sleep in the house.

- Left eyebrow: Unpleasant news, death of relative, someone is talking ill of you.

- Right eyebrow: Someone talking well of you.

- Nose: (in the morning) News, will become angry and hot-tempered later that day; a letter waits in the post office; will soon drink something good; someone loves you but cannot tell.

> If your nose itches, you will
> Be in danger,
> Meet a fool,
> Kiss a stranger.
> (Daniels and Stevans 1971.)

- Right nostril: Meet a stranger, receive a strange visitor.

- Left nostril: Someone is prying into your affairs.

- Lips: A kiss from a stranger; (upper lip) a kiss from someone taller; (lower lip) a kiss from someone shorter.

- Mustache: Girls are talking about you.

- Roof of the mouth: You are catching cold.

- Tongue: You will lie without knowing it.

- Sick person's tongue: Recovery.

- Right ear: Good news.

- Left ear: Bad news.

- Back of neck: Upcoming violent death of friend or relative.

- Neck and throat (woman): Will go to a wedding or christening.

- Back: Butter will be cheap.

- Back spine: Will carry a heavy load of trouble and care.

- Elbow: A change of circumstance, a new bedfellow; good tidings (right elbow); bad tidings (left elbow).

- Hand: Riches, money. Scratch itchy palms in your pockets to bring money. A bad omen (China). Spit on the palm and rub on side of hip to get money (Maine).

- Back of hand: Will pay an unknown debt.

- Thighs: A change of sleeping location.

- Knees: Will kneel in a strange church.

- Right knee: A remarkable change in life, a new subject, a change of bedfellows.

- Left knee: A shameful blunder of manners.
- Shins: Long and serious affliction.
- Feet: Will walk on strange ground, a journey, expect to dance a lot (Bohemia); (right foot) will go where welcome, (left foot) will go where unwelcome; (right foot) will ride, (left foot) will walk.
- Sole of the foot: Will walk on strange soil; (both feet) will begin journey immediately.
- Ankle joints: Imminent union with lover; (if married) an increase in home comforts.
- Old scar: Storm approaching.

FINGERS

- Second leaning toward third: Good fortune, large gains.
- Third leaning toward fourth: Celebrity in science, eloquence.
- Burning the thumb: Death of a child.
- Tips of first and fourth fingers capable of meeting over the back of the hand: Will attain any objective.
- See someone with more than five fingers: Will discover new relatives.
- Slippery fingers that drop objects: Visitor.
- Clasp hands together, interlacing the fingers: Right thumb on top, you will rule in married life; left, you will be ruled.
- If you twirl your thumbs and do not also unwind them, you wind trouble for yourself.
- If you snap your fingers while sitting down or walking along the street, you call Satan.
- Skin tearing at the root of a fingernail: Someone is jealous of you.
- Knuckles crack easily: Short lived.
- To know how many lovers you will have, pull your fingers once and count the number of cracks at the joints.

MOUTH

- Fever blister: Someone dreams of kissing you.

NOSE

- Small nose, distended nostrils (man): Will come to beggary.
- Small, pinched-up: Beware in business.
- Sharp ridge at top: Great powers of self-defense.
- Concavity between nose and forehead: A desirable feature.
- Vein on nose between eyes plainly visible: Short-lived.
- Wrinkles down the sides always at least somewhat visible: Acquisitive of money.

- Easily wrinkled: Good nature.
- Pointed: Meddlesome.
- Protruding nose and mouth: Self-confidence, impudence, rashness.
- Hooked: Will take care of self at expense of others.
- Swaybacked (concave): Beware in business.
- Bent (man): Unlucky to deal with.

TEETH

- Lying over one another: Will always live with mother.
- Ridgy: Will die of fever.
- Far apart: Will live far from parents, must seek fortune in foreign land, good luck; will marry twice (Persia).
- Close together: Will live close to parents.
- Chattering: Visit of a lost lover.
- Breaking a tooth: Death of a friend.
- If you can fit a nickel between your teeth, you will not live long.
- Tooth decay at lower edges: Will marry a widower.
- Tooth decay along sides: Will marry well.
- Top decay: Old maid.
- All teeth lost before age of seven means death before eleven.
- Lose a tooth: Death of friend, relative, evil luck (especially if on a rainy or stormy night), loss of money.

>   Pulled on Monday—approaching sadness.
>   Pulled on Tuesday—legacy from distant relative.
>   Pulled on Wednesday—loss and shame.
>   Pulled on Thursday—success in business.
>   Pulled on Friday—confusion in affairs.
>   Pulled on Saturday—discovery of a secret.
>   Pulled on Sunday—love quarrels.
>   Pulled without bleeding—something valuable found soon.
>   (Daniels and Stevans 1971.)

- Go to the dentist in a great storm: You will sicken and die.

WALKING

- Pigeon-toed woman: Will have more male than female children.
- Turning the left foot: Bad luck.

WARTS

- On the face: Tempestuous life.
- Under the left ear: Destined to hang.
- In general: A thief (Native American).

Taboos and Superstitions

- Never step over an eggshell. You will go mad (woman—Japan).
- Never throw your nail or hair clippings in the street, or someone might take them up and use them to work evil against you.
- Never kick the wall of a house, or you will cause the death of your grandmother or grandfather.
- Never reverse the pillows when making the bed, or someone will die.
- Never make the bed together with another person, especially if that person is sick, or someone in the family will die.
- Never drink liquor without blowing on the glass, or the Satanic influences of the drink will remain (Russia).
- Never take a drink of alcohol without making the sign of the cross to drive away the devil (Romania).
- Never blow into a bottle; you will die of starvation if you do.
- Never cut into the butter at both ends, or you will have bad luck.
- Never kill kittens, or you will have bad luck.
- Never walk over a cellar door, or you will have bad luck.
- Never sit down in a chair turned bottom up unless you first spit into it, or you will bring bad luck (Sweden).
- Never turn a chair on one leg—bad luck.
- Never turn a chair upside down—bad luck.
- Never lift a carpet on a Sunday—bad luck.
- Never stir the fire with tongs, or you will stir up anger.
- Never put your shoes and stockings on the table, or your feet will ache (Bohemia).
- Never wear cast-off shoes—bad luck.
- Never walk with one shoe off and the other one on. You will have one day of bad luck for each step taken.
- Never black a stove on a Friday, or your cooking will go awry.
- Never spit on a stove; you will get chapped lips.
- Never burn straw that someone else has slept on, or that person will have no rest.
- Never use milk, or you will have bad luck (Japan).

Never burn a broom—bad luck.
Never break a broom handle in two—death.
Never step over a broom (girl)—old maid.
Never sweep on New Year's Day—will sweep luck away (Japan).
Never move a broom across water—bad luck.
Never sweep the first snow with a new broom—bad luck.
Never loan a broom—bad luck.
Never give away a used broom—bad luck.
Never step over sweepings—bad luck.
Never put a broom on your head—bad luck.
Never sweep to the north—poverty (Madagascar).
Never sweep at night—poverty (Madagascar).
Never sweep outward toward a door.
Never sweep dirt from one room to another.
Never put a broom on a table.
Never sweep a table with a broom.
Never sweep a room immediately after a death (Japan).
Never step over a broom handle lying on the floor.
Never allow yourself to be touched by a broom handle when someone
    else is sweeping.
(Daniels and Stevans 1971.)

Pseudosciences

CABALISTIC CALCULATIONS
AND NUMEROLOGY

This example uses a table correlating letters and numbers to tell personal characteristics and fortunes.

Alphabetic Table

A	B	C	D	E	F	G	H
1	2	3	4	5	6	7	8

I	K	L	M	N	O	P	Q
9	10	20	30	40	50	60	70

R	S	T	U	X	Y	Z
80	90	100	200	300	400	500

J	V	Hi	Hu	W = V + V
600	700	800	900	1400

Number Significances

1.	Passion, ambition, design.	31.	Love of glory, virtue.
2.	Destruction, catastrophe.	32.	Marriage.
3.	Religion, destiny, the soul, charms.	33.	Purity.
4.	Solidity, wisdom, and power.	34.	Suffering, trouble of mind.
5.	The stars, happiness, graces, marriage.	35.	Beauty, harmony.
6.	Perfection, labor.	36.	Genius, vast conception.
7.	Imperfection, diminution, grief, expectation.	37.	Domestic virtues, conjugal love.
		38.	Imperfection, avarice, envy.
8.	Justice, preservation.	39.	Praise.
9.	Course of life, repose, liberty, perfect happiness.	40.	Festivals, weddings.
		41.	Ignominy.
10.	Success, reason, future happiness.	42.	A short, unhappy life, the tomb.
11.	Faults, discord, punishment, prevarication.	43.	Religious ceremonies, a priest.
		44.	Power, pomp, monarchy.
12.	Good omen, a town or city.	45.	Population.
13.	Impiety.	46.	Fertility.
14.	Sacrifice, purification.	47.	Long and happy life.
15.	Piety, self-culture.	48.	The tribunal, judgment, judge.
16.	Love, happiness, voluptuousness.	49.	Love of money.
17.	Misfortune, forgetfulness.	50.	Pardon, liberty.
18.	Hardening of the heart, misfortune.	60.	Widowhood.
19.	Folly.	70.	Initiation, science, the graces.
20.	Austerity, sadness.	75.	The world.
21.	Mystery, wisdom, the creation.	77.	Pardon, repentance.
22.	A scourge, the divine vengeance.	80.	A cure, physician.
23.	Ignorance of religion.	81.	An adept, occultism.
24.	Journeys.	90.	Blindness, error, affliction.
25.	Intelligence, a birth.	100.	Divine favor.
26.	Useful works.	120.	Patriotism, praises.
27.	Firmness, courage.	200.	Irresolution.
28.	Love tokens.	215.	Calamity.
29.	Letters.	300.	Safety, faith, belief, philosophy.
30.	Fame, a wedding.		

318. A divine messenger.

350. Hope, justice.

360. Home, society.

365. Astronomy.

400. Long and wearisome voyage, travel.

410. Priests, theology.

500. Holiness.

600. Perfection.

666. A malicious person, plots, enemies.

700. Strength.

800. Empire.

900. War, combat, struggles.

1000. Mercy.

1095. Taciturnity.

1260. Torments.

1390. Persecution.

Procedures

Write out the full name of the individual in question. Place the corresponding number value beneath each letter. Add the number values for each part of the name. Add these sums.

A	N	N	A					
1	40	40	1				=	82

M	A	R	I	A				
30	1	80	9	1			=	121

S	O	P	H	I	A			
90	50	60	8	9	1		=	218

N	I	N	S	T	I	L		
40	9	40	90	100	9	20	=	308

729

Reference this final sum in the list of significances.

729 = 700 (strength)
29 (letters)

To gain additional information, reference the parts of the name.

82 = 80 (a cure, physician)
2 (destruction, catastrophe)

121 = 100 (divine favor)
21 (mystery, wisdom, the creation)

218 = 200 (irresolution)
18 (hardening of the heart, misfortune)

308 = 300 (safety, faith, belief, philosophy)
8 (justice, preservation)

WOLFGANG AMADEUS MOZART sums to 2623. Eliminate the 2000 =

623 = 600 (perfection)
23 (ignorance of religion)

Wolfgang = 1531 (500: holiness; 31: love of glory, virtue)

Amadeus = 331 (300: safety, faith, belief, philosophy; 31: love of glory, virtue)

Mozart = 761 (700: strength; 60: widowhood; 1: passion, ambition, design)

JOHN JAMES AUDUBON sums to 1921. Eliminate the 1000 =

921 = 900 (war, combats, struggles)
21 (mystery, wisdom, the creation)

John = 698 (600: perfection; 90: blindness, error, affiction; 8: justice, preservation)

James = 726 (700: strength; 26: useful works)

Audubon = 497 (400: long and wearisome voyages, travel; 90: blindness, error, affliction; 7: imperfection, diminution, grief, expectation)

SUSAN BROWNELL ANTHONY sums to 2677. Eliminate the 2000 =

677 = 600 (perfection)
77 (pardon, repentance)

Susan = 421 (400: long and wearisome voyages, travel; 21: mystery, wisdom, the creation)

Brownell = 1617 (eliminate the 1000 = 617. 600: perfection; 17: misfortune, forgetfulness)

If 1000 or 2000 is eliminated from a sum, that amount can be presumed to mean "multiples of" the particular characteristic. For Susan B. Anthony, for instance, the 2000 would signify extra perfection, pardon, and repentance. More than one appearance of a characteristic can also mean extra. (Adapted from Daniels and Stevans 1971, vol. 1, 215-17.)

This example uses the same kind of table to determine personal qualities.

Numerology Table

1	2	3	4	5	6	7	8	9
A	B	C	D	E	F	G	H	I
J	K	L	M	N	O	P	Q	R
S	T	U	V	W	X	Y	Z	

Number Associations with Personal Characteristics

Number	Positive	Negative
1	Leader.	Arrogant, inferiority complex.
2	Tactful.	Overly sensitive, unsure.
3	Lucky, extroverted, creative, romantic.	Superficial.
4	Self-disciplined, hard-working, honest.	Stubborn, conservative.
5	Resourceful, sensual, adventurous.	Irresponsible, shortsighted.
6	Responsible, warm-hearted, peaceful.	Narrow-minded.
7	Intellectual, self-controlled.	Pessimistic, skeptical.
8	Practical, efficient.	Greedy, ruthless.
9	Selfless, visionary, compassionate.	Extremely selfish.
11	Idealistic, inventive, intuitive.	Fanatic, perverse.
22	Practically idealistic, creative, romantic.	Abusive of power, vicious.

Procedures

Write out the name of the individual in question. Assign numbers to the letters in the name using the correspondences given in the table. Sum the numbers. Add the numbers in the sum, repeating the process until one digit between 1 and 9 is derived. Interpret using the characteristics assigned to the numbers (Shadowitz and Walsh 1976, 130-31).

CHARLES ROBERT DARWIN

Charles = 30
Robert = 33
Darwin = 33
_____
96   9 + 6 = 15   1 + 5 = 6

6 = responsible, warm-hearted, peaceful, narrow-minded

WALTER ELIAS DISNEY

Walter = 25
Elias   = 19
Disney = 31
_____
75   7 + 5 = 12   1 + 2 = 3

3 = lucky, extroverted, creative, romantic, superficial

The special powers attributed to numbers and letters, and the magical properties of both, are an ancient lore, dating probably to the inception of written language. If oral language was a powerful medium—"In the beginning there was the Word, and the Word was God"—imagine the mystical and mysterious nature of written symbols which could encode and capture the word. Hence, letters and numbers together were imbued with a divinity which made them capable of speaking the mind(s) of the god or gods. Many manipulations of numbers and letters intended to read the divine have evolved in the lores of many cultures. There is little evidence that any of these were fashioned empirically. The second table, in fact, demonstrates a rather arbitrary and straightforward number-letter assignment. Presumably, magic and randomness are both implicit in the names of individuals. Shadowitz and Walsh (1976) suggest that numerology might be classed, along with astrology, Tarot, palmistry, and phrenology, as an art whose empirical substance consists of esoteric knowledge compiled slowly over many centuries. Though its reliability is questionable, people in many cultures trust to its results.

Chinese Numerology

Chinese numerology attempts to find the "soul age" by numerological techniques.

"There are nine numbers by which all calculations are made; beyond the number nine, all are repetition. No matter how large a sum, it can be reduced to a single figure by simple addition" (Ward 1982, 72). Write the numbers of month, date, and year of birth in vertical columns. Add these numbers. Place the numbers in the sum in a single column. Add these. Then add the single digits in this sum, until one single number between 1 and 9 is obtained.

October 7, 1984 becomes:

$$
\begin{array}{r}
10 \\
7 \\
1984 \\
\hline
2001
\end{array}
$$

$$
\begin{array}{r}
2 \\
0 \\
0 \\
1 \\
\hline
3
\end{array}
$$

February 6, 1943 becomes:

$$
\begin{array}{r}
2 \\
6 \\
1943 \\
\hline
1951
\end{array}
$$

$$
\begin{array}{r}
1 \\
9 \\
5 \\
1 \\
\hline
16
\end{array}
$$

$$
1 + 6 = 7
$$

- If you are *Aries* (March 22-April 20):

    Ruler/sign — Mars/Fire.

    General characteristics — forceful, ambitious, industrious, generous, idealistic, a starter, executive ability; obstinate, leaves things unfinished.

    Marriage/business partners — Aries, Leo, Sagittarius.

    Health — head injuries, stomach or kidney ailments, paralysis, apoplexy.

    Birthstone — sapphire.

    Vocations — soul age: 1, 2, 3: military, sailor, police force, firefighter, waiter, governess, school supervisor, playground superintendent, cashier, factory supervisor.

    soul age: 4, 5, 6: mechanic, radio technician, dentist, army captain, telegraph operator, department manager, tailor, dental assistant, secretary.

    soul age: 7, 8, 9: chemist, doctor, executive, banker, musician, singer, florist, storekeeper.

- If you are *Taurus* (April 21-May 21):

  Ruler/sign — Venus/Earth.

  General characteristics — calm, self-controlled, home lover, fond of children, enjoy creature comforts, quiet, forceful, undemonstrative, loyal, faithful mate, affectionate parent; unromantic lover.

  Marriage/business partners — Taurus, Virgo, Capricorn.

  Health — dropsy, kidney disease, problems of throat and generative system; avoid rich foods and wines.

  Birthstone — emerald.

  Vocations — soul age: 1, 2, 3: farmer, cattle/chicken husbandry, logger, dog fancier, housekeeper.

  soul age: 4, 5, 6: mill operator, sugar/flour manufacturer, grain/hay/produce dealer, service station operator, cannery operator, wine manufacturer, fruit storer/manufacturer, florist.

  soul age: 7, 8, 9: land owner, miner, potter, weaver, nurse, cheese maker, oil operator, smelter, gardener.

- If you are *Gemini* (May 22-June 21):

  Ruler/sign — Mercury/Air.

  General characteristics — charming, brilliant, good mental facility; mercurial, changeable, scattered forces, problems with concentration.

  Marriage/business partners — Gemini, Libra, Aquarius.

  Health — diseases of lungs/blood, abdominal operations.

  Birthstone — agate.

  Vocations — soul age: 1, 2, 3: restaurant owner, hotel manager, bank cashier, head waiter, employment agency operator, beautician, cashier, dietician, telephone operator.

  soul age: 4, 5, 6: sales, sales manager, office manager, musician, dancer, secretary, bookkeeper, file clerk, teacher.

  soul age: 7, 8, 9: artist, financier, chemist, doctor, musician, advertising, professor of languages, dance instructor.

- If you are *Cancer* (June 22-July 23):

  Ruler/sign — Moon/Water.

  General characteristics — sensitive, adaptable, charming, influenced by sympathy and kindness (but not driven by it), constant affection; given to worry, morbid introspection, misunderstandings.

  Marriage/business partners — Cancer, Scorpio, Pisces.

  Health — rheumatism, gout, poor circulation, trouble with lungs.

Birthstone — ruby.

Vocations — soul age: 1, 2, 3: stevedore, chef, fisherman, mail carrier, sales, elevator operator, telephone operator, file clerk.

soul age: 4, 5, 6: sales, conductor, railroad engineer, truck driver, billing clerk, timekeeper, housekeeper, bottler of liquids.

soul age: 7, 8, 9: importer, traveling salesperson, naval career, transportation manager, dealer in liquids, perfume manufacturer, wine merchant, cosmetic merchant, creamery operator.

- If you are *Leo* (July 24-August 23):

Ruler/sign — Sun/Fire.

General characteristics — leader, industrious, energetic, magnetic, generous, loyal, no harboring of grudges, usually deserves being looked up to; danger of uncontrolled love of power and authority, could be domineering, desire to be looked up to.

Marriage/business partners — Leo, Sagittarius, Aries.

Health — rheumatism, diseases of heart/liver/spleen.

Birthstone — sardonyx.

Vocations — soul age: 1, 2, 3: miner, carpenter, plumber, plasterer, laundry worker, raiser of small animals, kindergarten teacher, stone mason.

soul age: 4, 5, 6: supervisor, army captain, teacher, sales person, nurse, secretary, beautician.

soul age: 7, 8, 9: miner, coal/grain/hay merchant, office manager, shoe manufacturer, luggage merchant, florist, hospital manager, writer, head of nursery, school principal.

- If you are *Virgo* (August 24-September 23):

Ruler/sign — Mercury/Earth.

General characteristics — intellectual influences, inventive, analytical, critical, versatile, gifted conversation, unselfish work for others; overcritical, unemotional, intolerant.

Marriage/business partners — Virgo, Capricorn, Taurus.

Health — ulcers, stomach, and nervous system diseases.

Birthstone — chrysolite.

Vocations — soul age: 1, 2, 3: bookkeeper, bank teller, secretary, shipping clerk.

soul age: 4, 5, 6: law clerk, real estate sales, builder, draftsman, court clerk, court stenographer, accountant, designer.

soul age: 7, 8, 9: lawyer, court clerk, writer, professor of languages, judge, real estate dealer, professor of English.

- If you are *Libra* (September 24-October 23):

  Ruler/sign — Venus/Air.

  General characteristics — lover of beauty, despiser of ugliness or sham/deceit/crudity/grossness, honest, generous, socially gifted, delightful companion, steadfast affection; reluctance to marry.

  Marriage/business partners — Libra, Gemini, Aquarius.

  Health — Diseases of stomach, kidney, nerves, skin.

  Birthstone — opal.

  Vocations — soul age: 1, 2, 3: landscape gardener, electrician, painter, carpenter, mechanic, tailor, interior decorator, florist, housekeeper, sales.

  soul age: 4, 5, 6: mechanical engineer, architect, interior decorator, musician, designer of clothing, music teacher, manufacturer, art dealer.

  soul age: 7, 8, 9: doctor, sculptor, play producer, connoisseur of fine arts, writer, actor, artist.

- If you are *Scorpio* (October 24-November 22):

  Ruler/sign — Mars/Water.

  General characteristics — driving force to overcome all obstacles, passionate devotion, shrewd, analytical, strong, subtle; excess and folly in love, needing sympathetic understanding of others.

  Marriage/business partners — Scorpio, Cancer, Pisces.

  Health — gland trouble, fistula, diseases of bowels and generative system.

  Birthstone — topaz.

  Vocations — soul age: 1, 2, 3: draftsman, dealer in produce, trucking/shipping/storage estimator, designer, music teacher, school teacher, nurse.

  soul age: 4, 5, 6: lawyer, chemist, auctioneer, dealer in liquids, writer, perfume manufacturer, interior decorator.

  soul age: 7, 8, 9: distiller, druggist, publisher, advertiser, adventurer, actor, writer, singer, composer.

- If you are *Sagittarius* (November 23-December 22):

  Ruler/sign — Jupiter/Fire.

  General characteristics — honest, fearless, unselfish, insight, intuition, frank and direct, excellent business/marriage partner, appreciated when understood; brusque, overly fastidious in love, cold, sometimes misunderstood.

  Marriage/business partners — Sagittarious, Leo, Aries.

  Health — colds, bronchitis, diseases of liver and blood.

Birthstone — turquoise.

Vocations — soul age: 1, 2, 3: Bible student, lecturer, radio/television communicator, assayer, singer, chemical laboratory assistant.

soul age: 4, 5, 6: mechanical engineer, construction engineer, inventor, lecturer, writer, preacher, Bible teacher, actor, musician.

soul age: 7, 8, 9: traveler and lecturer, adventurer, philanthropist, journalist, magazine publisher, reporter, head of detention institution, publisher of religious subjects, writer of religious subjects, healer.

- If you are *Capricorn* (December 23-January 20):

Ruler/sign — Saturn/Earth.

General characteristics — ambition, dogged determination, work until success is achieved, hard worker, practical, independent, magnetic, cautious in love; will not fall in love until love is given.

Marriage/business partners — Capricorn, Taurus, Virgo.

Health — ulcers, diseases of gall bladder, bladder, and digestive organs.

Birthstone — garnet.

Vocations — soul age: 1, 2, 3: sales, organizing merchant, merchant, department manager, manufacturer, buyer.

soul age: 4, 5, 6: school teacher, bookkeeper, bank clerk, music teacher, secretary, chemist.

soul age: 7, 8, 9: advertiser, doctor, public speaker, lawyer, preacher.

- If you are *Aquarius* (January 21-February 19):

Ruler/sign — Uranus/Air.

General characteristics — quiet, reserved, modest, unselfish, give talents freely for good of others, impersonal view of life, loyal friend, gifted, rise to fame, mental poise, power over circumstance; learn to rely on own good judgment.

Marriage/business partners — Aquarius, Libra, Gemini.

Health — poor circulation, anemia, heart trouble, diseases of bladder and kidney.

Birthstone — amethyst.

Vocations — soul age: 1, 2, 3: worker in delivery service, butcher, baker, hairdresser, nurse, chef, beautician.

soul age: 4, 5, 6: writer, doctor, laboratory technician, chemist, dentist.

soul age: 7, 8, 9: executive, organizer, undertaker, dentist, doctor, lawyer.

- If you are *Pisces* (February 20-March 21):

    Ruler/Sign — Jupiter and Neptune/Water.

    General characteristics — popular, generous, socially charming, fine instincts, high ambition; indecisive, must learn to analyze, to design a course of action, to stick by decisions.

    Marriage/business partners — Pisces, Cancer, Scorpio.

    Health — nervous disorders, consumption, tumors, paralysis.

    Birthstone — bloodstone.

    Vocations — soul age: 1, 2, 3: stone mason, carpenter, machinist, electrician, designer, tailor, lacemaker, cutter, fitter.

               soul age: 3, 4, 5: play producer, advertiser, builder, architect, dance director, actor, writer, interior decorator.

               soul age: 7, 8, 9: builder of larger objects, theater business, musician, actor, singer, art of the stage.

When interpreting these characteristics, one should divide the period of one's birth sign into thirds. If one's birthdate falls into the first third of the sign, one should consider influences from the previous sign. The closer the proximity of the date to the end of the previous sign, the more pronounced the influence from that sign will be. If the date of birth is in the last third of the sign, one should also look at the characteristics of the following sign, using proximity of birthdate to the beginning of the next sign as a guide. Individuals whose birthdates fall into the middle third of their sign will be most powerfully influenced by the exclusive characteristics of that sign. (Adapted from Ward 1982.)

Chinese numerology, used as it is here in combination with astrology, refines astrological prognostication by incorporating elements of reincarnation. Young souls have had less experience, consequently have learned less than old ones. And, since the experiences of one incarnation integrate with those of others and carry forward into subsequent lifetimes, an older soul is more powerful and capable. A soul which has been born under the same sign repeatedly will exhibit a high degree of refinement and accomplishment of the characteristics of that sign. A soul which has been born under many signs is, by the seventh, eighth, or ninth life on Earth, well versed in many subjects, well rounded, a quick learner, and a good retainer of information. Such people are usually very wholesome and powerful persons, and have very powerful auras and presences (Ward 1982).

METOSCOPY

Metoscopy employs a combination of astrology, other body signs, and the nature of the forehead and the lines on the forehead.

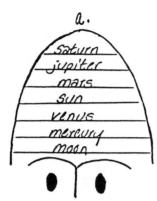

a.

(saturn / jupiter / mars / sun / venus / mercury / moon)

b.

c.

d.

e.

f.

g.

h.

i.

j.

k.

l.

m.

n.

o.

p.

q.

r.

s.

t.

a. Planetary influences (planes) on the forehead. The plane in which the lines on the forehead are located can further refine prognostication. Differences in interpretation exist for men and women. Apparently less concern was given to the fates of women using this method: all the illustrations in this list, with the exception of k and o, are for the male forehead and the male personality.

b. Peace, success.

c. Exaltation, priesthood.

d. Quarrelsome, murderous.

e. Will die a violent death.

f. Infirmity.

g. Poisoner.

h. Success in war.

i. Will be wounded in the head.

j. Will be drowned.

k. Happy, fortunate.

l. Instability.

m. Loving.

n. Upright, intelligent.

o. Vicious.

p. Immoderation, sickness.

q. Unintelligent.

r. Imbecile, long-lived.

s. Poet, musician.

t. Adventurer.

(Adapted from Seligmann 1948.)

If the forehead is:

- One deep perpendicular wrinkle with one or two lesser ones to each side of it (man): great, marked ability.

- Broad, straight lines: eventful life.

- Very crooked lines: evil sign.

- Lines bent at ends (woman): scold.

- Number of wrinkles (man): children he will beget.

- Number of horizontal wrinkles caused by frown: number of children.

- Number of creases between eyebrows when scowling: times married.

PHYSIOGNOMY

Developed by scholars in the 1500s, physiognomy was an attempt to organize folk observations into an orderly science and to add a degree of empiricism, the better to guarantee predictability. Physiognomy, nevertheless, remains more a folk art, albeit subjected to analysis, than a science.

In the nineteenth century, physiognomy abandoned much of its heritage in folk custom and took on the trappings of an empirical science. Hucksters and sincere scholars both made the practice of reading bumps and other features of the head—phrenology—into quite a fad before the emergence of modern psychology and the development of brain research. Their charts of the head, with its carefully numbered sections, are trotted out as curiosities from time to time, but the practice as it was known in the late 1800s is in disrepute. It is interesting that a divination practice that forsakes its ancient roots in folk tradition also forsakes its reliability.

CHIROMANCY/PALMISTRY

Chiromancy and palmistry use the hand as oracle.

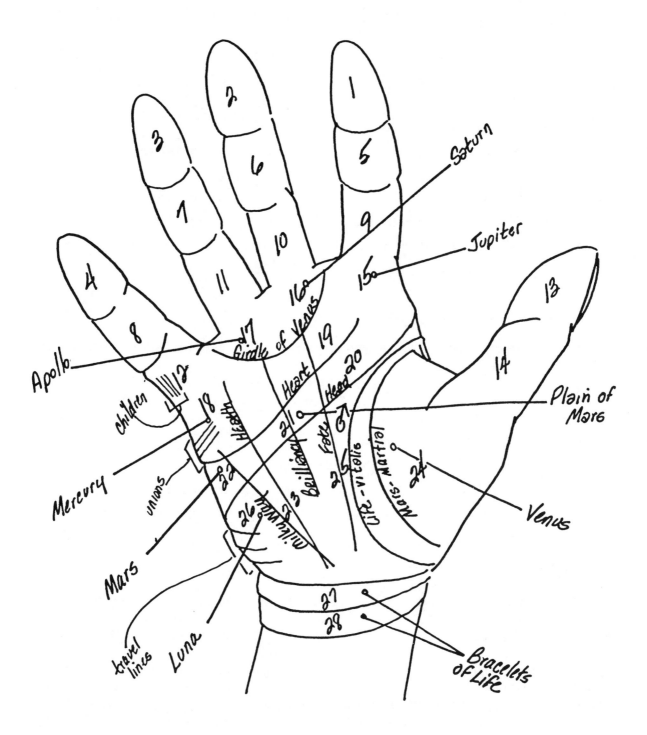

Modern divination by examination of the hand has ancient beginnings. As with the reading of other bodily characteristics, chiromancy became an object of study in the sixteenth century, when scholars and writers attempted to make its practice systematic. Chiromancy's claim to the status of science lies in its carefully organized and codified procedures. It cannot, however, escape the principal assumption upon which it is founded: that the gods imprint the pattern of one's life on the palm of one's hand. If we could but read the message, we could ascertain the divine will. In this respect, palmistry remains a folk art. Its practice can be traced back to Biblical times and beyond. In fact, chiromancers of the Middle Ages cited scripture as a mandate for their practice ("He seals up the hand of every man, that all men may know His work" [Job 37: 7]; "Long life is given in her right hand. In her left are riches and honor" [Prov. 3: 16]).

The thumb and fingers are divided into three *phalanges* by the joints. The first phalange (tips of fingers) represents intuitive faculties, the second (middle) is reasoning power, and the third (roots of the fingers) is material instinct. The *mounts* are the bumps at the bases of the fingers. The mount at the base of the thumb (Venus) is also the third phalange of the thumb. The center of the palm is called the "Plain of Mars"; the "Mound of Luna" is opposite the "Mound of Venus" at the base of the hand. The mound at the base of the little finger is the "Mound of Mercury." The "Mound of Mars" is the smaller bump sandwiched between Mercury and Luna.

Vitalis, the lifeline. A perfect lifeline completely encircles the Mound of Venus; is long, regular, narrow, deep, soft in color, and unbroken; and represents health, long life, and good character.

Martial, the line of Mars. Mars should be clear red. For a soldier, it indicates success in battle; for others, degree of violence of passion.

The line of Heart. The Heart line extends from the line of Jupiter to the Mound of Mercury. A deep, narrow line of good color means strength, a good heart, firm affection, and an even temper.

Head. The head line extends from the base of the Mound of Jupiter to the Mound of Mars. An even, narrow, long line means strong will and judgment, acute mental perception.

Fate, the line of Fortune. A straight, unbroken line from the bracelets to the base of the second finger. Broken lines mean trouble. Read both palms.

Brilliancy, the line of Apollo. A lucky line, which rises from the Plain of Mars or from the lifeline towards the third finger. When long and unbroken, it means fame in the arts and wealth.

Health. The line of Health starts at the wrist, extending on a diagonal to meet the head line close to the Mound of Mars or at the top of the Mound of Luna. A strong line means health.

Via Lasciva, the Milky Way. This line, which may extend from the wrist across the Mound of Luna, is rarely noticeable; when it is, it signifies faithless spirit and cunning.

The Girdle of Venus. This mark indicates bad character.

The Bracelets of Life. The bracelets, encircling the wrist, signify fortune, happiness, and length of life.

The Mound of Venus. If prominent, well-formed, and with many lines, the Mound of Venus signifies a cheerful, amorous, luxurious character; without lines, it signifies effeminacy, rudeness, and sorrowfulness.

The Mound of Luna. If well-proportioned and with many lines, Luna's Mound foretells fame, honesty, and honorable character; without lines, it signifies inconstancy.

THE DOCTRINE OF MOLES

Divination by moles is yet another dimension of folk knowledge given order and a set of formal and systematic rules by the scholars of the fifteenth and sixteenth centuries. Elaborate plates of the head and body were produced to illustrate the locations of prominent moles, the proximities between moles, and the astrological significance of mole placement. Like other so-called sciences of the features of the body, the doctrine of moles is more an organized folklore than an empirical science. Even so, moles have been objects of interest, whether considered marks of beauty or physical ugliness, since ancient times. In this century, moles or beauty marks have been alternately in and out of fashion.

Moles on Women

- Right knee—honesty, virtue; left knee—many children.
- Nose—travel on foot in different lands.
- Center forehead—discourteous, cruel, unpleasant discourse.
- Lower jaw—life of sorrow, physical pain.
- Honey-colored—beloved.
- Red—sullen and furious.
- Black—inexpert, wavering.
- Lip—great eater, amorous, much beloved.
- Chin—riches.
- Ear—riches, respect.
- Neck—money by the peck.
- Right breast—poverty.
- Near bottom of nostril—very lucky.
- Left side of belly—affliction.
- Right foot—wisdom.
- Left foot—dangerous, rash actions.
- Eyebrow—early, happy marriage.
- Wrist—ingenious mind.
- Between elbow and wrist—many crosses, ending in prosperity and joy.
- Side of chin—amiable, industrious, successful.

- Thighs — poverty, infelicity.
- Armhole — riches and honor.
- Right shoulder/arm — great wisdom.
- Left shoulder/arm — contention and debate.
- Raised like a wart — untidy; if black, treacherous and consenting to evil.

Moles on Men

- Throat — riches.
- Under left breast — unsettled mind.
- Ankle — courage.
- Right arm — undaunted courage, vigor.
- Left arm — resolution and victory in battle.
- Elbow — restlessness, unsteady temper, roving.
- Right ribs — slow to understand things which attend difficulties.
- Stomach — sloth, gluttony.
- Hip — healthy, patient.
- Either leg — Indolent, thoughtless, indifferent.
- Raised like a wart — very fortunate.

"I CHING," THE ORACLE OF CHANGE

The *I Ching* is a general philosophy which is organized for purposes of divination. Chinese legend gives its age at more than 4,000 years. It was first codified ca. 1200 BC, and has been revised and refined repeatedly since that time. The I Ching holds that nothing is static, and that the affairs of humanity and the universe are governed by cyclic patterns. By consulting the oracle, individuals can better fit their responses to their circumstances to the patterns of universal flow, rather than trying to swim against the current.

The book of I Ching contains sixty-four pages. Each of these is a self-contained text which has, at its head, a hexagram or figure specific to its content. The text on each page is divided into five subtexts which provide the meaning of the hexagram: 1 — *Decision*; 2 — *Commentary*; 3 — *Image*; 4 — *The Lines*; 5 — *Interpretation*. The old, conventional procedure for determining which of the sixty-four pages is applicable in a particular case involves a complicated and lengthy operation with piles of yarrow straws. The manipulator of the straws, perhaps in an altered state of consciousness, works to allow chance to determine which of the sixty-four hexagrams is the right one. A less time-consuming, but still somewhat difficult, operation, in which a set of three similar coins is tossed into the air six times, can also be employed. One side of each coin denotes *ying*, the other *yang*. Since the hexagrams are constructed of ying (short) and yang (long) lines in specific patterns, a record kept of the results of coin tossing will, in the end, identify the exact hexagram needed. The procedure is entirely governed by chance.

Once the hexagram is selected, the text must be interpreted in light of the circumstance brought to it; its meaning will be determined by that circumstance. As each page of text is sufficiently general, a message for the petitioner can be found.

RUNE STONES

The runes, a Tarot-like divination tool, are oracular, "a means of communication with the knowledge of our subconscious minds" (Blum 1982, 8). Like the I Ching, the twenty-five stones are "read" or interpreted using a systematic text. The rune stones can be cast in a variety of patterns or "spreads," which provide definition and help to explicate the text. One simply pulls the stones from their pouch (a blind draw) and lays them upon a surface, without looking at them, in order to allow even their position to flow from within.

Runes are an ancient form of divining, and were common among Northern European pagan peoples. Ordinarily, runes were smooth, flat pebbles that had glyphs or signs painted on one side. Rune casters (rune masters), many of whom were women, used the oracle to forecast, to make magic, and to cast spells. The runes had great magical and mystical potency. Like "Word," they had the power of making; that is, they had transformative capacities. They belonged to the Triple Goddess Freya, who originally created them. In order to gain enlightenment (part of which meant learning the secrets of the sacred runes), Odin chose to suffer the hero's death (he "gave himself to himself"), submitting to the common sacrificial hanging upon the great cosmic tree (Yggdrasil). Thus he learned of both the alphabetic and symbolic aspects of the runes. Many standing rune stones can still be found in Northern Europe, and remaining artifacts suggest wide employment of runes as amulets and signs of power and protection (Blum 1982).

> A King he was on a carven throne
> In many-pillared halls of stone
> With golden roof and silver floor,
> And runes of power upon the door.
> (J. R. R. Tolkien, *The Fellowship of the Ring*, 1986.)

FORTUNE TELLING

Using Dominoes

Lay the dominoes face down on a tabletop. Shuffle them, then draw twelve, turning and reading them one at a time.

- 6-6: receive money.
- 6-5: go to place of public amusement.
- 6-4: lawsuits, trouble.
- 6-3: ride in a carriage.
- 6-2: present of clothing.
- 6-1: will soon perform an act of friendliness.
- 6-0: guard against scandal or risk suffering.
- 5-5: advantageous new abode.
- 5-4: fortunate business speculation.
- 5-3: visit from a superior.
- 5-2: pleasant excursion on water.

- 5-1: love intrigue.

- 5-0: funeral of nonrelation.

- 4-4: drinking liquor at a distance.

- 4-3: false alarm at home.

- 4-2: beware thieves and swindlers, and, for women, greater danger.

- 4-1: trouble from creditors.

- 4-0: letter from an angry friend.

- 3-3: vexatious double wedding; you will lose a friend.

- 3-2: buy no lottery tickets, do not gamble; you will lose.

- 3-1: a great discovery soon.

- 3-0: an illegitimate child.

- 2-2: a jealous partner.

- 2-1: soon to find something advantageous in street.

- 2-0: lose money or something worth money.

- 1-1: loss of a friend, much missed.

- 1-0: very closely watched by someone you do not suspect.

- 0-0: trouble from a least expected quarter.

(Adapted from Daniels and Stevans 1971.)

These omens are good for one week. After that you must repeat the procedure.

Using Dice

Draw a circle on a tabletop. Shake three dice in a tumbler in your left hand. Toss. Only read dice which fall within the circle.

- 3—pleasant surprise.

- 4—disagreeable surprise.

- 5—stranger will prove a friend.

- 6—loss of property.

- 7—undeserved scandal.

- 8—merited reproach.

- 9—a wedding.

- 10—a christening.

- 11—a death that concerns you.

- 12—speedy letter.

- 13—tears, sighs.

- 14—beware getting drawn into plots and troubles initiated by a secret enemy.

- 15 — immediate prosperity.

- 16 — a pleasant journey.

- 17 — either a trip on water or advantageous dealings with those who have so journeyed.

- 18 — great profit, rise in life, immediate desirable good will.

- Same number twice — news from abroad.

- All dice outside circle — sharp words.

- Dice fall to floor — quarrel almost to blows.

- One die atop another — beware of trouble.

- Fall in triangle — (woman) will receive a ring; (man) will give a ring.

- Fall in straight line — bad luck.

- Fall in shape of a letter — first initial of husband or wife to be.

- If you are aged fifteen to twenty-five, you will have good luck with throwing of dice.

(Adapted from Daniels and Stevans 1971.)

Using Cards

Special fortune telling cards (Tarot) are used and interpreted according to precise design; however, playing cards will serve as well. Each card conveys a special meaning depending upon which question is being asked. These meanings are too lengthy, taken together, to list here. In general, however, clubs portend happiness and rarely carry a bad omen; hearts portend joy, liberality, and good temper; diamonds mean delay, quarrels, and annoyances; and spades signify grief, sickness, and loss of money. A few examples are:

- Ace of clubs — joy, money, good news; of short duration when reversed.

- Ace of hearts — a love letter, some pleasant news; a friend's visit when reversed.

- Ace of diamonds — a letter of importance, good news; bad news when reversed.

- Ace of spades — pleasure; bad news when reversed (when trouble comes, it comes in spades).

Shuffle the cards. Lay the deck face down on the table. Draw one card at a time until you draw an ace. The ace is your omen.

Shuffle the deck; draw twelve cards at random. Interpret according to proper card descriptions.

Shuffle the deck. Lay it face down on the table. Ask a question for which you wish a yes/no answer. Draw one card at a time until you draw an ace. If the ace is red, the answer is yes; black, no.

Remove all the face cards from the deck. Place them under your pillow before going to bed. In the morning, draw one card without looking. King: speedy marriage; Queen: delay or celibacy; Jack: a gay deceiver will give trouble. Diamonds: riches; hearts: true love; spades: thrift; clubs: poverty.

ASTROLOGY

Astrology is not an empirical science, and needs no apology for that fact. Astrology is, like other methods of divination, an organized, systematic, codified application of folk knowledge, along with the legitimate but mystical content of ancient science. It is an accumulated body of esoteric data consisting of the collective mysteries, experiences, and observations of antiquity. For those who might complain that astrology is misguided and uninformed science, we might consider that modern science has its roots in astrology, and also that astrology is not *about science*; it is about the social affairs of people.

The attitude of empiricists toward folklore in general is at its most arrogant over the subject of astrology. But, like folklore, astrology is not science at all: It is a method of divination. What matters is not what astrology explains about the nature of the scientific universe, but what people need in their lives. The lore of science and the lore of folk cultures do not occupy the same universe. When they pretend to do so, they become imposters. Science cannot replace the lore of the folk without becoming a lore and not a science. The lore of the folk cannot replace science; it is not science and should not pretend to be. These two roads to truth do not contradict one another, nor do they encroach upon one another's role in human affairs. Their domains are different, and they need not compete for the attentions of the human soul. Many contemporary tribal cultures illustrate an operational relationship between folklore and science in which each governs in its rightful sphere. Astrology, like any other practice of divination, is consensual. It becomes true for those for whom it has a real utility—and that utility is not about science.

(Occidental) astrological tables divide the calendar year into a zodiac consisting of twelve units, each approximately thirty days in length, which overlap common monthly divisions. (The months themselves are based in ancient astrological practice.) Each unit is called a *house*; each house is ruled (influenced) by certain planets and signs. (These are given in the section on Chinese numerology, p. 165.) A person born under a given sign will be influenced in character, behavior, and fortune by the special characteristics of that sign. The degree of influence and interactive influences of these characteristics on a person, and the degree to which influences from other houses will affect a person, depends upon when and where he or she was born: the day, year, minute, second, and the latitude of the birth location.

The construction of a horoscope is a complicated business. Today, as in ancient times, one must study to be an astrologer, though anyone can dabble, and many people do. Astrology is perhaps the best remaining example, at least in the "developed" world, of the operation of mystery, metaphor, and fascination in practices of divination. (References for both occidental and Oriental astrological information are given in the bibliography; see, for example, Walters 1987; Delsol 1969; Perrottet 1987a; Mark 1970; Parker and Parker 1971; Mayo 1964.)

11

Magic and Superstition

INTRODUCTION

Stories themselves are magical devices, having the power to entrance, transform, transport, and transcend. Magic is the fundamental and unifying element of story content as well. Story characters, actions, possessions, homes, and lands are not of the mundane world. The universe of story is governed by a very different set of rules. This is not to say that stories tell us about that which is unreal, for the stories and their contents are very real. Nor do we have to suspend disbelief in order to find a story acceptable; rather, we make use of a different kind of very human mentality. Story works in that other dimension of mind in which we know through experience, through communion, and through ecstasy and rapture—magic. In stories, magic is mundane reality. The knife of the warrior, embedded in a tree trunk, begins to rust at the moment of his death; the breadcrust and water of the youngest child is transformed into cake and wine; the child of innocence finds strawberries and violets in January's worst storms; animals speak; and children are transformed to swans. Magic is only magic if it is not real.

The following material is presented from the point of view of reason, and is therefore classified as magic (that is, improbable, irrational, or unreasonable). Charms, superstitions, curses, and the like belong to that larger body of folklore and folk practice which also includes stories and storying, and which, in an interesting inside-out maneuver, also operates intact within the larger contexts of stories. While the seemingly magical effects within stories are mundane if viewed from within the context of the storied world, stories and story characters also deliberately make magic—effects that are magical in the story world itself, and that magic is often the old magic of the folklore.

A charm of awful power ...
A spell that's older than the walls long buried,
Of Babylon; Ere Nineveh was dreamed
'Twas old beyond the power of computation.
They are seven, they are seven—seven they are:
They sit by the way. They sleep in the deep:
Down far—
Seven they are!
They are seven, they are seven—seven are they!

Out of the abyss they rise when day
Sinks into darkness.
Seven are they!
Born in the bowels o' the hills,
Evil ones, sowers of ills:
Setters of unseen snares,
Deaf to all pity, all prayers:
Male they are not,
Female they are not,
No wives have they known,
No children begot.
The fiends, they are seven:
Disturbers of heaven
They are seven, they are seven—seven they are!
(Ancient Chaldean conjuration of the seven spirits/demons of
the abyss, in Christian 1969, 431.)

A thorough discussion of what magic is requires side trips into considerations of what is real, and seen and unseen connections between cause and effect. It is complicated enough to say that magic has to do with mysteries—rites which, though we perform them, cannot be explained, because the direct connection between cause and effect is not clear. Because it is not, the whole of the experience seems supernatural. When people do magic, they control powers that cannot be seen to work ends that cannot be directly accounted for.

Whether magic is real or unreal has absolutely nothing to do with whether its effects can be attributed to its causes. Empirical science, which has determined to attack magical practices on these grounds, has entirely missed the mark. Magic is not bad science. Magic, though some of it has taken the form of a pseudoscience, is not about science. It is about people and society. It can exist quite comfortably side by side with science inside the same culture, because it does not occupy the same social space. It has an entirely different utility, although, for individuals who have abandoned magic, science has learned to play both roles.

Magic is real because people agree that it is. It works by consent. All religion is magic, because religion works with things unseen and requires faith. Medicine works when people let it work when they believe. Magic, therefore, uses the forces of nature in a manner that is different from the methods of science. Its principal instrument or tool is the power of the human mind. It works through belief, and sometimes through the effect of altered states of consciousness. Adler says that the spells, chants, and dances are "props" that help to "make" magic, and that the magic itself is the effect caused by the use of such tools (Adler 1986).

DEFINITIONS

Magic is divided into positive, negative, black, and white.

Positive magic. Positive magic is a sending of power designed to create or effect something. A taboo is positive because it prevents an action by an individual which might be harmful.

Negative magic. Negative magic is a repelling of power, a repelling of spells, charms, demons, witches, and other forces which would otherwise act to make a change that one might not desire.

Black magic. Black magic is evil magic which causes harm and which upsets the natural order. It is the force of chaos. Black magic can be both positive and negative. *Positive black magic* sends evil power for the purposes of creating an evil effect. *Negative black magic* repels the forces of good and light. Taken together, both positive and negative black magic work to maintain and extend the influence of undesirable and unsanctioned forces in the world.

White magic. White magic is good magic which causes harmony and well-being and which supports and strengthens the natural order. *Positive white magic* sends good power in order to effect good change. Cures and wonders—miracles—are examples. *Negative white magic* works to ward off evil and to keep the forces and works of witches, demons, and the like at bay.

- A spell or charm which sends to hurt is *positive, black.*
- A spell or charm which sends to help or heal is *positive, white.*
- A spell or charm which works to repel the effects of positive white is *negative, black.*
- A spell or charm which works to repel the effects of positive, black is *negative, white.*

We can see the interaction of these four types of magic with even the simplest of folk charms and remedies.

Sympathetic magic. Spells and charms are believed to work through the unseen cause and effect of *sympathy* (Frazer 1955). Things at some distance from one another can act upon one another because they are connected by an invisible "sympathetic" force. If we activate that force at one end, its effects will be felt at the other.

Homeopathic magic. Homeopathic magic (Frazer 1955) is that form of sympathetic magic which works on the *principle of similarity* and the *principle of imitation*. That is, if we create an effect on some thing that we have in our hands, the same effect will be repeated or imitated in the distant object that is the intended victim or recipient. The practice of creating a fetish which resembles an individual (similarity), then sticking pins into it to bring real suffering to that individual (imitation), is homeopathic magic. (Whatever is done to the image happens exactly to the real person.) Homeopathic magic can be positive white or positive black. Negative white and negative black would be used to block the homeopathic effect, and to prevent the imitation from taking place on the receiving end.

Contagious magic. Contagious magic (Frazer 1955) works by the *law of contact*. Here, resemblance is not important. What is important is the idea that a force can be transmitted to an end point if the point of origin (the object upon which the charm is worked), is a part of the victim or recipient. Thus, one should never leave hair trimmings or nail clippings or one's intimate belongings lying about—someone could take these things and work a charm on you. The magic would get back to you by "contagion" through the parts of your own body, however far removed they might be from you. Like homeopathic magic, contagious magic can be both positive white and positive black, and the negative aspects of black and white would be employed to intercept and cancel charms made by someone else. Thus, if you know that someone has secreted away a crop of your toenail clippings, and you are not feeling well or things are going wrong, you need a countercharm.

TYPES OF PRACTITIONERS

Witches, warlocks, wizards, sorcerers, diviners, healers, and common folk all work magic. The kind of magic practiced makes for less of a distinction between these folk than do the social provinces in which they practice it and the degree of power they claim to be able to control. Even the so-called "high magic" or scholarly magic is not that different in operation from "base magic" (kitchen magic), except for where and on whom it gets practiced, and perhaps the amount and kind of public recognition given to it. (During the witch hysteria, when thousands of common women were burned, the scholar magicians went relatively unscathed.)

The Christian church condemned magic as the work of the devil, yet practiced its own magic within the framework of a doctrine that was no less mystical and mysterious than that of pagan Europe. "Faith in magic was identical with faith in religion" (Walker 1983, 568). The pious called upon Christian deities, the pagans upon the older goddesses and gods. The heretical magician (witch) was the contemporary pagan, usually female, while both faithful practitioners of the magical arts and the ancient pagan knowledge of the occult were respected (Walker 1983). Most peasant magic was crude; often charms and cures were a part of the oral folk culture, while the better educated magician engaged (usually) his craft under the auspices of the church or in connection with the fledgling universities and colleges. The acceptable magician was often literate, and practiced a pseudoscience rather than a mumbo-jumbo.

Of course, the legitimacy of magic in terms of its effects was never at issue. Magic is belief, and the church was not able to tolerate differences in belief, even if practice was differentiated only by the character of a relic or amulet. In addition, the object of much pagan practice was a female deity; her worshippers often observed rite and ritual unclothed, as pagans believed in the magical power of nakedness. To the Christian, exposure of the body, particularly the female body, was sinful, degrading, and immodest. Such unsanctioned magic was deliberately and viciously suppressed.

A brief examination of the sorcerer's magic follows.

THE "MAGICIAN'S" MAGIC

The medicine man is sometimes a transformer. He can change into a wolf, fox, bear, coyote, bird, or whatever other shape is needed to do his work.

One ingredient in a medicine must always remain a secret, or the medicine will lose its potency.

The word has the power to heal, not only through the efforts of calling and making, but also as a physical essence. Early prescriptions consisted of a written incantation or formula, which the patient would then eat.

The "werewolf" is a sorcerer.

One northern sorcerer tried to make fogs by putting a goatskin over his head and saying, "Let it be foggy; Let it be magic." It worked, once, and he was burned for his success.

The sorcerer often has command of greater powers than does the witch. Sometimes a sorcerer can die, then be resurrected from a spell worked on one small part of his body, such as a lock of hair.

The sorcerer or wizard can sometimes change people from one form to another.

The sorcerer/necromancer can raise the dead.

The sorcerer is often the trained priest/diviner who can read the mysterious messages contained in letters, numbers, clouds, smoke, and the like.

The high magician often combines magic with scholarly activity to create a mystical pseudoscience.

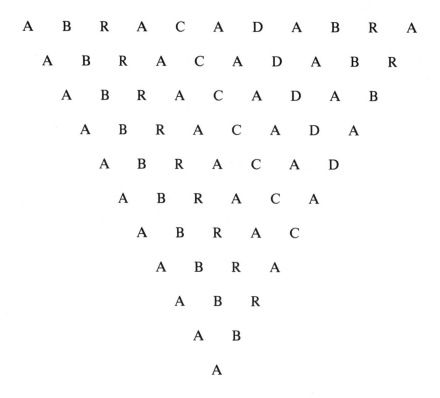

This most powerful of charms (only more recently the jargon of the trickster magician) is to be worn inscribed on a stone or, if one is already ill, on a piece of the purest white wax, and hung about the neck. It is said to be able to repel all evil and ward off all disease. The curative powers of this charm are said to derive from its suggestion of diminishing; the inverted pyramid, constructed all of powerful letters, which "shrinks" from top to bottom, will thus cause a disease to shrink (American Heritage Dictionaries 1986).

Holy water come and bring;
Cast in salt, for seasoning:
Set the brush for sprinkling:
Sacred spittle bring ye hither;
Meale and it now mix together;
And a little oyle to either:
Give the tapers here their light,
Ring the saints-bell, to affright
Far from hence the evil sp'rite.
(In Briggs 1962, 182.)

BELIEFS AND SUPERSTITIONS

Folk traditions include numerous references to magic worked by an unseen, presumably nonhuman, agent. Superstitions and beliefs suggest that magical effects are simply a regular part of the operation of the universe. Superstitions offer observations of unusually caused circumstances and events, cast as rhymes, aphorisms, and formulaic sayings. Though such observations certainly are not scientific, and seem devoid of logic and reason, the power of the human mind, once fixed on a "truth" (whether rational or irrational), to work as a causative agent cannot be discounted. If we believe something to be so, we can make it so, or at least we will "see" it, perhaps as a result of what we are then inclined to predict and perceive to be.

Beliefs from Various Cultures

- A Zuni superstition claimed that anyone who slumped before the tale was told would grow crooked before growing old.

- In China, lions are symbols of luck used to watch over businesses. Belief dictates that two lions, a male and a female, be placed on each side of the front door to watch the money for the business owner. If someone takes a lion, business will go bad because no one is watching the door.

- If someone steals a business's sign, it is considered very bad luck, and the business is closed up (Chinese).

- One of the most prevalent superstitions is found in the old nursery rhyme:

  > Monday's child is fair of face,
  > Tuesday's child is full of grace,
  > Wednesday's child is full of woe,
  > Thursday's child has far to go,
  > Friday's child is loving and giving,
  > Saturday's child must work for a living,
  > But the child that is born on the Sabbath Day
  > Is bonny and blithe, and good and gay.

- How many of us civilized, educated, sophisticated citizens of the twentieth century still check the auspices for the day we were born and either rejoice or frown? There is still a suspicion that this old rhyme has some validity!

- If a baby smiles in its sleep, it is because an angel has just kissed it.

- If a baby cries when he or she is being baptized, it is because of the pain caused by the evil spirits that are being driven out.

- If you place an ear of corn between the mother and her baby before the umbilical cord is cut, the child will have a happy and prosperous life.

- Women aboard ships are bad luck.

- Women in mines are bad luck.

- If a sailor sees a mermaid, the ship will sink with the loss of all hands.

- Since sailing ships were exposed to so many dangers at sea, those who built them always made sacrifices to the sea gods before the ships put out to sea for the first time. During the earlier days of sail, this was done by killing several domestic animals and tossing their carcasses into the sea. In later years, the custom was changed, and now the shipbuilder breaks a bottle of the best available wine or liquor across the bow of the ship just before she enters the water at her launching.

- Every year, on the seventh day of the seventh month, July, the festival of Tanabata is celebrated all over Japan. People write what they most wish for on pieces of paper and pin them to bamboo trees, as they believe this is a lucky time when wishes will come true.

- If you put any article of clothing on inside out in the morning, and then turn it right side out, you will have bad luck all day.

- If you wear any piece of clothing that has thirteen buttons on it, you will have bad luck.

- If you put a new pair of shoes on a table, you will have bad luck.

- If you hear an owl hoot close to your home in the daytime, you will have bad luck.

- If an owl perches near or outside your home, something terrible is on the way—death is knocking on your door (Navaho and Hispanic).

- Handling a frog causes warts (Navaho).

- Contact with snakes causes skin rashes (Navaho).

- If a lizard gets angry, it will chase a person and urinate on his head to poison him (Navaho).

- More than a hundred years ago, bears were a sacred part of Navaho rituals. The animal was considered to have strong psychological power and could hypnotize human beings. Therefore, in traditional Navaho society, there are taboos about touching a bear, its footprints, or anything it had touched.

- Navaho children are taught not to look people in the eye, for fear someone will bewitch them.

- Early Americans believed that sandwiches should always be cut in half so that two triangles will be formed. It was unlucky and unhealthy to cut the sandwiches so that the halves were rectangles. The Trinity was represented by the triangular shape.

- If you put on your left shoe before your right shoe in the morning, you will have bad luck.

- Two-dollar bills are bad luck.

- If a bluebird flies into your house, or if one builds its nest on your property, you will have an unexpected stroke of good luck a short time later.

- You will have thirty days of bad luck if you meet a hunchback on your way to church.

- If you rub the hunchback's hump, you will have good luck ("playing a hunch").

- Whenever your ears burn, it is a sign that someone is talking about you. If it is the left ear, the person is speaking ill of you; if it is the right ear, he or she is praising you.

- Whenever toads and frogs drop from the sky after a heavy rain, the farmers in the area will have an excellent harvest in the fall.

- If a person steps over a fishing pole or line, it means he or she will catch no more fish that day.

- It is bad luck to kill a spider.

- Long-legged spiders mean good luck.

- To kill a cricket is to kill the luck of the house.

- You cannot be harmed by the evil eye if you keep the wishbone of a female hummingbird on your person at all times. If you hang any three wishbones, open end up, over your bed, evil spirits will be unable to harm you while you are asleep.

- The seventh daughter of a seventh son is almost always gifted with spectral sight.

- If you and a companion are forced to walk on opposite sides of a tree, a pole, or any other obstruction in the sidewalk, your friendship will come to an end unless you press your face to some part of the obstruction and say "Bread and butter."

- If a dragonfly lands on your head, it will tangle your hair so badly that it will have to be cut off.

- If a dragonfly flies near your face, it will sew up your lips so tightly that you will never again be able to open them.

- If a girl who catches an apple with her teeth, when she dunks for apples on Halloween, sleeps with the apple under her pillow that night, she will dream of her future husband.

- When both ends of the crescent moon are pointing away from the earth, you will have thirty days of good luck if you spit on the ground three times and then rub the spit into the dirt with the sole of your right shoe.

- If you see the new moon for the first time through a window pane, you will have thirty days of bad luck.

- Friday the thirteenth is a doubly unlucky day. Jesus Christ was crucified on a Friday; there were thirteen people at the Last Supper; and one of them betrayed Jesus Christ for thirty pieces of silver.

- If your saltshakers are full on New Year's Day, you will have an abundance of food in your house the rest of the year.

- If you spill salt at the table, you will have bad luck for thirty days. Take a pinch of the spilled salt with the thumb and forefinger of the right hand and toss it over your left shoulder to offset the bad luck.

- The unmarried female to take the last piece of food from a plate will be an old maid.

- If you put thirteen pieces of the same food on one plate, you will have bad luck for the rest of the day.

- If you serve a wedge of pie with the sharp end pointing toward your guest, he will receive an important letter or telephone call in a short time.

- When one of your teeth falls out, throw it over your left shoulder with your right hand with all your strength. Close your eyes, turn around three times, then look for the tooth. If you cannot find it within five minutes, the tooth fairy will grant you one wish.

- Place a tooth you have lost under your pillow that night and the tooth fairy will replace it with money.

- Expect a visitor if your nose itches.

- If your left hand itches, expect to receive a gift or money.

- If the right hand itches, expect to shake hands with a stranger.

- If the right eye itches, it is lucky. If the left eye itches, expect a disappointment.

- If the joint of the thumb itches, expect an unwelcome visitor.

- If you sing at the table, expect bad luck.
- Misfortunes will come in groups of three.
- On New Year's Day, it is good luck if you eat black-eyed peas, sauerkraut and pork, put a dime under your plate, or wear red garters.
- Rubbing a rabbit's foot is good luck.
- It is lucky for people to sleep with their heads toward the North.

> See a pin, pick it up,
> All day long, have good luck.
> See a pin, let it lay,
> Have bad luck all the day.

- If two people happen to say the same word or phrase at the same time, they must not speak again until each makes a wish, hooks the little fingers together, and says:

> "Needles" "Pins" "Twins" "Triplets" "What goes up the chimney?" "Smoke!"

- If you see a shooting star, make a wish before it vanishes, and the wish is sure to come true.
- Wish on the first star you see at night and recite:

> Star light, star bright,
> First star I see tonight.
> I wish I may, I wish I might,
> Get the wish I wish tonight!"

- It is good luck to see a chimney sweep.
- You can learn to play the banjo if you meet the devil at a crossroads during the full moon.
- If you catch a butterfly and bite off its head, you will get a suit the color of the butterfly.
- Blow dandelion seeds to see how many children you will have.
- Put a dandelion under your chin. If it reflects yellow, you like butter.
- Blow all the dandelion seeds and make a wish. You can tell your sweetheart's initial by how many seeds float: A = 1, B = 2, C = 3, etc.
- When a firefly glows, pinch off the glow and put it on your love's finger for an engagement ring.
- A gap between the top two teeth in a woman is considered beautiful and desirable. She will bring good luck to her husband, especially in obtaining cattle. She has a tendency to be a healer and most likely will have twins (Nigerian).
- If you eat bread crusts, you will get curly hair.
- The Hmong believe that a person's life is bound up with that of a certain animal. The child is carried to a crossroads at exactly midnight and placed on a bed of ashes. His parents await until an animal approaches or is seen or heard nearby. From that point on, the animal is considered the guardian spirit of the child.
- The name of our summer "dog days," the hottest days of summer, comes from ancient times. A brown dog was sacrificed to Sirius, the Dog Star, whose dawn rising was considered the cause of the unbearable heat.

- Cranes are a bird of good omen for all Northern Europeans.
- Happy is the couple whose cottage chimney is the summer home of the female stork (storks bring babies).
- An old English superstition claims that fairies can surreptitiously substitute an ugly changeling for the natural child.
- If you are bitten by a snake, and you kill it, or it is killed immediately, you will not die (Masai).
- When you see a calf running, it means it is going to rain. When a coyote comes to your house and howls, he brings bad news (Cheyenne).
- Raccoon dogs gather in the full moon and play music, beating their big balloonlike bellies as if they were drums (Japanese).
- The morning dew of Midsummer Day has magical properties. Anyone who rolls in it naked can make a wish and may be cured of itching and other maladies (Iceland).
- Legend has it that the swallows of San Juan Capistrano, California, arrive in the spring on St. Joseph's Day and depart on St. John's Day.

Dropping Tableware

- If you drop a fork, you will have a female visitor before the day is over.
- If you drop a knife, the visitor will be a male.
- If you drop a teaspoon, a small child will drop in unexpectedly that day.
- If you drop a tablespoon, the visitor will either be an old man or an old woman.
- (In any case, the visitor will come from the direction in which the handle of the tableware is pointing.)

Weather Reports

- If you see a ring around the moon, a spell of bad weather will follow.
- If a cat washes its face before breakfast, it will rain sometime during the day.
- When cows return to the barn long before their usual time, it will rain very hard in a short time.

> Red sky at night, sailor's delight.
> Red sky in the morning, sailors take warning.
>
> If the sun rises red, the next day will be hot.
> If it sets red, it will not.
>
> Evening red and morning gray, sure sign of a fair day.
> Evening gray and morning red,
> You might as well stay in bed.

- Black flies will not disappear until after the first thunderstorm in June.

- If it rains on Easter Sunday, it will rain on the next seven Sundays.
- If the groundhog sees his shadow anytime during the day on February 2, there will be six more weeks of winter.
- If March comes in like a lion, it will go out like a lamb.

Death

- If a cow moos after midnight, someone in her owner's immediate family will soon die.
- If a bat flies into your house, a very close friend will soon die.
- If a dog howls after midnight, someone in the immediate neighborhood will soon die.
- If someone counts the vehicles in a funeral procession or points his finger at any of them, someone in his family will die before a year has passed.
- If anyone holds an open umbrella over his or her head in the house, a close relative will die within six months.
- If three crows fly over your house, someone very close to you will die within a year.
- Whenever a death occurred in a family, in some rural areas, one of the family was sent out to the beehives to turn them around and tell the bees the sad news.
- Anyone speaking ill of a dead person will lose a close member of his or her own family within a year.

Vampires

- Vampires could change weather at will.
- Vampires were excellent cooks with a fine taste for spices.
- To keep a suspected vampire from rising from the grave after death, the head was cut off and placed between the corpse's legs before burial. Suspects were also buried with sharp sickles across their necks so they would cut their throats if they tried to rise from the grave. Suspects were buried face down so they would dig down rather than up.
- A clove of garlic will ward off vampires.

Wedding Customs

In olden times, people believed that the bride's adornments had mystical value, and tried to grab a piece of her outfit. The bride threw the bouquet away from herself so the crowd would have something to grab for, and she could then escape with her clothes intact. Today, the bridesmaid who catches the bouquet thrown by the bride will be the next person in the wedding party to get married.

The wedding ring worn on the third finger of the left hand is from Egyptian custom handed down by the pharaohs. They believed that the *vena amoris* ran from that finger directly to the heart. Today, the wedding rings that the bride and groom place on each other's fingers symbolize the wish that the union will last forever, since there is no beginning or end in a circle.

There is ancient symbolism in the custom for the bride to wear "something old, something new, something borrowed, and something blue." Most of the bridal clothing is new, as a portent of future plenty. Wearing something old is a sign of continuity with the past. Something borrowed follows the superstition that happiness can rub off, so if you wear a borrowed item from a happily married friend, your marriage will be happy too. Blue is associated with purity, fidelity, and love.

Sew a small pouch filled with a tiny piece of bread, cloth, wood, or a dollar bill into the wedding dress. This is meant to protect against future shortages in food, clothing, and shelter. The dollar bill is a hostage to fortune.

WEDDING CAKES

In early Roman days, a simple wheaten cake was broken during the ceremony. The first morsels were eaten by the bride and groom and the rest of the cake was crumbled over the bride's head in a fertility rite, to guarantee many children and a life of plenty.

By Elizabethan times in England, small sweet buns were a centerpiece on the table. The bride and groom were playfully challenged to kill each other over the cakes, which were stacked into a mountainous bundle. In the seventeenth century, a French chef frosted the small cakes with white sugar so that they held together and stood upright. Today in France, *croquembouche*, a cake composed of cream puffs held together in a cylindrical form with melted caramelized sugar, is still a wedding cake of choice. Today's tiered wedding cake is the result in the United States.

Today it is believed that if the unmarried girls who attend the wedding sleep with a piece of the wedding cake under their pillows, they will dream of their future husbands.

THRESHOLD CUSTOMS

The bride is carried over the threshold because, in the ancient world, it was thought that evil spirits were in the house, unseen but there. The groom carried his bride over the threshold to avoid any demons lurking on the doorstep, and also to keep the bride from tracking in any spirits on the soles of her feet.

In some Hungarian villages, it is still the custom for the wedding guests to escort the bride and groom to their bedroom and then dance around the house nine times to drive away evil spirits. The next day, a married woman's cap is placed on the bride's head and a fire is lighted in the village square. All dance around the fire, but the bride jumps over the flames, thus evading any remaining demons.

Wedding motto: Start as you mean to go on.

RICE THROWING

Although rice, which is an ancient symbol of fertility, is thrown at the newly married couple to ensure that the marriage will be blessed with many children, it also serves other purposes. The evil spirits who attend all weddings will be kept so busy looking for and eating all the tiny grains that they will have no time to cast any spells on the young couple or harm them in any other way.

Today, instead of throwing rice (since birds can die from eating it), it is recommended that people throw bird seed.

TRADITIONS

It will be a happy marriage if the sun shines any time during the day of the wedding.

The old shoes that are a traditional part of the post-wedding ceremony are meant to express the wish that the couple will walk together for a long time.

MARRIAGE BELIEFS

If the groom falls asleep before the bride on the wedding night, he will die before she does. It is bad luck if:

- An uninvited man in uniform is in the church during the ceremony.

- A one-armed relative of the bride attends the ceremony.

- Someone other than the bride is the first to cut into the wedding cake.

- A runaway horse races down the street as the bride is entering the church.

- The bride puts her wedding dress on more than one hour before the ceremony begins.

- The couple's new home burns down before they return from their honeymoon.

- The wedding is held on a Friday or a Saturday.

- The groom does not dance with the oldest female guest at the reception.

- The bride steps over the sill at the entrance to the church with her left foot.

- A dog enters the church before the ceremony is over.

- Anyone sneezes three times during the ceremony.

- The wedding ring is lost.

- A wedding guest appears at the ceremony dressed completely in black.

- If more than three babies less than a year old are at the wedding ceremony.

12

Games

> She had two hairs upon her head;
> One was alive and the other was dead.
> Kathaleena, macaleena
> Uppa sala wala vala
> Oca poca noca was her name.
>
> — Children's traditional

INTRODUCTION

A game is a drama, a play on human circumstances. Some games are dances, some are songs, some are dramatic activity. Games are reenactments of ritual, of work, of daily living, of war, of politics, of historical events, of religious mysteries. Perhaps games arose as the inevitable product of the development of human awareness of self and surroundings, combined with what seems to be the species' characteristic of playfulness. Games are certainly related to the human attributes of reflectivity, creativity, humor, and the ability to solve problems. They may also, to some significant extent, be connected to the human ability to make language, and to the power of language as a creative force in its own right. Gaming and games are important and potent aspects of human behavior. Far from operating only within the isolated province of the worlds of children, games and gaming are in force everywhere in human activity. Games have great social utility, and the understanding of "game" and its various applications insinuates itself into every dimension of human endeavor. The language that we use in the most mundane of circumstances is laced with metaphoric references that prove the ubiquity of play: a game plan, to make points, to be a team player, to be a winner/loser.

Two of the most basic characteristics of game—perhaps its original characteristics—have to do with rules and magic. These two things, within the idea of game, are so interdependent that they seem almost inseparable. They are the elements of creativity upon which a game depends for definition as *game*. As newer forms of adult play and adult-organized children's play abandon these elements to the seductions of commerce, modern games cease to be real games.

Game rules. Little observation is required to see that games have rules. (Of course games have rules!) What is less obvious, but what makes perfect sense once realized, is that the rules of games have the power to create an entirely new reality—a reality which exists only inside the game. The rules also protect that reality against the encroachments and violations of the non-game world. The game becomes the world all around.

Magic. Insides and outsides exist in the universe of games. When we play, and agree to the rules, we create a boundary. We are on the inside; the rest of the world is not. Children are so clearly aware of the invisible line separating in from out that they employ special rules to close a game; anyone who wants to get into the game after it has been closed is "locked out." Adults do this, too, but are less overt about it. In the world of adults, one cannot simply tell someone that they are locked out. Lock-outs are often illegal—no fair.

The inside of the game is magic. Things happen and can be made on the inside that cannot be on the outside. The rules and the very idea of game act as a shield which surrounds the sacred space of the game.

The game may also be a charm. Some games, though today we do not play them with that understanding, may be enactments designed to work sympathetic magic, raise power, or work as repellents of evil.

THE UTILITIES OF GAMES

Games are fun, and provide recreation, but they do not suspend reality altogether. Instead, they replace one reality with another. Sometimes, from the perspective of the altered state of consciousness of the game, we gain a better understanding of all our other activities. The game can be a special window through which we can better see our regular circumstances. It is a place in which we can be allowed to experiment with alternatives without fear of harmful consequence, punishment, or retaliation. The socializing function of the game and play is readily apparent: they help people learn to cooperate, to use strategy, and to solve problems. They also help people to experience the mysteries of their world, to remember their origins, to take necessary responsibilities, and to learn their identities. Games are very empowering, provided that one is *in* the game and not merely a spectator.

WHAT IS A GAME?

In order to limit the field of games eligible for discussion here, we must set some defining criteria. Our criteria are related to who gets to play, and what is the utility of the play. As a consequence, we first exclude so-called games that are spectator sports, on the grounds that the game exists only for those who are in it—a cardinal rule. People who watch others play a game cannot be empowered by the game. The magic does not work on the outside; the magic fails for the spectator. This is not to say that the spectator might not enjoy the experience of watching, nor do we suggest that it is wrong to watch. We are only saying that the sacred space defined by the game takes its very existence from the experiences of the players of the game. The spectator has an entirely different experience. The real game does not exclude; everyone can have a chance to play.

Our second criterion excludes games the sole purpose of which has to do with winning and losing. The principal utilities of games have to do with cooperation, socializing, development of a moral sense, and play with intelligence. While some games do act out memories of battles, these games are not themselves battles. Games which actually *are* battles may not really be games, and may not, despite protest, teach anything but enmity. Many games have teams, winners, and losers, but winning and losing is not the reason for playing the game. The game is played so that people can join together in a mutually empowering experience. A test might work like this: Can we walk away from a game with no feelings of rancor, no concern about who won or lost? Can we truly say, "Well, it's only a game"? Can we truly say that we played for fun? If winning or losing matters to such a degree that we cannot lay down the sword at game's end, then the game may not really be a game.

Our criteria, boiled down to their essentials, have to do with who owns the game and who is empowered by it. In the games of the folk tradition, everyone owns the game and everyone is empowered by it. *Pom Pom Pull-Away*, generic chasing games such as *Tag*, pushing and shoving games such as *Shoving Winter Out* (Vinton 1970), and circle games like *Pass the Shoe* are good illustrations. Everybody plays; everybody has fun; everybody is served by the game according to his or her needs. There may be scrapes and bruises, and egos may get dented when disagreements occur, but the design of the game itself does not work to systematically undermine the worthiness of individuals.

TYPES OF NONSINGING GAMES

The categories used here are those set out by Opie and Opie (1984). These categories are generic, and exhibit many parallels to a listing of universal story motifs. One might, in fact, think of them as play motifs. Additional categories, subcategories, and games are included from Skolnik (1974); Knapp and Knapp (1976); and Newell (1963). Also see Fluegelman (1976) and Vinton (1970).

Chasing Games

The chasing game is universal. Specific versions with variant rules exist, but the common distinguishing feature of all games of chase is the "it." Somebody chases and tries to tag or touch, while other players must keep from being touched.

The basic game. Within a designated space, the it chases and touches another player, who becomes it in his place. There are no outs and no safeties.

Hand substitute variants. The chaser must tag other players with another object—a scarf, stick, ball, rope, or with the hands held to make an effigy of some other object (bull's horns). In some versions, a ball may be thrown at a runner; if it hits her, it constitutes a tag.

Bad touch variants. The touch of the chaser has power. The person tagged must hold the place where he was tagged until another player has been touched. The tag "freezes" a runner, who must stand immobilized.

Immunity from touch variants. A runner cannot be tagged if she is touching a "safety," has both feet off the ground when touched, has assumed a particular posture when touched (*Stoop Tag*), has been able to reach a safety location, or does not have a shadow when touched. In reverse versions, a player loses immunity from touch by stepping across a line or by going into a designated area.

Proliferation of chasers variants. When a person is tagged, he also becomes a chaser, until many chasers run after a few remaining "free" players. In alternate versions, chasers must hold hands, thus making a longer and longer chain (*Chain Tag*).

Suspense start variants. Players do not know when the chaser will begin chasing, and/or do not know who the chaser is. The runners give a signal for the chaser to begin, or runners do not know where the chaser is hiding.

Runner assist variants. One player helps another by diverting the chaser away from another runner and to herself. Players who are free can touch and free those who have been tagged out. In a version of this last, tagged players make a chain, perhaps along a sideline, stretching away from the location (a tree or wall) of "tagged out." A runner can then get to the end of this chain to free several players. In some versions, a runner who goes all the way to the tree or wall to touch the very first person in the chain automatically frees all the others. If the chain is not allowed, a free player must touch each caught player individually. ("Electricity" is the operative principle.)

Chaser disadvantaged variants. The chaser is blindfolded, or has to hop or skip, etc., while the others can run. Alternatives command that the chaser remain seated or be obstructed.

Catching Games

A group of players risks being caught by another or a group of others when they have to run, skip, or hop across a stretch of open ground, usually bounded on either side by parallel lines or walls.

The basic game. Players line up as two facing teams on either side of an open middle ground. On command, often on a particular word in a verse (*Blackberries* in Vinton 1970), players run across in both directions. They have to avoid getting caught. Caught players are out, or have to join the ranks of the catchers.

Chain variants. All runners who are caught must link hands with the catcher.

Movement variants. Players must come across as commanded. "Pom Pom Pullaway, let your horses RUN away" (SKIP away, HOP away, WALK away, etc.).

Immunity variants. The catcher names a color, article of clothing, etc. If a player is wearing this article or color, he can come across without being caught.

Special challenge variants. The catcher names one, two, or three players by name who must then come across. Or the chaser calls across everyone wearing green, etc.

No command variants. Runners run across at will.

Catch by force variants. The catcher must use force to catch; runners are given the option of submitting.

Prisoner rescue variants. Two opposing teams guard rear goals, where they imprison captured opposing players and/or hold a treasure (*Capture the Flag*). The object is to steal the other team's flag and release imprisoned teammates. Prisoner chains can reach out for rescue by "electricity."

Seeking Games

One player, who is it, must try to find other hidden players. These other players are safe as long as they remain undiscovered. Often they must run for a safety (sanctuary) and touch it without being tagged.

The basic game. A single player, chosen by lot, blindfolds herself or hides her eyes, then counts to a designated number, while others secret themselves away in hiding places. When finished counting, the seeker must announce that she is seeking. Players she finds are out. Others that she does not find must make a run for a specified tree or wall either before the seeker tags them or before the seeker can tag the safety.

Unequal numbers of seekers/hiders variants. One seeker looks for all other players; one seeker is assisted by those he finds; one hider is sought by all other players; hiders are automatically caught when found; hiders must still be tagged when found. In one version, all players individually seek one player and hide with her upon finding her.

Equal numbers of seekers/hiders. In this variation, there is a hider team and a seeker team. Seekers try to find and capture hiders; hiders must get back to the starting place or safety. Hiders try to smuggle a particular object back to the starting place. Hiders chase seekers when found. Hiders must release team members already held captive.

Hunting Games

These are no-boundary team games in which one team chases and catches the other. The hunters are guided in their search for the hunted: the hunted wave scarves, make an agreed-upon noise, make a trail for the hunters to follow, or leave signs. When played at night, the hunted may blink flashlights to tell the hunters of their whereabouts.

Racing Games

Racing games are those in which players must reach the end of a course first. Sometimes ability to skip, run, jump, or hop fast is not a factor in the outcome.

Hesitation start variants. Runners do not know when the signal to start will be given.

Command and condition variants. In order to be able to move forward, a player must satisfy a certain condition (be wearing a named color, etc.), or must move only in the direction, as far as, and with the movement specified by a third-party player (*Simon Says*).

Stop and start variants. The catcher gives a command to start/stop (*Red Light/Green Light*). Any runner who cannot stop on command, but takes an extra step, is out. Or, runners may go only when the catcher's back is turned. If a runner is caught moving when the catcher faces forward again, he is out.

Two-competitor variants. Two players may run against only one another. Sometimes all players run against one.

Different location start variants. Players race from different starting points, or keep changing places, while the odd one out runs to claim one of these locations.

Duelling Games

Duelling games pit two contestants against one another.

Contests of strength. Arm-wrestling, leg-wrestling, lifting one's opponent from a sitting position while sitting oneself, tagging with sticks, cockfighting, pushing an opponent off a branch (a diving board), piggy-back fighting.

Contests of skill and nerve. Knife throwing, unseating one another from bicycles.

Contests of fortitude. Knuckle mashing or bashing, finger rapping, hitting the back of the opponent's hand, trying to slap the backs of one another's hands, foot stamping, wrist hitting with *Rock, Paper, Scissors*.

Proxy duels. Duels with stalks or sticks; smashing acorns or chestnuts together.

Exerting Games

Exerting games include attacking and defending positions, *Crack the Whip*, tug of war, breaking out of a circle, pushing others off a mound of dirt, breaking through a line of opposing players (*Red Rover*), breaking through a pair of players, varieties of leap-frog, vaulting sticks, long jumping, and holding a difficult pose.

Daring Games

In daring games, players take dares to do as commanded or are challenged to do what a leader does (sometimes leading to the attempting of foolhardy stunts). One player, chosen by lot, has to do as commanded. Players see who will be bravest, or last to cross a line to safety (*Chicken*).

Guessing Games

Players may run, chase, catch, etc., if they can answer a question correctly or identify an unseen fellow player. In some games, the guesser is punished until she can make a correct guess.

Acting Games

In the acting games, players assume roles, then act out a standard ritual play. In some of these games, a chase is the result; in others, one player ends by having to seek and find the others (*Fox and Chickens*). Often the "mother's" children are stolen, and she must rescue them.

Pretending Games

In these dramas, children choose (usually adult) roles: doctor, nurse, teacher, mother and father, then act them out. Though these dramas will have the standard features of child expectation and perception, plots are inventive. Children step in and out of character to make and redefine the rules of the play. In some games, children become animals or book characters, or act out adult activities such as war.

Ball Games

Newell (1963) provides a somewhat different set of categories: love games, history games, work plays, animal games, motion games, humor games, mythology games, and ball games. Many of his listings appear under Singing and Dancing Games (p. 205 in this treatment); however, his list of games played with balls is worth note. He describes *Stool Ball* (one player protecting a stool from being hit with a ball thrown by other players); *Call Ball* (a player throws a ball against a wall while naming another player who must catch it); *Haley Over* (players on either side of a house throw a ball back and forth); *Roll Ball/Hat Ball* (a ball is rolled into a hat or hole belonging to one of a group of players); *Corner Ball* (*Four Square*); and *Marbles*.

Other Games

Jumprope. Skolnik (1974) gives directions for a host of jumprope terms that refer to turning and jumping styles and techniques (Back Door, Black Sheep, Bluebells, Bullets, Bumps, Call in — Call out, Continues!, Crossie, Double Dutch, Enders, Fireys, French Ropes, Front Door, High Water, Hopsies, Hot Peas, Hot Pepper, Kiss, Licking, Loops, Low Waters, Mustard, Old Maid, One Hundred, On Time, Out My Window, Over the Moon, Over the Water, Pass the Baker, Pennies, Pepper, Red-hot Bricks, Salt, Scolding, Scotch, Single Jumping, Skin, Steady Enders, Straight Rope, Turners, Up the Ladder, Vinegar, Wavie, Whipping, White Sheep). He classifies jumprope rhymes, many of which seem to have been adapted to jumprope from other traditions, into rhymes which count, predict, fortune tell, or call in, and those which specify multi-jumping, pushing, (dramatic) action, and fast jumping (*pepper*) (Skolnik 1974).

Hop scotch. Players draw one of several varying diagrams on a flat, hard surface. The figure in use will depend upon the region of the country in which the game is played. The figure must be approximately twelve feet long. Players throw stones into the squares each by turns, beginning with square one. If the player's stone lands in square one, she must hop the entire figure, stooping to retrieve her stone on the way back. She may not step on a line, on a square that contains another player's marker (stone), or in the square containing her own. Where hopping must be done on one foot, she may not lose balance and have to touch the ground with any other part of her body. If she does, she loses her turn and must leave her marker in its place. If she does a round successfully, she can throw her marker to the next square in sequence. If she misses, she must retrieve the marker and wait for another turn. The winner is the first player to complete the figure. Sample hopscotch figures appear in Knapp and Knapp (1976).

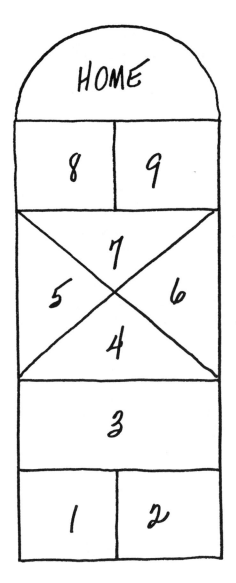

SCHOOLYARD
MILWAUKEE
1955

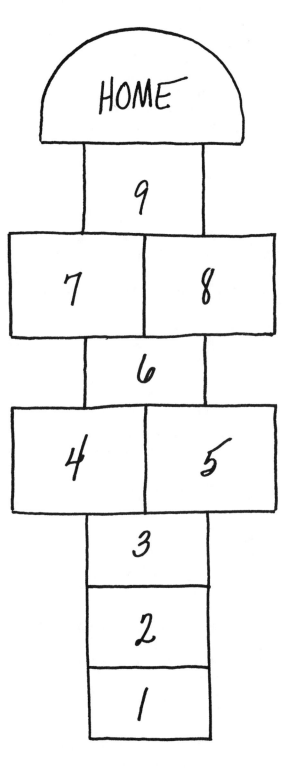

DRIVEWAY
MONTANA
1987

Jacks. Jacks is a game of skill in which each player in turn must pick up a set of jacks, first each singly (onesies), then in pairs (twosies), then in triplets (threesies), etc. Each pick-up must be done to the bounce of a small rubber ball. The player tosses the ball up, picks up the jacks, and catches the ball after a specified number of bounces. All this must be done one-handed. As the game progresses, the manner in which the ball is bounced changes. The maneuver called "jump the fence" ("over the moon") requires that the player scoop up the jacks, then jump the hand over the ball before catching it. "Around the moon" explains itself.

Ball bouncing. Ball bouncing is a game of skill. The rules change and the maneuvers become more difficult as the game advances. Bouncers usually recite rhymes to establish a rhythm. A familiar routine is swinging the leg over the ball while saying:

> One, two, three O'Leary,
> Four, five, six, O'Leary,
> Seven, eight, nine, O'Leary,
> Ten, O'Leary postman!

Marbles. A discussion of the intricacies of marbles would require another volume. Suffice to say that matters of propriety, making of rules, and determining of spoils occupies much attention. Knapp and Knapp (1976) list several variants of marble games: Chase, Shooting marbles from a circle, Line, Chinese, Pots and Ring, Bombsies, Poison, and Marble Shoe.

Clapping games. Clapping games are games of speed and skill. Chanted rhymes accompany this play, and hands and arms fly to prescribed motions. Clapping is usually done in pairs.

>   /   /   /   /
> Did you ever, ever, ever,
>   /   /
> In your long-legged life,
>   /   /
> See a long-legged sailor
>   /   /
> With a short-legged wife.
>
> No, I never, never, never,
>
> In my bow-legged life,
>
> Saw a knock-kneed sailor,
>
> With a spider-legged wife.

Changes to this verse include all "leggeds," in scrambled combinations: bow-legged, knock-kneed, spider-legged, wobble-legged, one-legged, etc. The clap motions incorporate the look of the different kinds of legs.

Columbus went to sea, sea, sea,
To see what he could see, see, see.
And all that he could see, see, see,
Was the bottom of the deep blue sea, sea, sea.

Kathaleena, macaleena,
Uppa sala wala vala
Oca poca noca was her name.
She had two eyes in the front of her head;
One was green and the other was red.
Kathaleena ...
She had two teeth in the front of her mouth,
One pointed north and the other pointed south.
Kathaleena ...
She had two hairs upon her head;
One was alive and the other was dead ...

Reverse catch games.

I AM A GOLD LOCK.
I am a gold key.
I AM A SILVER LOCK.
I am a silver key.
I AM A BRASS LOCK.
I am a brass key.
I AM A MONK LOCK.
I am a monkey.

I WENT UP ONE STEP.
So did I.
I WENT UP TWO STEPS.
So did I.
I WENT UP THREE STEPS.
So did I.
I WENT UP FOUR STEPS.
So did I.
I SAW A CAT.
So did I.
I SAW A RAT.
So did I.
THE CAT ATE THE RAT.
So did I.
(Opie and Opie 1959.)

String figure games. The most common string figure game is *Cat's Cradle*, played with two people. Many other string figures have been recorded in Jayne (1962). Some of the more practiced ones are Candles, Crows Feet, Lightning, and My Grandmother's Bra. Children will occasionally duel with string figures—a contest to see who can make the most, taking turns, and allowing no repeats.

Puzzle games. Puzzle games include mazes, number teasers, magic word squares, dot riddles, and more (Kaufman 1940).

Word and letter games. Word games and letter games may be anagrams, rebuses, riddles, charades, and more (Shipley 1960).

SINGING AND DANCING GAMES

Singing and dancing games are games that are built into songs or that are a part of a singing dance.

Song Games

Cumulative patterns. Children, Go Where I Send Thee; The Green Grass Grew All Around; Hi Ho the Rattlin' Bog; The Ford Song; The Peanut Song; The Ladies in the Harem; The Wind Blow East; Bought Me a Cat; By'm Bye; On This Hill; There's a Hole in the Bottom of the Sea; When I First Came to This Land; The Barnyard Song; The Greenberry Tree; There Was an Old Lady; She'll Be Comin' Round the Mountain; Old MacDonald; The Twelve Days of Christmas; The Twelve Apostles; The Horse Went Around; There Was a Man and He Was Mad; Green Bottles; Roll Over, Roll Over; Wiggle the Wool; Mrs. Murphy's Chowder; Once an Austrian Went Yodeling; Eyewinker; John Brown's Body; The Instrument Song.

Language invention songs. I Love My Shirt; Mary Wore Her Red Dress; Circle Left; Frog's in the Meadow; Here We Are Together; Sally Go Round the Sun; Down Came a Lady; Jim Along Josie; Here Sits a Monkey; Clap Your Hands; All Around the Kitchen; Little Bird, Little Bird; Walk Along John; Old Mister Rabbit; Who's That Knockin' at My Window?; The Barnyard Song; A-Huntin' We Will Go; The Mailboat; London Hill; Galloping Horses; When I First Came to This Land; The Greenberry Tree; The Peanut Song; Oh, Watch the Stars; The Wind Blows East; Such a Getting Upstairs; There's a Little Wheel A-Turnin' in My Heart; I Got a Letter This Morning; Roll That Brown Jug; Old Molly Hare; Sweet Water Rollin; This Old Man; Toodala; By'm Bye; What Shall We Do When We All Go Out?; Oh, Oh, the Sunshine; Juba; Hop, Old Squirrel; Do, Do, Pity My Case; Skip to My Lou; The Train Is A-Comin'; When the Train Comes Along; Deep Blue Sea; The Tide Rolls High; If I Had the Wings of a Turtledove; Oh, You Can't Get to Heaven; Roll, Jordan, Roll; Throw It out the Window; Polly Wolly Doodle.

Swapping (echo) songs. Who's That Knockin' at My Window?; What Shall We Do When We All Go Out; How Old Are You?; Billy Barlow; Did You Go to the Barney?; Blow Boys, Blow; Old Molly Hare; Mommy Buy Me a China Doll; The Button and the Key; Milking Pails; Who Built the Ark?; Jenny Jenkins; There's a Hole in the Bucket; What Shall We Do with a Drunken Sailor?; Who Killed Cock Robin; Soldier, Soldier, Won't You Marry Me?; Buffalo Boy; The Deaf Woman's Courtship; Henery My Boy; The Cutty Wren.

"Bad taste" songs. Mrs. Murphy's Chowder; The Tattooed Lady; On Mules We Find; Pink Pajamas; The Hearse Song; My Bonnie; There'll Be a Hot Time in the Old Town; The Cow Kicked Nellie; Johnny Vrobeck; The Pig and the Inebriate; Ol' Joe Clark; The Ship Titanic; Throw It Out the Window; Junior Birdmen; My Nuthouse; Do Your Ears Hang Low?; In a Cabin in a Wood; Green; Bottles; 100 in the Bed; 100 Bottles of Beer; The Ant Song; The Ford Song; The Peanut Song; The Ladies in the Harem; The Horse Went Around.

Rounds. Rose, Rose; Music Alone Shall Live; Sarasponda; One Bottle Pop; Little Tommy Tinker; A Boat, A Boat; Row Row Row; Sandy McNab; Banbury Ale; Now We'll Make the Rafters Ring; Christmas Is Coming; Zum Gali Gali; Ducks on a Pond; Heigh Ho, Nobody Home.

Ballads. Bluebeard; Clementine; Shootin' with Rasputin'; The Ship Titanic; The Mermaid; The Crocodile; Bow Down; The Greenland Whale Fishery; Polly Von; Barbara Allen; The Turkish Roveree; The Farmer's Curst Wife; The Fox Went Out; As I Stepped Out One Evening; The Grey Goose.

Song/Dance Games

Line games. Milking Pails; Jennie Jenkins; Paper of Pins; Walking up the Hillside; Jenny Jones; The Butcher's Shop; Hark! The Robbers; Queen Mary.

Circle games. Green Gravel; Poor Mary Sits A-Weeping; The Farmer in the Dell; Where Has My Little Dog Gone?; Skip to My Lou; Dona Rosa; Marchin' Round the Levee (Valley); Shoo Fly; Dollar, Dollar; Ring on a String; Bluebell, Bluebell; Four in a Boat; Buffalo Gals; Did You Ever See a Lassie?; Pick a Bale of Cotton; Knick Knack (This Old Man); Roselil; Pig in the Parlor; A Tisket, A Tasket; Turn the Glasses Over; Send My Brown Jug Down to Town; Pass the Shoe; Farm Boy's Bonny; Old Joe Clark; Oats, Peas, Beans and Barley Grow; Fox in a Box; Old Roger; Skating Away; Hullabaloo; Lady on the Mountain; Draw a Bucket of Water; B-I-N-G-O; One Morning in May; Trick-A-Ma-Jig; Jump Jim Crow; King William Was King George's Son; Push the Business On; Two Jolly Sailor Boys; Wall Flowers; Sally Go Round; The Two Pigeons; Ring-A-Ring-O-Roses.

Reel-Type games. Old Lady Sally; Turkey in the Straw; Down the River; Willowbee; The Grand Old Duke of York; Way up the Holler; Old Joe Clark; O Belinda; Goin' to Boston; Paw-Paw Patch; Weevily Wheat; The Bear Went over the Mountain; Charley over the Water.

Catching games. London Bridge; Open the Gates; I Want to Be a Farmer; How Many Miles to Bethlehem?; Paw-Paw Patch.

Team games. The Roman Soldiers; Here We Come Gathering Nuts in May; Walking up the Hillside.

Winding games. The Allee Allee O; Wind up the Apple Tree; How Many Miles to Bethlehem?

Rough and tumble games. The Allee Allee O; Wind up the Apple Tree.

Pairs games. Four in a Boat; Up on a Mountain; Old Woman; Buffalo Gals; Happy Is the Miller; Pop Goes the Weasel; Coffee Grows on a White Oak Tree; Captain Jinks.

Dramatic play games. Old Roger; When I Was a Young Girl; Jenny Jones; Here We Go Round the Mulberry Bush; Annie the Miller's Daughter; My Good Old Man; Froggie Went A-Courtin'; Little Brown Jug; Pick a Bale of Cotton; When I Was Single; Old Woman; The Cooper of Fife; King of the Barbarees; The Two Pigeons.

History games. Three Dukes A-Riding; The Rovers; Riflemen of Bennington; King William; The Noble Duke of York; The Roman Soldiers; King of the Barbarees; Queen Mary; Captain Jinks.

Chasing games. Oh Where Has My Little Dog Gone?; Che' Weh; Frog's in the Middle (Meadow).

Choosing games. The Farmers; Oats, Peas, Beans and Barley Grow; The Farmer in the Dell; One Morning in May; King William Was King George's Son.

Odd man out games. Oats, Peas, Beans and Barley Grow; Rosie; Darling Rosie; I Want to Be a Farmer; Four in a Boat; Pig in the Parlor; A Tisket, A Tasket; Turn the Glasses Over; Carousel; Farm Boy's Bonny; Send My Brown Jug Down to Town.

Follow the leader games. Hokey Pokey; Did You Ever See a Lassie; B-I-N-G-O; Looby Loo.

Other Dramatic Play

- Chick-Ma-Craney-Ma-Crow (a witch drama).

- Molly Bright (a witch drama).

- Old Tom (a play on the Circe story in *The Odyssey*).

- Tug-of-War (see Vinton [1970] for "Pushing Winter Out" and "Ptarmigans Against the Ducks," seasonal and sun calendar games).

COUNTING OUT AND CHOOSING RITUALS

Introduction

Games work by social consent. Players who agree to play a game cannot always proceed directly to the game itself without first negotiating terms. Certain preliminary formalities must sometimes be observed. Everyone must agree to the play, to the rules of the play, and cooperate in assignment of roles which exist in the game—leader, captain, "it." Consequently, one game often begins with the playing of another. The formula beginning that initiates a game provides the consensus necessary to the success of the game. Unadulterated children's play is not about winning, losing, or final scores. It is about society and about cooperation in a mutual effort; hence the often-rigid invocation of the game in order for the game to work without argument. Ritual beginnings are especially necessary for games in which one player must be it.

It is a role to be avoided. The it must do the chasing or catching and is often left alone while the other players hide. Though children can leave a game behind, knowing that it is only a game, while they are in the play, the game has a reality of its own. Players run from the it with genuine purpose, screaming in terror. The it is at once an outcast and a figure of power in the game. The touch of the it catches, freezes, or kills. Once a player is selected as the it, the object of the game has to do with staying free, while the it tries to become free by transferring the odious role of untouchable to another player. Within the context of the game, the power of the it engenders real fear, perhaps the same kind of titillation experienced while watching a horror movie.

The Opies (Opie and Opie 1969) observe that the it may represent an evil or supernatural being: a witch, a wolf, the devil, the Evil One. Since naming the Evil One or evil power was taboo in Western Europe, and still is in many cultures, people simply said "he" or "him." Many names for it in old games still in use may be references to the powers of evil. The Opies list numerous curious versions of the name *it*, most of which reflect superstitious origins, and which in turn raise questions about the ancient meanings of games of chase, tag, and other play employing an it. Chants and ritual game-initiating procedures may also recall routines that developed in ancient times in order to randomize the selection of a sacrificial victim from a group of qualified individuals. The it might have been the one chosen to propitiate a water spirit during the construction of a bridge, to be walled into the foundation of a new building in order to ensure its strength, or to be burned or otherwise killed for religious purposes (Knapp and Knapp 1976). (Walling a human sacrifice into a building was a common practice in pre-Christian Europe. Some fortifications and "common houses" required four victims, one per corner of the structure.) Perhaps, once the individual was selected as it, he or she ceased to exist for friends and relatives, and became outcast immediately, already beyond reach of the living.

The unpopularity of the role of it in contemporary children's games is deep and intense. (Some children *want* to be it, because they like to exercise the power associated with the role, but the role itself is not modified.) Since the traditions of child society tend to be exclusively oral (dependent upon memory), conservation of form through repetition rather than original invention is valued. Children are, therefore, a most useful source of historical material. The it in children's games, and the manner in which children react to and act out the role, may be a memory, preserved in play, of a more terrible reality.

There are many variations on the name for *it*:

- *It* (most widely used in Great Britain and the United States). Also *on it*, *on*, *hit*, or *het*.

- *Wolf* (Germany and France).

- *El Dimoni* (Spain).

- *Oni* (Japan; a reference to a witch or demon).

- *Old Mr. Wolf*, *Old Mother Witch*, *the Devil* (Great Britain; however, in very limited use, since naming the evil one is taboo).

- *He* (Great Britain; also *hee* or *'e*, often thought to be *E*).

- *Catcher* (Great Britain; very restricted use).

- *Daddy* (Great Britain; very restricted use).

- *Done* (Perth; "You're done," meaning, "You're it").

- *Has it on* (Orkney; a reference to having the "touch" on you; then you are it and must put it "on" someone else).

- *Het* (Holland).

- *Him* (Shetland).

- *In* (Devon).

- *King* (the chief player in a game; king is not, apparently, the same role as it. The king is the leader, the captain).

- *Man, mannie, old man* (Great Britain).

- *On, on it* (Great Britain; the player who has the special and awesome power of it in a game. He or she attempts to be rid of this power by putting it "on" another player; the touch of the it is imbued with evil power).

- *Outer* (Scotland, parts of England; the "outer" is the outcast, the player who must be separated from all the other players).

- *Tag, Tagger, ticker, tig, tigger, tiggy* (Great Britain, Scotland).

- *Ten* (Great Britain; regional).

- *Touch* (rare in contemporary play; old form).

- *Under* (Great Britain; regional).

- *Up* (Great Britain; regional).

(See Opie and Opie 1969.)

Even in contemporary play, the *it* remains a powerfully negative archetypal figure in the game. Though children today may not identify the it with some form of evil, or with the terror of being chosen for sacrifice, they are acting on the memory of some old fear. (This author has observed three-year-olds playing *Duck-Duck-Goose*. Though the children enjoy the game of chase, nobody wants to be the goose, an it. What kind of combination of human mind and folklore is at work such that children of three, who cannot be told such things, already know them?) It is taboo: a powerful, frightening, untouchable evil, a state to be avoided. The malignancy of the it can be spread by touch. Historical origins excepted, the it is, at least, the worst among bad guys. Nobody wants to be it. Nobody wants to be the one to have to say "you're it" without the protection of a procedure to make the choice random.

In the lore of children, many forms of counting off, or choosing work in the manner of divination practices. Just as no child wishes to be it, no child wishes to be responsible for choosing who the it will be, particularly if she has to choose someone other than herself. The common practice of yelling "not it" ("not on") and bestowing the title of it or on upon the slowest and last to yell can lead to dispute, as can tests of endurance or of who flinched. Divination works to eliminate dispute. Counting off rhymes are obligatory rituals that cast the blame for choosing who will be taboo on some higher power. Game-starter formulas serve the same social purposes for children that similar divination routines serve for adults. (If the it was originally a sacrificial offering, then choosing routines which removed selection from human control would have been essential.)

The Opies (1969), Newell (1963), and other collectors describe many pregame rituals which children conduct with extreme care and precision. Formulas for starting games are games of chance. The blinded player who points and turns in the center of a circle of players, who throws a ball to hit a player at random, or who bounces a ball through the legs of one hapless participant is a version of the spinning bottle or the wheel at the gaming table. The game of chance is also replicated in guessing procedures. The chooser selects a number, color, or holds up a number of fingers behind his back. The unfortunate whose guess matches this choice is it. Quite often, the chooser will have been the it in the previous round, and hence is exempted from the choosing ritual for the next game.

Choosings

One player dips her hand in mud. The other players each then choose a finger. When the muddy hand is displayed, the player who has chosen the finger with the most mud is it.

One player wets all his fingers, then rubs his hand in the dirt. As with the preceding method, the players choose fingers. The player whose choice is the wettest (dirtiest) is it.

While all the other children turn away, one player makes as many identical piles of dirt as there are players, hiding a stone in one of the piles. Each player then chooses a pile and picks it up. The player who picks the stone is it.

One player makes a pool of spit on the back of her hand, then whacks it with an index finger. The player in whose direction the spit flies is it.

Drawing lots, cuts, or straws is common practice. It seems to be the operation of choice in literary reference, and is a preferred method for choosing an it or for settling disputes in many cultures. The it is sometimes the person who is charged with an unpopular job. Just as children do not want to be it in a game, adults do not want to take on a dangerous or unpleasant duty.

ODD MAN OUT

The "odd man out" ("chinging-up"; Opie and Opie 1969) routine is known in the United States as *Rock, Paper, Scissors* and by many other titles in many other countries: *Ching, Chanh, Cholly*; *Dish, Dash, Dosh*; *Hick, Hack, Hock* (parts of England); *Jan, Kan, Pon* (Japan). It may have its antecedents in the finger flashing games recorded in Egyptian tomb paintings dating to 2000 BC (Opie and Opie 1969). The same game was played for purposes of choosing in ancient Greece and Rome, and was used by the gods themselves to divine the unfortunates who would have to undertake some unpleasant toil.

Players chant three ritual words, usually raising and lowering fists with each. (Often, a player will raise one fist, then slam it down against the open palm of the other hand.) On the down stroke accompanying the last word, each player makes one of three established hand signals, which are then interpreted in order to determine a winner.

Scissors: Fist with forefinger and middle finger extended and separated, to resemble an opened scissors.

Rock: Fist.

Paper: Hand open, palm down, fingers together and extended.

Formula: Scissors cut paper; paper covers rock; rock breaks scissors.

Players divide into pairs. Each pair does the procedure until a winner emerges. (If one player gives the rock signal, and the other the sign for scissors, the rock wins: rock breaks scissors. Two identical signals "thrown" together result in a draw.) Winners from the first round pair off again; eventually, only two players remain. The winner of this last match is it. In this type of reverse catch, the losers are the lucky ones.

In many parts of the world (especially the United States and Great Britain, China, Japan, and other Oriental countries), the hand signals are the same, though the words or syllables accompanying the game differ (Opie and Opie 1969). Some folk cultures employ different objects in sets of three. Indonesians use earwig, elephant, and man (Opie and Opie 1969). Enterprising gamesters in the United States have borrowed this old idea for the game of *Giants, Dwarves, Wizards* (Giants stomp dwarves; dwarves frighten wizards; wizards make giants disappear). The idea of the triangle of objects of equal and unequal power is an ancient one, and an interesting play with paradox.

COIN TOSSING

Coin tossing is universally practiced. Eliminations are often accomplished in pairs, as in *Rock, Paper, Scissors*. Or all players may flip coins simultaneously. If "tails" has been established as the losing side, then all tails are out. All "heads" must flip again. Eventually, only one player remains. If all coins on a particular flip come up tails, or all heads, it is a bad sign — perhaps then the game should not be played.

STONE HIDING

Choosing is also accomplished by hiding of stones. One player holds both hands behind her back. One hand holds a stone (marble, coin). Another player must guess which hand is empty in order to be out. The player who chooses the stone is it. Because stones sometimes move from one hand to another after a choice has been made, this method requires some regulation. Sometimes a player will stand behind the stone holder to ensure that no willful manipulation takes place; or the stone holder must hold both hands forward in view of the one who has to guess. If this last method is used, the hands are held in fists, with wrists flexed down and backs of hands facing out. The stone must also be small enough to keep from making one hand look too big. Even so, the guesser will often inspect the hands carefully to try to detect differences. A guesser who spends too much time deliberating will suffer threats and verbal abuse from the others.

Counting Out

Counting out routines are games of elimination by chance. The first player counted out could become the it, but ordinarily counting outs are reverse catches. The players counted out are winners, because they do not have to stand in the circle to be counted again and run the ever-increasing risk of being the last player left, or it. In some counting outs, the player (priest?) who does the chanting and counting is immune. In most formulas, however, the center player must also count himself.

Though many counting rhymes in common use do not name numbers (any nursery rhyme, rhythmic child invention, or commercial jingle will do), verses with roots in old folk practice actually do count. Most of these rhymes are distortions of real number names. Those which play on contemporary language forms are more easily recognized as counts, however fanciful.

One-ery, two-ery, tickery, seven,
Hallibo, crackibo, ten and eleven,
Spin, span, muskidan,
Twiddle-um, twaddle-um, twenty-one.
(Opie and Opie 1951.)

Counting rhymes whose distorted numbers derive from older forms or from ancient languages sound more like gibberish. Newell, writing in 1963, expressed some uncertainty that such rhymes were anything more than meaningless nonsense, and suggested that they might not contain any significant historical or linguistic content other than that imposed upon them by folklorists. Children in the United States call these rhymes "Indian counting," because Native Americans living on the Eastern seaboard learned them from white settlers and then were heard using them (Newell 1963). In England, children call the same rhymes "Chinese counting" (Opie and Opie 1951; 1969). The forms of such rhymes as "Eenie, Meenie" and "Intery, Mintery" are Indo-European in origin (Newell 1963; Opie and Opie 1951, 1969).

Ena, mena, mona, my,
Panalona, bona, stry,
Ee wee, fowl's neck,
Hallibone, crackabone, ten and eleven,
O-U-T spells OUT!
(United States [Newell 1963].)

Eny, meny, mony, my,
Tuska, leina, bona stry,
Kay bell, broken well,
We, wo, wack.
(Massachusetts [Newell 1963].)

Ene, tene, mone, mei,
Paster Lone, bone, strei,
Ene, fune, herke, berke,
Wer? Wie? Wo? Was?
(North Germany [Newell 1963].)

Counting out is the ritual of choice for beginning games in which someone must be taboo. Child folk cultures name the practice differently from country to country and region to region (Opie and Opie 1969):

- "Clappin' out" (Scotland; child reference to choosing by lot).

- "Counting a pie" (Aberdeen; also, in the nineteenth century, counting out of fingers, after each player puts a finger into one player's cap).

- "Counting out" (most common term in Scotland, North England, Canada, and the United States).

• "Dipping" (Great Britain). The term is derived from the practice of the counter beginning each round of counting with a count to the ground on "dip":

> Dip
> Eeny, meeny, miney, mo.
> Catch a tiger by the toe.
> If he hollers, let him go.
> Eeny, meeny, miney, mo.

The object of the dip to the ground before beginning the rhyme may be to make the ritual seem less under the arbitrary control of the counter, and thus more magical (Opie and Opie 1969). Dipping was observed in practice in the nineteenth century, but did not come into general use until the 1940s. The term "dip" refers to specific counting out rituals; "One Potato, Two Potato" is a dip. In France, the term is "pouce."

• "Dishing up" ("dipping up," "dipping out").

• "Picking" (West Riding; older forms include "picking out," "knocking out").

• "Telling out" (telling out rhymes are called "tells").

• "Titting out" (southern Scotland) (Opie and Opie 1969).

ONE-ROUND COUNTS

More straightforward counting out procedures identify the it on the first round, by recitations of the letters of the alphabet, chanting of sequences of numbers, or use of simple formula verses. First-out-as-it routines seem less magical. They certainly are less trustworthy, in that a counter can possibly choose the it beforehand by doing some preliminary calculation.

A B C D E F G H I for IT!

A B C D E F G H I J K L M N O P Q R S T U means YOU! (U are OUT!)

A E I O U means YOU!

A B C D E F G H I J K L M N O P Q R S T U are IT!

1 2 3 4 5 6 7 8 9 10 11 12 13 14 15 16 17 18 19 20 21 is IT!

One, two, sky blue; all out but YOU!

Red, white, and blue; all out but YOU!

Tom Tit; you are IT! (Opie and Opie 1969.)

ELIMINATION COUNTS

Elimination counts are more equitable; they remove control of the outcome from the counter. In an elimination count, the counter, like the diviner, is more a manager of a randomizing procedure than an arbitrator. Elimination routines take on magical qualities, as the counter removes one child after another from the count, until only one remains—the it. The outcomes of eliminations which count each player out twice (two fists), or five or ten times (five or ten fingers), are that much more removed from the control of the counter, and their magical powers are multiplied. Counts that ask the players for choices of numbers or letters add a second randomizing effect. The memory of the belief in the working of divine authority through the exercise is, perhaps, illustrated in the following elimination rhyme:

> Dip
> Ip, dip, sky blue,
> Who's it? Not you.
> God's words are true,
> It must not be YOU!
> (Opie and Opie 1969.)

One might think that these preliminaries delay the game unnecessarily, and that children could find a more expedient means of choosing the bad guy. However, children's games are much more about socializing than about winning or losing. Every elimination, no matter how time-consuming, is a game in its own right, an end as well as a means. It is executed with great and absolute precision and with an intensity of purpose that is almost religious. Mystery is an essential ingredient. Violations would be unthinkable, perhaps punishable. (Woe unto the unfortunate counter who, by reason of accident or will, takes liberties with the formula!) The ritual nature of elimination counts in children's play hints at their original utilities in adult society. Children have become the conservators of oral traditions no longer practiced by the mainstream adult community.

Fists and Fingers

> /   /
> One potato, two potato,
>
> /   /
> Three potato, four!
>
> /   /
> Five potato, six potato,
>
> /   /
> Seven potato, MORE!
> (Authors.)

> /   /
> (Seven potato, OR!)
> (Knapp and Knapp 1976.)

All players stand in a circle facing center, fists extended. The counter (Potato, Potato Man, Potato Masher) stands in the center of the circle, fists also extended. The counter begins with herself, hitting right fist with left (one potato), then left with right (two potato), then continuing on with the children in the circle. The child whose fist is counted out on "more" must put that hand behind his back. Counting continues with all remaining fists. When both of a child's fists have been counted out, that child is out of the circle. The counter must always count her own fists with each pass around the circle. If one of the counter's fists is counted out, then the counter counts her remaining fist with the chin. (See Bley 1957.) The following fist rhymes can be found in the Opie collection (1969).

     /   /
Olicka, bolicka,

 /   /
Susan solicka,

  /   /
Olicka, bolicka,

 /
Nob (Great Britain).

  /   /
Olleke, bolleke,

  / /
Rubisolleke,

  /   /
Olleke, bolleke,

 /
Knol (Netherlands).

   /   /   /
Sancta, femina, goda,

    /   /
Caracas et Quito,

    /   /   /
Villes principales Cayenne

    /   /
Et Paramaribo

   /   /   /   /
Cache ton poing derriere ton dos
     (France).

Newell (1963, 142) describes a rather complicated operation in use in Massachusetts. Parts of this rhyme appear in other counting out chants.

  /   /   /   /
Intery, mintery, cutery, corn,

  /   /   /   /
Apple seed and apple thorn,

  /   / /   /
Wire, briar, limber, lock.

   /   / /   /
Twelve geese in a flock

  /   /   /   /
Sit and sing by a spring.

  /   /   /   /
OUT spells out and in again.

  /   /   /   /
Over yonder steep hills,

  /   /   /   /
Where my father, he dwells;

  /   /   /   /
He has jewels. He has rings,

  /   /   /   /
And very many pretty things.

  /   /   /   /
Strike Jack! Lick Tom!

  /   /
Blow the bellows—

   /
BLACKFINGER!

  /   /
OUT OF THE GAME!

In this time-consuming and precise counting out, children sit in a circle facing center, hands on knees, finger spread wide. The counter chants and touches fingers, one per beat. As soon as a child's finger is counted out, he or she must tuck it under quickly, as the counter will try to flick it or slap it ("Blackfinger"). Once all of a child's fingers have been counted out, the child is eliminated from the circle. The last child left is not only it, but must also endure continued counting until all of his or her fingers are counted out. This child is likely to get flicked or slapped in the process.

Feet

/   /
The sky is blue,

/   /
How old are you?

/ /   / /   /   /   /
One, two, three, four, five, six, seven ...

Players stand in a circle with one foot extended toward the counter in center. The counter chants, stooping down to touch one foot per beat, beginning with his own foot. When the counter chants "you," the child whose foot was touched must state her age. The counter then resumes, counting numbers, up to the age given. The child whose foot is counted with the given age is eliminated (Bley 1957).

/ /   / /   /   /   /
Your shoes are dirty, please change them!

Players are positioned as above, with right feet forward. When "them" is counted on a child's right foot, he puts the left foot forward, the right being counted out. A child is eliminated when both feet are counted out. On occasion, a special punishment is reserved for the poor soul who remains at the end of the elimination (Opie and Opie 1969). Variations:

Your shoes are dirty; your shoes
   are clean,
Your shoes are not fit to be seen by
   the queen.
Please change them.

Ladhar-pocan,
Ladhar-pocan,
Pocan seipinn
Seipinn seonaid
Da mheur mheadhon (Scotland).

Di pi tic
Di pi toc
Carabou azinel
Vire, vire, forekel (France).

Alaghena,
Chalaghena,
Akh dedi,
Chekh dedi (Armenia).

(Opie and Opie 1969.)

Touching/Tapping

In many eliminations, players stand in a line or circle. The counter touches or taps one player with each count or beat of the rhyme. The player who gets tapped on the last beat goes out. Tapping can vary from pointing, to touching shoulders or heads, to gently slapping faces, chins, ears. Some rhymes describe the kind of wallop the person who gets counted out receives on that last beat: "and out you go, with a jolly good clout upon your big nose," "out you must go for saying so, with a clip across your ear-hole," "and run away, with a jolly good smack across your face, JUST LIKE THIS" (Opie and Opie 1969).

    /   /   /   /
Inka, bink, a bottle of ink!

      /   /   /   /
Pull out the cork and take a drink!

    /   /   /   /
Red, white, blue, black.

    /   /   /   /
Pour the rest down the kitchen SINK!
(Bley 1957.)

Red, white, and blue,
The cat's got the flu,
The baby has the whooping cough
And out goes YOU!
(Opie and Opie 1969.)

Piggy on the railroad
Picking up stones;
Along came an engine
And broke Piggy's bones.
Oh, said Piggy,
That's not fair.
Oh! cried the engineer,
I don't care.
(Montana, 1975 [Knapp and
    Knapp 1976].)

Engine, engine number nine,
Ring the bell when it's time.
O-U-T spells out goes he,
Into the middle of the dark blue sea.
(Pennsylvvania, 1888 [Opie and
    Opie 1969].)

Engine, engine number nine,
Coming down that railroad line,
O-U-T spells out goes she,
Right in the middle of the deep blue sea.
(Authors.)

Engine, engine number nine,
Running on Chicago line;
When she's polished, she will shine.
Engine, engine number nine.
(North Carolina, 1925 [Opie and
    Opie 1969].)

Engine, engine number nine,
Goin' down Chicago line.
If the train should jump the track,
Do you want your money back?
[YES/NO response]
Y-E-S spells YES ...
You are NOT IT!
(Knapp and Knapp 1966.)

Fireman, fireman, number eight,
Hit his head against the gate.
The gate flew in; the gate flew out.
O-U-T spells OUT!
And OUT YOU GO!
(Skolnik 1974.)

Dip, dip, dip,
My blue ship,
Sailing on the water
Like a cup and saucer.
Dip, dip, dip,
You are not IT!
(Opie and Opie 1969.)

Inky, pinky, ponky,
My daddy bought a donkey.
The donkey died,
Daddy cried,
Inky, pinky, ponky.
(Opie and Opie 1969.)

Oh deary me,
Mother caught a flea,
Put it in the kettle
To make a cup of tea.
The flea jumped out,
And bit mother's snout.
In come daddy
With his shirt hanging out.
(Opie and Opie 1969.)

One, two, three, four, five, six, seven,
All good children go to heaven.
Penny on the water,
Tuppence on the sea,
Threepence on the railway,
Out goes SHE!
(Opie and Opie 1969.)

Bake a pudding, bake a pie.
Did you ever tell a lie?
Yes, you did. I know you did.
You broke your mother's teapot lid.
O-U-T spells out,
And out you must go,
Right in the middle of the deep blue sea.
(Skolnik 1974.)

As I went up the apple tree,
All the apples fell on me;
Bake a pudding, bake a pie,
Did you ever tell a lie?
Yes, you did. You know you did.
You broke your mother's teapot lid.
L-I-D, that spells LID!
(Cincinnati [Newell 1963].)

One, two, three, four,
Mother washed the kitchen floor.
Floor dried, mother cried,
One, two, three, FOUR!
(Skolnik 1974.)

One, two, three,
The bumblebee.
The rooster crows,
OUT goes SHE!
(Skolnik 1974.)

Mickey Mouse
In a public house
Drinking pints of beer.
Where's your money?
In my pocket.
Where's your pocket?
I forgot it.
Please walk out.
(England [Opie and Opie 1959].)

As I was walking up a scabb't lane,
I met a scabb't horse.
I one it.   [counter to count self]
I two it.   [recited by first child in circle]
I three it.   [recited by second child in circle]
I four it.   [recited by third child]
I five it.   [fourth child]
I six it.   [fifth]
I seven it.   [sixth]
I ATE it!   [seventh: this child goes out, and counter begins again with
                eighth child, who will say, "I one it."]
(Opie and Opie 1969.)

Eexie, peeksie, pearie, plum,
Out steps Tom Thumb;
Tom Thumb in a basin,
Out steps James Mason;
James Mason in a cellar,
Out steps Cinderella;
Cinderella in a fix,
Out pops Tom Mix;
Tom Mix is a star,
S-T-A-R!
(Opie and Opie 1959.)

[Author's note: This rhyme uses the same formula as "There Was an Old Man and He Was Mad" (see Seeger 1948):

> There was an old man and he was mad,
> So he jumped into a pudding bag.
> The pudding bag it was so fine,
> That he jumped into a bottle of wine.
> The bottle of wine it was so clear,
> That he jumped into a bottle of beer ...
> When singers have finished invention, they say "Poof! Poof! Poof!"]

Mickey Mouse was in a house
Wondering what to do.
So he scratched his bun-tiddly-um;
Out goes YOU!
(Opie and Opie 1959.)

William A. Trimbletoe,
He's a good fisherman,
Catch his hands, put them in pans,
Some fly East, some fly West,
Some fly over the cuckoo's nest—
O-U-T spells out and be GONE!
(Georgia [Newell 1963].)

Stick, stock, stone dead,
Blind man can't see,
Every knave will have a slave,
And you must be HE!
(Opie and Opie 1969.)

Stick, stock, stone dead,
Set him up,
Set him down,
Set him in the old man's crown.
(Philadelphia [Newell 1963].)

Eggs, butter, cheese, bread,
Stick, stock, stone dead.
Set him up and set him down,
Set him in the old man's crown.
(Skolnik 1974.)

Errie, orrie, round the table,
Eat as much as you are able;
If you're able, eat the table,
Errie, orrie, OUT!
(Opie and Opie 1969.)

Oh dear me,
Ma grannie catcht a flea.
She roastit it an toastit it,
An' took it till her tea.
(Opie and Opie 1969.)

Interactive Counting

Interactive counting employs a formula verse that requires a player to answer a question, the answer to which will determine who goes out. For instance, using feet (see p. 216) is an interactive routine. The counter counts to the end of the rhyme, then asks for the age of the player taking the last count. This player gives her age. The counter must then continue the count from one to the given number. The player upon whom the given number falls goes out. Perhaps this extra effort makes the counting ritual seem more mystical. It does further remove control for choosing from the counter. A counter can add a syllable, count a two-word beat on each word, count an eight-word, four-beat line as eight beats, or append an additional formula ending, such as "right in the middle of the deep blue sea," or, "with a dirty dishrag on your snout." Any such changes will affect the outcome. Should a counter wish to ensure that a certain individual becomes the it, a few simple deviations can guarantee it. But if the rhyme asks a question which, in turn, calls for more counting to a given number or letter, the process of elimination becomes more random. An additional dollop of insurance against caprice can be had by requiring that the answer be spelled. To make sure that the player who answers the question cannot choose by doing some quick counting, that player might be asked to close his eyes before giving the answer. If the answer is a color, the person upon whom the count finally falls can be required to prove that he or she is wearing that color in order to go out. The more chancey the business, the better. The function of divination procedures in eliminating disputes and maintaining social order is nowhere better illustrated than in these elaborate efforts to guarantee randomness while choosing the it. Some rhymes even incorporate a line which begs the question: "and it's as *fair* as *fair* can be."

The sky is blue,
How old are you?
(Bley 1957.)

Blue shoe, blue shoe,
How old are you?
(Knapp and Knapp 1976.)

My mother made a nice seedy cake:
Guess how many seeds were in the cake.
(Opie and Opie 1969.)

Charlie Chaplin
Sat on a pin.
How many inches
Did it go in?
[Four]
One, two, three, FOUR!
(Opie and Opie 1969.)

Dic-dic-tation,
Corporation.
How many buses
Are in the station?
(Opie and Opie 1969.)

As I went down the Icky Picky lane
I met some Icky Picky people.
What colour were they dressed in—
Red, white, or blue?
[Red]
R-E-D spells red.
And that's as fair as fair can be,
That you were not to be IT!
(Opie and Opie 1969.)

Father Christmas
Grew some whiskers.
How many inches long?
[Four]
One, two, three, FOUR!
And if you do not want to play,
Just take your joy and run away,
With a jolly good smack across
          your face,
Just like this!
(Opie and Opie 1969.)

Engine, engine number nine,
Running on Chicago line.
If the train should jump the track,
Do you want your money back?
[Yes]
Y-E-S spells YES!
So, if you do not want to play,
Take your hoop and run away.
(Opie and Opie 1969.)

... Do you want your money back?
[Yes]
Y-E-S spells YES!
And you are NOT IT!
(Knapp and Knapp 1976.)

My mother and your mother
Were hanging out clothes.
My mother hit your mother
Right on the nose.
What color blood came out?
[Green]
G-R-E-E-N!
And you are out!
(Knapp and Knapp 1976.)

My mother and your mother
Were chopping sticks.
My mother cut her fingertips.
What colour was the blood?
[Pink]
P-I-N-K spells PINK,
So pink you must have on.
[If the player is wearing something pink,
then he or she is out.]
(Opie and Opie 1969.)

Monkey, monkey, bottle of pop,
On which monkey do we stop?
[Three]
One, two, THREE!
Out goes he!
(Knapp and Knapp 1976.)

Mickey Mouse bought a house,
What colour did he paint it?
[Blue]
B-L-U-E spells blue,
And you must have it on you.
(Opie and Opie 1959.)

Mr. Brown went to the store to buy a
      bucket of paint.
What color did he buy?
(Knapp and Knapp 1976.)

Eachie, peachie, pear, plum.
When does your birthday come?
[Fourteenth of December]
1, 2, 3, 4, 5, 6, 7, 8, 9, 10, 11, 12, 13, 14.
D-E-C-E-M-B-E-R!
You are out!
(Opie and Opie 1969.)

As I climbed the apple tree,
All the apples fell on me.
Bake an apple; bake a pie;
Have you ever told a lie?
[No]
Yes you did, you know you did.
You broke your mother's teapot lid.
What colour was it?
[Blue]
No, it wasn't. It was gold.
Now that's another lie you've told.
(Opie and Opie 1969.)

Bubble gum, bubble gum in a dish,
How many pieces do you wish?
[Two]
T-W-O!
And YOU are NOT IT!
(Knapp and Knapp 1976.)

Pennies, pennies in a fountain.
How many pennies make a mountain?
(Knapp and Knapp 1976.)

Quick Counts

Some counting outs are "quick and dirty." What they lack in ensuring chance, they compensate for by saving time — unless a player calls the counter for rigging.

I lit a candle,
And it went OUT!

Three horses in a stable;
One runs OUT!

Tarzan, tarzan in a tree.
Tarzan fell OUT!

Superman, superman, fly around,
Around, around,
OUT!

Dog shit, you're it.
OUT!
(Knapp and Knapp 1976.)

Mickey Mouse bought a house,
Couldn't pay the rent,
And got kicked OUT!
(Skolnik 1974.)

Pig's snout, walk out.

Oot Scoot, you're oot.

Ice cream sold OUT.

Wring the dirty dishcloth OUT.

Eggshells inside OUT.

In pin, safety pin, in pin, OUT.

Little Minnie washed her pinnie
    inside out.
I-N spells IN,
O-U-T spells OUT!

Eggs and ham, out you scram.

Smack, wallop, thump; you're knocked
    out.

A car went up the hill and conked out.

Black shoe, brown shoe, black shoe out.
(Opie and Opie 1969.)

Apples and oranges, two for a penny,
Takes a good scholar to count as many;
O-U-T, out goes she!
(Philadelphia.)

1, 2, 3, 4,
Mary at the kitchen door.
5, 6, 7, 8,
Mary at the garden gate.
(Massachusetts, 1820.)

1, 2, 3, 4,
Lily at the kitchen door,
Eating grapes off the plate,
5, 6, 7, 8.
(Philadelphia, 1880.)

1, 2, 3, 4, 5, 6, 7.
All good children go to heaven.
(Massachusetts to Pennsylvania.)

1, 2, 3, 4, 5, 6, 7, 8.
All bad children have to wait.
(Massachusetts.)

Monkey, monkey, bottle of beer.
How many monkeys are there here?
1, 2, 3,
You are he! (she)
(Massachusetts to Georgia.)

School's up, school's down.
School's all around the town.

Three potatoes in a pot,
Take one out and leave it hot.
(Philadelphia.)

Engine No. 9,
Out goes she.
(Philadelphia.)

Little man, driving cattle,
Don't you hear his money rattle?
One, two, three,
Out goes HE! (she)
(Massachusetts [Newell 1963].)

The Opies also offer a listing of "spell-like jingle[s]" and their many local variations.

Iggy oggy
Black froggy,
Iggy, oggy out.

Ibble ubble,
Black bubble,
Ibble ubble out.

Ickle ockle,
Black bottle [ink bottle, chockle bockle, chocolate bottle, chockle chockle],
Ickle ockle out.

Eettle ottle,
Black bottle,
Eettle ottle out [you are out, my dog's died].

Ingle angle,
Silver bangle, [golden bangle]
Ingle angle out.

Sometimes these jingles are used with extending lines: "If you want a piece of bread and jam, please step out." "If you want a lump of jelly, please walk out." "If you see a policeman, punch him in the snout." "If you want another bangle, please walk out." "Turn the dirty dish cloth in-side-out." "If you had been where I had been, you would not have been out." "Tea and sugar is my delight, and O-U-T spells out (and tea and sugar's out)." "Shines on the mantle piece, just like a three penny piece, O-U-T spells out." Other end lines include, "Out goes a bonny lass, out goes she, out goes a bonny lass, one, two, three." "Raggle taggle dish cloth torn in two, out goes you." "O-U-T spells out, so out you must go, with a dirty dishrag on your head because I said so (with a dirty wet dishcloth wrapped around your big toe, because the king and queen say so)" (Opie and Opie 1969). Since lines that extend the jingle also change the result, counter and players had best agree to the extension before beginning the counting out, to avoid charges of rigging and cheating.

Chinese Counting

I went to a Chinese laundry
To buy a loaf of bread;
They wrapped it up in a tablecloth
And this is what they said:

Ibbity, bibbity, sabbity, sab.
Ibbety, bibbety, can-a-bah.
Dictionary. Down the ferry.
Out goes Y-O-U!
(Bley 1957.)

Ibbity, bibbity, sibbity, sa,
Ibbity, bibbity, vanill-a.
Dictionary, down the ferry.
Fun, fun, American gum
Eighteen hundred and ninety one.
(Chicago [Opie and Opie 1969].)

Iberdi, biberdi, ziberdi, zab,
Iberdi, biberdi, kanalie.
(Denmark [Opie and Opie 1969].)

Ipetty, sipetty, ippetty sap,
Ipetty, sipetty, kinella kinack,
Kinella up, kinella down,
Kinella run round the monkey o' town.
(Scotland [Opie and Opie 1969].)

Ellerli, Sellerli, Sigerli, Sa,
Ribedi, Rabedi, Knoll.
(Germany [Opie and Opie 1969].)

One-ry, two-ry, dickery seven.
Hallibo, crackibo, ten, eleven.
Pee, po, must be done.
Twinkle, twankle, twenty-one!
(St. Simon's Island, United States
    [Jones and Hawes 1972].)

Onery, uery, ickory, a,
Hallibone, crackabone, ninery-lay,
Whisko, bango, poker my stick,
Mejoliky one leg!
(Massachusetts, 1800 [Newell 1963].)

Onery, uery, hickory, able,
Hallowbone, crackabone, Timothy
    ladle,
Whisko, bango, poker my stick,
Mejoliky one leg!
(Massachusetts [Newell 1963].)

One-amy, urey, hickory, seven,
Hallibone, crackabone, ten and eleven,
Peep-O, it must be done,
Twiggle, twaggle, twenty-one.
(Georgia [Newell 1963].)

Onery, uery, ickery, see,
Huckabone, crackabone, tillibonee;
Ram, pang, muski dan,
Striddledum straddledum, twenty-one.
(Connecticut [Newell 1963].)

One-ery, two-ery, ziccary, zan;
Hollow bone, crackabone ninery ten:
Spittery spot, it must be done;
Twiddleum, twaddleum, twenty-one.
Hink spink, the puddings stink,
The fat begins to fry,
Nobody's at home, but jumping Joan,
Father, mother and I.
Stick, stock, stone dead,
Blind men can't see,
Every knave will have a slave,
And YOU must be HE!
(England, 1810 [Opie and Opie 1969].)

Anery, twaery, tickery, seven,
Aliby, crackiby, ten or eleven;
Pin-pan, muskidan,
Tweedlum, twodlum, twenty-one.
(Scotland, 1821 [Opie and Opie 1969].)

Onery, uery, hickory, Ann,
Fillison, follason, Nicholas John,
Queevy, quavy, Virgin Mary,
Singalum, sangalum, buck.
(Philadelphia, 1820 [Newell 1963].)

Onery, uery, ickory, Ann,
Filisy, folasy, Nicholas John,
Queevy, quavy, Irish Mary,
Stingalum, stangalum, buck.
(New England, 1820 [Newell 1963].)

Onery, uery, ickory, Ann,
Fillison, follason, Nicholas John,
Queevy, quavy, English Navy,
Stinkalum, stankalum, John Buck.
B-U-C-K spells Buck.
(Cincinnati, 1880 [Newell 1963].)

Wonery, twoery, tickery, seven;
Alibi, crackaby, ten and eleven;
Pin, pan, musky, dan;
Tweedle-um, twoddle-um, twenty-wan;
Eeerie, Orie, ourie,
You are out.
(Opie and Opie 1951.)

One's all, zuzall, titterall, tann.
Bobtailed vinegar, little Paul ran,
Harum, scarum, merchant marum,
Nigger, turnpike, toll-house, OUT!
(Massachusetts, 1800s [Newell 1963].)

Ehne Dehne du,
Kappernelle wu,
Isabelle, Pempernelle,
Ibille, Pibille,
Geh weg!
(Germany, 1851 [Opie and Opie 1951].)

One saw, two saw, ziggy-zaw-zo.
Bob-tail, dominicker, deedle-dall-do.
Hail-em, scail-em, Virgin Mary.
Ike to my link-tom Buck!
(St. Simon's Island, United States
     [Jones and Hawes 1972].)

One-ery, two-ery, tickery, seven,
Hallibo, crackibo, ten and eleven.
Spin, span, muskidan,
Twiddle-um, twaddle-um, twenty-one.
(Opie and Opie, 1955.)

One-erum, two-erum,
Cockerum, shu-erum,
Shetherum, shatherum,
Wineberry, wagtail,
Tarrydiddle, den.
(Opie and Opie 1955.)

Zinti, tinti,
Tethera, methera,
Bumfa, litera,
Hover, dover,
Dicket, dicket,
As I sat on my sooty kin,
I saw the king of Irel pirel
Playing on Jerusalem pipes.
(England, 1820 [Opie and Opie 1969].)

Zeenty teenty
Heathery bethery
Bumful oorie
Over Dover
Saw the king of easel diesel
Jumping over Jerusalem wall.
Black fish, white trout,
Eerie, oarie, you are out.
(England, contemporary [Opie and
     Opie 1969].)

Eenty teenty haligalum,
The cat went out to get some fun,
It got some fun on Toddy's grond,
Eenty teenty haligalum.
(Scotland, contemporary [Opie and
     Opie 1969].)

Eenty-peenty, halligo lum,
The cat gaed oot to get some fun;
It got some fun on Toddy's grun —
Eenty-peenty, halligo lum.
(Scotland, 1855 [Opie and Opie 1969].)

Indi tindi alego Mary,
Ax toe, alligo slum.
Orgy porgy, peel-a-gum;
Itty Gritty, francis itty,
Ordellum joodlum pipes.
(Australia, 1895 [Opie and Opie 1969].)

Eener, deener, abber, dasher,
Ooner, eye-sher,
Om, pom, tosh,
Iggery-eye, eggery-eye,
Pop the vinegar in the pie,
Harum, scarum, pop, canarum,
Skin it.
(England [Opie and Opie 1969].)

Zeetum, peetum, penny pie,
Poppy-lorry, jinkum, jie,
Fish guts, caller troot,
Gibbie, gabbie, ye're oot.
(Scotland [Opie and Opie 1969].)

Eenty, teenty, figury, fell,
Ell, dell, dominell,
Irky, pirky, tarry rope,
An, tan, tousy, Jock.
(Scotland [Opie and Opie 1969].)

Ecklie, picklie, eleka fa,
Fix Q, salty fa,
Sonti fonti, eleka fee,
Trons.
(England [Opie and Opie 1969].)

Ickama, dickama, aliga, mo,
Dixue, aliga, sum,
Hulka, pulka, Peter's gun,
Francis.
(San Francisco, 1888 [Opie and
    Opie 1969].)

Ikkamy, dukkamy, alligar mole,
Dick slew alligar slum,
Hukka, pukka, Peter's gum,
Francis.
(Massachusetts and Maryland, 1848.)

Ickery, ahry, oary, ah,
Biddy, barber, oary, sah,
Peer, pear, mizter, meer,
Pit, pat, out one.
(Opie and Opie 1969.)

Ip, dip, alaba-da,
Dutch cheese, chentie ma,
Chentie ma, alaba-da,
Dutch cheese, Scram.
(England [Opie and Opie 1969].)

Eenie, meenie, mackeracka,
Hi, di, dominacka,
Stickeracka, roomeracka,
Om, pom, push.
(Opie and Opie 1955.)

Ah, ra, chickera,
Roly, poly, pickena,
Kinny, minny, festi,
Shanti-poo,
Ickerman, chickerman, chinee-choo.
(Opie and Opie 1955.)

Icka backa, icka backa,
Icka backa boo;
Icka backa, soda cracka,
Out goes you.
(Opie and Opie 1969.)

Acca bacca soda cracker,
Acca bacca boo.
If your father chews tobacco,
Out goes you.
(Knapp and Knapp 1976.)

Eeny, meeny, tiptty, te,
Teena, dinah, domine,
Hocca, proach, domma noach,
Hi, pon, tus.
(Philadelphia, 1855 [Opie and
    Opie 1969].)

Eenie, meenie, tipsy, toe,
Olla, bolla, domino;
Okka, pocha, dominocha,
Hy, pon, tush.
O-U-T spells out goes he,
Right in the middle of the dark blue sea.
(Washington, DC, 1888 [Opie and
    Opie 1969].)

Inty, minty, tippety, fig,
Delia, dilia, dominig,
Otcha, potcha, dominotcha,
Hi, pon, tusk.
Huldy, guildy, boo,
Out goes you.
(Hartford, Connecticut, 1888 [Opie
and Opie 1969].)

Inty, minty, tibbity, fee,
Delia, dona, domini;
Eenchi, peenchi, domineenchi,
Alm, palm, pus.
Alicka, balicka, boo,
Out goes Y-O-U.
(New York City, 1938 [Opie and
Opie 1969].)

Impty, dimpty, tibbity, fig,
Delia, dauma, nauma, nig,
Heitcha, peitcha, dauma neitcha,
Ein, pine, pug,
Ullaga, bullaga, boo,
Out goes YOU!
(San Francisco, 1956 [Opie and
Opie 1969].)

Eenie, meenie, tipsie, tee,
Alabama, dominee,
Hocus, pocus, deminocus
I pon tus.
(Pasadena, California, 1938 [Opie
and Opie 1969].)

Engete, pengete, zukate, me,
Abri, fabri, domine,
Enx, penx,
Du bist drauss.
(German colony, Hungary, 1855
[Opie and Opie 1969].)

Anemane, mikkelemee,
Hobbel, den dobbel, den dominee,
Flik, flak, floot, eik en lood,
Jij bent dood.
(Netherlands, 1874 [Opie and
Opie 1969].)

Eckati, peckati, zuckait, me,
Awi, schwavi, domine,
Quitum, quitum, habine,
Nuss, puff, kern,
Du bist drauss.
(Austro/Czechoslovakian border,
ca. 1855 [Opie and Opie 1969].)

Scores and Counting Words

Although "Chinese" counting is often used to determine the it, such counting may be a real, if distorted, form of keeping a score. Though Newell (1963) doubts that the rhymes have their roots in old language forms, the Opies (1951; 1969) find some evidence for the theory. They cite old Welsh and Cornish (Celtic) shepherds' counts or scores and the universality of similar rhymes on the European continent as evidence of the existence of some common linguistic ancestor. Henry Carrington Bolton, a folklorist collecting in the 1800s, recorded and reported related rhyme families held in common amongst the children of England, Ireland, Scotland, Wales, Germany, Sweden, Holland, France, Spain, Italy, Portugal, Greece, western India, Turkey, parts of Arabia, Armenia, and Bulgaria. He also found that jingles with similar or identical rhyme schemes and rhythms, but different language forms, were indigenous to Japan, Malaysia, the Hawaiian Islands, and the Penobscot cultures of North America. Newell himself remembers women counting stitches in their knitting using the old scores.

SCORES

Anglo-Cymric (Massachusetts, ca. 1880 — English version) (Newell 1963).

1.	ane	11.	een dick
2.	tane	12.	teen dick
3.	tother	13.	tother dick
4.	feather	14.	feather dick
5.	fip	15.	bumfrey
6.	sother	16.	een bumfrey
7.	lother	17.	teen bumfrey
8.	co	18.	tother bumfrey
9.	deffrey	19.	feather bumfrey
10.	dick	20.	gig it

Native American (Massachusetts, ca. 1800 — Native American version as recited by an Anglo child) (Newell 1963).

1.	een	11.	een dick
2.	teen	12.	teen dick
3.	tuther	13.	tuther dick
4.	futher	14.	futher dick
5.	fip	15.	bumpit
6.	sother	16.	een bumpit
7.	tother	17.	teen bumpit
8.	porter	18.	tuther bumpit
9.	dubber	19.	futher bumpit
10.	dick	20.	gig it.

English (ca. 1877) (Newell 1963).

1.	aina	11.	ain-a-dig
2.	peina	12.	pein-a-dig
3.	para	13.	para-a-dig
4.	peddera	14.	pedder-a-dig
5.	pimp	15.	bumfit
6.	ithy	16.	ain-a-bumfit
7.	mithy	17.	pein-a-bumfit
8.	owera	18.	par-a-bumfit
9.	lowera	19.	peddar-a-bumfit
10.	dig	20.	giggy

Irish (ca. 1877) (Newell 1963).

1.	eina	11.	eina dickera
2.	mina	12.	mina dickera
3.	pera	13.	pera dickera
4.	peppera	14.	pappera dickera
5.	pinn	15.	pumpi
6.	chester	16.	eina pumpi
7.	nester	17.	mina pumpi
8.	nera	18.	pera pumpi
9.	dickera	19.	peppera pumpi
10.	nin	20.	ticket

Score from Bishopdale (Opie and Opie 1969).

1.	een	11.	tine-er-giggle
2.	teen	12.	pear-er-giggle
3.	peever	13.	pepper-er-giggle
4.	pepperer	14.	pomfit
5.	pence	15.	heen-er-bun
6.	sather	16.	teen-er-bun
7.	lather	17.	pear-er-bun
8.	luther	18.	mepper-er-bun
9.	nogger-go-lence	19.	pepper-er-bun
10.	hine-er-giggle	20.	figgit

Score from Borrowdale (Opie and Opie 1969).

1.	yan	11.	yan-dick
2.	tan	12.	tan-dick
3.	tethera	13.	tether-dick
4.	methera	14.	mether-dick
5.	pimp	15.	bunfit (bumfit)
6.	sethera	16.	yaner-bunfit
7.	lethera	17.	taner-bunfit
8.	hothera	18.	tethera-bunfit
9.	dothera	19.	methera-bunfit
10.	dick	20.	gigert

Score from Connecticut (Opie and Opie 1969).

1. rene	11. rene-dit
2. tene	12. tene-dit
3. tother	13. tother-dit
4. feather	14. feather-dit
5. fib	15. bumpum
6. solter	16. rene-bumpum
7. lolter	17. tene-bumpum
8. poler	18. tother-bumpum
9. deborah	19. feather-bumpum
10. dit	20. giggit

Early Celtic numerals:

	Welsh	(pronunciation)	Cornish	Irish	Breton
1.	un	/een/	ouyn	aon	unan
2.	dau	/daay/	dow	do	daou
3.	tri	/tree/	tray	tri	tri
4.	pedwar	/pai'dwaar/	peswar	ceathair	pevar*
5.	pump	/pimp/	pimp	cuig	pemp

———————

*(fem. peder)

The Opies (1951) list samples of counting lines:

Eena, meena, mona, my/Barcelona, bona, stry/Air, ware, frum, dy/Araca baraca, wee, wo, wack.

Eeny, meeny, mony, my/Barcelona, bona stry (Wisconsin).

Ena, mena, mona, mite/Basca, lora, hora, bite (Cornwall).

Hana, mana, mona, mike/Barcelona, bona, strike/Hare, ware, frown, venac/Harrico, warrico, we, wo, wac (New York, ca. 1821).

Ene, tene, mone, mei/Pastor, lone, bone, strei/Ene, fune, herke, berke/ Wer? Wie? Wo? Was? (Germany).

Inty, tinty, tethera, methery/Bank for over, dover, ding. (Edinburgh).

Ya, ta, tethera, pethera, pip/Slata, lata, covera, dick.

Een, teen, tether, fether, fip/Sather, lather, gother, dather, dix
(United States, 1969).

Yan, tan, tethera, methera, pip/Seeaza, leeaza, catra, coan, dick
(Bransdale).

Yen, tane, tether-me, leather-me, dick/Caesar, lazy-cat, or-a-horn, or-a-tick
(Weardale).

Newell (1963) adds:

Unichi, dunichi, tipel-ti/Tibel, tabel, domine (Germany).

Eckati, peckati, zuchati-me/Avi, schavi, domine (Germany).

Aeniga, maniga, tumpel-ti/Tifel, tafel, numine (Germany).

Anigl, panigl, subtra-hi/Tivi, tavi, domine (Germany).

Endeli, bandeli, deffen-de/Gloria, tibi, domine (Germany).

Eeny, meeny, tipti-te/Teena, Dinah, domine (United States).

Unemi, dunemi, tronemi, ronemi, donemi/Ronza, konza, jewla, dewla,
tschok (Transylvania).

Aketum, taketum, tinum, tanum (Transylvania).

Knapp and Knapp (1976) record these:

Een, meen sahri, mahri, teen (India).

Een, tean, tether, mether, pimp (England).

Eina, peina, paira, puffera, pith (England).

Eina, mina, pera, peppera, pinn (Ireland).

Een, teen, tuther, futher, fip (United States).

Children habitually play and invent using language forms that they have heard, and are especially attracted to rhythmic and rhyming play. They like alliterative language, reduplication of sounds, and seem to find special (physical?) pleasures in certain kinds of articulations. Counting scores are ideal material for play, and children might very easily have adapted these forms to their own purposes at a time when counting was still done in the old way, just as children today make games of counting. Distortions occur because children substitute (intrude) language and sound sequences that are familiar for parts of rhymes which they do not recognize. One-ery, two-ery rhymes are distortions of contemporary number names. *Can-a-bah*, *canal boat*, and *vanilla* seem to be North American sound and word substitutions for the Danish *kanali*, the Scottish *kinella-knack*, or the German *knoll*.

Evidence that counting out rhymes may contain the distorted remnants of ancient folk practice can be seen in the regional variations and gabblings of chants which contain recognizable meanings. Adult societies change, and the contexts which provide meanings for certain words and phrases can disappear from adult cultures. In the year 3989 AD, adult folklorists will probably have difficulty assigning meaning to rhymed references to "the Queen," Listerine, jelly bean, submarines, pork and beans, blue jeans, Hawaiian punch, Abe Lincoln, Turpentine, Valentine, Mexico or Texaco. Who, adult or child, would remember Shirley Temple, James Mason, Tom Mix, Charlie Chaplin, Raggedy Ann, Raggedy Andy, Andy Panda, Dennis the Menace, or Blondie and Dagwood? (Mickey Mouse probably has a better chance.) Even if children were able to repeat these words precisely as they are spoken today, some, if not all of them, would sound like gibberish? Language forms for which meanings are lost become gibberish, because meaning resides in the practices and memories of people, not in language itself. If adults can resist the compulsion to organize children's play—it *looks* so disorganized—and allow some room for child culture to operate, children will conserve, and perhaps garble, dead language forms. If today's children are using words which once belonged to long-abandoned practices, through repetition of their own rhymes, the rhymes present interesting linguistic artifacts of some historical significance.

COUNTING WORD DERIVATIONS

"Right in the middle of the deep blue sea."

> Come, let us cast lots, that we may know for whose cause this evil is upon us. So they cast lots, and the lot fell upon Jonah.
> Then they said unto him, What shall we do unto thee, that the sea may be calm unto us?
> And he said, Take me up and cast me forth into the sea; so the sea shall be calm unto you.
> So they took up Jonah, and cast him forth into the sea: and the sea ceased from her raging.
> (Jonah 1:7, 1:11-12, 1:15.)

"Hora, lora." Latin for "binding straps," "hour."

"Bucca." Cornish for "goblin."

"Mona." A place name. Former name of the island called Anglesea on which the Druid priests maintained a sacred grove of trees, possibly an oracle. Ritual sacrifices are known to have been performed there. In 61 AD, the Romans cut down and destroyed the trees as part of a campaign to rid the entire country of its pagan traditions.

"Eggs, butter, cheese, bread." These foods were (and are) associated with magical practices, divination, and the working of charms.

"Stick, stock." The Druids (pagan Celtic priests) burned their human sacrifices in wicker baskets or cages made of sticks (stocks). Sometimes, these baskets or cages were hung from a high place (e.g., a tree limb) with ropes. The Druids may also have hoisted the victim after the sacrifice, perhaps to make the offering, just as priests today continue to raise the sacrifice (the Host) for consecration. The sacrifice hero whose blood was used to fertilize the earth was commonly hung on a cross, a pole, or on a tree, all of which represented the great world/cosmic tree. Human and animal sacrifices were also burned in towering effigies constructed of branches.

Sticks, arrows, and rods were common divination tools. Marked sticks could have been used to do choosings.

"Stone dead." A possible reference to the stone upon which human and animal sacrifices were sometimes carried out. Traces of blood have been found on certain of the stones of the ancient stone monuments in Great Britain. Today we use the term "stone cold dead" without much thought to its derivation. Could *stone dead* be "dead of the stone," as in "dead of a heart attack," a way of saying that someone died (was sacrificed) on the stone? "Cold" might refer to the stone—"stone-cold" or "cold stone," in which case, cold might have a slightly altered meaning. The cold stone might be the death stone. Stones were also associated with the goddess, to whom many sacrifices were made.

"Old man's crown." Katherine Elwes Thomas noted that "old man" comes from the Saxon *onwel-man*, which was a "well known name for priests" (Thomas 1930, 131). "Crown," she writes, derives from the Saxon *grouen*, plural for *grouw*, meaning "horror, a detestable act, infamous conduct." From this clue, she concludes that the "Stick Stock" rhymes are references to the despicable conduct of the clergy during the years immediately preceding and following the rise of the House of Tudor in England. "The 'stick, stock stone dead' indicates fraud and bad actions" (Thomas 1930, 131). The Opies (1951) and Baring-Goulds (1962) make no such claims, but do cast serious doubt on many of Thomas's fanciful speculations. Unless we wish to blunder as deeply into fantasy as did Thomas, we cannot write with her certainty. But one would suspect that the Saxon from which "old man" and "crown" derive predates the Tudor line by some centuries, and probably predates Christianity as well. We might speculate that, if the Saxon meanings for *onwel-man* and *grouen* were applied to Christian clergy in the sixteenth century, that application was made because those words were used in an earlier time to refer to a different class of priests. (The contemporary given name of *Dru*—listed in name books as Celtic, and short for Druce, Drud, or Druid—means "old wise man.") Sure the "old man's crown" is not of Christian origin, Thomas's unconvincing interpretation of "stick stock" is not supported by the single clue which she finds in the Saxon derivations. Divination practices using sticks and stocks are ancient, and might be a better—or at least a more interesting—consideration. In any case, "old man's crown" has about it the same flavor as "my father's throne": "And bids me at my Father's throne/ Make all my wants and wishes known" (Cramblet and Smith 1953). One additional and very likely association has to do with the burning of human and animal sacrifice victims in very large wicker (human) effigies. Victims probably stood on a platform within the structure that was placed some distance from the ground, possibly in the head of the construction. "It" might also refer to "The Anointed One" (the Christos), the sacrifice hero chosen to die to keep the sacred covenant. Translated into a children's game, everyone runs away from the it. In some later pagan practice, the sacrifice was a simulation, wherein the intended victim died in sham (bluff), but then suffered ritual shunning for a year, as an it from whom people would run.

Just for fun, look once again at the following rhyme, a jumprope jingle collected in the United States (Skolnik 1974).

/   /   /   /
EGGS, BUTTER, CHEESE, BREAD,

/   /   /   /
STICK, STOCK, STONE DEAD.

/   /   /   /
SET HIM UP, SET HIM DOWN,

/   /   /   /
SET HIM IN THE OLD MAN'S CROWN.

Or, try this.

/   /   /   /
EENA, MEENA, MONA, MITE,

/   /   /   /
BASCA, LORA, HORA, BITE.

/   /   /
HOGGA, BUCCA, BAU;

/   /   /   /
EGGS, BUTTER, CHEESE, BREAD,

/   /   /   /   / / /
STICK, STOCK, STONE DEAD, O-U-T!

Are these rhymes, which serve the games of children, very abbreviated and frightening stories in which only the most essential elements have been retained?

"EENY, MEENY, MINEY, MO"

Eeny, meeny, miney, mo.
Catch a tiger by the toe.
When he hollers, let him go!
Eeny, meeny, miney, mo.
My mother said to choose the very best one.
One, two, three,
Out goes she,
Right in the middle of the deep blue sea.
(Milwaukee, 1955 [Authors].)

This little jingle, in its many versions, is the most popular and used rhyme among all English speaking children (Opie and Opie 1951). Its universality can hardly be attributed to its utility, since it serves the same game-initiating purposes as other counting out rhymes, and without the mystery of the extra randomizing safeguards found in some. Its ubiquity might have more to do with its structure: its simple rhyme scheme, its alliteration and repetition, its exact sixteen-count length, and the relative flexibility of lines two and three for allowing modification. (Also, it feels good.) For this and recent generations, in any case, "Eenie, Meeny, Miney, Mo" is the quintessential formula, the perfect pattern—the first learned and the last forgotten.

Eeny, meeny, miney, mo,
Catch a tiger by his toe,
If he hollers, let him go!
My mother told me to choose this ver-ry
    one.
O-U-T spells out goes he,
Right in the middle of the deep blue sea.
(United States [Knapp and Knapp
    1976].)

Eeny, meeny, miney, mo,
Sit the baby on the po.
When he's done,
Wipe his bum,
Tell his mummy what he's done.
(Opie and Opie 1969.)

Eeny, meeny, miney, mo,
Sit the baby on the po.
When it's done,
Clean its bum,
And give it a lump of sugar plum.
(Northern Ireland [Skolnik 1974].)

Eeny, meeny, tipsy, teeny,
Apple Jack, Paul Sweeny,
Dotchy, potchy, Don Morotchy,
Oh, par, dar, see,
Out goes Y-O-U!
(Skolnik 1974.)

Eeny, meeny, miney, mo,
Catch a tiger by the toe,
If he hollers, let him go.
Eeny, meeny, miney, mo,
Out goes Y-O-U!
(Bley 1957.)

Eine, meine, mine, mu;
Und draust bist DU!
(Austria [Opie and Opie 1951].)

Iene, miene, mutten,
Tien, pond, grutten,
Tien, pond, kass,
Iene, miene, mutten is de bass.
(Netherlands [Knapp and Knapp 1976].)

Ene, mene, mu,
Muller's Kuh;
Muller's Esel,
Da bist DU!
(Germany [Knapp and Knapp 1976].)

Eenie, meenie, miney, mo,
Crack-a-feeny, finey, foe,
Alma, nuger, papa, tuger,
Rif, bif, bam, bo.
(Knapp and Knapp 1976.)

Eeny, meeny, and cho-cha-leeny,
I buy gum-baleeny,
Achee, pachee, liver-achee
Out you go!
(Knapp and Knapp 1976.)

Eny, meny, mone, mite;
Butter, lather, bony, strike.
Hair cut, froth neck,
Halico, balico,
We, wo, wack.
(Philadelphia [Newell 1963].)

Eny, meny, miny, mo,
Catch a Nigger by his toe.
If he hollers, make him pay
Fifty dollars every day.
O-U-T spells out,
And out goes she,
In the middle of the deep blue sea.
(United States, 1947 [Opie and
    Opie 1951].)

Eendy, beenby, bandy, roe,
Catch a chicken by the toe.
If he screams, let him go.
Eendy, beendy, bandy, roe.
(Opie and Opie 1951.)

Ena, meena, mina, mo,
Catch a tinker by his toe.
If he screams, let him go.
Ena, meena, mina, mo.
(Opie and Opie 1951.)

Eny, meny, mony, mine,
Hadsy, pasky, daily, ine,
Agy, dagy, walk.
(Connecticut [Newell 1963].)

Eeny, weeny, winey, wo.
Where do all the Frenchmen go?
To the east and to the west,
And into the old crow's nest.
(Opie and Opie 1955.)

Eeny, meeny, macca, racca,
Rae, rye, doma, naca,
Chicca, racca,
Old Tom Thumb.
(Scotland [Opie and Opie 1969].)

Eeny, meeny, macker, acker,
Ere, o, dominacker,
Ala, packa, pucker acker,
Um, pum, push.
(Scotland [Opie and Opie 1969].)

Ena, mena, macka, racka,
Rai, ri, domi nacka,
Chicka lolla, lolla poppa,
Whiz, bang, push.
(England [Opie and Opie 1969].)

Eeny, meeny, macca, racca,
Ere, ree, dominacca,
Icaracca, omaracca,
Om, pom, push.
(Wales [Opie and Opie 1969].)

Eena, meena, micka, macka,
Eyre, eye, domma nacka,
Icky, chicky,
Om, pom, puss.
(Australia [Opie and Opie 1969].)

Eeny, meeny, macka, racka,
Rare, rye, domma nacka,
Chicka pocka, ellie focka,
Om, pom, puss.
(New Zealand [Opie and Opie 1969].)

Any, many, mony, my,
Barcelony, stony, sty,
Harum, scarum, frownum ack,
Harricum, barricum, wee, wi, wo, wack.
(England [Opie and Opie 1969].)

Hana, mana, mona, mike,
Barcelona, bona, strike,
Hare, ware, frown, venac,
Harrico, warrico, we, wo, wac.
(New York, 1815 [Opie and Opie 1969].)

Eeny, meeny, moany, mite,
Butter, lather, boney, strike,
Hair, bit, frost, neck,
Harrico, barrico, we, wo, wack.
(Philadelphia, 1855 [Opie and
    Opie 1969].)

Eena, meena, mona, my,
Pasca, lara, bona, by,
Elke, belke, boh,
Eggs, butter, cheese, bread,
Stick, stock, stone dead.
(England, 1882 [Opie and Opie 1969].)

Une, mine, mane, mo,
Une, fine, fane, fo,
Maticaire et matico,
Mets la main derrier ton dos.
(France, 1961 [Opie and Opie 1969].)

Ina, mina, maina, mau,
Katta, lita, bobbi, sau,
Di va, noksa gau,
Ina, mina, maina, mau.
(Norway, 1959 [Opie and Opie 1969].)

Eeny, meeny, mink, monk,
Chink, chonk, charla,
Isa, visa, varla,
Vick.
(England [Opie and Opie 1969].)

Eena, meena, ming, mong,
Ting, tay, tong,
Ooza, vooza, voka, tooza,
Vis, vos, vay.
(White Rhodesia [Opie and Opie 1969].)

Ene, mene, ming, mang,
Kling, klang,
Osse, bosse, bakke, disse,
Eje, veje, vaek.
(Denmark, 1965 [Opie and Opie 1965].)

Ala, mala, ming, mong,
Mong, mong, mosey.
Oosey, oosey, ackedy,
I, vi, vack.
(England [Opie and Opie 1969].)

Ene, mene, mink, monk,
Klink, klank,
Ose, Pose, Packedich,
Eia, weia, weh.
(Germany, 1857 [Opie and Opie 1969].)

Eeny, meeny, mink, monk,
Chink, chonk, chow,
Oozy, boozy, vacadooza,
Vay, vie, vo — vanish.
(Australia [Opie and Opie 1969].)

Counting out rhymes bear so much resemblance to old college cheers that one might wonder if the remembered lore of children's games has not found its way into team yells.

Ah-ricka, racka, ree;
Ah-ricka, racka RAH!
Ricka, racka, dommin-acka,
RAH! RAH! RAH!
RAH! RAH! RAH!
SIS! BOOM! BAH!
Racka, racka,
Macka, racka,
RAH! RAH! RAH!

RANDOM CHOICE CHILDREN'S GAMES

Each of these games involves choosing teams or trading the role of it.

- *Bingo* (Chase 1949).

- *Bird, Beast, or Fish?* (Newell 1963).

- *Birds* (Newell 1963).

- *Blue Birds and Yellow Birds* (Newell 1963).

- *Bob-a-Needle* (Jones and Hawes 1972).

- *Carousel* (Bley 1957).

- *Charlie Over the Water* (Collins 1973).

- *Chicka-Ma-Craney-Ma-Crow* (Collins 1973).

- *Club First* (Newell 1963).

- *Did You Ever See a Lassie?* (Bley 1957).

- *Ding, Dong, Bell* (Nancrede and Smith 1940).

- *Dollar, Dollar* (Bley 1957).

- *El Conejo de Esperanza*—the rabbit of hope (Prieto 1973).

- *El Juego del Panuelo*—the handkerchief game (Prieto 1973).

- *El Mendego*—the beggar (Prieto 1973).

- *Farm Boy's Bonny* (Bley 1957).

- *Farmer in the Dell* (Bley 1957).

- *The Farmer in the Dell* (Chase 1972; Newell 1963; Cano 1973).

- *The Farmer's in His Dell* (Gomme and Sharp 1976).

- *The Farmers* (Collins 1973).

- *Fly Little Bluebird* (Collins 1973).

- *Four in a Boat* (Bley 1957).

- *Fox in a Box* (Bley 1957).

- *Frog in the Sea* (Newell 1963).

- *Go In and Out the Window* (Chase 1949; Collins 1973; Bley 1957; Jones and Hawes 1972).

- *Go Round and Round the Valley* (Newell 1963).

- *Happy Is the Miller* (Newell 1963).

- *Here I Bow and Here I Bake* (Newell 1963).

- *How Many Miles to Babylon?* (Newell 1963).

- *Hunt the Squirrel* (Newell 1963).

- *Jolly Is the Miller* (Collins 1973).

- *The Jolly Miller* (Gomme and Sharp 1976).

- *Juba* (Jones and Hawes 1972).

- *Juego de los Pavos*—the turkey game (Prieto 1973).

- *King Arthur Was King William's Son* (Newell 1963).

- *King George's Horses* (Collins 1973).

- *King William Was King George's Son* (Collins 1973; Newell 1963).

- *Little Bird, Little Bird* (Seeger 1948).

- *Little Sally Walker* (Jones and Hawes 1972).

- *Little Sally Waters* (Newell 1963).

- *London Bridge* (Cano 1973; Gomme and Sharp 1976; Bley 1957; Collins 1973; Jones and Hawes 1972).

- *Marching 'Round the Levee* (Cano 1973).
- *Mientes Tu'* — you fib (Prieto 1973).
- *Mollie Bright* (Collins 1973).
- *Moneyfoot* (Jones and Hawes 1972).
- *My Good Ol' Man* (Bley 1957).
- *The Needle's Eye* (Newell 1963).
- *Oats and Beans* (Chase 1972).
- *Oats, Peas, Beans* (Gomme and Sharp 1976).
- *Oats, Peas, Beans and Barley Grow* (Collins 1973; Bley 1957; Newell 1963).
- *One Morning in May* (Collins 1973).
- *Open the Gates* (Newell 1963).
- *Our Shoes Are Made of Leather* (Gomme and Sharp 1976).
- *Pepito* (Prieto 1973).
- *Perrito Goloso* — little dog with a sweet tooth (Prieto 1973).
- *Pig in the Parlor* (Bley 1957).
- *Prendas* — forfeits (Prieto 1973).
- *Pussy Wants a Corner* (Newell 1963).
- *Ring Around the Rosie* (Newell 1963).
- *Ring on a String* (Bley 1957).
- *Ring-A-Ring O' Roses* (Gomme and Sharp 1976).
- *Rosie, Darling Rosie* (Cano 1973).
- *Send My Brown Jug Down to Town* (Bley 1957).
- *Skating Away* (Chase 1949).
- *Skip to My Lou* (Bley 1957; Collins 1973).
- *A Tisket, A Tasket* (Bley 1957).
- *Threading the Needle* (Newell 1963).
- *Turn the Glasses Over* (Chase 1949; Bley 1957).
- *Uncle Jessie* (Jones and Hawes 1972).
- *Way Down Yonder in the Brickyard* (Jones and Hawes 1972).
- *Way Go Lily* (Jones and Hawes 1972).
- *What Color?* (Newell 1963).
- *Wheel of Fortune* (Newell 1963).
- *Who'll Be the Bonder?* (Newell 1963).

5

The Devices of Memory in the Oral Narrative

Perhaps the most difficult task facing the literate revivalist storyteller is the overall effect of discontinuity of tradition. Not only do revivalist tellers often know very little of the lore of in-story references which give the story meaning, they do not think in the language and structure of oral narrative. As a result, the efforts of the literate storyteller are necessarily based in the habits of literacy. We work from printed materials, which, though they might be accurate transcriptions of orally composed texts, lack the critical characteristics of oral language. Or we work from texts of *recomposed* oral stories, the language of which is no longer a genuine oral construction. Though we understand that the oral composition is a stitching together of formulaic patterns in the oral tradition, and not a recitation of memorized material, we do not have those formulae firmly in memory. Often, we are obliged to discover the patterns of oral narrative in much the same way that we learn a native language, through trial and error and through exposure to and experimentation with countless stories.

When we are separated, as we all are, from the experiences of primary orality (meaning that we have not learned by natural means to make oral stories as they would be composed in oral, preliterate cultures), we have to resort to other strategies to learn to make oral narrative. Though a seeming contradiction, the analytic, reflective nature of study of transcribed oral art forms can help us to identify those features of oral text which, when in memory, support the making of oral narrative. Examination of linguistic patterns and text organizations can help us to tell a more coherent story, and one that is more genuinely oral in nature. It can also help us to avoid the making of a literary story from honest oral material.

Converting back to a mentality of orality may not be entirely possible for storytellers who are steeped in literacy. However, some knowledge of the nature and organization of the language and construction of oral text can help us learn to tell a more authentic and genuine story. Over time, and with much practice, we might even accumulate a sufficient amount of memory for oral formulae to be able to invent a bit. One notable milestone in the development of a revivalist story-teller is the eventual ability to retell a "heard" story without having to use print as a mediator.

The following chapters are designed to provide some insight regarding the formulaic content and organization of the oral narrative. They cover text structure and language formulae, motifs, numbers, and humor.

13

The Language of Story

A wise man will hear, and will increase learning; and a man of understanding shall attain unto wise counsels: To understand a proverb and the interpretation; the words of the wise and their dark sayings.
—Proverbs 1: 5-6

INTRODUCTION

Because oral traditions and the knowledge they preserve must be trusted to in-mind memory, thoughts are cast in regular, predictable, highly conventional language—prescriptive formulae. In order to conserve both oral text and its contents, strict adherence to such formulae is necessary. Ritualized and elaborated sayings are patterns or recipes, and are almost always metaphoric: "The early bird catches the worm." "For every rip there is a patch." "Never look a gift horse in the mouth." "Let sleeping dogs lie." Formula encodes important, lasting thought (Ong 1982).

Remembering and composing oral art forms depends upon set patterns which are regular, repetitive, predictable, and conventional. Discrepant content and nonformula language is not likely to become a part of the community tradition. Stories are constructed from prescriptive devices which organize language itself into predictable structures in order to ensure memory. Rhyme, meter, alliteration, synecdoche, metaphor, simile, metonymy, onomatopoeia, chant and rhythm, proverb, allegory, riddle, joke, epithet, and other formula sayings are contrivances forged by oral cultures to preserve cultural wit and wisdom, and to support the oral composition of such extended text as the story. Story often amplifies and organizes these devices, fitting them into its own structure and using them to provide internal text coherence.

SOUND DEVICES

Rhyme, meter, alliteration, onomatopoeia, chant, and rhythm are memory devices which are constructed using sound. Memory is obviously enhanced by patterns of repetitive sound (moon, spoon, June, tune, croon [rhyme]; one flea fly flew up the flue, the other flea fly flew down [alliteration]). Onomatopoeia uses sound in an almost metaphoric manner, the perceived pattern of sound intended to duplicate its nonlinguistic counterpart: schwooush, smash, crash, pop, plop, bif, bam, whack! "Whickety whack, jump into my sack!" combines rhyme, alliteration, and onomatopoeia in a single formula, and is most memorable. Meter organizes sound sequences into repetitive patterns of stress—beat rhythms.

WHICKETY WHACK, JUMP INTO MY SACK!

LITTLE PIG, LITTLE PIG, LET ME COME IN.

NOT BY THE HAIR ON MY CHINNY-CHIN-CHIN.

Oral art forms combine sound devices to make language that stays in memory as a whole, extended unit, and that invites chanting and participation. Melody (pitch patterns), when added to formulaic constructions, enhances both recall and audience involvement.

DEVICES OF COMPARISON AND ASSOCIATION

Simile, metaphor, synecdoche, metonymy, and allegory preserve memory and conserve information and language through comparison and association. Simile and metaphor provide simple and extended one-on-one comparisons, both indirect (*simile*: as white as the driven snow, as black as pitch) and direct (*metaphor*: the sun is a golden earring, the rain is a silver curtain, the grass is a carpet of down). Metaphor is a particularly complex invention of oral cultures. A metaphor can be limited to a single phrase, extended to a sequence of references which elaborate the same comparison, or expanded to encompass a story. Origin stories, such as those explaining the appearance of sun, moon, and stars in the heavens, are metaphors in story form.

Synecdoche is a figure of speech in which a reference to a part of or one aspect of a thing is taken for the whole ("the pawing and prancing of each little hoof"; "she finally earned her wings"; "he was showing off his new wheels"), or in which a reference to the whole is understood to represent only a part (a Midas touch, a Machiavellian solution, an atomistic approach). *Metonymy* is a rhetorical use of terminology in which the name for one thing can stand for something else, provided that an association between the two is commonly understood. "Hitting the bottle" (drinking heavy stuff), "the crown" (the monarchy), "counting noses" or "counting heads" (counting people) all exemplify metonymy.

Allegory is a form which represents a usually abstract and/or spiritual meaning by referencing something concrete which conveys the intended image or association. The simple allegory is a single, direct allusion: mankind as God's flock, God as shepherd. Stories in their entirety can also be allegories. Aesop uses the ant to represent the wisdom of industry, the grasshopper to represent indolence and sloth, the bullfrog to represent pride and vanity, and the stories themselves to count for human behavior. Many fables are allegorical, as are a considerable number of stories in the traditions of the great religions.

FORMULA SAYINGS

Formula sayings commonly incorporate the devices of sound, comparison, and association to construct witticisms and to make the recipes for remembering critical information. Question/ answer riddles, knock-knocks, the rhyming riddle, the limerick, proverbs, expressions, sayings, and countless mnemonic inventions ("Thirty days hath September ...") account for a substantial proportion of the oral text that has survived the literacy revolution. Formula sayings often stand alone; however, they are commonly incorporated into stories, or they represent the story boiled down to an absolute minimum.

Formula sayings also include epithets ("wicked witch"; "graceful swan") and other aggregative units (phrases and clauses) from which stories and epic poems are constructed. Lord (1981) lists aggregative units collected from Yugoslavian epic poets:

> "Shout comrade, and help us, God!"
>
> "So it shall be, if God grants ..."
>
> "To help and entertain ..."
>
> "To protect us from all torment ..."
>
> "One morning when it was dawn ..."
>
> "The chilly dew fell ..."
>
> "The green garden blossomed ..."
>
> "What was once in time ..."
>
> "What our elders accomplished ..."
>
> (Lord 1981, 70.)

Such units are wholes which are stitched together much as an author/writer in a literary tradition combines word units into larger chunks of text.

THE LANGUAGE UNIT

Because the idea of *word* (wordness) evolved along with the development of written language (Ong 1982; Downing 1982; Smith 1988), the language unit for composition of oral text is not a word. It is a phrase, clause, or sentence (a sound unit). A word is a visual unit resulting from the need to segment written text into minimal meaning units to accommodate a visual process. Literate people can hear words in oral language, despite the fact that sound units are not broken up into words by breaks in articulation, because literate people know how written language is segmented. For the individual who reads, the idea of word is *retroactive* to oral language (Ong 1982).

The oral art form is constructed by combining sound units (not words). Sound units are the recipes or formulae, the oral patterns which compound the devices of sound, comparison, association, and saying. Sound units are aggregative wholes (Ong 1982). They are intact truths without internal segmentation, and are unsegmentable. Difficult as this notion is for the literate to fathom—"word" is a powerful idea—the sound unit of the oral art form is remembered and known as a singular item and not as a unit composed of smaller recognizable parts. For instance, the epithetic formulae /dirtydog/, /sturdyoak/, /mightyhunter/, /swiftrunner/, /uglytroll/, /meanwitch/, and /beautifulmaiden/ are whole sound units. In written language, these would be segmented, e.g., dirty dog. Written language therefore suggests a different kind of syntax, specifically, an adjective/noun relationship. "Rover was a dirty dog." We would presume that the dog is dirty, and that if he were to have a bath, he might be (temporarily) clean. The epithet /dirtydog/ cannot be segmented; it has no internal syntax. It is as small as it can possibly be. /Mightyhunter/ has meaning as an unsegmentable unit. In a genuinely oral tradition, we would never entertain the possibility that the hunter might have a few off days. The contents of the epithet, "mighty" and "hunter," do not work together in the reasoned relationship of the literate world as adjective/noun.

The units of the oral art form are chunks that, in written language, would have considerable internal structure. In the traditions of composition of oral text, however, no such internal baggage exists. The oral units are the equivalent, perhaps, of written words, in that the storyteller puts the story together by organizing such formulaic wholes into larger units of discourse. These larger units are themselves segmentable. They can be *de*composed into the formulae or the units that constitute them. Alfred B. Lord (1981) lists the unsegmentable units (phrases and clauses) that comprise the orally composed texts of the Yugoslavian epic poets whose performances he documents. He suggests that such units are, along with memory for overall text structure, the basic pieces for construction. The storytellers use the rules or methods (also formulaic) for putting the smaller units together. Combination by formula is the guiding principle of the oral composition (Ong 1982), and the formulae themselves are what the teller holds in memory (Lord 1981). Perhaps the best residual oral unit left to literate societies is /ONCEUPONATIME/. The most literate individuals among us have no difficulty in perceiving that phrase as a basic and unsegmentable whole.

Composition of oral text is difficult for the literate, revivalist storyteller: first, because so much of the primary oral material has been transformed into written language, and second, because the teller has to learn many stories before memory for the basic units of the oral art form develops. While beginning storytellers are urged never to memorize stories—a telling is a *composition*, not a *recitation*—the formulae that make a story regular and aid memory and oral composition may not be readily apparent. Perhaps revivalist storytellers can measure their maturity as practitioners by the evolution of a telling from an oral text that is literate (that is, nonformulaic) to composition that is based in formula.

NAMING

Word in oral traditions does not mean what literates take it to mean—a unit of print. *Word* is a reference to the power of language to make or create. *Word* is an event, not a thing (Ong 1982). The word is a dynamic force, a power, a magical potency, and is conceived of as action. The primary oral conception of *word* is closely associated with names and naming. When we use the word to name something, we make it; we take its power. By naming a thing, we gain control over it, and the ability to call it or to invoke it. The gods of the ancient world had names which people could use in common conversation, sacred names by which they could be invoked, and sacred, secret names which were not to be used except in times of great peril. In many cultures, children are given many names, one of which is secret and must never be revealed lest others gain power over one's thoughts and actions by using it. In many cultures, the names of the deceased are never to be used. Instead, euphemisms substitute for such references.

Name is a powerful tool and an equally potent force. Naming can be used to take power and to give it. Names do not simply have meanings; they bequeath the magical essences of their referents. Neither the giving nor the calling of a name are frivolous acts.

Names of people, places, and things are symbols with many cultural meanings. The scholarly study of names is called *onomastics* (quite a name itself). When we meet people, the first thing we usually exchange is our names. What is behind our family names and our first, middle, and nicknames?

No matter where you travel, places have names. Of course place names help us communicate specific information, but where did countries, cities, towns, rivers, lakes, oceans, and continents get their names? The same goes for everything in life: It has a name. Someone gave it that name for some reason. Some names are apparently purely descriptive. Other reasons for names could be romantic, hopeful, imaginative, cultural, or despairing.

Stop and think about it. What if we did not have names? How would we ask for food? Drink? Shelter? Clothes? Each other? Of course we are much more organized today in our naming of people than before; we have to be. How could we operate without telephone directories, atlases, and road map information?

Most family names refer to a locality, a relationship, an occupation, or a description or characteristic of the person named. Native Americans have special beliefs about names. It was believed that the name had to fit the person. Secret names were given, and the wrong name could bring on illness. Milton Meltzer wrote, "In ancient times Chinese doctors would write a patient's name on a piece of paper, then burn the paper and mix the ashes with medicine to guarantee that the medicine would cure the sick person" (Meltzer 1984).

The following information is only a brief look at and sampling of names and naming. There are stories for all of the names, and storytellers may be able to embed naming stories in the tales they tell.

Names of Minerals

Garnet. Derived from the Latin word for *pomegranate* because of the resemblance between this mineral and the seeds of that fruit. Legends about garnets attribute it with many virtues, among which is the ability to protect the wearer from accidents during travel. Garnet bullets were employed against the British in 1892 in the war in Kashmir.

Mica. Probably from the Latin word *micare* which means "to shine or glitter." Sheet and leaf mica are from a fascinating group called *muscovite*. Muscovite earned its name several centuries ago when it was used as window panes in Russia, a use which extended even to the portholes of old Russian man-of-war ships. It was commonly called "Muscovy Glass."

Place Names

- Alamosa, Colorado, was named by an early settler for the Spanish word *alamosa*, which means "cottonwood grove."

- Arapahoe is a common name in Colorado. It is not only the name of a place, but is also a name given to mountains, peaks, and a county. The Arapaho Indians lived in this region. Their own name for themselves was *Inunaina*, or "our people."

- Basalt, Colorado, was named for Basalt Peak which rises from the center of a large outcrop of basaltic lava.

- Beulah, Colorado, was chosen at a social gathering, and is a Hebraic word meaning "married" or "inhabited."

- Bow Mar, Colorado, got its name because it is located between Bowles and Marston Lakes. It is a combination of the first syllables from each of the lakes.

- Columbine, Colorado, is named for the flower that grew there in profusion. The columbine is also Colorado's state flower.

- Cripple Creek, Colorado, was named by early cowboys because a cow was crippled attempting to cross it.

- Deer Trail, Colorado, was a natural place name for the place where deer drank from Bijou Creek.

- Delhi, Colorado, may have gotten its name from the city in India, but it could have also been an exotic name chosen without any reason.

- Egnar, Colorado, is unique because it is the reverse spelling of "range." It was adopted after the range land was thrown open to homesteading and a post office was established. One account has it that the name Range was desired, but was already in use by another town.

- Eldora, Colorado, was chosen for a similar reason. It was established as a gold mining camp and people wanted to call it *Eldorado*, which is Spanish for "golden." However, when the application for a post office was made, there was a prior claim, so the name was shortened to Eldora.

- Fairplay, Colorado, was founded by gold seekers who were angered to find the best placers at the nearby Tarryall diggings taken. They found other rich deposits and established their own camp, called Fair Play as a jeer at their rivals' camp which they nicknamed "Graball." Fairplay, officially one word, indicated there would be fair play for all.

- Galetea, Colorado, got its name either for the heroine of Cervantes's novel *La Galatea* or from the heroine of a Greek legend.

- Greeley, Colorado, was named for Horace Greeley of the *New York Tribune*, who was impressed with the agricultural possibilities of the country.

- Hesperus, Colorado, was named for the Latin word for Venus, the evening star.

- Hygiene, Colorado, was named by a Dunkard pastor after an early sanitarium, Hygiene Home.

- Idaho Springs, Colorado, has a controversial background. One version says it is a derivation from the Indian word meaning "gem of the mountains." Another translates it to "rocks." It also could have come from *Idahi*, the Kiowa-Apache name for the Comanches.

- Silver Plume, Colorado, was named for the silver ore found there, which was in the shape of a perfect feather.

- Wild Horse, Colorado, was once a watering place for immense bands of wild horses. Zebulon Pike said, "They came charging up making the earth tremble under them like a charge of cavalry."

From just this sampling of Colorado place names, it is evident that names were given in a variety of ways. The first settlers, animals, plants, minerals, geology, names from other cultures, mistakes, romance, and sometimes just plain fooling around were all involved in places naming. All states have a rich history as to how places there got their names. All you have to do is look for them.

Terminology for Groups of Animals, Birds, and People

The traditional use of figures of speech for collective terms for birds, animals, and people has come to us from a variety of inspirations. The first type of group terms developed from onomatopoeia. For example, "a murmuration of starlings" and "a gaggle of geese" contain this element. Next, some terms derive from a characteristic of the animal such as "a leap of leopards" and "a skulk of foxes." This group is the largest. Third, the terms may be associated with appearance. "A knot of toads" and "a bouquet of pheasants" demonstrates this. Fourth, the habitat of the creature may be responsible for the term, such as "a shoal of bass" and "a nest of rabbits." Fifth, a comment or point of view gives the group name. "A richness of martens" and "a cowardice of curs" fit here. Sixth, an error or incorrect transcription can stick. "A school of fish" is an example of this: "school" originally was "shoal."

The following terms might be useful in developing and embellishing a story.

- An abominable sight of monks.
- An army of caterpillars.
- A balding of ducks.
- A bale of turtles.
- A band of men (hence, a group of musicians is a *band*).
- A barren of mules.
- A bevy of beauties.
- A bevy of roebucks.
- A blackening of shoemakers.
- A blast of hunters.
- A boast of soldiers.
- A bouquet of pheasants.
- A brood of hens.
- A building of rooks.

- A business of ferrets.
- A cajolery of taverners.
- A cast of hawks.
- A cete of badgers.
- A charm of finches.
- A clowder of cats.
- A cluster of churls.
- A cluster of grapes.
- A cluster of knots.
- A clutch of eggs.
- A colony of ants.
- A congregation of plovers.
- A converting of preachers.
- A covey of partridges.

- A cowardice of curs.
- A crash of rhinoceroses.
- A cry of players.
- A cutting of cobblers.
- A deceit of lapwings.
- A descent of woodpeckers.
- A dignity of canons.
- A diligence of messengers.
- A discretion of priests.
- A dissimulation of birds.
- A disworship of scots.
- A doctrine of doctors.
- A draught of bottlers.
- A dray of squirrels.
- A drift of fishermen.
- A drift of hogs.
- A drove of cattle.
- A drunkenness of cobblers.
- A dule of doves.
- An eloquence of lawyers.
- An exaltation of larks.
- An example of masters.
- An execution of officers.
- A faith of merchants.
- A fall of woodcock.
- A fighting of beggars.
- A flight of swallows.
- A flock of sheep.
- A foresight of housekeepers.
- A gaggle of geese.
- A gaggle of women.
- A gam of whales.
- A gang of elk.
- A goring of butchers.
- A harras of horses.

- A herd of elephants.
- A herd of harlots.
- A host of angels.
- A host of men.
- A host of sparrows.
- A hover of trout.
- A husk of hares.
- An illusion of painters.
- An impatience of wives.
- An impertinence of peddlers.
- An incredulity of cuckolds.
- A kindle of kittens.
- A knot of toads.
- A labor of moles.
- A lash of carters.
- A laughter of hostlers.
- A litter of pups.
- A lying of pardoners.
- A melody of harpists.
- A murder of crows.
- A murmuration of starlings.
- A mustering of storks.
- A neverthriving of jugglers.
- A nye of pheasants.
- An obeisance of servants.
- An observance of hermits.
- An ostentation of peacocks.
- A pace of asses.
- A paddling of ducks.
- A plague of locusts.
- A parliament of owls.
- A passel of brats.
- A peep of chickens.
- A pencil of lines.
- A pitying of turtledoves.

- A pod of seals.
- A pontificality of prelates.
- A poverty of pipers.
- A pride of lions.
- A promise of tapsters.
- A proud showing of tailors.
- A prudence of vicars.
- A rafter of turkeys.
- A rag of colts.
- A rage of maidens.
- A rascal of boys.
- A richness of martens.
- A riffraff of knaves.
- A route of knights.
- A route of wolves.
- A safeguard of porters.
- A school of clerks.
- A scolding of seamstresses.
- A sentence of judges.
- A set of ushers.
- A shrewdness of apes.
- A siege of herons.
- A singular of boars.
- A skein of geese (in flight).
- A skulk of foxes.
- A skulk of friars.
- A skulk of thieves.

- A slate of candidates.
- A sloth of bears.
- A smack of jellyfish.
- A smirk of couriers.
- A sounder of swine.
- A spring of teal.
- A squat of daubers.
- A stalk of foresters.
- A state of princes.
- A string of ponies.
- A subtlety of sergeants.
- A superfluity of nuns.
- A swarm of bees.
- A temperance of cooks.
- A thrave of threshers.
- A threatening of courtiers.
- A tidings of magpies.
- A trip of goats.
- A troop of kangaroos.
- An unkindness of ravens.
- An untruth of summoners.
- A walk of snipe.
- A wandering of tinkers.
- A watch of nightingales.
- A waywardness of herdsmen.
- A wisp of snipe.
- A worship of writers.

PROVERBS

As snow in summer, and as rain in harvest, so honor is not seemingly for a fool.

As the bird by wandering, as the swallow by flying, so the curse causeless shall not come.

Answer not a fool according to his folly, lest thou also be like unto him.

As a dog returneth to his vomit, so a fool returneth to his folly.

As the door turneth upon his hinges, so doth the slothful upon his bed.

He that passeth by and meddleth with strife belonging not to him is like one that taketh a dog by the ears.

Where no wood is, there the fire goeth out; so where there is no talebearer, the strife ceaseth.

The words of a talebearer are as wounds, and they go down into the innermost parts of the belly.

He that hateth dissembleth with his lips and layeth up deceit within him.

Whoso diggeth a pit shall fall therein, and he that rolleth a stone, it will return upon him.

(Prov. 26: 1, 2, 4, 11, 14, 17, 20, 24, 27).

Proverbs are defined as the "wisdom of many, and the wit of one." These lean, didactic, aphoristic statements are nuggets of truth. Proverbs come to us from many sources, places, and times. Plain people making everyday observations, philosophers, and writers of literature have contributed to our collections of proverbs.

The true proverb is couched in metaphoric language. The universal message is expressed in concrete, poetic language, but the meaning is deeper and more abstract. People who grapple with proverbs will come eventually to the deep meaning by learning how to bridge the subtle symbols.

The word *proverb* means literally "before the word." The proverbs are guides through the thicket of social life. There are proverbs for paying respect; expressing pleasure, sympathy, or regret; to make people laugh; to blame or criticize; to apologize; to insult, thank, or cajole; to ask a favor; or to say farewell. Proverbs deal with the fundamental stuff of life: love and war, birth and death, sickness and health, work and play, wealth and poverty.

Proverbs can be used to add to the authenticity of the ethnic background of the story or to make a moral point emphatic. Sometimes, in storytelling, the right proverb can be woven into substories within the larger story. These pithy embellishments can be demonstrations of a character's speaking mannerism. Whole, new stories can be developed around proverbs. Sayings as story beginnings work very well. They seem more direct and precise before the story rather than after the fact. The initiating proverb acts to stimulate prediction.

Proverbs can also be chosen to suit the theme of the story or to fit the story subject. A story about a wise person would be a natural spot for a related proverb. However you choose to use them, appreciate and enjoy them also.

- "Take the Proverb to thy heart,
  Take, and hold it fast.
  Men live Now and Tomorrow;
  Learning, always, from the past" (Anonymous).

- When the heart overflows, it comes out through the mouth (Ethiopian).

- A proverb is the horse which can carry one swiftly to the discovery of ideas (Yoruba of Nigeria).

- It is better to live one day as a lion than a hundred years as a sheep (Italian).

- Spring is sooner recognized by plants than by men (Chinese).

- If you plan for the year, plant a seed. If you plan for a decade, plant a tree. If you plan for the century, educate the people (Chinese).

- The frog does not drink up the pond in which he lives (Native American).

- All mankind is divided into three classes: those that are immovable, those that are movable, and those that move (Arab).

- Measure your patience with pebbles. Mark every grievance by putting a pebble in a pouch. When the pouch is full, go to war (Native American).

- A good story fills the belly (Irish).

- People who bathe together can work together (Japanese).

- A book, tight shut, is but a block of paper (Chinese).

- The early bird catches the worm.

- A rolling stone gathers no moss.

- The grass is always greener on the other side.

- People who live in glass houses shouldn't throw stones.

- One good turn deserves another.

- A bird in the hand is worth two in the bush.

- Early to bed and early to rise, makes a man healthy, wealthy, and wise.

- Waste not, want not.

- Look before you leap.

- Silence is golden.

- A stitch in time saves nine.

- A penny saved is a penny earned.

- With seven nurses, the child has no eye (Russian).

- Too many cooks spoil the broth.

- Two midwives will deliver a baby with a crooked head (Iranian).

- With so many roosters crowing, the sun never comes up (Italian).

- Too many boatmen run the boat up to the top of the mountain (Japanese).

- It leaks at the gunwale, it leaks in the keel (Samoan).

- An eye for an eye, a tooth for a tooth (Bible).

- A goat's hide buys a goat's hide and a gourd a gourd (Nandi tribe, East Africa).

- A soft answer turneth away wrath.

- Handsome is as handsome does.

- Like father, like son.

- Don't count your chickens before they hatch.

- The burned child fears the fire.

- He whom the serpent hath bitten is terrified at a rope.

- The proof of the pudding is in the eating.

- The acorn does not fall far from the tree.

- The pot calling the kettle black.

- Money talks.

- A man is known by the company he keeps.

- Birds of a feather flock together.

- Many hands make light work.

- He who pays the piper, calls the tune.

- When ignorance is bliss, 'tis folly to be wise.

- Fine feathers make fine birds.

- You can't judge a book by its cover.

- He who hesitates is lost.

- Stolen fruit is the sweetest.

- Nothing ventured, nothing gained.

- The wood for a temple does not come from one tree (Chinese).

- There's more than one way to skin a cat.

- Many roads lead to Rome.

- Don't put all your eggs in one basket.

- Patients with the same disease sympathize with each other (Japanese).

- Misery loves company.

- To grind a blunt axe into a needle requires only hard labor (Chinese).

- When the kettle boils over, it overflows its own sides (Hebrew).

- What is the vulture to eat, if the horses and donkeys don't die? (Hausa).
- One ass nicknames another "Longears" (German).
- The bee hath sweetness and a sting (Hausa).
- Never a rose without a thorn.
- Even the longest journey begins with one step.
- It's an ill wind that blows no good.
- Don't cut off your nose to spite your face.
- All that glitters is not gold.
- Strike while the iron is hot.
- Never put off till tomorrow what you can do today.
- Half a loaf is better than none.
- Hell hath no fury like a woman scorned.
- When the cat's away, the mice will play.
- No news is good news.
- It takes two to tango.
- If the shoe fits, wear it.
- Woman's work is never done.
- The early bird catches the worm.
- Beauty is only skin deep.
- If at first you don't succeed, try, try again.
- A watched pot never boils.
- Chickens always come home to roost.
- Ice three feet thick isn't frozen in a day (Chinese).
- Young gambler — old beggar (German).
- Where the river is deepest, it makes the least noise (Italy).
- Still waters run deep.
- If you climb up a tree, you must climb down that same tree (Ghana).
- You cannot get two skins from one cow (England).
- Eggs must not quarrel with stones (Chinese).
- A horse that arrives early gets good drinking water (African).
- The love of money is the root of all evil (Hebrew).
- The wife at another's house has the pretty eyes (African).
- God gives the milk but not the pail (German).
- Punch yourself to know how painful it is to others (Japanese).

- A bird in the hand is worth a hundred flying (Mexican).
- Sing and cares disappear (Polish).
- One man's story is no story; hear both sides (Japanese).
- God is a good worker but he loves to be helped (Spanish).
- Many a good man is to be found under a shabby hat (Chinese).
- Fine clothes don't make the man (Japanese).
- Two captains sink the ship (Japanese).
- Little by little grow the bananas (Dahomey).
- If you want to go fast, go the old road (Burma).
- Six feet of earth makes all men equal (Italy).
- Eat to live, not live to eat (Greece).
- He who stands with his feet on two ships will be drowned (Russian).
- A little in your own pocket is better than much in another's purse (Spain).
- Joy, moderation, and rest shut out the doctors (Germany).
- He who rides the tiger finds it difficult to dismount (Chinese).
- You can lead a horse to water but you can't make him drink.
- A miss is as good as a mile.
- Don't cross your bridges before you come to them.
- Laugh and the world laughs with you; cry and you cry alone.
- It is always darkest before the dawn.
- He was so learned that he could name a horse in nine languages; so ignorant that he bought a cow to ride on.
- Write injuries in dust, benefits in marble.
- A slip of the lip can sink the ship.
- When it is a question of money, everybody is of the same opinion.
- You can't sell the cow and have the milk too.
- You can't tell the depth of the well by the length of the handle on the pump.
- He must hunger in the frost who will not work in the heat.
- Work is fire for frozen fingers.
- You can't have your cake and eat it too.
- You can't judge wine by its barrel.
- You can't grow hair on a billiard ball.
- You can't squeeze blood from a turnip.

- You can't make a silk purse out of a sow's ear.
- You can't make cookies when you haven't got the dough.
- Be it ever so humble, there's no place like home.
- It is easy to be generous with another man's money.
- Don't burn your candle at both ends.
- One man's meat is another man's poison.
- It is better to be safe than sorry.
- Figures never lie, but liars can figure.
- There are two sure things—death and taxes.
- All things come to him who waits.
- A new broom sweeps clean.
- It is the squeaky wheel that gets oiled.
- You make your bed, so you must lie on it.
- Don't buy a pig in a poke.
- Better late than never.
- As the twig is bent, so grows the tree.
- Life is not a problem to be solved, but a gift to be enjoyed.
- You're never too old to learn.
- You can't teach an old dog new tricks.
- Where there is smoke there is fire.
- Two wrongs don't make a right.
- The higher they stand, the farther they fall.
- Two is company, three is a crowd.
- Prevention is better than cure.
- Spare the rod and spoil the child.
- Jack of all trades, master of none.
- Little pitchers have big ears.
- If it ain't broke, don't fix it.
- If it isn't worth doing right, it isn't worth doing.
- Never trouble trouble until trouble troubles you.
- Absence makes the heart grow fonder.
- Too soon old, too late smart.
- Time and tide wait for no man.
- Time heals all wounds.

- Don't throw the baby out with the bath water.
- Don't hide your light under a bushel.
- Every tub must stand on its own bottom.
- The old forget, the young don't know.
- You can't put an old head on young shoulders.
- Experience is the best teacher.
- A smart mouse has more than one hole.
- The spirit is willing but the flesh is weak.
- A fool and his money are soon parted.
- Better to let them wonder why you didn't talk than why you did.
- Love is blind.
- What is sauce for the goose is sauce for the gander.
- Marry in haste, repent in leisure.
- A prophet is without honor in his own country.
- Practice what you preach.
- Evil words cut far worse than swords.
- It's too late to lock the barn door after the horses are stolen.
- Don't bite off more than you can chew.
- You catch more flies with honey than with vinegar.
- No use crying over spilled milk.
- One rotten apple spoils the barrel.
- It's the last straw that breaks the camel's back.
- Rats desert a sinking ship.
- Don't rub salt into a wound.
- Don't try to teach fishes to swim.
- You scratch my back and I'll scratch yours.
- You reap what you sow.
- Let sleeping dogs lie.
- The leopard can't change its spots.

- I hear, and I forget
  I see, and I remember
  I do, and I understand (Chinese).

- For every rip, there is a patch (Spanish).

- He who has little to lose has little to worry about (Spanish).

- A fair exchange is no robbery.

- A frog would leap from a throne of gold into a puddle.

- The frog's own croak betrays him.

- A frog in the well knows not of the ocean (Japanese).

- The frog flew into a passion and the pond knew nothing about it.

- When you live with a goat, you must get used to the bad smell (Russian).

- The YOO HOO you YOO HOO into the forest is the YOO HOO you get back.

- You can't tell how deep a puddle is until you step into it.

- One picture is worth more than ten thousand words (Chinese).

- A book is like a garden carried in the pocket (Chinese).

- Sharp bargains make fat purses.

- When someone has a debt, he must be kind and speak gently to whomever he has borrowed from. It is better to do good to them than evil (Hmong).

- To ask is no sin and to be refused is no calamity (Russian).

- Think much, speak little, and write less (Russian).

- If heaven wishes to rain, or your mother to remarry, there is no way to stop them (Chinese).

- Throw a lucky man into the sea, and he will come up with a fish in his mouth (Arabian).

- If you are born lucky even your rooster will lay eggs (Russian).

- Good luck beats early rising (Irish).

- Without perserverance, talent is a barren bed (Welsh).

- He who knows not and knows not he knows not:

    He is a fool—shun him.

  He who knows not and knows he knows not:

    He is simple—teach him.

  He who knows and knows not he knows:

    He is asleep—wake him.

  He who knows and knows he knows:

    He is wise—follow him (Arabian).

- Slow and steady wins the race (Aesop).

- Take your good fortune as it comes (Aesop).

- If you grab for more, you may lose what you already have (Aesop).

- Those who lie are not believed when they finally tell the truth (Aesop).

- Don't try to be what you can't be (Aesop).

- If you try to please everyone, you may very well please no one at all (Aesop).

- If something seems impossible to obtain, try using your brain (Aesop).

- There is no wealth where there are no children (African).

- Wisdom is not like money which should be kept in a safe (African).

- You send a wise person on an important mission, not a long-legged person (African).

- One must come out of one's house to begin learning (African).

- Truth came to the market and could not be sold; we buy lies with ready cash (African).

- If you see wrongdoing or evil and say nothing against it, you become its victim (African).

- Even the greatest bird must come down from the sky to find a tree to roost upon (African).

- If a quantity of water does not suffice for a bath, it will at least be sufficient for drinking (African).

- One does not make a shield in the battlefield (African).

- A house containing a bad person is better than an empty one (African).

- People are the home (African).

- When two antelopes are fighting and a lion approaches, the antelopes run off together (African).

- To get the warmth of the fire, one must stir the embers (African).

- Better be quarreling than lonesome (Irish).

- When whales fight, shrimp are eaten (Korean).

- A man would have to keep his mouth open a long, long time before a roast pheasant flies into it (Irish).

- Rooster, do not be so proud. Your mother was only an eggshell (African).

- Many things are lost for want of asking (English).

- When the drummer beats his drum, people far and near enjoy it (African).

- If the town people are all happy, look for the chief (African).

- Better than a hundred rubles is to have a hundred friends (Russian).

- He who knows a proverb can resolve conflicts (Nigerian).

- When spiders unite they can tie up a lion (Nigerian).

- When the storyteller speaks, the sun and the clouds stop to listen (Irish).

- Call no man happy until he is dead (Greek).

- A word is not a bird—if it flies out, you'll never catch it again (Russian).

- Examine the contents, not the bottle (Talmud).

- A wise man makes his own decisions; an ignorant man follows the public opinion (Chinese).

- Use it up; wear it out; make it do; or do without (New England).

- What may be done at any time will be done at no time (Scottish).

- A little learning makes the whole world kin (Prov. 32: 7).

- He is a good driver who knows how to turn (Danish).

- When a Jewish farmer eats a chicken, one of them is sick (Jewish).

- If you are patient in one moment of anger, you will escape a hundred days of sorrow (Chinese).

- If you wish to know what a man is, place him in authority (Yugoslavian).

- He who tells the truth should have one foot in the stirrup (Arabian).

- To know the truth is easy. But ah, how difficult to follow it (Chinese).

- Hard times will make a monkey eat pepper (African).

- In the council of the chickens, the cockroach has no say (Cuban).

- What is to come, even a bird with a long neck cannot see (Sierra Leone).

- One worm will spoil the whole soup pan (Vietnamese).

- The rock will be worn out from the flowing water (Vietnamese).

- Fatherless children eat rice without fish. Motherless children lick leaves on the street (Vietnamese).

- Distant relatives are not as helpful as neighbors (Vietnamese).

- The first man to raise his voice has lost the argument (Japanese).

- There's nothing in the world you don't need (Chinese).

- If your heart is honest, it is like a straight road (Chinese).

- Clean the river's way before the river comes (Ethiopian).

- Trees have ears (Ethiopian).

- A hungry eye sees far (Irish).

- Never bolt your door with a boiled carrot (Irish).

- Slow is every foot on an unknown path (Irish).

- There is no overtaking the shot once fired (Irish).

- The absent are always in the wrong (English).

- Write down the advice of him who loves you, though you like it not at present.

- The gem cannot be polished without friction, nor man perfected without trials (Chinese).

- The woman who tells her age is either too young to have anything to lose or too old to have anything to gain (Chinese).

- Anger is as a stone cast into a wasp's nest (Malabar).

- A wicked book cannot repent.

- He who borrows sells his freedom (German).

- Creditors have better memories than debtors.
- Examine what is said, not him who speaks (Arabian).
- Never swap horses crossing a stream (New England).
- Charity sees the need, not the cause (German).
- Charm is more than beauty (Yiddish).
- Children are poor men's riches (English).
- Better bend than break (Scottish).
- Open confession is good for the soul (Scottish).
- He who sacrifices his conscience to ambition burns a picture to obtain the ashes (Chinese).
- Since we cannot get what we like, let us like what we get (Spanish).
- To speak kindly does not hurt the tongue.
- A pig bought on credit is forever grunting (Spanish).
- Good men must die, but death cannot kill their names.
- One meets his destiny often in the road he takes to avoid it (French).
- The man who lives only by hope will die with despair (Italian).
- If a man is destined to drown, he will drown even in a spoonful of water (Yiddish).
- Who is not satisfied with himself will grow; who is not sure of his own correctness will learn many things (Chinese).
- Better lose the anchor than the whole ship (Dutch).
- When the Czar has a cold all Russia coughs (Russian).
- Clothes make the man (Latin).
- The only real equality is in the cemetery (German).
- Not the cry, but the flight of the wild duck, leads the flock to fly and follow (Chinese).
- He who buys what he needs not, sells what he needs (Japanese).
- What the fool does in the end, the wise man does in the beginning.
- No gain is so certain as that which proceeds from the economical use of what you already have (Latin).
- A homely girl hates mirrors.

CONVERSATION AS A MARTIAL ART

People have spoken and written of others using words as weapons. The following folk sayings constitute effective war with words. The creators of these sayings probably will not be sued for what they have said about others, but they have certainly managed to say it with originality and pithy observation.

- "If I saw Mr. Haughey buried at midnight at a crossroads, with a stake driven through his heart—politically speaking—I should continue to wear a clove of garlic around my neck, just in case" (speculation about a general election in Ireland).

- "Well now, do you remember what they said about Conor Cruise when he was minister of posts, telephones and telegraph? They said he was about as effective as a lighthouse on the Bog of Allen." (The bog happens to be a huge dismal swamp of peat, which when dried is the fuel of turf fires.)

- Daniel O'Connell, the great champion of Irish home rule, once likened British prime minister Robert Peel's smile to "the silver plate on a coffin."

- The mother who reared him would drown nothing.

- For her, the honeymoon was just a busman's holiday.

- The foreman sent him for an x-ray to see if there was a trace of work left in him.

- A tenement dweller pouring out her anguish to a Dublin court trying her three teenaged sons on drug-dealing charges: "I'm heart-scalded with the lot of them."

- An old Irish "shawlie" telling her parish priest what it was like to be visited by the ghost of her dead husband: "It felt like a wind from the sea coming bechuxst me skin and me blood."

- A venerable cleric telling a waitress in the Gresham Hotel to serve the old-fashioned brandy fruitcake: "At our age it's nice to have archaic and eat it."

- English spoken in Ireland, as playwright Brian Friel noted, has a "syntax opulent with tomorrows."

- God took mud to create the world, man takes words to create his own world. While God's men die, their words live" (Hungarian).

- She was so buck-toothed she could eat corn on the cob through a fence" (Southeast United States).

- He was so short he could sit on cigarette paper and still dangle his legs" (Southeast United States).

- When we were kids and played kick-the-can, it was so pitch-dark out there that you couldn't hear the can, let alone see it.

- Our town is so small, even the dogs are subject to gossip.

WESTERNISMS

Throughout the years, the authors have gathered wonderful uses of language—language that painted pictures. These quotations are, among other things, social commentaries and occupational observations, and again might fit perfectly in a specific story to add some color. Since these were collected out in the West, we call them "Westernisms." Wherever you live, you will also find Southernisms, Easternisms, and Northernisms. Tune your ears to recognize and discover them.

- "We saw what we had to do and it didn't work." (A newly built water tower collapsed in Texas after it was built.)

- "The small miner is one that has less than four attorneys. I've got two and I'm not even operating" (Norm Blake of Blackhawk, Colorado).

- "A mine is a hole in the ground owned by a liar" (Mark Twain).

- "To hell with any mine that won't pay under mismanagement" (Choppo Fedderhoff of Idaho Springs, Colorado).

- An old timer was talking with someone on a hot day; the other person was complaining about the heat. They had just experienced a hard winter, and the old timer retorted, "I never shoveled sunshine!"

- God doesn't give babies to women over 50 because they would forget where they put them.

- It's hard not to get something when you already have something.

- "I am 82 years old, you know. When I was a younger man, I din' remember nothin, and now I remember less" (Ben Ortega of Chimayo, New Mexico).

- How hot was it? — a real scorcher.

  - hot enough to bake a snake's bellybutton.

  - hot enough to fry an egg on a lily pad.

  - hot enough to steam the hide off a heifer.

  - hot enough to melt a feller's coloring book crayons.

- Only a fool argues with a skunk, a mule, or a camp cook.

- "One of the symptoms of an approaching nervous breakdown is the belief that one's work is terribly important" (Bertrand Russell).

- "He was so slow flies died on him" (Lee Pennington).

- Never lend a man your horse, your gun, or your wife.

- Never camp this side of the stream — always cross to the further side.

- Talk is cheap and lies worth nothing.

- Never go down a cliff that you can't climb back up.

- Do not drink water you cannot see and sign no paper you do not read.

- Hope does not fatten but it keeps you going.

- Cowboys used horse stuff on their lips. It doesn't cut down on chapped lips but it sure keeps you from licking them.

- For someone who pays attention and understands, you don't need many words to explain.

- A person who does not look back at his past will never reach his destination.

- Better run than fight badly.

- Nothing scratches your own skin like your own fingernails.

- Men are like steel, of little use when they lose their temper.

- Don't say hello before you have crossed the creek.

- When a beautiful woman smiles, some man's purse weeps.

- "Do you believe in free speech? I need you to present _____."

- Sergeant Preston said the scenery only changes for the lead dog.

- As tight as a gnat's ass stretched over a barrel.

- "Nothing is a bung hole with a barrel around it" (Eleanor Hoch).

- "Securities are our illusions" (Ashley Bryan).

- "We can get there from here" (Glenn McGlathery).

- "He who hesitates is lost. He who is lost hesitates" (George Livo).

- "Don't shake your dog finger [index] at me" (the finger used to sic the dogs on runaway blacks) (Lee Pennington).

- "Fine as frog's hair cut lengthwise four times with a broad ax" (Jimmy Neil Smith).

- True friends are like diamonds, precious but rare; false ones like autumn leaves, found everywhere.

- My hogs are so poor it takes six of them to cast a shadow.

- My hogs are so poor that every morning I have to get up a half hour early and soak them in the horse tank before they will hold slop.

- He's so cheap he used to sit in the shade of the cottonwood tree so he could save the shade on the porch.

- He's so tender hearted that he can't stand to see his wife work, so he puts on his hat and goes to town.

- We were too poor to paint and too proud to whitewash.

- His kid was so ugly they used to have to tie a pork chop around his neck so the dog would play with him.

- The kid was so ugly when he was a baby they had to dunk him in the water and look for bubbles so they'd know which end to put the diaper on.

- When I was little I was born a twin and my parents could only afford one, so they threw the ugliest one in the river — and that's where I learned to swim.

- I was the runt of the family, and I was so ugly that when my mother put me out to play in the sandbox, the neighbor's cat covered me up three times.

- This girl was so ugly that in the dictionary they put her picture under the word *ugly*.

- She's uglier than homemade sin, dipped in misery.

- She has a face on her like a fried egg.

- She's uglier than a mud fence.

- Up the creek without a paddle.

- That team won't pull the hat off your head.

- He rides like a sack of wet meal.

- She looks like a sack of oats tied in the middle.

- Going to hell in a handbasket.

- Slap you up to a peak and then slap the peak off.

- Stomp a mudhole in you and stomp the mudhole dry.

- You're about as handy as a whistle on a plow.

- Whistling girls and cackling hens never come to very good ends.

- If you want the oats before they go through the horse, you have to pay more.

- He is such a liar he had to get a neighbor to call his own dog for him.

- That stream is too thick to drink and not thick enough to plow.

- They threw her in a lake and it boiled up so much no fish have lived in it since.

- I live in a house that grows dust.

- I was born before cellophane.

- It was like giving dry birth to a porcupine.

- He'd complain even if you hanged him with a brand new rope.

- He's got the world by the tail with a downhill pull.

- Slow as the seven-year itch, seven years behind scratching.

- Slick as warm snot on a door knob.

- There never was a lane so long that it doesn't have a turning.

- Kitchen is so small you can't cuss a cat without getting hair in your mouth.

- As low as a snake's belly in a wagon rut.

- Don't start chopping till you have treed the raccoon.

- Big enough to go bear hunting with a switch.

- Nervous as a long-tailed cat in a room full of rocking chairs.

- Slick as a wax snake on a marble floor.

- That hen was so tough you couldn't stick a fork in her gravy.

- To become a bigger liar, he'd have to put on weight.

- He could talk your arm off, then curse you for being crippled.

- Walks like an old hen with an egg broken inside her.

- You don't need that anymore than a tomcat needs a marriage license.

- Terms for liquor: sleep disturber, gum tickler, anti-fogmatic, nose tickler, wild mare's juice, gut warmer, nose paint, neck warmer, bottle courage, neck oil, Taos lightning, tangle legs.

- Drinking was "laying on a little more kindling wood."

- Terms for the cook: bean artist, bean master, belly cheater, biscuit shooter, greasy belly, dough wrangler, grub spoiler, gut robber.

- Terms for death: cashed in his chips, got a halo gratis, no breakfast forever, grass is waving over him, sawdust in his beard, shaking hands with Saint Peter, sacked his saddle, fried gent, took the big jump, gone over the range and landed in a shallow grave, pushing up daisies.

Obituaries

- Coroner's report: He came to his death from heart disease. We found two bullet holes and a knife in that organ. We recommend that Bill Younger be lynched to prevent spreading of the disease.

- He committed suicide at a distance of a hundred yards. He opened fire with a pistol against a man armed with a rifle.

- The deceased came to his death at the hands of an unknown party who was a damned good pistol shot.

- He committed suicide trying to outrun a bullet.

Cowland Terminology

- Airin' his lungs: cussing.

- Air tights: canned goods.

- Alkalied: acclimated to country.

- Angoras: chaps made of goat skin.

- Antelope big: butchered stolen beef for sale.

- Apple: saddle horn.

- An Arbuckle: a green hand.

- Basto: saddle skirt.

- Blocker: a large loop made with a rope.

- Brasada: evergreen oak.

- Brush popper: a cowhand who works in the brush.

- Bug on a rail: a type of brand.

- Cattalo: a hybrid offspring of a buffalo and cattle.

- Cheekin: to grab a horse by its head.

- Chihuahuas: nickname for big spurs.

- Churn-heads: horses who are bull-headed and with little sense.

- Cimarron: a human or an animal of any kind who runs by itself.

- Cloud-hunter: a horse bucking high.

- Coasters or sea lions: cattle raised along the Texas coast.

- Cold-jawed: a horse's mouth which is numb to a bit.

- Converter: a minister of the gospel.

- Count book: a little book to tally the number of cattle and brands.

- Coyotin' around: just fooling around any place.

- Crump incubator: a dirty undershirt.

- Drags: cattle in the tail end of the herd.
- To dry-gulch: to waylay and kill a man.
- Forging: a horse who strikes the heels of his front shoe with the back shoes.
- Grappling-irons: a pair of spurs.
- Gut-hooks: spurs.
- Hard tails: mules.
- Heeled: carrying a gun.
- Hobbled stirrups: when they are tied together under a horse.
- Hornswoggling: when a steer throws a rope off his neck or horns.
- Jerk-lines: a line to the lead mule of a freighting team.
- Jingle-bob: a mark made on an animal's hide with a knife.
- Leppy: an orphan calf.
- Lick: syrup or a salt lick.
- Long rope: a cow thief.
- Man-stopper: bullet.
- Moonshinin': working with a pack outfit.
- Night hawk: a night wrangler.
- Oklahoma rain: a sand storm.
- Orejana: an unbranded animal.
- Pie-biter: a horse who is a camp robber.
- Pilgrims: newcomers.
- Prairie lawyers: coyotes.
- Ramrod: cow boss.
- Ranahan: cowhand.
- Reefing: a term used when raking a horse with spurs.
- Reps: a man at a roundup representing some owner's brand.
- Ring bit: a Mexican bit, with a ring encircling the lower jaw.
- Road agents: hold-up men.
- Rosadero: a leather protection.
- Saddle warmer: slang for a cowhand.
- Sallie or old woman: pet name for a roundup cook.
- Segundo: straw boss.
- Slow elk: stolen beef.
- Snortin' post: a post to tie broncs to.
- Soogans: homemade quilts.
- Squeezin' em down: trimming a herd on the trail on a long narrow line.

- Strayman: an outsider working with the roundup.
- Sudadero: sweat pad under the saddle.
- Talk-box: a human mouth.
- Wattle: marking a cow's hide with a knife.
- Wisdom-bringers: professors or teachers.
- Woolies: sheep.
- Wrangatang: a day horse wrangler.

OTHER WAYS TO SAY "DUMB"

At a storytelling conference, Jackie Torrence regaled the audience with her description of one of the story characters. She said he was crazy and dumb; she then reeled off six or seven other rich ways to say the same thing. The listeners roared with laughter. Several people wrote to the conference organizer about how marvelous Jackie had been and they all included references to her quaint insults. Therefore, here is a collection of ways to describe "dumb" in clever terminology, so that you too can add some moments of humor to your stories whenever it is appropriate.

- He isn't driving with a full tank.
- He's so ignorant he can't drive nails into snow.
- He's not hauling a full load of bricks.
- The Lord poured in her brains with a teaspoon and someone joggled his arm.
- His elevator doesn't go to the top floor.
- Her library card hasn't been stamped.
- He doesn't have both oars in the water.
- She doesn't have a full knitting bag.
- Her porchlight doesn't go on.
- His ladder doesn't have a top rung.
- His oil is two quarts low.
- There's no cherry in her sundae.
- He's playing without a full deck.
- She got off the road of life two exits early.
- The stork lost some of her luggage.
- His alphabet doesn't go to "z."
- There's no cross on the top of her steeple.
- He's two tricks shy of a load.
- Someone didn't put the sandwiches in her lunchbox.
- There's no pilot in his cockpit.

- Her "vacancy" sign hangs out permanently.
- His book of life has no table of contents.
- Her apartment building is minus the penthouse.
- He doesn't have all the clubs in his bag.
- He doesn't have 11 men on the field.
- There are no strings in her tennis racquet.
- Her flag doesn't go all the way up the staff.
- Her beacon doesn't swing full-circle.
- His pilot light went out.
- Her porch lights flicker.
- His pilot light is on dim.
- She's all over the road.
- He just fell off the turnip truck.
- She is one bubble off plumb.
- He couldn't unfold his deck chair.
- She has a leak in the attic.
- His encyclopedia has several volumes missing.
- Her go cart has only three wheels.
- He is a flower pot with no flower.
- Her dice are missing a few dots.
- He acts as if he were casting for fish with an empty reel.
- She is running with one wheel in the sand.
- He is still missing some spare parts.
- She still has parts on order.
- All the butter has slipped off his noodles.
- His dip stick doesn't reach the oil.
- She is quietly knitting without needles.
- He couldn't manage a two-car funeral.
- Her transmitter is working but the receiver isn't.
- He is not wrapped too tight.
- She is a bale short of a stack.
- She doesn't have a full string of beads.
- His light is on but nobody is home.
- He's a wee bit away with the birds (Scottish).
- She couldn't lead a silent prayer.
- He couldn't find a stick with two ends.

SLANG TERMS FROM THE 1920s

In telling a story about or from the 1920s, the slang of the time will add authenticity to the tale. Here are some slang terms from the twenties that have been collected from folks who were there.

- All wet: wrong, arguing a mistaken notion or event, as in "you're all wet."
- Applesauce: a term of derogation, nonsense, same as boloney and bunk.
- Banana oil: hokum or horsefeathers.
- Bee's knees: a superb person or thing.
- Berries: anything wonderful, similar to bee's knees.
- Bible belt: an area in the South or Midwest where a fundamentalist religion prevails.
- Big cheese: a very important person.
- Bump off: to murder.
- Cake eater: a lady's man; the same as lounge lizard.
- Carry a torch: to suffer from unrequited love.
- Cat's meow: anything wonderful.
- Cheaters: eyeglasses.
- Copacetic: all right.
- Dogs: human feet.
- Drugstore cowboy: an idler who hangs around public places to pick up young girls; generally fashionably dressed.
- Dumb Dora: a stupid girl.
- Fall guy: a scapegoat.
- Flapper: the typical young girl of the twenties, usually with bobbed hair, short skirts, and rolled stockings.
- Flat tire: a dull, boring person.
- Gam: a girl's leg; from the French "gambe."
- Gin mill: a speakeasy or saloon selling bootleg whiskey.
- Gold digger: a woman who uses feminine charm to extract money from a man.
- Hard-boiled: tough and without sentiment.
- Heebie jeebies: the jitters.
- Hep: someone who is with it or wise.
- High hat: to put on airs and snub people.
- Hooch: bootleg liquor.
- Hotsy totsy: pleasing.
- Keen: appealing.

- Kiddo: a familiar form of address.
- Kisser: the mouth.
- Line: insincere flattery.
- Neck: to pet or caress intimately.
- Nerts: an expression of disgust.
- Ossified: drunk.
- Pinch: to arrest.
- Red neck: Catholic.
- Ritzy: elegant.
- Scram: to leave in a hurry.
- Sheba: a young woman with sex appeal.
- Sheik: a young man with sex appeal.
- Smeller: the nose.
- Spiffy: having an elegant or fashionable appearance.
- Splifflicated: drunk.
- Struggle buggy: a car; comes from being a place to seduce girls.
- Torpedo: a hired gunman.

FAN LANGUAGE

Just as words have meanings, so do gestures, use of objects and other non-verbal messages. The fan has been used throughout the ages for communication. If your story's characters have an occasion to use fans, these details can amplify and enrich their actions. Some of the ways women have given romantic encouragement or discouragement with their fans follow.

- With the fan handle to the lips, the woman is saying KISS ME.
- If the lady carries the fan in her right hand in front of her face, she is saying FOLLOW ME.
- If she carries the fan in her left hand, she is saying I AM DESIROUS OF YOUR ACQUAINTANCE.
- If she places it on her left ear, the message is YOU HAVE CHANGED.
- When she twirls the fan in her left hand, she is saying I WISH TO GET RID OF YOU.
- When she draws the fan across her forehead, she is saying WE ARE WATCHED.
- If she carries the fan in her right hand, she means YOU ARE TOO WILLING.
- When she draws the fan across her cheek, she is saying I LOVE YOU.
- If she draws the fan through her hand, she means I HATE YOU.

- When she twirls the fan in her right hand, the message is I LOVE ANOTHER.
- When she closes the fan, she says I WISH TO SPEAK TO YOU.
- If she draws the fan across her eyes, she means I AM SORRY.
- When she lets the fan rest on her right cheek, the message is YES.
- If she lets the fan rest on her left cheek, the message is NO.
- If she opens and shuts the fan, she means YOU ARE CRUEL.
- When she drops the fan, she is saying WE ARE FRIENDS.
- If she fans herself slowly, the message is I AM MARRIED.
- If she fans herself fast, she is saying I AM ENGAGED.
- If she holds the fan open wide, she is signaling WAIT FOR ME.

14

Numbers

INTRODUCTION

Number is in the story and is the story. Before the advent of written language, oral art forms (traditions) were entrusted to human memory. The experiences of living, boiled down to their essences, were cast into narrative patterns that may very well be evidence of the structure and organization of the human mind. "[A] common possession [oral narrative] of humankind was not ipso facto of little account but rather an indicator of the functioning of the mind, a part of the deep structure of the grammar of our world" (Rosen 1985, 7). "[N]arrative is a disposition of the mind, a valid and perhaps ineradicable mode of human experience" (Eagleton 1981, in Rosen 1985, 8). "[T]he drive to represent experience as narrative is indestructible" (Rosen 1985, 9).

The patterns of narrative discourse, including the habit of employing archetypal formulae, language "chunked" in epithetic phrases and clauses, parallel structures, and backloops made possible the storage in memory of large bodies of "unmemorized" oral text. Though people very likely made stories of all their experiences, stories which were told again and again were those that could be remembered, that were patterned for easy retrieval (could be constructed or stitched together from formulae in memory), and that dealt with the greater truths (Ong 1982). The structures and contents of such stories are of a universal nature.

The primary characteristic of oral narrative is its uniquely predictable and very mathematical grammar. Stories are organized around number formulae, based in elementary number, though traditional tellers in primary oral societies most probably did not study or analyze stories in order to determine their number patterns or understand their mathematical properties. The arithmetic nature of the stories is in all likelihood a reflection of the magical powers and spiritual potency of elementary numbers, and not at all related to "how many." Just as elementary numbers were originally situation-dependent, arising as an integral and inseparable part of a context and not as an analysis of it, the mathematics of stories was probably also emergent. Number in story evolved as a natural part of the making and remembering of narrative (its grammaticality and its meaning) and not as a set of abstractions applied to the deliberate invention of discourse. The numbers are in the stories and govern the stories, because the numbers figured profoundly in people's lives.

The mathematics of story is a very special semantic component of traditional narrative. This usually overlooked aspect of story meaning can be better apprehended by examination of the meanings of elementary and abstract numbers in folk traditions. Storytellers who unwittingly or otherwise change the number configuration of a story violate its grammaticality, damage the meanings which are inseparable from the structure of the text, and undo the spiritual potency of the narrative.

I'll sing you twelve — O.
Green grow the rushes — Ho.
What is your twelve — O?
Twelve for the twelve Apostles,
'Leven for the 'leven who went to heaven,
And ten for the Ten Commandments;
Nine for the nine bright shiners,
And eight for the April rainers;
Seven for the seven stars in the sky,
And six for the six proud walkers;
Five for the cymbals at your door,
And four for the Gospel makers;
Three, three, the rivals —
Two, two little white boys
Clothed all in green — O.
One is one,
And all alone,
And ever more shall be so.
(Traditional.)

Numbers provide a great deal more information about the universe than the answer to "How many?" Numbers are symbols of significant power. They possess innate mystical and mysterious attributes that make them much more than the tools of the empiricist. Numbers are magic. What a people believes about numbers will influence their entire world view and the basic structure of their cosmology. A system of beliefs and practices — superstitions, taboos, ritual formulae, dances, games, riddles and rhymes, the nature of the godhead, the structure and organization of an entire body of oral narrative — is fixed by the community's perception of the meanings of numbers. Numbers are spiritually potent and are at the foundation of the construction of all mental models.

Perhaps the magic of numbers can be more easily understood in terms of the function of language. Language is a *representative* system. Words, sentences, and larger discourses stand for the realities of things and experiences. The word *re-presents* the thing. Because the very existence of language guarantees it a separate reality of its own, what the word represents also becomes real. Language can create realities: That is magic. When language is used to tell about something that has already happened, or something that has not yet happened, it makes realities out of things which do not exist concretely in present time. That is magic, too. Language has the power to make, and that is a great power indeed. This is the heart and soul of storytelling. This is what storytelling is, and what storytelling does: storytelling is creation by the power of the word. It is magic and it makes magic.

In the beginning was the Word,
And the Word was with God,
And the Word was God.
(John 1: 1.)

... by the Word of God
The heavens were of old,
And the earth standing out of the water,
And in the water.
(2 Peter 3: 5.)

... the worlds were framed
By the Word of God,
So that things which are seen
Were not made of things which do appear.
(Hebrews 11:3.)

God used words to make. The creation was, in Judeo-Christian tradition, and in all other traditions, too, the first great magical act. God created something out of nothing, and did it by using words to name. Even today, we use language to make. Naming is making: By saying it, it becomes. Written words have even more magic. They can be used to make over extended times and distances. (Letters were—and are—believed by some to be imbued with special mystical qualities.)

Numbers are a different kind of language, but the power to make resides in numbers just as it does in words. Numbers make structures, frameworks, patterns. If words can make a reality, numbers decree the repetitions of the words which are necessary in order for the magic of the language to work. Numbers organize the manner in which other kinds of magic are accomplished. Numbers make the world of language and the world of experience sensible. It is no accident that a substantial portion of traditional oral discourse is organized in "sets": sets of twos, sets of threes, sets of fours, etc. Nor is it accident that formula incantations are constructions of sets. Cosmological dualities and trilogies are no coincidence either. We create after the nature of our perceptions, and humans perceive in numbers.

Number is primordial. In its capacity to organize the structure of human memory, it is a sister, in its antiquity, to language. Hopper suggests that we might understand this effect if we consider that certain numbers are "elementary." By *elementary*, he means playing a primary role in the structuring of human thought.

Nothing in the history of number symbolism is so striking as the unanimity of all ages and climates in regard to the meanings of a certain few number symbols. Inasmuch as these same number beliefs color the literature of the ancient world and recur in the superstitions of our own contemporary primitives, we are justified in classifying them as "elementary" and in isolating them, in order to define the nature of at least one fixed and universal type of number symbolism" (Hopper 1969, 3).

Like language, numbers can be used to create abstract realities. However, also like language, numbers probably began as associations with concrete, present-time objects. We can understand the development of number as abstraction by considering the specific, concrete associations which are necessary in order for children to learn number symbols (both oral and written), to grasp the basic ideas of summing and subtracting, and to develop the concept of "number" itself. Children learn language contextually, by associating the known meaning of the concrete context with the articulations accompanying it. We assume that number learning is equally, and necessarily, contextual. "These associations must originally have been more real than the number itself, 3 trees more real than the abstract 3, so that particularly prominent and fixed numerical groups might readily come to be thought of as attributes of the numbers themselves" (Hopper 1969, 3).

ELEMENTARY NUMBERS

Elementary numbers are numbers derived from nonnumerical contexts. They are, like the meanings attached to the forms of language, contextual discoveries. Elementary numbers might thus be distinguished from non-elementary numbers as the primary numbers, derived from experience and environment and not from numerical contexts. Non-elementary numbers are numbers that derive from other numbers.

Hopper contends that cultural communities "pass through ... stages" in their development of number concepts, that each of these stages represents the emergence of an elementary number, that each stage marks a new moment of conscious awareness of the organization of the environment, and that each is arrived at by a "half-instinctive mode of reasoning [which is] one of the curiosities of human logic" (Hopper 1969, 5).

The Number ONE

ONE is the number of the separate soul. As the song says, "One is the loneliest number that you'll ever know."

In the beginning there was only one, and that one was everything. The evidence available from megalithic and neolithic cultures and the contents of earlier myth cycles suggests a single Great Mother figure emerging out of the collective unconscious. She would be the original "one," synonomous with "void" or "chaos," out of whom all other things emerged (Neumann 1963). Her power to transform matter is, in the beginning, purely physical (Neumann 1963), but she is the source and sustenance for the eventual development of human consciousness. She is the creatress of the word, which has its own transformative powers. Later patriarchal cultures adopted a male creator god whose power to transform resided in the word.

The next step represents a substantial leap—to the designation of "one" of a thing as opposed to "many" of that thing. Hopper notes Brazilian Indians who use the word *etama*, meaning "alone," to distinguish between a single object or an object which is one of a group. Hopper characterizes this awareness as a differentiation of the single ego from that of the group (Hopper 1969); Neumann views it as the emergence of the individual psyche from the collective unconscious. (When the Spirit of God moved over the face of the deep, there was the *one* and there was everything else.)

We now have two numerical terms:

> *one*—this "one" object.
>
> *many*—these "many" objects.

Any reference to objects in any group of two or more objects does not differentiate further. Two is "many," as is three, thirty-three, or three million.

CASES

The primordial (single) archetype which contains everything else is that of the archetypal feminine—the one which is everything. This oneness is a state of mind (Neumann 1963).

Hayya (EHYH) the Great Mother, later Jehovah (YHWH) the Great Father, is singular, the ego which is the "one" distinguishable from all else. Numerous creation legends identify this one, alone in the void.

The Hopi creator, Taiowa, creates Sotuknang, another single soul. Sotuknang creates twins—a dyad with complementary creative powers of their own (Waters 1963).

The Number TWO

TWO is the number of diversity and antithetical pairs. The number two probably developed in direct association with dualities in nature—pairs, for which the single most striking characteristic must have been antithesis: male/female, day/night, light/dark, sun/moon, earth/sky, earth/water. (God divided the void into light/dark, day/night, morning/evening, heaven/earth, land/water, sun/moon, plant/animal, male/female, toil/rest.)

This primary awareness is everywhere demonstrated in literary and religious reference. We find dualities in countless cosmologies. The history of Semitic development traces in scripture the evolution of the duality of good/evil, characterized, eventually, by the fall of Satan. By the fourteenth century, the direct association of the duality of male/female with that of good/evil was made clear in woodcuts which depicted the snake in the Garden of Eden with the face of a woman. (This association may help to explain the preponderance of females prosecuted as witches during the years of the Inquisition.) The Etruscan goddess Anna Perenna has two faces (Prorsa and Postuerta) which look, respectively, to the past (history) and to the future (prophecy). She was later masculinized as the dual-personalitied Janus (Walker 1983). The Egyptian diety Horus is double-headed, one head representing truth and right and the other wickedness (Hopper 1969). Many royal coats of arms illustrate dualities.

Hopper offers the possibility that the first words for *two* were words which also represented a dual state of being, such as "marriage" (male/female). This is a preliminary and contextually referenced association, and not yet the abstract concept of *two*. *Two* would emerge from the synthesis of a collection of many such cases of duality into the single underlying principle of twoness. This more global construct could then also find application in cases in which two things were not antithetical.

We now have three numerical terms:

One—the single, separate ego.

two—the pair; antithetical/not antithetical/any two things.

many—a group of three or more.

CASES

Certain African tribal groups admit to the existence of only two colors. That is, their languages have words for only two differentiations of the entire spectrum—red (or brown) and green. These two colors represent a dyad which exists in association with another dyad: life/death, or animate/inanimate. All things which are "green" (falling within that subdivision of the spectrum so identified) are animate/living. All things which fall into the other part of the color spectrum, red, are inanimate/dead. (Since the spectrum of colors is itself innocent of divisions and absolutes, each culture can divide it differently, making its own truth which will be reflected in language. The European cultures divide the spectrum into sets of three.)

The Number THREE

THREE is the number of "all," of superlatives, and of the holiness of triads and trinities: the Triple Goddess (three female); the Three of the Eleusinian mysteries (mother, daughter, and divine child or sun hero), the divine family (father, mother, and divine child or sun hero), the father, son (sun hero), and the holy ghost (three male).

The number three is implicit in the concept of *two*. Three is "many," an identification which is widespread in literature and language even in contemporary times. We see it in the ideas of singularity, duality, and plurality—distinctions made in Arabic, Egyptian, Sanskrit, Hebrew, Greek, and Gothic (Hopper 1969). We use it every time we apply the superlative English endings to make forms like "big," "bigger," "biggest," or when we imply "good," "better," "best." *Three* still retains the character of superlative. We say "this one," or "these two," but of three, we say "all of these." Three is the first number to which we can apply the word *all*. Three still connotes infinity, and the power of countless numbers. This may be why so many references to triune godheads appear in religious doctrine. The one goddess or god, who is really three, is all-powerful (Hopper 1969).

The abstract idea of *three* very likely emerged as a set of three things with the discovery of natural triads (contextual associations): morning/noon/night; male/female/child (the exact pattern in many celestial families); heaven/earth/water; heaven/earth/hell (a later theological invention); sun/moon/stars; birth/life/death; beginning/middle/end.

The triad of beginning/middle/end is of particular significance in the idea of story. Beginning/middle/end is the simplest construction of elements that can make a story. If a body of discourse is lacking any one of these three, we would not call it a story. The triad which makes a story a story also makes a story its own reality or truth. When we "story" an event, we must reconstruct the event so that it fits the triad. We take the truth of the event and bend it, making it into a new truth. Because the triad is already true, the new, storied version of the event is also equally true, even though we may have had to do some inventing to get a fit.

If we impose the idea of three/all on the idea of the triad, our triads become infinitely powerful. Our folk literature, our theologies, and our other cultural traditions prove the invincibility of the three. Perhaps, by such imposition, we also believe in the "trial of three" as the perfect proof—the original significant statistic. (If the car stalls once, it's an isolated incident. If it stalls twice, it's a coincidence. If it stalls three times, there's a reason.) We will take the best two out of three: toss a coin three times, play three games in a series, race from the pole to the tree three times. Three is all; three is law. In many, many folk stories, the protagonist acts three times—throws down three golden apples, shoots three arrows, runs three races. All we need to know from the story is that the character took three tries, and we understand the presence of all other labor. There is no need to exhaust the patience of listener and storyteller alike by repeating the next twenty-five events. We know all about them; they are implicit in the power of the number three.

Three is perhaps the most pervasive and dominating idea in ancient and contemporary cultural cosmologies. It is so powerful a construct that it becomes the rule against which sensibility itself is judged. For example, consultants who help others to learn effective communication skills have one rule for making a point in oral and written expression: either make three points, or divide the single message into three parts—never two, never four. A second rule is to list words, phrases, or clauses in series in sets of three—never two, never four. If we must repeat ourselves, say it three times, and it will be true.

It is enough to take cognizance of the fact that at the dawn of history the number three had already robed itself in manifold meanings, and bore a ruling and godly aspect from whose dominion man was not soon to escape (Hopper 1969, 8).

Now we have a collection of numerical terms and concepts.

one—as singular, and as the sum of the triad, the three in one.

two—the antithetical pair and the two in the set of two objects.

three—as many/all/infinity; as triad, all powerful; as the set of three things; as the number of trials or tests which provides the rule; as the proof of truth.

CASES

Symbols of greatness and power in antiquity were made in threes: the trident; the triple thunderbolt; the Triple Goddess as maid, mother, and crone; Trefuilngid Tre-Eochair, Irish god of the shamrock, the "Triple Bearer of the Triple Key" (Walker 1983); Trevia, the "Three Ways" or name of the triple goddess Hecate; the Great Triangle, Tantric symbol for female, sign of the "Primordial Image," Triangle of Life; Trident, the phallic symbol representing the male principle and god consort.

The three faces of Hecate presided over all three-way crossroads.

Noah sent the dove out three times to look for land.

In the flood legend of ancient Babylon, Utnapishtim (Noah) sent a dove, a raven, and a swallow.

In numerous Native American tales, the creator forms the earth from mud which is brought from the depths of the waters (the deep) by a turtle who dives three times, a duck who dives three times, or three different animals who each dive only once.

The number of folk tales and legends which incorporate the ideas of three trials, three tries, three objects, three brothers, three sisters, three forks in the road, three witches, three magical gifts, three wishes, and/or three suitors reaches, like the number three, almost to infinity.

"A threefold cord is not quickly broken" (Eccles. 4: 12).

Christ hung on the cross for three hours.

Christ was entombed for three days.

Three is the most universal number for expressing the idea of the deity. Where panoplies of gods appear in a cosmology, they appear in multiples of three: three, then three times three (nine), then three times three times three (twenty-seven). The three principle deities of the *Rig Veda* are so elaborated. Often, the triple triad of gods is a subdivision of the primary three. In such cases, the twenty-seven merge mystically into the nine, and these into the three. This magical collapsing of numbers into numbers is also one of the principal rules in cabalistic calculation.

The oldest known divine triad is Anu (heaven), Enlil (earth), and Enki (water), a Sumerian trilogy circa 2400 BC. Interestingly, the original creation triad is heaven, earth, water. The Genesis triad bears this out. God does not create an underworld, nor does he provide for hell. These ideas were later theological developments (Howland 1957). The equation of good/evil and heaven/hell came even later. The original Satan (Lucifer) was the angel whose responsibility it was to bring bad fortune and death to men. He was God's ally, not his enemy. He was rewritten later, perhaps to explain theological perturbations on earth rather than in heaven (Howland 1957).

Later versions of this triad have substituted the underworld for the world of water: Anu (heaven), Baal (earth), and Hea (underworld).

The Greek version is Zeus (heaven), Poseidon/Demeter (earth), Hades (underworld).

Vishnu takes three strides across the heavens—the rising, the midday, and the setting sun.

In India, where autumn and winter are alike, there are three seasons.

The Egyptian sun god Ra is a trinity rather than a triad. He is the three-in-one Horus (the morning sun), Ra (the midday sun), and Atun (the setting sun). (The *triadic* godhead cannot be collapsed from three to one; the *triune* god is three in one.) The earliest known triune god is Gilgamesh of Sumerian tradition, circa 2000 BC. Gilgamesh was two-thirds god and one-third man, collapsed into one personality. Hopper (1969) speculates that this model is the antecedent of the more elaborated Christian trinity.

The triad of living—birth, life, death—takes many traditional forms. All are metaphoric and mystical.

The Fates (Greek)	Birth—Klotho, the spinner.
	Life—Lachesis, the giver of lots/the weaver.
	Death—Atropos, the thread cutter.
The Norns (Scandinavian)	Urd—Past.
	Verdandi—Present.
	Skuld—Future.
(India)	Brahma—Beginning/birth.
	Vishnu—Middle/life.
	Siva—End/death.

Inasmuch as Zeus is considered to be the beginning, middle, and end of all things, his aspect seems more like that of the triune god.

European cultures divide the color spectrum into three primary and three secondary colors. Black/white is a diad which has metaphoric connotations.

Some folk stories, often quest tales, employ the three, three times three, and three times three times three model. In such stories, the hero encounters a monster (dragon) with three heads. In one version of this motif, three heads appear for each one that he cuts off; thus he faces first a three-headed, then a nine-headed, and finally, a twenty-seven-headed beast. In other versions, the hero meets and vanquishes the three-headed creature, only to be confronted later with its nine-headed relative, and lastly with the twenty-seven-headed animal.

Yggdrasil has three roots.

Scandinavian mythology names three colors of the rainbow.

Many Celtic gods had three heads.

The ancient Irish held three annual festivals.

The Number FOUR

FOUR is the number of earth. The number four is also, most certainly, the product of initial contextual associations. Just as the concept of three was first embedded in natural triads, the concept of four was first implicit in natural sets of fours. The first and primary of these fours, the points of the compass, probably originated as a product of sun worship and observation, just as did the sun triads: sunrise/sunset/summer, sun/winter/sun, or, eventually, north/south/east/west. If we take into account the respective horizontal and vertical lines drawn by the daily east/west and the yearly north/south courses of the sun, we have a rough equal-armed cross, a symbol dating to antiquity, which enjoyed original, separate invention worldwide, and which most assuredly is the model for later cruciform figures. Crosses and swastikas are to be found in early carvings and in tomb and wall murals, and are ubiquitous among petroglyphs and pictoglyphs in the American Southwest. In fact, what the cult of three is to European and Middle Eastern peoples, the cult of four is to many Native American cultures. The number four is the primary organizing principle of cosmology, affecting both base and lofty aspects of culture, and lending structure to the literature.

Other natural fours would have become apparent once the first (the sun "cross") became obvious: the four winds, the seasons, the four physical influences (earth, air, fire, water), the humours (hot, cold, moist, dry), the "points" of the body (head, foot, left, right) and, with astronomical observation, the combined pairs of summer/winter solstice and spring/fall equinox. Fourness became a natural way of understanding the cycles and influences of the planet.

The abstract concept *four* — four things as separate from the many and as distinct from one, two, or three, was the eventual conclusion of counting related things in fours. One can postulate an early four count in which the names of the compass directions were used to determine the existence of four objects. The idea of the whole being apportioned naturally into four different aspects persists in explanations of mind, personality, learning styles, etc.

The collection of numerical terms and concepts thus expands with four:

> *four* — the model for the nature of earth and earthly phenomena; the four different aspects of or manifestations of a single characteristic, such as personality; four objects, the abstract *four*.

CASES

The agricultural tribes of the American Southwest name four Corn Mothers, which are associated with the four points of the compass: white/blue/red/yellow and north/south/east/west.

The Hopi people believe in four worlds. The first is *Tokpela* (Endless Space). Tokpela is the world of the creation. *Tokpa* (Dark Midnight), the second world, is a second creation, formed after the fiery, volcanic destruction of the first, when its people forgot their origins and became sinful. Some of the people from the first world were saved to populate the second. The third world, *Kuskurza*, was created for the remaining faithful after the people of the second world turned to wickedness. The second world was destroyed when the earth rolled over twice on its axis. When the people of the third world also turned from the path, it too was destroyed. Floods were loosed upon it. Only those few who remembered their original emergence were saved; they were sealed into hollow reeds to float upon the waters. Eventually these people came into the fourth world, *Tuwaqachi* (World Complete). The first world was the most beautiful, and in it, the people lived in harmony with the animals. Its color was yellow, its appointed direction west. The second world was a little less a paradise. Its direction was south, its color blue, and in it people developed handicrafts, homes, and villages. In the third world (the red world and east world), people constructed great cities and powerful civilizations. The evil of these things was washed away; all of the physical remains of this world are now beneath the sea. The fourth world is the world in which mankind must choose to carry out the plan of creation. If he fails, this world too, will be destroyed. Its color is yellow-white; its direction is north (Waters 1963).

When Spider Woman made mankind, she gathered earth of four colors: red, yellow, black, and white. She then made one male and one female of each color—a set of four men, a set of four women (Hopi).

There were four phases to the creation of man. At the first phase, the time of purple light, man was formed. At the second phase, the time of yellow light, life was breathed into the forms. The third phase, the time of red light, was a time of teaching, in which man learned of the creator and creation. The fourth phase gave the power of speech, so that man could praise the creator. These four phases are the mystery of creation, the breath of life, the warmth of love, and the power of language (Hopi) (Waters 1963).

When a Hopi child is born, four lines are painted on each of the four walls and on the ceiling (Waters 1963).

The Hopi identify four of the seven chakras of Eastern mysticism. The first is the soft spot on the top of the head, which is found in infants. This spot is the first vibratory center, the *kopavi*, the open door, through which the soul enters and departs the body, and through which the infant communicates with the creator. The second vibratory center is the brain. Its true function is to help man achieve the plan of the creation. The third center, in the throat, is the one through which the breath of life was received and the place of language. The function of language is to sing the praises of the creator. The fourth center, the heart, is the focus of purpose. A singularly focussed person, one whose only intent is to work within the plan of creation, is said to be of one heart. A two-hearted person is an individual who has allowed evil to enter, and who works to evil ends (Waters 1963).

The Hopi also employ the swastica to prophesy the circular wanderings of their people in their gradual evolution toward the center.

The perfect ear of corn is the one which ends at the tip with four fully formed kernels (Hopi).

Many gods are depicted as having four eyes and/or four ears, hearing and seeing in all directions.

The Egyptian roof of heaven is supported by four pillars, or four mountains, or four women, placed at the cardinal points of the compass. Some Egyptian illustrations show a woman bending over the earth, with arms and legs extended to the four cardinal points. In other similar illustrations, a cow is depicted.

Living individuals were sometimes walled into the four corners of community buildings in pre-Christian Europe to provide the fortification with magical strength and to ensure protection.

Eddic mythology identifies four world regions and four streams of milk which flow from the sacred cow.

Rabbinical writings identify four powerful tribal matriarchs: Rachel, Sarah, Rebecca, and Leah.

A *tetragrammaton* is a four-letter word representing the secret name of the god. The tetragrammaton for Yahweh is *YHWH*, which derives from the three-letter HWH, meaning "woman." The tetragrammaton *EHYH* represents Hayya, the goddess, or female, life-giving principle (Walker 1983).

The Number FIVE

FIVE is the number of the hand, of the flower, and of the star. The number five surely had its beginnings in the discovery of fingers and toes as adding machines (Hopper 1969). Finger and toes supplied the specifics of contextual association. Some tribal cultures still use their word for "hand" to connote "five of," two hands to mean "ten of" and certain references to a "man" to mean "twenty."

The number five initiated the birth of arithmetic. Its antecedents in context—the hands and feet—clearly demonstrated multiples. The adoption of a number system with a base of ten makes good anatomical sense. Four is easily demonstrated as one less than five, three as two less than five, and so on. Nine is one less than ten, eight is two less than ten, five is one half of the full complement of fingers or half of two hands. The advent of the idea of *five*, even with the less abstract anatomical meaning in force, begs for the abstraction of the numbers represented by counts of fingers. (The three-year-old who holds up fingers and says, "I want these many," begins early with the use of the hand to denote elementary numbers.) Pictorial representation would be an easy step.

> One finger—a hand with one finger up, or, more cryptically, I
>
> Two fingers—II
>
> Three fingers—III
>
> Four fingers—IIII, or one less than five, IV (if V means hand)
>
> Five—hand—IIIII, or V (if V means one hand)
>
> Six—hand plus one, VI
>
> Seven—hand plus two, VII
>
> Eight—hand plus three, VIII
>
> Nine—VIIII, or one less than ten, IX (when X means two hands)

CASES

Five is the "Marian" (Great Mother/Triple Goddess) number (Walker 1983). Five is the number of petals in the rose (rose"mary") and in the apple blossom. Five represents the maid aspect of the Triple Goddess.

Five is a virginity symbol: Mary = maid = rose/apple blossom.

The apple has five lobes. The apple is the symbol of the mother aspect of the Triple Goddess (Walker 1983). The apple is also a symbol of death and resurrection. Five is the sacred number of death and rebirth. An apple, cut transversely, reveals a core (ovary wall) that is a five-pointed star. The maid (Mary) is the earlier *Kore* ("core") (Walker 1983).

The sacred symbol of the Triple Goddess Ishtar was the five-pointed star. The five-pointed star is the Egyptian symbol of the uterine underworld and rebirth. The pagan pentacle is a sacred and powerful sign.

Five times three (fifteen) is also a sacred number of the virgin goddess Kore (Persephone). Three times five is the Triple Goddess (maid, mother, crone—beginning, middle, end).

The Number TEN

TEN is the number of completeness, finality, and perfection: the finished cycle, the unbroken circle. The number ten (two hands, or two times five) came to be an important number. Because two hands is "all," ten became attached to the meaning of finality or completeness (Hopper 1969). Even when used to its powers, it signifies wholeness: 100, 1000. The number 500 denotes half of completeness. Ten and its powers also became associated with the idea of "full cycle" and came to be thought of as round. Perhaps this is why memory of place in counting is served by tens and multiples of tens. If, when we count, we must stop, we can better go back to our place if we stop on a number of significance. When we "round" a number, we do a simple operation to get closer to wholeness, completion, or a full complement. Rounding is a metaphoric reference to the idea of the number ten as the symbol of finality and perfection (Hopper 1969).

The number ten, two hands, makes multiplication and the advent of other numbers all but inevitable. With the idea of ten, the powers of the forces represented by the other numbers can be mystically extended. Forty-four is four and ten times the four. Seventy-seven, a very important number, might have had its origin as a charm. If the number seven is powerful, because it has certain innate qualities, then seven plus ten times seven is a blockbuster. Numbers beyond the number nine, in fact, are not considered by the ancients to be real, in the sense that they are always representing the actual numbers of things. Ancient number mysticism saw numbers as magical and creative forces. The number seventy-seven as a charm can exist by the principle of seven and ten times the seven without any reference to the numbers one through seventy-six. In like violation of contemporary mathematical logic, any number larger than nine can be collapsed into itself through addition to obtain one number between one and nine. (The number 9561, for instance, sums to 21, which, in turn, can be collapsed to 3. Then all the portents and powers attributed to 3 can be applied, depending upon the situation.) Numbers beyond the number twenty may not have their origins in the contexts of situation. They may have been abstractions at their inceptions, invented to "power" the elementary numbers. Thomas Aquinas, who determined that the mystical number of the beast in Revelation is 666, discussed the meaning of the number six, and the power of that meaning achieved by tens and hundreds. "The meaning of the number 6 does not change by reason of its decimal position" (Hopper 1969, 10).

CASES

On the tenth day of the Babylonian (3500-1900 BC) spring festival, all the gods took part in a procession (Hopper 1969). The Babylonians also believed that ten ages (ten kings) preceded the flood. There are ten guardians for the Babylonian city.

The *Rig Veda* (1200-800 BC) contains ten books of hymns.

Athens had ten divisions.

The tithe is, by tradition, one-tenth.

The Egyptians counted 100 (ten times ten) days for the rising of the Nile.

Oracles were often consulted on the "round" numbered days, the tenth day, the hundredth day, etc., from an auspicious event.

The Ten Commandments signify total law, perfect law, complete divine will.

In cabalistic theology, there are ten divine names, ten archangels, ten divisions of the material world, ten orders of angels, ten orders of demons, and ten archdevils.

The Number NINE

NINE is the "almost" number — almost perfect, almost complete, almost ten. The number nine came to prominence after the number ten gave it definition (Hopper 1969). Nine is the number of almost completeness. The mystery of nine is derived from the magic of ten. Nine is the omen of completion; it signals that the end is at hand. The idea of nine as the almost number is probably as old as is the idea of ten as perfection. Both numbers, and their respective metaphoric references, share a great age.

CASES

Troy was besieged for nine years. It fell in the tenth.

Homer's Odysseus wandered for nine years. He arrived home in the tenth.

The number nine is associated, by medieval Christian theologians, with the nine orders of angels in heaven. Nine were left after the fall of Satan, who, according to the parable, is the lost piece of silver. Man is the potential tenth heavenly order; no wonder the common occurrence of the motif of the battle between good and evil for the soul of man. Specific stories include those in which a man makes a bargain with the devil.

Nine is also synonomous with the ninefold goddess of pagan belief. She is portrayed as giver of knowledge, wisdom, law, and inspiration in multiples of three: the nine muses, the nine sisters who ruled the Fortunate Isles where the dead were taken (Walker 1983).

Nine seems to be the favorite number for winter in Nordic tradition.

Skaldi lives for three months out of each year with her husband. When she leaves her homeland, summer comes there. Skaldi, the goddess of the Snow-Skates, unlike Proserpine, brings the winter with her; warmth can only come in her absence.

Animal and vegetable life remain hidden in the womb of the earth in northern climes for the same number of months as the baby remains in the womb of the human mother. After nine months is the time of birth.

The Valkyries are numbered according to the pattern of triples. There are three, three times three, and three times three times three.

Odin suffers torture during the nine winter months.

The nine worlds of *Niflhel* ("dark hell where dead men dwell") are at the roots of the great world tree.

Every ninth year, a fertility feast is held for nine days in some northern communities.

Frey was forced to wait nine nights before his marriage to Gerda.

Heimdall was born of nine giantesses.

Thor makes nine great strides against the serpent sea, but is defeated by winter.

The number nine is the northern equivalent of the southern number seven, and signifies fertility, religion, and magic.

The Celtic "need fire" was kindled by eighty-one men, nine at a time. Beltane rites also required sets of nines.

There were nine witches of Gloucester.

Nine "nicors" were slain in *Beowulf*.

The Nine Maidens is one of the best known stone circles.

The cauldron of the head of Hades was kept boiling by the breath of nine maidens.

The Irish employ the term *nomaid*, to denote a nine-month interval of time.

The patterns of threes and three times threes recur throughout Arthurian legend. Merlin had nine bards. Kei could exist nine days and nine nights without sleep. Bedwyr's spear made nine wounds when it was pulled out.

Northern peoples often make reference to "the nine days' wonder."

ASTROLOGICAL NUMBERS

While astrological numbers can include elementary numbers, they are also numbers which are derived by manipulating elementary numbers. Because the elementary numbers were already imbued with powerful significances, numbers derived from them also had special meanings and portents. All numbers had occult and magical powers.

> The corn which stands upright
> Shall come to the end of its prosperous growth;
> The number [magic force to produce this]
> We know it.
> The corn of abundance
> Shall come to the end of its prosperous growth;
> The number _____
> We know it.
> (Akkad [Hopper 1969, 12].)

The number was the supreme secret, a tool of magic and sorcery. *Number* is a maker.

Astronomical activity, a natural and necessary concomitant to religion, was less science, at first, than a study of the gods in an effort to know their will and predict their actions. The ancients believed that the divine plan of the gods was written in the stars; man had but to unravel the secrets of the heavens, and it could be revealed. Such investigations led to the discovery of new numbers.

The Number SEVEN

Seven was originally the baleful number. It was probably discovered as a natural product of observation of the moon, the easiest of all planets to assess. The number of beginnings, middles, and endings (sunrises, middays, and sunsets) in its cycle could be counted, placing the number three in prominence. The total of days in the cycle, divided into four equal parts (perhaps because four is the earth number and the moon is close to the earth, or because the seasons gave precedent), gives a count of seven days per part. Coincidentally, three and four sum to seven. This is magic.

The Babylonians, who observed a lunar calendar, avoided performance of important acts on all seventh days and on all days whose numbers were multiples of seven. This taboo also included the nineteenth of every month, because it was the forty-ninth—seven times seven—day after the first of the preceding month. These were "evil days" (Hopper 1969), on which one had to work against evil or pray.

The magical relationship between three, four, and seven becomes evident with creations, in some cosmogonies, of three to add to the four, to make an all-powerful seven. The Babylonians added to the four winds of the points of the compass the evil wind (tempest/hurricane), the four-fold wind, and the threefold wind, to make a total of seven winds.

As other patterns of seven were discerned in the stars, the number seven became more strongly associated with the positive powers of wisdom and godliness.

CASES

The Bear contains seven stars. The seven stars of the Bear may be the antecedents for the seven gods of the Brahmanas who precede the flood, and also for the seven who follow to dispense the secrets of divination, magic, and wisdom.

Seven-starred constellations may have given rise to the seven Hathors of Egypt, the seven seers of Vedic ritual, and the seven sages of Greece.

Eastern mysticism identifies seven *chakras* or points of vibration in the human body.

The Pleiades contains seven stars. The number forty is the number of days of the rainy season during which the Pleiades were not visible to the Babylonians. These forty days, on land and sea, were times of tempest and danger, for the sailor who could not see the stars for navigation, and for the land dweller, who was always fearful of flood and inundation. When the Pleiades reappeared after forty days, the New Year Festival was celebrated. The people burned forty reeds to destroy the forty devils who had held the stars hostage for forty days. The darkness and tribulation associated with forty days is apparent in the period of Lent, the years spent by the Hebrews wandering in the desert, and the original forty days of *quarantine* in Roman ports. In one version of Genesis, the flood lasts forty days. Purification after childbirth lasts forty or twice forty days. The Philistines ruled in Israel for forty years. Moses was on Sinai for forty days.

The Pleiades, despite their utility, were considered to be evil demons. Magic cords were knotted seven times, incantations were repeated seven times, and seven corn loaves were roasted to protect against their merciless destruction.

> Seven are they! Seven are they!
> In the Ocean Deep, seven are they!
> Battening in heaven, seven are they
> Bred in the depths of ocean;
> Nor male nor female are they,
> But are as the roaring wind-blast,
> No wife have they, no son can they beget;
> Knowing neither mercy nor pity,
> They hearken not to prayer or supplication.
> They are as horses reared amid the hills,
> The Evil Ones of Ea;
> Throne-bearers of the gods are they,
> They stand in the highway to befoul the path;
> Evil are they! Evil are they!
> (Babylonian tablet [Hopper 1969, 16].)

Astronomers assumed the existence of seven planets, then searched for them. Once they were found, the search ended. The seven planets became gods who decided the fates of man. The days of the week are named for these seven.

There are seven "windows" to the human head.

The Zoroastrian temple, the Ziggurat, was built of seven stories, one for each of the seven divisions of the world. Each step was dedicated to one of the seven planets, was faced with one of the seven principal colors, and represented the seven steps to heaven.

The great tree of life (Semitic) has seven branches, each of which bears seven leaves. The seven-branched candlestick of Hebrew tradition may be a symbol of the tree.

The positive sevens have their negative counterparts, antithetical dyads of sevens: seven gods/seven devils, seven steps to heaven/seven steps to hell.

There are seven ledges on the mount of Purgatory, hence seven stages in purification.

In medieval lore, seven is the common number necessary for attainment of perfection.

Many creation stories tell of seven acts of creation done in seven days. (At some earlier time in the history of scripture, man was said to have been created on the seventh day. Later, to account for the baleful aspect of the seventh day, his creation was moved back to the sixth. One should do no creative sabbatical act.)

Adam's descendents through Cain number seven. The seventh, Lamech, lived 777 years.

Seven is the number of servitude years.

Seven is a traditional number for sacrifice.

Seven is a number for punishment—seven times, seven years.

In Genesis 7:2-3, we learn that the animals entered the Ark by sevens. Seven and multiples of seven are used repeatedly in the Old Testament. For example, seven days of Passover; seven days of fasting. Seven good years/seven lean years; seven years of plenty/seven years of famine.

Seven is a common number in the folk literature, usually specifying seven of something: seven brothers, seven swans, seven beds. Some cumulative pattern stories have seven items in the cumulative list.

Seven is generally a propitious and a lucky number.

Salome's Dance of the Seven Veils represented the surrogate (sacrifice) king's descent into the underworld and his passage through the seven underworld gates. She (the goddess) rescued the hero from death by taking off one veil at each gate, thus securing him passage.

The River Styx wound through the underworld seven times.

The ancients believed that it took seven months to traverse the underworld between death and rebirth.

Egyptians identified seven Hathors or planetary spheres: the seven heavenly midwives, the seven-gated holy city, the seven gates of heaven, the seven gates to the underworld, the seven recesses, abysses, or pits (Walker 1983).

Osiris's descent into the underworld took him fourteen days; his ascent to heaven took him an additional fourteen, accounting for the number of days in the lunar month. He was thought to be twenty-eight years old at the time of his passion (sacrifice), or in the twenty-eighth year of his reign on earth (Walker 1983).

Artemis is represented by a set of seven stars.

Both Ursa Major, the Great She Bear (Aphrodite's totem), and Aphrodite are associated with the seven pillars of wisdom.

The Number EIGHT

The number EIGHT seems to have derived from seven, by the same—if reverse—logic by which the number nine comes from the number ten. If something takes seven years, seven steps, seven objects, seven days of uncleanness, seven incantations, or seven sacrifices, eight is the number marking completion, fulfillment, salvation, payment, freedom, or an answer to one's prayers. Seven seems to represent the task, and eight the end of toil. Eight is a blessed number; it means purification, sanctity, the end of trial and privation.

CASES

The eighth day after a seven-day fast is the day of the feast.

The eighth day is the day of purification and of circumcision.

Specifically eight sons, neither seven nor nine, is a blessing from God.

In Norse myth, the seven-day week is usually referred to in terms of "eight nights." The use of the numbers eight and nine together in this reference suggest an eight-day week, which would account for the eight rings which drop from Odin's ring every ninth night, and also for his eight-legged steed *Sleipnnir* (Hopper 1969).

In northern Europe, the winters are long (eight to nine months) and dark. The eight winters that Loki remains underground in the form of a woman may refer to the cold months of the year in which life is dormant.

Thrym, the Frost Giant, hides Thor's hammer eight miles down in the earth. Thor can win it back only when Freya agrees to become his bride.

The Great Wheel of Fate (karma) has eight spokes leading from the rim to the center.

The Number TWELVE

The number TWELVE has two possible derivations. Twelve is the number of lunar cycles that would have been observed in the heavens within the span of one solar cycle, plus five "intercalary" days coming at the end of the year. (Among the Aztecs and other Central American civilizations, the intercalary days were dark and dangerous times in which ordinary laws of the universe were suspended. One did not go outside. All foodstuffs and other necessities were brought indoors prior to the beginning of this period.) Each month was ruled by its appropriate zodiacal sign, twelve in all, as early as 2000 BC. With the pattern of twelve established for months, each day was also divided, initially into four parts, then into halves. Each half was divided into twelve portions. The day was a double-twelve arrangement, which eventually became a twenty-four-"hour" pattern when the double twelve was summed. Magically, three sets of four make twelve, as do four sets of three. Astronomers lost no time in finding obliging twelve-star constellations in both hemispheres, and twenty-four judges of the living and the dead emerged.

The second possible derivation, probably more ancient, is the set of four tetrads. In the older "Jahwistic" version of the legend of creation, the use of four is regular: four rivers, four parts of the world, four winds, etc. In I Kings 7: 25, the sea of the temple is supported at four points, by oxen — three to each point, twelve altogether. Perhaps the number three comes from the habit of assigning tetrads to the divisions of fours which marked the description of the planet, thus combining god (in three) and earth (in four) and resulting in another sacred number, twelve.

CASES

There are twelve spokes in the wheel of the Hindu Rta.

Hercules accomplished twelve labors.

The Egyptian god Ra must spend twelve hours of each day in the underworld next to the twelve gates of hell.

There are twelve winds.

There were twelve gods of Greece and also of Rome.

There were twelve tables of Roman law.

Solomon divided his kingdom into twelve sections in order to collect taxes.

Numerous folk stories employ the number twelve, either as a full complement of twelve things (brothers, sisters, a dragon with twelve heads), or as a sum of sets (three quadrads or four tetrads). Some cumulative stories include twelve items in the list.

The Number ELEVEN

The significance of ELEVEN is derived from twelve in much the way the number nine is related to ten. Eleven is an "almost" number, but with a special twist. If twelve represents the full complement, then eleven represents those who remain true, or faithful, who do not deviate. There are twelve disciples, but one falls away, leaving eleven to go to heaven. Some folktales employ the motif of the eleven who are cursed, and who must depend upon the twelfth to effect a rescue. Twelve is the full company, one of whom is somehow different from the rest. Eleven, since the time of St. Augustine, has been a number associated with sin, and figures in the dimensions of the architecture of hell (Hopper 1969, 152).

The Number SIX

Six is very probably a derivative of twelve, and an invention imitating the pattern of antithetical dyads—seven feast years/seven famine years. The full complement of twelve, divided into two equal sets, yields sixes, which can then be set in antithesis. The twelve signs of the zodiac are thus divided into six and six: male/female and left/right. The twelve hours of the day and night, respectively, can be likewise divided.

Hex, the word associated with witches' spells, also means "six." The number six was sacred in the pagan world, because it represented the sacred union between the Triple Goddess and Triplotemus (the triple god consort). "666," therefore, was the number of fertility and plenty—333 and 333. Ancient Egyptians saw magic in the numbers three, six, and seven. "37" (a combination of three and seven, and not thirty-seven) had particular potential, because it could be multiplied by any multiple of three to yield a triple-digit number—a perfect trinity: "111, 222, 333, 444, 555, etc. The miraculous number 666 is a product of $3 \times 6 \times 37$" (Walker 1983, 401). Later, Christian doctrine converted the pagan 666 to a number of evil, the number of the beast.

The Number THIRTEEN

The number THIRTEEN generally strikes dread. While gnostic tradition viewed thirteen as a sign of wisdom and unity, and the Christian church associates thirteen with Epiphany as a holy number, thirteen tends, in contemporary lore, to inspire fear, loathing, and avoidance. It has even earned its own place in the world of psychiatry in the label "triskaidekaphobia." It is thought by some to be the number of sin, because it exceeds by one the correct number of the twelve Apostles. It is a prime number, which cannot be formed by any equal combinations of other significant numbers, such as three or four; nor can it be conveniently divided into dyads.

The fear of the number thirteen may be related to the need, periodically, to insert a thirteenth month in a year in order to account for intercalary days. The thirteenth month was believed to be a time of ill fortune and discord. Astrologers were obliged to account for the extra month in an intercalary-month year. Its symbol was the raven. Cabalistic lore may have introduced thirteen as a magical number. The idea of a company of thirteen being unlucky, or thirteen at the table being a bad omen, perhaps stems from the fate of Christ, who with the Disciples made a thirteenth.

Perhaps an equally sensible explanation for the dread of thirteen may stem from the Druidic practice of using thirteen as the right number of people for ceremonial practices. The strong association of the number with witchcraft haunts the modern world. The Druidic use of thirteen was very likely innocent of any such fearful connotations, unless it was connected to the practice of sacrifice. What is more likely is that thirteen was part of the Celtic and pagan tradition which was attacked by the Christian church, and became associated, as did many pagan traditions, with devil worship. The practices of witchcraft are, today, attached to thirteen and its multiple numbers, since thirteen is the usual number for membership in a coven. However, to assume that contemporary witches choose the number because of its association with Satan and evil is to confuse cause and effect during the rise of Christianity in Europe.

The pagan world was ruled by lunar, not solar, cycles. Each year, then, has thirteen (lunar) months plus a day ("a year and a day"). The lunar calendar, most likely based upon the menstrual cycle (Neumann 1963), had its own zodiacal constellations: the sword basket, the drinking horn, the chariot, the halter, the knife, the cauldron, the whetstone, the garment, the pan, the platter, the chessboard, and the mantle. Thirteen, throughout the pagan world, was the number of the matriarchate. The goddess, when represented as a fertile female animal (e.g., Cerridwen as the Great Sow) has thirteen teats. On twelfth night, pagan ceremony required the kindling of twelve small and one great fire, the large one signifying the moon of the New Year (Walker 1983). Thirteen was the number of fortune in pagan Europe, sacred to the goddess, and lucky. Friday the thirteenth was an especially good day, since all Fridays were the given days of the Scandinavian Mother, Triple Goddess Freya.

Contemporary dislike of the number thirteen is undoubtedly due to propaganda and deliberately concocted bad press associated with religious and consequent political strife. Whether the number thirteen's plight is deserved or not, it still suffers the ill fortune of an outcast number. It is quite often associated with taboo: Never seat thirteen people at a table; never sneeze thirteen times; never number a floor or a room in a building with the number thirteen. If you see thirteen of almost anything, cross yourself three times, thus using the positive magic of one number to dispel the negative magic of another.

SUMMARY

One can see how the influences and aspects of numbers have become a part of divination, whether the practice is as sophisticated as astrology or as informal as casting stones. One can also see the effects of conservation of folk culture. Five-thousand-year-old magical associations with numbers are alive and well today, affecting our decisions, directing our activity, and organizing our language.

15

Motifs

INTRODUCTION

Motifs are formulaic universals: circumstances or situations which are generic, recur with great frequency and in more than one story, and characterize all oral narrative. The motif is a part of the conventional pattern of oral discourse, a schematic, a piece of language and formulaic meaning which can be "stitched," with other such pieces, into a story. The children abandoned in the forest, the youth and maiden who change shapes to escape capture, the woman who must be a frog by night, the mother's warning to her children to beware of strangers at the door, the devil who is outwitted by the common man, the mistreated girl (Cinderella) who prays for help at her natural mother's grave, the quest, the race, the deception, the falsehood, and the innocent error that must be undone are typical of the motifs that provide much of the content of stories.

Storytellers in the oral tradition did not and do not memorize stories. Rather, they learn to tell stories much as a child learns to talk, by inductively discerning the rules governing the grammars and grammatical operations of making oral narrative. Storytellers make a story from such patterns in memory much as others generate sentences from linguistic rules governing syntax and semantics. Motifs, their structures, and their meanings are implicit in deep structure, providing much of the substance from which a story takes form. They might be thought of as substructures of oral discourse which, like words, phrases, and clauses in sentence construction, are knit together according to culture-specific guidelines. Certain motifs appear clustered together according to a given rule or pattern. The teller and listener would both recognize a story as "wrong" somehow if motifs which did not belong together were mixed without regard to traditional formulae. Other cultures' stories can also seem strange if common motifs are organized according to different, but equally logical and legitimate, sets of conventions. One of the reasons that the literary story *Heckedy Peg* (Wood and Wood 1986) is so successful is that it uses the "right" (western European) traditional motifs in the "correct" (western European) relationships.

Motifs are the teachers in the story. Along with the theme (and a theme might also be a motif), the motif summons a cluster of powerful associated memories. Its placement in the story, its emphasis, and the way in which it interacts with other such structures to make meaning tells much about what is right and good in a given culture. Many story motifs have such significance that they also appear separately as sayings and proverbs, presumably to deliver the same message more directly.

... [T]hen he sighed and said to his wife, "What's to become of us? How can we feed our poor children when we don't even have enough for ourselves?"

"I'll tell you what," answered his wife. "Early tomorrow morning we'll take the children out in the forest where it's most dense...."

And when the full moon had risen, Hansel took his little sister by the hand and followed the pebbles that glittered like newly minted silver coins and showed them the way.

But little by little, Hansel managed to scatter all the bread crumbs on the path.

When the moon rose, they set out but could not find the crumbs, because the many thousands of birds that fly about in the forest and fields had devoured them.

... [T]hey kept going deeper and deeper into the forest.... [T]hey saw a beautiful bird as white as snow sitting on a branch. It sang with such a lovely voice that the children stood still and listened to it. When the bird had finished its song, it flapped its wings and flew ahead of them. They followed it until they came to a little house....

Hansel reached up high and broke off a piece of the roof to see how it tasted, and Gretel leaned against the windowpanes and nibbled on them.

As soon as she had any children in her power, she would kill, cook, and eat them.

... Hansel stuck out a little bone.... [S]he thought the bone was Hansel's finger ... [and] was puzzled that Hansel did not get any fatter....

The witch intended to close the oven door once Gretel had climbed inside ... but Gretel sensed what she had in mind and said, "I don't know how to do it. How do I get in?"

Then Gretel gave her a push that sent her flying inside ... and the godless witch was miserably burned to death.

... [T]hey went into the witch's house, and there they found chests filled with pearls and jewels all over the place.

... [T]hey reached a large river. "We can't get across," said Hansel ... "but there's a white duck swimming over there. Help us, help us, little duck! It's Hansel and Gretel...."

... [I]n the meantime, the man's wife had died....

... [T]he pearls and jewels bounced about the room ... now all their troubles were over.

("Hansel and Gretel" [Grimm 1987 58-64].)

The motifs which appear in oral narrative have been a topic of study for many years (Thompson 1955-58). While a story topic or theme can be a motif, characters, character actions, and circumstances are also motif contents within stories. A single story can use several motifs. For instance, "Coyote and Locust" (Hayes 1983) contains mythological motifs (origins of animal characteristics), animal motifs (magical animals and animals with human traits), taboo motifs (ownership of songs), wisdom and foolishness motifs (disregard of facts, short-sightedness, bungling, literal foolishness, and an easy problem made hard), deception motifs (thefts and cheats, a deceptive bargain, escape by deception), reversal-of-fortune motifs (triumph of the weak, pride brought low), reward and punishment motifs (deeds rewarded by punishment), traits-of-character motifs (unfavorable traits of character), and humor motifs (humor of lies, exaggeration, character behavior, language physical disability, and discomfiture).

A full collection of stories belonging to a people presents a diverse and rich set of motifs which, in turn, are a form of cosmological content within the literature. Each story is a construction of a select number of the total of motifs available to a culture. Not only are story structures generated when one tells stories, but also specific organizations, juxtapositions, and interactions of motifs are created. (One might almost think of motifs as modules from which stories are built.) The motif contents of stories represent a wealth of cultural understanding presented in the most direct and simple form—the stories themselves.

Motifs are symbols which represent and reconstruct deeper, unconscious, basic, archetypal memories. Their appearance in stories (and in other forms of folk art) evidences an architecture of mind residing at a level of knowing which is elemental and inaccessible. Such basic archetypes give rise to creative impulses, inventions which take regular surface forms—"symbol sets" (Neumann 1963). These projections into the outside world make an external reality of archetypal constructs, setting consciousness in motion, and engaging the individual and the culture in the riddles which they signify. Motifs constitute a principal expression of archetypal memory in story.

NATIVE AMERICAN STORY MOTIFS

The following Native American stories are collected here by major motif, as given in MacDonald (1982). Minor motifs are not included, but can be discovered easily enough by cross-referencing a given story with the Thompson index (Thompson 1955-58). Stories are limited to collections in print by 1980 and to those materials which derive from collective (oral) folk traditions. While this particular listing is reduced to minor motif, tribe, author, and publication date for the sake of brevity, even such a simplified representation clearly indicates the wealth and breadth of motif-centered material existing within the folk stories of a people. Stories and motifs of other cultures can be located by referring to an appropriate index (MacDonald 1982; Thompson 1955-58) or by visiting the folk literature collections of any library. Additional stories can be obtained, under the correct conditions, from live storytellings.

Mythological Motifs

GODS

- Origin of thunderbird: Winnebago (Chafetz 1964, 3-13; DeWit 1979, 27-33).
- Origin of thunderbird: tribe unspecified (Field 1929, 40-54).
- Disappearance of thunderbird: Bering Strait Eskimo (Melzack 1967, 85-92).
- Seasonal habits of thunder: tribe unspecified (Field 1929, 55-61).
- Goddess of lightning: Hawaiian (Thompson 1966, 20-27).
- Goddess of snow: Hawaiian (Thompson 1966, 28-32).
- Seasonal habits of snow king: Naskapi (Cunningham 1939, 60-65).
- Habits of blowing and drifting snow: California (Curry 1965, 90-100).
- Goddess of world of dead: Hawaiian (Berry 1968, 89-97).
- Goddess of fire: Hawaiian (Thompson 1966, 15-19).
- Spider woman: Hopi (full collection: Mullett 1982).

DEMIGODS AND CULTURE HEROES

- Coyote as culture hero: collective (full collections: Courlander 1978; Curry 1965; Fisher 1957; Hayes 1983; Heady 1970; Martin 1950).
- Raven as culture hero: collective (full collections: Martin 1951; Melzack 1970).
- Invincible culture hero: Oglala Sioux (Matson 1972, 42-43).
- Culture hero overcomes monsters—Raven: Eskimo (Melzack 1970, 83-91).

COSMOLOGIES

- Earth Magician creates universe: Pima (Baker 1978, 1-6).
- Universe created from calabash: Hawaiian (Thompson 1966, 11-14).
- Raven creates universe: Eskimo (Melzack 1970, 15-24).
- Maui pushes sky up: Hawaiian (Colum 1937, 38-64; Williams 1979, 13).
- All tribes raise sky together: Snohomish (Matson 1968, 90-93).
- Many creations: Papago and Pima (Baker 1978, 1-6).
- Creation of sun, moon, and stars: Greenland Eskimo (Leach 1967, 37-38).
- Coyote creates sun and moon: Southern Pomo (Fisher 1957, 16-23).
- Raven rescues sun, creates stars: tribe unspecified (Manning-Sanders 1971, 81-84).
- Bluejay and Ground Squirrel rescue Dawn: California (Curry 1965, 38-47).
- Arctic Hare and Eagle rescue Sun: Chuckee (Newell 1970, 51-62).

- Fox rescues Sun: tribe unspecified (Marriott 1947, 3-12; Haviland 1979, 60-64).

- Coyote steals sun; brings light: Yokuts (Curry 1965, 22-37; Leach 1967, 44).

- Sun, moon, and stars rescued: Hawaiian (Thompson 1966, 33-39).

- Sun rescued, returned to sky: Snohomish (Matson 1968, 80-86).

- Sun falls to earth, is pushed back into sky: Achomawi (Belting 1961, 51-53).

- Cottontail shoots down sun to make it cooler: California (Curry 1965, 48-50).

- Animals free Sun from trap: Algonquin (Jablow and Withers 1969, 79-80).

- Sun caught in snare, released: Menominee (Field 1929, 71-73; Cunningham 1939, 66-69).

- Sun caught and slowed down: Hawaiian (Colum 1937, 38-64; Cathon 1962, 104-9; Thompson 1966, 60-64; Williams 1979, 17).

- Sun is brought closer to Earth: Cree (Belting 1961, 79-84).

- Origins of sun and moon: Eskimo (Field 1973, 14-16).

- Moon's light dims, moon disappears: Eskimo (Caswell 1968, 19-23).

- Origin of sun, moon, and stars: Nez Perce (Heady 1970, 15-20).

- Origin of eclipses: Swinomish (Matson 1968, 123-27).

- Boy becomes "man in the moon": Loucheux (Jablow and Withers 1969, 21).

- Crane carries rabbit to moon: Cree (Belting 1961, 67-70).

- Frogs sit on the face of the moon: Lillooet (Jablow and Withers 1969, 24; Leach 1967, 31-33).

- Waxing and waning of moon: Iroquois (Jablow and Withers 1969, 14); Kutchin (Jablow and Withers 1969, 39-40).

- Goddess in moon: Hawaiian (Colum 1937, 173-75; Colum 1937, 117-19; Thompson 1966, 76-80).

- Girl marries moon: Eskimo (Maher 1969, 139-58; Caswell 1968, 19-23).

- Girl marries star husband: Blackfeet (Cunningham 1939, 87-94); Algonquin (Williams 1963, 223-30); Cheyenne (Field 1929, 13-31); Skagit (Matson 1968, 63-74); plains (Mobley 1979).

- Girl marries "old man" in sky world: Arapaho-Caddo (Brown 1979, 39-42).

- Coyote makes stars: Hopi (Courlander 1978, 25-26); tribe unspecified (Baker 1978).

- Origins of specific stars and constellations: Cheyenne (Haviland 1979, 40-43; Penny 1953); Micmac (Leach 1967, 133-34); Chippewa (Leekley 1965, 76-78); Snohomish (Matson 1968, 90-93); Eskimo (Leach 1967, 138-39); Mono (DeWit 1979, 117-21; Fisher 1957, 54-59); Blackfeet and Assiniboin (Hulpach 1965, 43-45); Cherokee (Leach 1967, 136-37); Onondaga (Cunningham 1939, 37-40); Luiseno (Leach 1967, 112); Hawaiian (Thompson 1966, 40-44); tribe unspecified (Marriott 1947, 83); Seneca (DeWit 1979, 9-12); Shoshone (Hulpach 1965, 40-41); Achomaloi (Fisher 1957, 60-73); Eskimo (Maher 1969, 39-54); Hawaiian (Thompson 1966, 65-69).

- Origin of earth: northwest (Martin 1975, 6-18 and 11-15; Haviland 1979, 40-43; Yokuts (Leach 1967, 44); Yuchi-Creek (Leach 1967, 15-16); tribe unspecified (Curry 1965, 9-21); Shoshone (Heady 1973, 15-19); Cherokee (Bell 1955, 4-7); Chippewa (Leekley 1965, 35-49); California (Fisher 1957, 10-15).

EARTH TOPOGRAPHY

- Tides: Tahltan (Leach 1967, 25-27).

- Coyote Lake and San Francisco Bay: California (Curry 1965, 9-21).

- Columbia River: Nez Perce (Matson 1972, 64-69).

- Snake River: Shoshone (Heady 1973, 23-26).

- Idaho, Twin, American, and Shoshone Falls—Snake River: Shoshone (Heady 1973, 20-23).

- Lakes and springs: Tlingit (Hardendorff 1969, 121-26; Martin 1951, 6-18; Martin 1975, 11-15; Haviland 1979, 40-43).

- Polar ice cap: Tahltan (Leach 1967, 25-27).

- Shapes of islands: Chippewa (Leekley 1965, 111-17).

- Origins of islands: Hawaiian (Courlander 1955, 14-19; Thompson 1969, 66-71; Williams 1979, 21); Eskimo (Melzack 1970, 15-24).

- Irregularities of coastline: Skagit/Swinomish (Matson 1972, 105-11).

- Hills and valleys: Yuchi/Creek (Leach 1967, 15-16); Cherokee (Bell 1955, 4-7); Papago/Pima (Baker 1973, 1-6).

- Mountain ranges: California (Curry 1965, 9-21); Jicarilla Apache (Leach 1967, 23-24).

- Mount Shasta: tribe unspecified (Fisher 1957, 24-35).

- Gorge on Oahu: Hawaiian (Thompson 1969, 45-52).

- Rock formations: Sioux (Matson 1972, 55-58); Eskimo (Field 1973, 64-66); Chuckee (Newell 1970, 107-18); Nez Perce (Matson 1972, 64-69; Heady 1970, 29-34, 57-61, 95-100).

- Wind Cave: Oglala Sioux (Matson 1972, 39-42).

GLOBAL CATASTROPHE: PUNISHMENTS AND RENEWALS

- How the world will end: Tahltan (Leach 1967, 135); Eskimo (Newell 1970, 81-84).

- Floods: Chippewa (Leekley 1965, 35-49); Eskimo (Caswell 1968, 88-95); Pima (Baker 1973, 8-15); Arikara (Brown 1979, 65-70); Eskimo (Newell 1970, 91-98).

NATURAL ORDER

- How water is controlled: Tlingit (Hardendorff 1969, 121-26; Martin 1951, 6-18; Martin 1975, 11-15; Haviland 1979, 40-43).

- Winds: Eskimo (Cothran 1956, 13-17); Hawaiian (Thompson 1966, 70-75); Eskimo (Newell 1970, 119-24); Nez Perce (Heady 1970, 62-66).

- Rains: Lillooet (Leach 1967, 31-33).

- Clouds and mists: Lakota (Yellow Robe 1979, 24-30); Nez Perce (Heady 1970, 21-24); Eskimo (Hardendorff 1969, 56-57; Caswell 1968, 68-71); Cherokee (Bell 1955, 78-80; Cathon 1972, 133-34).

- Thunder and lightning: Eskimo (Newell 1970, 69-74; Field 1973, 18-30; Maher 1969, 99-105); California (Curry 1965, 68-79); Lakota (Yellow Robe 1979, 24-30).

- Earthquakes: California (Fisher 1957, 10-15); Eskimo (Caswell 1968, 96-106).

- Determination of seasons: Shoshone (Heady 1973, 35-38); tribe unspecified (Field 1929, 32-39; Bleecker 1946, 153-60); Kootenai (Cothran 1954, 76-83; DeWit 1979, 113-17); plains (Jones 1974, 1-13); Micmac (Haviland 1979, 58-59; Toye 1969; Macmillan 1918; DeWit 1979, 39-43); Chippewa (Brown 1979, 79-80; Cathon 1972, 130-32); Canadian (Littledale 1970, 111-20; Macmillan 1918).

- Night and day/Light and dark: Eskimo (Newell 1970, 63-68; 85-90; Field 1973, 10-11); Menomoni (Hardendorff 1969, 22-23); Nez Perce (Heady 1970, 25-28); Iroquois (Leach 1967, 75-76); Creek (Brown 1979, 62-63); Modoc (Cunningham 1939, 16-18); Chuckchee (Leach 1967, 41-43).

HUMAN ORIGINS

- From earth: Greenland Eskimo (Leach 1967, 37-38).

- From blood: Yuchi-Creek (Leach 1967, 15-16).

- From bone: Chuckee (Leach 1967, 41-43).

- Coyote creates: tribe unspecified (Frost 1943, 161-64).

ORDERING OF HUMAN LIFE

- Origin of death: Yokuts (Leach 1967, 44); tribe unspecified (Marriott 1947, 31-35); Swinomish (Matson 1972, 119-23); Greenland Eskimo (Leach 1967, 37-38); Nez Perce (Heady 1970, 109-18); Blackfeet (Brown 1979, 59-62).

- Language: Seneca (Brown 1979, 71-74).

- Origin of disease: Cherokee (Bell 1955, 7-12); Pima (Baker 1973, 8-15); tribe unspecified (Chafetz 1964, 15-26).

- Why women chatter: Shasta (Fisher 1957, 104-10).

- Origin of hatred: Nez Perce (Matson 1972, 69-75).

- Miscellaneous human characteristics: Chuckchee (Leach 1967, 41-43); Penobscot (Gruenberg 1955, 333-35).

HUMAN CULTURE

- Environment: Eskimo (Melzack 1967, 51-59; Melzack 1970, 61-69; Cothran 1956, 3-7; Caswell 1968, 64-67; Cunningham 1939, 19-23; Maher 1969, 39-54); northwest (Martin 1951, 6-18; Martin 1975, 17-25; Haviland 1979, 44-51); Haida (Robinson and Hill 1976, 35-40); Navaho (Hulpach 1965, 12-16); Yuchi-Creek (Leach 1967, 15-16).

- Fire: Luiseno (Leach 1967, 108); Chuckchee (Leach 1967, 41-43); Cherokee (Bell 1955, 15-18, 41-43; Leach 1967, 49-51; Parker 1970, 85-94; Scheer 1968, 25-30); Eskimo (Newell 1970, 91-98); Catawba (Leach 1967, 47-48); Shoshone (Heady 1973, 30-34); Hawaiian (Colum 1937, 38-64; Cothran 1956, 45-48; Williams 1979, 25-29); Menominee (Cunningham 1939, 33-36); Chippewa (Leekley 1965, 11-19); Creek (Brown 1979, 70-71); Hitchiti (DeWit 1979, 49-51); Eskimo (Gillham 1943, 44-50); Karok (Fisher 1957, 46-53); tribe unspecified (Hardendorff 1969, 73-77; Haviland 1979, 52-56); Wintu (Belting 1961, 34-36); Crow (Robinson and Hill 1976, 79-84); California (Curry 1965, 51-79); Paiute (Hodges 1972); Nisqually (Matson 1972, 28-31).

- Game: tribe unspecified (Fisher 1957, 96-102); Nez Perce (Heady 1970, 50-56; Martin 1950, 46-53).

- Plants and crops—agriculture: California (Curry 1965, 38-47); Shoshone (Heady 1973, 46-50); Eskimo (Newell 1970, 99-106); Cherokee (Bell 1955, 7-12); Hawaiian (Thompson 1966, 53-59).

- Weapons: Shoshone (Heady 1973, 85-88).

- Origin of stories: Seneca (Cunningham 1939, 3-15; DeWit 1979, 5-9); Iroquois (Bruchac 1975, 15-16).

- Origin of language: Snohomish (Matson 1968, 90-93).

TRADITIONS

- Social ceremonies: tribe unspecified (Chafetz 1964, 27-41); Kutenai (Arnott 1971, 1-5); Oglala Sioux (Matson 1968, 36-39); Cheyenne (Brown 1979, 46-59).

- Dancing: Eskimo (Haviland 1979, 101-6); Kwakiutl (Curtis 1978, 21-30).

- Worship: Skagit (Matson 1968, 114-17).

- Clan totems: Tsimshian (DeWit 1979, 137-42; Harris 1963, 5-30; Martin 1951, 43-46; Martin 1975, 53-60; Toye 1969).

- Hospitality: Tlingit (Cothran 1956, 8-12).

DIFFERENTIATION OF PEOPLES

- Tribal origins: Pima (Baker 1973, 25-32); Nez Perce (Heady 1970, 101-8); Eskimo (Caswell 1968, 24-25); Swinomish, Kikiallus (Matson 1968, 31-38); Makah (Matson 1972, 106-9); Yokut (Fisher 1957, 36-45); Tsimshian (Harris 1963, 115-48).

- Origins of different peoples: Eskimo (Caswell 1968, 24-25).

CREATION OF ANIMAL LIFE

- Origins of animals: tribe unspecified (Haviland 1979, 97-100).

- Origins of mammals: Lakota (Yellow Robe 1979, 42-51); Nez Perce (Heady 1970, 119-24); Eskimo (Melzack 1967, 77-84); tribe unspecified (Hardendorff 1969, 42-43; Field 1929, 3-12; Marriott 1947, 12-24); Apache/Comanche (Brown 1979, 63-65); Kond (Leach 1967, 66); Sioux (Matson 1972, 53-55); Blackfeet (Brown 1979, 98-101).

- Origins of birds: Chippewa (Leekley 1965, 92-99); Canadian (Frost 1943, 287-94); Hawaiian (Williams 1979, 9); Iroquois (Jones 1972); tribe unspecified (Haviland 1979, 97-100); Eskimo (Gillham 1943, 35-40; Maher 1969, 79-88).

- Origins of insects: Northwest (Harris 1963, 89-111; Martin 1951, 38-42; Martin 1975, 45-52); Shoshone (Heady 1973, 65-69); Zuni (Brown 1979, 115-23).

- Origins of fish: Eskimo (Caswell 1968, 26-34, 41-47, 54-56; Haviland 1979, 60-64; DeWit 1979, 39-46; Field 1973, 46-48; McDermott 1975; Melzack 1967, 27-34; Maher 1969, 17-30, 79-98); Chippewa (Leekley 1965, 79-91); Northwest (Martin 1951, 6-18, 55-60; Martin 1975, 11-15, 83-88; Haviland 1979, 40-43; DeWit 1979, 149-54; Robinson 1976, 103-12); Pomo (Fisher 1957, 80-86); Hawaiian (Thompson 1966, 45-52; Cothran 1956, 49-52); Iroquois (Jones 1972); Haida (Harris 1963, 33-58).

ANIMAL CHARACTERISTICS

Note: Animal characteristics are given by tribe rather than by minor motif.

- Acoma (Belting 1961, 93-94).

- Assiniboin (Belting 1961, 37-38, 85-88).

- Caddo (Brown 1979, 26-28).

- Cherokee (Bell 1955, 4-7, 18-21, 41-47, 51-53, 61-64, 67-69, 70-73, 78-83; Scheer 19, 33-36, 43-46, 55-60, 62-74; Belting 1961, 15-25, 57-59, 62-66; Cathon 1972, 133-34).

- Chippewa (Leach 1967, 96; Leekley 1965, 27-34, 79-91; Haviland 1979, 19-20).

- Cree (Belting 1961, 67-70).

- Creek (Belting 1961, 15-25, 46-50, 54-56; Brown 1979, 62-63).

- Eskimo (Gillham 1943, 17-50, 68-105, 117-20, 127-34; Melzack 1969, 21-25; Melzack 1970, 47-60; Gruenberg 1948, 113-18; Cathon 1972, 48-52; Caswell 1968, 33-34; Newell 1970, 75-80).

- Hawaiian (Thompson 1969; Cothran 1956, 45-48).

- Hopi (Courlander 1978, 46-49, 60-62).

- Iroquois (Bruchac 1975, 26-29; Leach 1967, 75-76).

- Karok (Fisher 1957, 46-53, 74-79; Belting 1961, 76-78).

- Kiowa (Marriott 1947, 25-35).

- Lipan and Apache (Belting 1961, 26-28; Leach 1967, 62).

- Luiseno (Leach 1967, 112).

- Makah (Matson 1972, 106-9).

- Navaho (DeWit 1979, 75-79).

- Nez Perce (Heady 1970, 25-28, 50-56, 81-85).

- Nisqually (Matson 1972, 19-28).

- Northwest (DeWit 1979, 142-49; Martin 1951, 27-30; Martin 1975, 37-43; Matson 1972, 115-21).

- Passamaquoddy (Leach 1967, 97).

- Pawnee (Belting 1961, 42-45).

- Penobscot (Leach 1967, 109-10).

- Piegan (Hulpach 1965, 139-41).

- Pima (Baker, 1973, 43-49, 146; Brown 1979, 146).

- Pueblo (Cothran 1956, 44-48; Dolch and Dolch 1956, 79-85).

- Sahaptian (Belting 1961, 74-75).

- Seneca (Parker 1970).

- Shasta (Fisher 1957, 24-25).

- Shawnee (Belting 1961, 71-73).

- Shoshone (Heady 1973, 24-29, 39-45, 51-53, 61-64, 80-84; Hulpac 1965, 99-100).

- Tahltan (Belting 1961, 37-38, 85-88).

- Tewa (Belting 1961, 89-92).

- Upper Skagit (Matson 1972, 41-48, 77-82).

- Wishosk and Wiyot (Leach 1967, 84).

- Yokut (Fisher 1957, 36-45).

- Zuni (DeWit 1979, 80-87).

- Tribes unspecified (Field 1929, 62-70; Leekley 1965, 64-68; Marriott 1947, 62-70; Martin 1950, 23-30; Bierhorst 1969, 42-46; Green 1965, 55-56).

ORIGINS OF PLANTS

- Flowers: Cherokee (Bell 1955, 78-80; Cathon 1972, 133-34); Shoshone (Heady 1973, 42-45).

- Trees: Hawaiian (Cothran 1956, 49-52).

- Moss: Choctaw (Arbuthnot 1961, 392).

- Corn: Iroquois (Leach 1967, 100).

- Berries: Cherokee (Bell 1955, 23-26; Hulpac 1965, 131; Cathon 1972, 19-21).

- Lichen: tribe unspecified (Leekley 1965, 64-68).

- Tobacco: Canada (Frost 1943, 283-86).

PLANT CHARACTERISTICS

- Why leaves fall: Canada (Frost 1943, 287-94); Cherokee (Bell 1955, 4-7; Leach 1967, 125); Micmac (1967, 133-34).

- Why conifers remain green: Seneca (Parker 1970, 153-58).

Animal Motifs

MYTHICAL ANIMALS

- Monsters and monster animals: Hawaiian (Thompson 1966, 65-69; Berry 1968, 13-21); Chinook (Robinson and Hill 1976, 73-78); Arikara (Brown 1979, 22-26); Seneca (Parker 1970, 183-89).

- Beast men: Swinomish (Matson 1968, 117-19).

- Birds: Samish (Matson 1968, 19-27).

MAGICAL ANIMALS

- Geese: Eskimo (Gillham 1943, 1-16).

- Dog: Swinomish (Matson 1968, 85-90).

ANIMAL WARFARE

- Games: Cree (Brown 1979, 147); Creek, Cherokee (Belting 1961, 16-25); Cherokee (Bell 1955, 87-91).

ANIMAL FAMILIARS

- Helpful animals: Northwest (Martin 1951, 31-37; Martin 1975, 75-82); Navaho (Brown 1979, 28-39); southeast (Arnott 1971, 23-30).

- Healing by animals: Iroquois (Jones 1972); Lakota (Yellow Robe 1979, 66-85).

- Animals saving or caring for people: Iroquois (Bruchac 1975, 51-57, 59-61); Sioux (Matson 1968, 51-52); tribe unspecified (Bierhorst 1969, 65-70).

- Animals as paramours: tribe unspecified (Manning-Sanders 1968, 54-58).

- Marriage to animals: Iroquois (Cunningham 1939, 95-97); Eskimo (Melzack 1970, 53-60); Caddo (Brown 1979, 123-28); Abenbaki (Crompton 1975).

ANIMAL HABITS

- Animals call the dawn: Hopi (Courlander 1978, 126-28; Brown 1979, 14-18).

GIANT ANIMALS

- Whales: Eskimo (Maher 1969, 31-38).

Taboo Motifs

TABOOS CONNECTED WITH
SUPERNATURAL BEINGS

- Taboos against offending animal spouse: Eskimo (Caswell 1968, 76-80).

- Taboos against offending animal relative: Eskimo (Cunningham 1939, 98-104; Melzack 1970, 53-60).

- Taboos against offending the gods: Salish-Blackfeet (Brown 1979, 109-11).

SPEAKING TABOOS

- Contests and games: tribe unspecified (Parker 1970, 13-22).

MISCELLANEOUS TABOOS

- Supernatural creatures cannot be abroad in daylight: northwest (Martin 1951, 47-50; Martin 1975, 69-74).

Magic Motifs

TRANSFORMATIONS

- Human to animal: Eskimo (Caswell 1968, 72-75).

- Animal to human: tribe unspecified (Bierhorst 1969, 11).

- Object to object: Nez Perce (Heady 1970, 35-40); Pueblo (Wiggin 1967, 281-90; Fisher 1957, 88-95).

- Other transformations: Pawnee (DeWit 1979, 99-107).

- Transformations to escape detection: Eskimo (Hardendorff 1969, 88-91; Maher 1969, 115-31).

MAGIC CLOTHING, IMPLEMENTS,
AND OBJECTS

- Snowshoes: Micmac (DeWit 1979, 192-97).

- Needles: Eskimo (Cothran 1956, 18-21; Leach 1961, 83).

- Trees: Chippewa (Leekley 1965, 58-63); tribe unspecified (Marriott 1941, 54-60).

- Mountains and rocks: Eskimo (Caswell 1968, 64-67); Nisqually (Matson 1968, 24-28).

- Fruits: Hawaii (Berry 1968, 13-21).

INVULNERABILITY

- People transported to magical places: Wiyot (Curtis 1978, 35-41); Shoshone (Heady 1973, 89-94).

INJURIES AND CURES CAUSED BY MAGIC

- Paralyses: Eskimo (Curtis 1978, 99-110).
- Cures: tribe unspecified (Hill 1965, 66-74).

Death Motifs

RETURN FROM THE DEAD

- Resuscitation: Chippewa (Cunningham 1939, 58-59).
- Dead return to be helpful: Tlingit (Littledale 1970, 13-20); northwest (Martin 1951, 19-26; Martin 1975, 27-35).
- Dead return to repay obligation or to do penance: Arapaho (Brown 1979, 159).
- Dead return to receive proper burial: Lakota (Yellow Robe 1979, 94-101).

GHOSTS

- Ghosts in human form: Hawaiian (Thompson 1969, 38-42).
- Ghosts in animal form: Seneca (DeWit 1979, 9-12); tribe unspecified (Bierhorst 1969, 47-57); Hawaiian (Thompson 1969, 9-13).
- Human conflicts with ghosts: Hawaiian (Thompson 1969, 28-37); Sioux (Brown 1979, 66-67).
- Marriage to ghosts: tribe unspecified (Bierhorst 1969, 78-89); Nisquali (Curtis 1978, 5-20).
- Reincarnation: Eskimo (Leach 1967, 37-38).

Marvel Motifs

OTHER-WORLD JOURNEYS

- Visits to the star world: Navaho (Curtis 1978, 81-95); Tlingit (Cunningham 1939, 70-79; Dolch and Dolch 1956, 11-25); Eskimo (Caswell 1968, 83-87; Bella Coola (Jablow and Withers 1969, 86-87).
- Visits to the lower world: Nez Perce (Heady 1970, 109-18); Cherokee (Cunningham 1939, 41-44); Canada (Littledale 1970, 111-20); Yakima (Robinson and Hill 1976, 113-24); tribe unspecified (Bierhorst 1969, 29-38).

MARVELOUS CREATURES

- Fairies: Hawaiian (Berry 1968, 22-29); tribe unspecified (Bierhorst 1970; Haviland 1979, 97-100).

- Spirits and demons: Hawaiian (Belting 1961, 66-69); Eskimo (Belting 1961, 47-52); Onondaga (Belting 1961, 27-34); Eskimo (Maher 1969, 107-14); Arapaho (Brown 1979, 114-15).

PERSONS WITH EXTRAORDINARY POWERS

- Tasks and rewards: Hawaiian (Cothran 1956, 31-37); Thompson River (DeWit 1979, 161-68).

- Extraordinary occurrences: Eskimo (Caswell 1968, 88-92; Field 1973, 81-82; Melzack 1970, 42-44; Robinson 1976, 85-94); Hawaiian (Thompson 1969, 23-27); Haida (Harris 1963, 33-58); tribe unspecified (Field 1929, 62-70); Sioux (Garner 1969, 1-2); Chippewa (Leekley 1965, 79-91; Haviland 1979, 19-20); Nez Perce (DeWit 1970, 122-26; Heady 1970, 101-8; Martin 1950, 53-60; Matson 1970, 64-79); North Cheyenne (Field 1929, 13-31); Cherokee (Brown 1979, 132-33); plains (Jones 1974, 41-49).

- Marvelous cures: Eskimo (Caswell 1968, 41-47; Maher 1969, 17-30; Toye 1969).

- Other events: tribe unspecified (Bruchac 1970, 26-29; Parker 1970, 159-64).

Ogre Motifs

WITCHES

- Evil deeds: Upper Skagit (Matson 1968, 49-59); Cherokee (DeWit 1979, 52-56; Bell 1955, 27-33); Nez Perce (Heady 1970, 75-80).

- Devils and witches: Tsimshian (Harris 1963, 81-85); Eskimo (Caswell 1968, 57-63).

OGRES

- Capture of children: Eskimo (Melzack 1967, 59-67).

- Ogres defeated: tribe unspecified (Parker 1970, 196-203); Snohomish (Matson 1968, 86-90); Navaho (Robinson 1976, 23-24).

- Rescues from ogres: Hopi (Courlander 1978, 82-85); tribe unspecified (Curry 1965, 104-10).

Test Motifs

MARRIAGE TESTS

- Suitor tests and trials: Hawaiian (Cothran 1956, 27-30); Thompson River (DeWit 1979, 161-68; Newell 1970, 125-42); Eskimo (Melzack 1967, 69-75).

RIDDLES

- Riddle contests and games: Hawaiian (Thompson 1969, 43-48, 54-65, 72-79, 86-99); Seneca (Parker 1970, 52-59).

SUPERHUMAN TASKS

- Lakota (Yellow Robe 1979, 59-65).

ENCHANTMENTS

- Eskimo (Maher 1969, 79-98).

CONTESTS

- Hopi (DeWit 1979, 63-75).

Wisdom and Foolishness Motifs

WISE AND UNWISE CONDUCT

- Choices—values and people: Chippewa (Leekley 1965, 20-26); Cochiti (Brown 1979, 148-50); Eskimo (Gillham 1943, 106-16; Bleecker 1946, 81-89).

CLEVERNESS

- Acts and retorts: tribe unspecified (Bierhorst 1969, 39-42); California (Curry 1965, 111-20).
- Tricks avenged: Hopi (Courlander 1978, 47-100, 143-44).

ABSURD IGNORANCE

- Absurd misunderstandings: Eskimo (Melzack 1967, 35-40); Kwakiutl (Arnott 1971, 71-75).
- Mistaken identities: Eskimo (Caswell 1968, 81-82); Pueblo (Dolch and Dolch 1956, 105-17); southern plains (Robinson and Hill 1976, 41-42).

ABSURD DISREGARD OF FACTS

- Disregard of danger: California (Curry 1965, 101-3); Eskimo (Gillham 1943, 51-67).
- Shortsighted acts: Northwest (Robinson and Hill 1976, 63-72); Eskimo (Gillham 1943, 76-85).

ABSURD FOOLISHNESS

- Fools: Seneca (Parker 1970, 60-67); Chippewa (Leekley 1965, 55-57); Alaska (Dolch and Dolch 1961, 119-23); Shoshone (Heady 1973, 42-45); California (Curry 1965, 88-89).

- Literal fools: Hawaiian (Thompson 1969, 49-53).

- Easy problems made hard: Yorok (Robinson 1976, 95-105).

Deception Motifs

GAMES AND CONTESTS

- Contests won by deception: Cherokee (Bell 1955, 58-60, 67-69; Scheer 1968, 37-42, 55-57); Seneca (Parker 1970, 165-86; Bruchac 1975, 20-22); Iroquois (Bruchac 1975, 23-25); plains (Jones 1974, 15-22); Yokut (Cothran 1954, 56-64); tribe unspecified (Marriott 1947, 45-54).

COOPERATIVE UNDERTAKINGS
AND BARGAINS

- Deceptive division of profits: tribe unspecified (Baker 1978); Abenaki (DeWit 1979, 183-87); Pueblo (Dolch 1956, 17-25).

- Deceptive bargains: Hawaiian (Thompson 1969, 80-85).

LIES AND CHEATS

- Hoodwinking to accomplish goal: Eskimo (Caswell 1968, 41-47; Maher 1969, 17-30, 133-37; Gillham 1943, 51-67); Hawaiian (Thompson 1969, 23-27; Colum 1937, 92-96; Colum 1966, 44-49; Mohan 1964).

- Thefts: Seneca (Parker 1970, 109-16).

DECEPTIONS TO CONTROL OR
ESCAPE CONTROL

- Escape deceptions: Eskimo (Cothran 1956, 22-24; DeWit 1979, 174-77; Gillham 1943, 121-26; Melzack 1967, 13-20; Melzack 1970, 71-78); Sia (DeWit 1979, 127-30); southern plains (Robinson 1976, 41-52); tribe unspecified (Firethunder 1963; Matson 1972, 103-6); Cherokee (Bell 1955, 80-86; Scheer 1968, 31-32, 47-50, 65-68; Belting 1961, 29-33); Seneca (Parker 1970, 68-81); Lakota (Yellow Robe 1979, 52-58); Hawaiian (Thompson 1969, 14-22).

- Capture deceptions: Pueblo (Dolch and Dolch 1956, 79-85); Plains (Jones 1974, 15-22; Robinson and Hill 1976, 53-62); Cherokee (Bell 1955, 54-56; Scheer 1968, 47-50); tribe unspecified (Haviland 1979, 71-75; Marriott 1947, 47-54; Bierhorst 1969, 42-46); northwest (Harris 1963, 89-111); Wintu (Cothran 1954, 65-66); Chippewa (Leekley 1965, 50-54); Sioux (Matson, 1972, 48-50); Seneca (Parker 1970, 43-51); Lakota (Yellow Robe 1979, 86-93); Dakota (DeWit 1979, 93-98); Comanche (Brown 1979, 111-13); Blackfeet (Hardendorff 1969, 82-84); Shoshone (Heady 1973, 74-79).

INJURY AND MURDER

• Murder by deception: Nez Perce (Heady 1970, 90-94).

• Self-injury by deception: Iroquois (Bruchac 1975, 31-33); Cheyenne, Choctaw, Micmac (Hulpach 1965, 192-97); Seneca (Parker 1970, 23-30, 102-8); Loucheux (Belting 1961, 13-15); Pueblo (Cothran 1954, 44-48); Nez Perce (Heady 1970, 67-74); Chuckee (Newell 1970, 51-62); Eskimo (Melzack 1970, 25-31; Edmonds 1966, 21-29); Creek (Brown 1979, 106-9); Lakota (Yellow Robe 1979, 86-93); tribe unspecified (Leekley 1965, 69-75).

HUMILIATIONS, ENTRAPMENTS, BLUFFS, DISGUISES, IMPOSTURES, HYPOCRISIES

• Deception into humiliating positions: Creek (Brown 1979, 106-9); tribe unspecified (Haviland 1979, 71-75); southern plains (Robinson and Hill 1976, 41-52).

• Deceiver falls into own trap: Ojibwa (Cothran 1954, 84-89); Eskimo (Gillham 1943, 51-67).

• Deception through bluffing: Cherokee (Bell 1955, 80-83; Scheer 1968, 65-68).

• Deception through disguise: Hopi (Curtis 1978, 73-80); Cree (Curtis 1978, 61-69).

• Deception through imposture: Nez Perce (Martin 1950, 23-30).

• Deception through hypocrisy: Comanche (Curtis 1978, 54-57).

Reversal-of-Fortune Motifs

UNPROMISING HEROES AND HEROINES

• Character types: Eskimo (Caswell 1968, 96-106).

PRIDE BROUGHT LOW

• The humble and weak overcome the prideful and strong: Algonquin (Garner 1969, 210-12); tribe unspecified (Wiggin 1954, 400).

Chance and Fate Motifs

WAGERS AND GAMBLING

• Wives/husbands as wagers: Seneca (Parker 1970, 95-101).

HELPERS

• Human helpers: Eskimo (Melzack 1970, 53-60).

Society Motifs

FAMILY

• Family solidarity: tribe unspecified (Bierhorst 1969, 58-65).

Captive and Fugitive Motifs

RESCUES

• Flight from difficult family situations: Micmac (Arbuthnot 1961, 109-201, 392-93 (anthology)); Algonquin (DeWit 1979, 34-38); Zuni (Haviland 1979, 76-82); tribe unspecified (Association 1930, 156-61; Cunningham 1939, 105-12; Child Study 1958, 59-67; Sheehan 1970, 141-48; Haviland 1979, 94-96; Macmillan 1918).

ESCAPES

• Animal helpers: Micmac, Passamaquoddy (Williams 1963, 208-16); Comanche (Jablow and Withers 1961, 15-17); Shoshone (Heady 1973, 74-79).

Unnatural Cruelty Motifs

CRUEL RELATIVES

• Eskimo (Maher 1969, 53-71).

ABANDONMENT AND MURDER

• Abandonment of children: Gros Ventre (Curtis 1978, 45-51).

Sex Motifs

LOVE

• Courting rivalries: Cherokee (Bell 1955, 51-53; Scheer 1968, 33-36).
• Rejection of suitors: Eskimo (Maher 1969, 73-78; Caswell 1968, 76-80).

MARRIAGE

• Uniting of tribes through marriage: Crow (Brown 1979, 135-41).

BIRTHING

- Miraculous births: Makah (Matson 1972, 97-102); Canada (Frost 1943, 278-82).

Traits-of-Character Motifs

FAVORABLE TRAITS

- Kindness: Eskimo (Caswell 1968, 48-53).

UNFAVORABLE TRAITS

- Laziness: Eskimo (Field 1973, 29-30; Melzack 1970, 79-84); Thompson (Newell 1970, 23-28); Menominee (Hardendorff 1969, 24-25).
- Unpredictability: Eskimo (Field 1973, 80-82).

Miscellaneous Motifs

FORMULAS

- Stronger and strongest: Eskimo (Cunningham 1939, 46-57).
- Series: Eskimo (Melzack 1970, 71-78).

SYMBOLS

- Personifications: tribe unspecified (Marriott 1947, 70-74).

UNIQUE EXCEPTIONS

- Special vulnerabilities: Chippewa (Leekley 1965, 100-110).

MOTIF CATEGORIES

The following abbreviated motif listing (Thompson 1955-58) provides sufficient argument for considering the universal contents of oral narrative as the ancient basis for thought, for function of mind, as the genesis of invention, as the moving force in much human activity, and as a primary agenda for learning.

Mythological motifs. Creator, gods, demigods and culture heroes, cosmology and cosmogony, earth topography, world calamities, establishment of natural orders, creation and ordering of human life, creation of animal and plant life, origins of animal and plant characteristics.

Animal motifs. Mythical animals, magic animals, animals with human traits, friendly animals, marriages of people to animals, fanciful traits of animals.

Taboo motifs. Taboos connected with supernatural beings, sex taboos, eating/drinking/speaking/looking/touching taboos, class taboos, unique prohibitions and compulsions, punishments for breaking taboos.

Magic motifs. Transformations, enchantments and disenchantments, magic objects, magic powers, and manifestations.

Death motifs. Resuscitation, ghosts, reincarnation, the soul.

Marvel motifs. Other-world journeys, marvelous creatures, extraordinary places/things/occurrences.

Ogre motifs. Kinds of ogres, falling into an ogre's power, ogres defeated.

Test motifs. Tests of identity, truth, marriage, cleverness, prowess, fear, vigilance, endurance, survival, character; quests, natures of quests.

Wisdom and foolishness motifs. Acquisition/possession of wisdom/knowledge, wise and unwise conduct, cleverness, fools/foolishness/absurdities, types of fools.

Deception motifs. Contests, bargains, thefts, cheats, lies, escapes and captures, fatalities, self-injuries, humiliations, seductions and deceptive marriages, adultery, destruction of property, shams, bluffs, disguises, illusions, traps, impostures, hypocrisies, false accusations, villains and traitors.

Reversal-of-fortune motifs. Victory of youngest/weakest, modesty rewarded, pride brought low.

Ordaining-the-future motifs. Judgments, decrees, oaths, vows, bargains, promises, prophecies, and curses.

Chance and fate motifs. Wagers and gambling, lucky and unlucky accidents, luck and fate.

Society motifs. Royalty, nobility, social orders/relationships, families, trades and professions, government, customs.

Reward and punishment motifs. Deeds rewarded/punished, nature of rewards/punishments.

Captive and fugitive motifs. Captivities, rescues, escapes and pursuits, refuges and recaptures.

Unnatural cruelty motifs. Cruel relatives, murders and mutilations, sacrifices, abandonment, persecution.

Sex motifs. Love, marriage, married life, chastity and celibacy, illicit sexual relations, conception, birth, child care.

Nature-of-life motifs. Life's inequalities.

Religious motifs. Services and ceremonies, edifices and objects, sacred persons, beliefs, charity and charities, religious orders.

Traits-of-character motifs. Favorable/unfavorable traits.

Humor motifs. Discomfiture, disability, social classes/races/nations and nationalities, sex, drunkenness, lies and exaggerations.

Miscellaneous motifs. Formulas, symbolism, heroes, unique exceptions, horror/terror, historical/genealogical/biographical.

CHAPTER

16

Humor

All sorrows can be borne
if you put them into a story,
or tell a story about them.

— Isak Dinesen

He deserves paradise
who makes his companions laugh.

— *Koran*

INTRODUCTION

There are several truisms about humor: People do not agree as to what is funny; people laugh at things they are too old to cry over; we laugh when we feel superior to others; and finally, in the words of Winston Churchill, "Before we understand the most serious things in life, we must first be able to laugh at them."

The values of humor are just as varied as the truisms. Humor expands the imagination. When we are able to play with words, language, and ideas, the imagination must be involved.

Humor conveys harsh truths and is often used as a means to overcome sorrow or depression. We have stories and jokes that deal with the human condition and our frailities. It is no coincidence that there are so many mother-in-law jokes and jokes about tragedies (such as the spate of one-liners that came out after the explosion of the space shuttle *Challenger*). There are also jokes about financial depressions, occupations, and even stories about towns in countries populated by silly people.

Humor helps us release repression of fears (such as white-knuckle airplane flights) and develop a sense of superiority (we of course aren't as foolish as the drolls or sillies).

Humor can be found in a variety of ways.

- Characters can be funny.

- Word play can provide humor (groan-provoking puns).

- The situation may be the source of humor.

- Satire can generate humor.

- The unexpected or a surprise produces humor.

- The impossible or exaggeration is the source of humor.

- The absurd or incongruous carries the fun.

- Whimsy (truth in an imaginative or fanciful way) contains the humor.

- Mischief and pranks (sometimes to the point of slapstick) may be used.

- Recognizing the familiar (the basis of Bill Cosby's humor) can be funny.

- Breaking expectations achieves humor.

- Breaking taboos is the foundation of many nightclub comedians' successes.

- Poking fun at ourselves is a way of survival (it is easier if we do it before someone else pokes fun at us).

Here we consider humor through jokes and riddles, funny stories, tall tales, and linguistic play.

DROLLS

The *droll* or fool folk tale is a gentle form of humor which is found universally and has served to poke fun at absurd behavior for thousands of years. *Droll* means to be amusing in an odd or wry way. The stories of astonishing simpletons, sillies, numbskulls, dolts, noodleheads, and ninnies are not as popular as other folk stories. This could be because the events, however improbable, are painfully possible. Where are our heroes and heroines of noble proportions whom we would all like to emulate when we hear stories of the drolls? Instead, each of us can identify someone else as the silly, but never ourselves—of course. This is the aspect that makes these stories less than comfortable sometimes; yet these same tales are the ancestors of many of our current moron and ethnic stories. Droll stories, further, are examples of the use of humor to establish a feeling of superiority to someone else. In other folktales in which the silly character is an animal, we can freely enjoy the foolishness, but when the character is a human, we tend to become uncomfortable.

There are many examples of nationalities with stories about these wonderful sillies.

African. "Why Wisdom Is Found Everywhere" (Courlander and Kofi-Prempeh 1957) features Anansi, who did not want to share his wisdom with other creatures. From his abortive effort to hide wisdom comes the saying, "One head can't exchange ideas with itself." Another picture-book retold version is *Pot Full of Luck* (Rose 1982).

American black. "Epaminondas" is a variant on "Lazy Jack." Because an earlier picture-book version contained controversial artwork, Merriam updated the story with her 1968 illustrated picture book.

Arabian. Goha is an Arabian folklore character, an anti-hero who manages to disentangle himself from embarrassing situations through guile or simple wisdom. Some of the Goha stories are droll, though, such as the time Goha is convinced that the moon is following him, because he sees the moon move when he moves and stop when he stops.

English. "Lazy Jack" is always one step behind instructions for carrying things home, but all ends well for him.

Finnish. "Seven Silly Wise Men" (Bowman and Bianco 1964) is a time-and-motion study on reaping grain or installing solar lighting. These Finnish drolls have established a prototype for how not to do it.

German. "Clever Elsie" from Grimm's collections does not provide belly laughs, just a gentle awareness of folly. Elsie is sent to the cellar to fetch some beer and, because she is so "clever," she discovers all sorts of possible future tragedies. She is being wooed by a young man who insists she should be really called wise. Who is the silly?

Italian. The Italian version of "Clever Elsie" is "Clever Elsie and Her Companion." In the "Fearless Simpleton," the uncle who is a priest is called upon to teach the simpleton and winds up with a murder on his hands.

Middle Eastern. There is a sizable collection of Mulla (Mullah) Nasreddin (Nasrudin), the wise fool, stories. An example of a Nasreddin story tells of a man who comes upon Nasrudin, who is on all fours in the grass. "What are you doing, Mullah?"
"I am looking for my key." So the man joins Nasrudin on the ground searching for the key. After quite some time the man asks, "Just where did you lose your key?"
"In my house."
"Why are you looking for it here, Mullah?"
"Because it is too dark in my house."

Norwegian. "Gudbrand on the Hillside" (Asbjornsen and Moe 1960) is a variant on other "foolish people" stories. Gudbrand starts out with a cow and makes a series of foolish exchanges for it; however, his kind wife unknowingly helps him win a bet. "Mr. Vinegar" involves a series of barters starting with a cow and ending with a cudgeling.

Polish. Anne Pellowski, in her picture book *The Nine Crying Dolls* (1980) gives a sure-fire recipe for an epidemic of crying babies.

Russian. "Simple Ivanushka" (Morton 1967) is a hero of Russian folktales. Ivanushka is an example of a paradoxical droll. As in many tales, he is the third son, almost automatically qualifying him as stupid, simple, guileless, and not attractive; however, he experiences fairy-tale justice, and the good simple soul triumphs.

Spanish. Juan Bobo stories are told in all cultures with Hispanic influence.

Yiddish. "The Mixed-Up Feet and the Silly Bridegroom" (Singer 1966) is the Yiddish version of "Lazy Jack" and "Epaminondas."

The pattern of the character of the third son is evident in many droll stories. The amusing character is rewarded for his or her silly antics, and makes the princess laugh or is misjudged as wise by a suitor or observer.

The droll characters are perceived as fools. However, some of them evolve to be the most exceptional of people in spite of their supposedly eccentric behavior. After all, fools rush in where angels fear to tread, or, as the Hassidic poem says, "A man must descend very low before he can rise up again."

Within a country, people tell with gusto about fellow countrymen and their silly ways. In England, it is the men of Gotham; in Switzerland, it is the folk of Meiringen; in Finland, it is the wise men of Holmola; in the United States, it is the hillbillies; in Yiddish stories, it is the fools of Helm (or Chelm). Helm is a small town located in the deep forests of Poland and populated by very religious Jews. Some believe that the reason there are so many fools concentrated in one area is because an angel carrying a sackful of foolish souls to heaven for repairs got lost in a storm while flying over Helm. As the angel struggled through the storm, the bottom of the sack ripped and all the damaged souls spilled out and fell into Helm, where they have stayed to this day.

How foolish are these Helmites?

- Helmites built a wall around the city to keep the cold out.

- Helmites say the sea is salty because of salty herring.

- Helmites also came up with the solution to make their town bigger — push the mountain further away.

- A Helm community spokesman and respected scholar woke up with a terrible toothache. He made his dentist prove he was a good dentist — the dentist had to find the bad tooth on his own. Ten pulled teeth later, the dentist hit on the troublesome tooth and pulled it, leaving the respected scholar with two teeth. The scholar praised the dentist for good workmanship in finding the correct tooth.

Modern writers have used droll tales and talent to make readers laugh. For instance, James Thurber, Andy Rooney, Shel Silverstein, Mark Twain, Erma Bombeck, Art Buchwald, and Will Rogers have all been able to help us see humor in the world around us, with a wry twist.

Folk heroes, such as Superman (the mild-mannered Clark Kent), and the Scarlet Pimpernel pass themselves off as drolls so they can escape detection and perform their feats of derring-do. The *Star Wars* droids R2D2 and 3CPO are drolls in hardware form.

Humor, like clothing fashions, seems to go in cycles, but the drolls will always be with us. We need them to help us laugh at our own foibles as well as the eccentricities of others. It is still a gentle way to help us survive.

OUTHOUSES

Outhouses have always been an integral part of the culture. Before plumbing and running water, and even after these great technologies, outhouses have provided important services. Along with the services, many stories have come into historical and current outhouse folklore. An ancient Persian story of the Mulla is an example of these stories.

> The door was shut on the outhouse facility. The Mulla needed to use the outhouse desperately. He shifted from foot to foot and jiggled around. Finally, he could stand it no longer, so Mulla knocked on the door as a precaution. Not hearing anyone inside, he opened the door and found the outhouse empty. As he hurried in he said, "Why the hell didn't you tell me you are not here sooner?"

Jokes abound about outhouses. A current riddle is, "What is the organization of the wooden outhouses called?" Answer: "The Birch John Society."

An old miner who still works a single-man mine near Idaho Springs, Colorado, told this one.

"Miner's Dilemma"

> Back in the heyday of the gold mines here, two miners, Pat and Mike, were taking a relief break in one of the two-seater facilities. Mike had finished and stood up and started adjusting his trousers. A quarter and a dime rolled out of his pocket into the open hole. He looked into the hole and then continued to hitch his pants up, buckle his buckle, and zipper the zipper. Then, before Pat's eyes, Mike reached into his back pocket and took out his wallet. He looked in it and took out a dollar. He threw the dollar into the hole. Pat, who was still sitting, was flabbergasted. Before he could ask what was going on, Mike deliberated again and took a five dollar bill out of his wallet and threw it in too.
>
> "What's got hold of you, Mike? Are you gone daft?" asked Pat.
>
> Mike's answer was short, "You don't think I'd go in there for 35 cents, do you?"

Many old timers remember stories connected with outhouses. Quilter Jewell Wolk was collecting stories from the one-room schoolhouse era from old timers in Cut Bank, Montana. One of the stories told to her concerned how you knew if you were popular or not. An eighty-year-old woman told her, "If you went into the outhouse during the lunch break and the kids threw stones at the outhouse, you knew you were popular. If you went in and it was silent, you knew you weren't."

Another schoolhouse outhouse story tells of a young girl who dropped her pocketbook and lunch bucket down the outhouse hole. She came home and handed her lunch bucket to her mother and happily reported that they hadn't been able to get her pocketbook out but that they got her lunch bucket out.

Many a country prankster took part in the annual Halloween pranks. A favorite one was to gather outhouses and set them on fire. Everyone in town gathered at such a burning, and the town sheriff was laughing right along with everyone else, until he recognized his own outhouse in the pile.

We had tales in our family about a little kid who skedaddled out of the farm outhouse as fast as he could. Have you ever exposed your bottom to a band of yellowjackets who had just found a place to build their nest?

Another old timer also told me that you had to plan ahead and not drink any liquid after dinner because you did not want to have to go to the outhouse during the night. If you forgot about drinking liquids and nature called, you had to take an oil lantern and hike up the hill to the outhouse. She also mentioned toilet paper substitutes—Sears and Roebuck catalog pages and sometimes corn cobs.

Charles Eagle Plume, owner of an Indian trading post at Allenspark, Colorado, told the author this one.

"The Depression and the Outhouse"

Back in the early 1930s, when the federal government had an agency called the W.P.A., they sent a crew of men out every month on Colorado State Highway 7. They tore it up and then repaved it. Every month, mind you!

It raised the devil with our business. The tourists could not get to us. The road was always torn up. So in indignation I wrote a letter directly to President Franklin Delano Roosevelt.

Courteously I said, "Dear President: What we country people need the most is not a brand new paved highway every month. We need a good outhouse," and I just signed it with my Indian name, Charles Eagle Plume.

Roosevelt called the Secretary of the Interior, Harold Ickes (and I'd like to say Mr. Ickes was the first and last completely honest Secretary of the Interior we ever had). Roosevelt said, "He wants an outhouse. Let's give him one."

One day into my store walked three government gentlemen. Typical government employees—blue serge suits, white shirts, and correct ties. With great awe they said, "We have a letter from the White House saying you want an—um—ah—um—" and I said, "An outhouse."

"Well," they said, "What should we do?"

"I'll just show you what to do," I said. I showed them the spot and sure enough, within several days, men came and built one.

The three government employees came back and said, "Now you have to pay something on that. You will have to pay $10 for materials and for 30 days you will be required to go in each morning and evening and count how many flies are in there."

So every day for 30 days I went faithfully morning and night to count the flies. To my amazement, there were no flies and no odor. So I reported that.

They said, "That is great. This will be the model we will use for the national parks and wayside stops."

This same outhouse is still in use behind Charles Eagle Plume's store. He chuckled after he told me this story and shared some recent stories about sweet little old ladies and their magnificent broad jumps as they left this historic landmark, which has a strong spring with a built-in door slam that is like a gunshot. The modern facility inside his shop is not available for shoppers to use. I have been in this inside room, though, and Charles Eagle Plume has a sign above the toilet: "When in the land of fun and sun, we don't flush for number one."

The most recent outhouse story the author has heard was told by Mary Hamilton about her younger brother. She told this story at the October 1987 National Association for the Preservation and Perpetuation of Storytelling Festival, which was held in Jonesborough, Tennessee.

> Mary's younger brother had finally reached the age (eleven) when he was allowed to ride all the county fair rides alone. The whole family went to the fair and their father gave each child enough money to pay for every ride there.
>
> They were all instructed where and when to meet at the end of the day. All went well. On the ride home, everyone was eager to find out if the brother had managed to ride on everything. He was animated as he told them the thrills of the day. However, in answer to their question, "Had he ridden them all?" he had to say no.
>
> When asked which ride he missed, he told the family, "There was one with a row of tall white boxes with a door in front of each box. Everyone was lined up in deep lines to take this ride. They always had a long line. I really wanted to take this ride because I noticed when people came out they all had pleased smiles on their faces. I knew it had to be a good ride."
>
> When asked the name of the ride, he answered, "I never did see a ticket booth for them or a name. I walked around behind them and I think that they must have been called 'Port O Pot.'"

And so even today, modern stories of modern outhouse folklore are being told.

OCCUPATIONAL AND NEWS-ITEM JOKES

News items, current events, and occupations continually spawn new jokes, even while last week's jokes get stale and fall out of circulation. Although many are obviously culture-bound and currency-dependent, they can be surprisingly adaptable if the storyteller is inventive. Here are some samples of Russian underground jokes:

- Brezhnev to cosmonauts: "The Americans were first to land on the moon, so we will be the first to land on the sun."

    Cosmonauts: "But Comrade, we will be burned to death."

    "Do you think we know nothing?" replied Brezhnev. "We arranged for you to land at night.

- If communism takes over the world, where will we buy wheat?

- During the Stalinist terror, one rabbit asked another rabbit why he was running. "They're going to castrate all the camels," the second rabbit said.

    "But we are not camels."

    "After they castrate you, convince them you are not a camel."

- "I am prepared to give my blood for the working class, drop by drop," said Stalin in a speech to the masses. A voice from the audience said, "Why drag things out, beloved comrade? Give it all at once."

- Pravda reported that a two-man foot race between President John Kennedy and Premier Nikita Khrushchev was won by Kennedy. "Our beloved Nikita Sergeivitch won a respectable second, but the American president barely managed to finish next to last."

- "Why are our troops staying so long in Afghanistan?"
  "They are still looking for the people who invited them."

- Leonid Brezhnev arrived at the Kremlin wearing a yellow shoe and a black shoe. An aide assured him, "Do not worry, comrade Chairman. We will send the chauffeur for other shoes."
  "That won't help," said Brezhnev, "the other pair looks just like these."

Regional Humor

The people of New England are noted for their wry, earthy humor. These are some of the stories passed along by New Englanders:

- One day a nurse was walking a couple of patients at the local state hospital for mental patients. A passing bird dropped a calling card on the bald head of one of the men, and the nurse, in an effort to soothe him, said, "Don't worry. Stay right here. I'll go in the building and get a piece of toilet paper." While she was gone the decorated fellow told his companion, "Ain't she a damn fool? That bird will be miles away before she gets back."

- Samuel Langhorne Clemens (Mark Twain) gave one of his humorous lectures in New England. The response wasn't at all what he was used to getting, so he hurried his talk along and stopped ahead of schedule. He then went out to see if he could find out what had gone wrong. Out came a nice old couple who had driven down from their rocky hill farm with their horse and buggy. Clemens overheard the old gentleman tell his wife, "Wasn't he funny? Dang, if he wasn't funny! I had all I could do to keep from laughing."

- A minister went back into the hills to substitute at a service. The entire congregation proved to be one man. The preacher asked him if he thought they should go on with the service anyway. The fellow thought for a while and then said, "Well, Reverend, if I put some hay in the wagon and go down to the pasture to feed the cows and only one cow shows up, I feed her."
  So the visiting preacher went through most of the service, including a full-length, heavy-duty sermon. Afterwards, he asked his congregation what he thought of it.
  "Well, preacher, it's this way. If I put some hay in the wagon and go down to the pasture to feed the cows and only one cow shows up, I don't give her the whole dang load."

- At a trial in Vermont, a witness gave a familiar name, and the judge asked if there hadn't been another witness with that same name in the courtroom earlier. The witness replied, "Yes, Your Honor. He is my father."
  A voice came from the back of the courtroom, "Well, Judge, now that is a fact that has been disputed."

Humor similar to that of the New Englanders can be found in the town of Kuopio, Finland. Kuopio's biggest and best-known tourist attraction is humor. Kuopio is located on Lake Kallavesi in Eastern Finland, not far from the Soviet border. Their humor is laced with a philosophy that seems almost Zen-like, and an understatement that is almost Judaic, while still retaining Scandinavian fatalism. Here are some samples:

- A visitor asked a Kuopion man on the street, "If I go around the corner, will the cathedral be there?"

  "Even if you don't go around the corner, the cathedral will be there," was the answer.

- "Have you ever been to Kuopio?"

  "No, never."

  "Then you must know my brother-in-law. He's never been to Kuopio either."

- How did the people from Kuopio discover that beautiful region? "When we emigrated to the East many centuries ago, we came to a crossroads and one sign said, 'To Kuopio.' We were the only people able to read, so we went there."

- *Miettonen* is one of the commonest names in this part of Finland. A common rule of behavior in Kuopio is if there are three boys fighting in the street and blocking your way, all you do is yell, "Miettonen's son, come here." At least two of the boys will come over right away and the fighting will stop.

Mining and Oil Business Jokes

- Most miners nowadays are losing the war on poverty. As one grizzled old miner said, "Shucks, if they take away our poverty, we won't have anything."

- Mark Twain described a mine as a hole in the ground owned by a liar. One Securities and Exchange Commissioner recommended, "When a company hires its first geologists, it is time to sell your stock."

- "To hell with any mine that won't pay under mismanagement," says Choppo Fedderhoff, a Colorado miner for nearly fifty years.

- Norman Blake, member of an historic Colorado mining family and a retired official of the Colorado Division of Mining, says, "The small miner is one who has less than four attorneys. I've got two and I'm not even operating."

- An observation after Norm Blake's remark, "The chief by-product of any mine is litigation."

- At last count, there were only 8.3 oilmen left in Denver after the oil market crashed. One of them asked another, "What's the difference between a pigeon and an oilman?" He answered his own question, "A pigeon can still make a small deposit on a Mercedes-Benz."

- "How do you get an oilman down from a tree?" Answer: "Cut the rope."

- Two lovely secretaries were taking a lunchtime stroll down the 16th Street Mall in Denver. On one of the corners there was a frog. The frog said, "Kiss me and I'll turn into a geologist."

  One of the secretaries scooped the frog up and put him into her purse. Her friend said, "But he said if you kissed him he would turn into a geologist. Why did you put him in your purse?"

  "Because a talking frog is worth more than a geologist these days," was the answer.

- Oilman's prayer: "Please Lord, let there be one more oil boom. I promise not to throw it all away this time."

- You know times are bad when a barrel of crude oil costs less than a good bottle of Scotch.

- "Do you know the difference between the *Titanic* and the oil business?" asks an oilman. Answer: "The *Titanic* had a band."

- "Do you know where the best oil exploration department in the U.S. works?" Answer: "At the Sears and Roebuck in Tulsa."

- In a speech to other unemployed oilmen, one speaker summed it up, "We can see the light at the end of the tunnel. There's only one problem: it's a train."

- Oil prices had plummeted. In a restructuring of the company, the president was fired. As he was cleaning out his desk, the newly appointed president asked him if he had any advice to give before he left. The old president told him he had already taken care of that problem. "In the desk I left three envelopes. On the outside they are marked #1, #2, and #3. When things get rough get the first envelope, open it, and follow the instructions inside."

  Things were calm for a while, and then there were rumblings about some financial investments the company had made. The president left the board meeting, rushed into his office, opened the desk drawer, and took out envelope #1. "Blame the old president," was written on a slip of paper inside.

  He went back to the board room and blamed everything on the old president. It worked, and then the board started rumbling about the high company overhead. The new president calmly got up, left the room, went to his office, opened the desk drawer, and took out envelope #2. It said, "Reorganize."

  Yes, indeed, that was the answer, so he returned to the board room and announced new reorganization plans. That satisfied the board for a while, and then real attacks were hurled at the president. He left the meeting, went to his office, opened the desk drawer, took out envelope #3, opened it, and read, "Prepare three envelopes."

Lawyer Jokes

- One day, two accidents were reported in the police blotter. In one of the accidents, a lawyer was hit by a car. In the other accident, a skunk was hit by a car. The only difference was that there were skid marks in front of the body of the skunk.

- What's black and brown and looks good on a lawyer? A Doberman pinscher.

- Why didn't the shark attack the lawyer swimming in the ocean? Professional courtesy.

- Three lawyers are at the beach, buried up to their necks in sand. What's wrong with this scenario? Not enough sand.

Football Player Jokes

- What did the star Nebraska football player answer when asked what the big white N stood for at the end of the football field? "Knowledge."

- The football player was asked to tell how tall he was, so he measured himself. When asked to tell how old he was, he started counting his fingers. When asked to tell what his name was, he started singing, "Happy birthday to...."

Farmer Jokes

- What's the difference between a pigeon and a farmer? Answer: Only the pigeon can make a deposit on a tractor. [Remember the mining jokes?]

- A newspaper writer went to interview a farmer about the economic bad times on the farm. He saw a pig with a wooden leg outside the farmhouse. When he asked the farmer why the pig had a wooden leg, the answer was, "We have such good feelings for him that we eat him only a little at a time."

- An elderly rancher lost his cattle herd in a heavy winter blizzard. That summer, it was a wonderful season with good tall grass covering his ranch. In the fall, he harvested the grass and bought more cattle. To buy the cattle, he went to the bank to get a loan. He was smiling as he came out of the bank. A friend asked him how he could smile about another chance to fight blizzards to feed the cattle in the winter and cut hay on 100-degree summer days.

  "Because, I have won," he said. "There's no way I'll live long enough to have to pay this note off."

- A common western insult: "There's no one as dumb as a busload of agricultural extension agents."

- By tradition, a successful rancher is one who takes his whole life to go broke.

- A rancher spotted a government pickup truck on the edge of his pasture by a stream. When he went to investigate, a young Bureau of Land Management agent explained he was naming all the streams. "What name do you use for this stream?" the agent asked the rancher.

  The rancher growled, "The crik."

  A month later, a sign appears, "Crik Creek." When the rancher saw it he muttered, "It figures. The kid got the name backwards."

- The farmer couldn't get any more loans to grow wheat, but his banker suggested he try growing peanuts instead. The farmer said he didn't know anything about peanuts, so the banker sent him to the local extension agent to get some information. Based on the figures from the extension agent, the banker decided it would be feasible to grow peanuts.

  The farmer made lots of money growing peanuts, paid off his loans, and was doing really well. He ran into the banker, who asked him how things were going.

  "Well, I have made enough money so I can afford to go back to growing wheat."

- A farmer won $1 million in the state lottery. Asked what he would do with the winnings he replied, "I'll stick with farming until I lose it all."

- President Reagan bet he could walk across the reflecting pool in Washington, DC. He got halfway across and then fell in. Three boys pulled him out. After Reagan thanked them, he offered them anything they wanted as a reward. One boy said he wanted to go to West Point; the second boy asked for an appointment to Annapolis. The third boy said he wanted to be buried at the military cemetery at Arlington. Reagan agreed to all three, but said the last request was an odd one for such a young man. The boy explained, "My dad's a farmer, and if he finds out who I just saved, I'm going to need a place to be buried."

Wall Street (Post-Crash) Jokes

- "I slept like a baby last night," one financial adviser deadpanned to another. "I woke up every hour and cried."

- A sign hanging above a trading post at the American Stock Exchange: "Lost: Three-legged dog, blind in one eye, recently castrated. Answers to the name of Lucky."

- What's the difference between a yuppie arbitrageur and a pigeon? The pigeon can still make a deposit on a BMW. [Does that begin to sound familiar?]

- "How do you know when it's really cold outside?" Answer: "The stockbroker has his hands in his own pockets."

- "How many stockbrokers can you get in the back of a pickup truck?" Answer: "Two—with their lawnmowers."

- "How do you get a yuppie stockbroker out of a tree?" Answer: "Cut the rope." [Familiar?]

- Have you heard the new Smith Barney slogan? "We make money the old-fashioned way ... We sell apples."

- A man comes home to his penthouse and tells his wife they have lost it all—their savings in the market, their home, car, everything. She opens a window and jumps. As she plummets earthward, the man sighs, "Thank you, Paine Webber."

- There are a lot of good buys on Wall Street ... Goodbye house, goodbye car, goodbye American Express Platinum Card....

The familiar patterns of gallows humor appear in these examples of economic hard times. These stories and jokes have been around for years in other forms, and with other characters. They will be back again, too. What comes around, goes around.

PUNS

Puns are an excellent way to give people a love for language. The Shakespeare era was the real golden age of puns. More than a thousand puns appear in Shakespeare's plays, but they have lost a lot of their timeliness because of changes in language, events, and customs. Puns sharpen the ear to the sounds of words and the many different possibilities of meaning.

If you enjoy puns, the following examples will bring you joy. If you do not enjoy puns, why not? Sit back and browse through the linguistic, intellectual gems that follow.

- Good music is still a hit at the Bach's office.

- A man was walking along a pier one day watching his feet. Another man asked him what he was doing. The first man stated that he was just counting the slits in the pier, so the second man joined him. As they were walking along counting the slits, they didn't notice the end of the pier and both fell off into the water. Just proves one thing: When you're out of slits, you're out of pier.

- What would you call Jabba the Hutt's Dog? "Jabba the Mutt."

- Speaking of *Star Wars*, who is R2D2's psychiatrist? [Sigmund Droid.]

- What did the manic-depressive say? "Easy glum, easy glow."

- What is the name of the new movie about a friendly bear who wants to become a rabbi? "Yentl Ben."

- When the geneticist crossed an owl with a goat, she got a hootenanny.

- There is a famous singing group that drinks nothing but diet drinks and eats nothing but fruit. It's known as the "Tab and Apple Choir."

- Doctors are now telling us that our attitudes have an influence on infection. The surly bird catches the germ.

- Roy Rogers climbed on trusty old Trigger for a ride on the ranch. Shortly after they left, Roy returned with his new shiny boots all ripped, scratched, and mauled. He grabbed his gun from the mantle, jumped back on his horse, and took off in a cloud of dust. When he came back to the ranchhouse, Dale Evans was standing on the porch. She saw him ride in with a mountain lion slung across his saddle. Dale asked Roy, "Pardon me, Roy, is that the cat that chewed your new shoes?"

- What did Snow White say to the photographer? "Some day my prints will come."

- Joe Murmur and his brothers were pickpockets. They worked all the county fairs. People knew their pockets were being picked when a Murmur ran through the crowd.

- A famous rock star has been cloned. The singing group is called "Cher and Cher alike."

- What is white, fleecy, and writes classical music? "Cloud Debussy."

- What is white, puffy, and skis? "Jean Cloud Killy."

- If you are lonely you should go to Missouri; Missouri loves company.

- What is a tone deaf person called? "The Van Gogh of music—he doesn't have an ear."

- The first-grade teacher married the local coroner. They took the class on a tour of a wig factory. One little kid couldn't see the conveyor belt with the wigs because it was too high, so the coroner let him stand on his back. Then the little kid was standing on the coroner watching all the curls go by.

- What is it called when you can catch a fly in the air with your bare hand? "The hand is quicker than the fly."

- The art gallery was burglarized but the thief didn't get away with the Monet—he couldn't make his Van Gogh.

- What is Irish and rusty and stays out all night? "Paddy O'Furniture."

- A painter was painting the church. He ran low on paint so he thinned the remaining paint to do the steeple. Just then a huge cloud opened up, a golden finger appeared, and a booming voice said, "Repaint and thin no more."

- The symphony orchestra was playing Beethoven's Ninth when the wind blew up so hard that the musicians tried to keep the music from blowing away by lashing it down. The bass players got disgusted and went to have a few drinks. That was the night that in the bottom of the Ninth, the scores were tied, and the basses were loaded.

- The world's richest man raised porpoises. They developed an exotic disease and a marine biologist said the only cure would be to give them a transfusion of a quart of seagull blood. That night, the rich man went to the beach and trapped twenty-four seagulls, stuffed them into the trunk of his limousine, and raced to the gates of the estate. Just as he was turning in the estate lane, he saw the flashing lights of a police car behind him. He drove through the gates and before he could stop he drove into the guard lions standing in the driveway. The patrolman got out and put him under arrest. The charge was crossing estate lions with young gulls for immortal porpoises.

- What is a Communist plot? "Stalin's grave."

- A clever duck convinced the drug store clerk to put some Chapstick on him. When asked how he would pay for it, the duck said, "Just put it on my bill."

- In the early days, surveyors found the compass to be indispensable. There were many brands of compasses available, but the best known was the Tate Compass. It was relatively cheap, so many surveyors bought it. Unfortunately, along with being cheap, it was also highly inaccurate. The sad result was that virtually every surveyor who ventured into the wilderness using one of them was never seen again; hence the saying, "He who has a Tates is lost."

- Another saying might be that he who is lost, hesitates.

- In Australia, the bush people rely on prayer to protect them from severe winter conditions. They huddle together when they pray, and that is why many are cold but few are frozen.

- The frog went to the bank for a loan. When the loan officer, whose name was Paddywack, asked for collateral, the frog offered his lily pad and a small memento from his father. Puzzled, Paddywack went to the bank manager, showed him the memento, and asked for a decision. The bank manager puffed on his cigar and said, "That's a knickknack, Paddywack. Give the frog a loan."

- The bankrupt owner of a Chinese restaurant says he's caught between a wok and a hard place.

- A parent asked his son about his final grades. He was told that they were under water: below C level.

- The music teacher left the following sign on the door: "Bach at 2. Offenbach sooner."

- The local marina had a sign: "Out to launch."

- J. Paul Getty was thinking of opening some baths at Pagosa Springs in Colorado to take advantage of the hot springs. He planned to call it "spa-Getty."

- The foo bird of Africa has amazing powers. If a foo bird drops a deposit on you and you wash it off, you will drop dead. Everyone knows, "If the foo shits, wear it."

- If you spend a lot of time thinking about traveling orthodontists, you're obviously into transient dental meditation.

- A man worked in a bakery and was paid according to the number of loaves of bread he could slice. He got a knife long enough to slice two loaves at once and he doubled his money. Immediately he began looking for a knife that could slice three loaves at once, and found one, so he tripled his money. Being ambitious, he wanted to quadruple his money, so he looked for a knife that would cut four loaves at once. Finally, he found one in an antique store. The store owner wrapped it up in a long slender package. On his way back to the bakery, he saw a friend who asked him why he was so happy. The baker replied, "This is my lucky day. I just found a four loaf cleaver."

- Mr. Chan owned a shop with exquisite carvings of teak, stuffed panda bears, jade jewelry, and ivory carvings. One day a young man went into the shop to browse. He saw two teak carvings he coveted but he didn't have the money for them. The fellow went down the street to the costume store and asked to rent a panda bear outfit. The clerk told him the only one they had had just been returned and the feet were missing. The fellow told him not to worry, rented the costume, left the costume store, and went back to Mr. Chan's shop. While still outside he put on the panda bear suit and started slowly into the shop. When he got beside the two teak carvings he wanted, he snatched them and started running out of the shop. Just then Mr. Chan looked up and screamed, "Help, help. Boy foot bear with teaks of Chan."

- Bruno Opporknockity is a Bulgarian immigrant working in Denver as a piano tuner. He tunes pianos only for great musicians and for the very wealthy. Bruno takes great pride in his appearance and wears a white tie, top hat, and tails when he tunes pianos. One day, he went to one of Denver's wealthy dowagers to tune her concert grand. When he was finished, he played a tremendous arpeggio. He got up and bowed to the woman. Then she told him, "That sounds terrible. You will have to tune it again." With hatred in his eyes Bruno said, "Madame, Opporknockity only tunes once."

- When geologists reached the edge of Mount St. Helens, the volcanic crater, they heard music coming from deep inside. They flew a recording engineer in by helicopter. He lowered a microphone into the crater, and sure enough, there was music: the volcano was humming, "Lava, Come Back to Me."

- The French chef discovered that frogs sauteed in eggs and milk were delicious. He gave us the breakfast dish French toads.

- When the farmer in Iowa heard that his two college-bound daughters planned to specialize in research on ancient Egyptian plumbing, he telephoned them and said, "Under no circumstances will I support a couple of pharoah faucet majors."

- The producers of a major ice-skating show have made a deal with a medical-research firm so they can offer everyone who attends a free ice queen clone.

RIDDLES

Riddles are among the earliest and most universal form of story. It has been said that each is a little metaphor that often includes not only a mystery but a contest.

> Samson was traveling on foot through the desert when he was attacked by a young lion. He stood his ground and fought back. With his bare hands, he tore the lion limb from limb. Several weeks later he passed that way again and came upon the lion's carcass, only now the carcass was filled with a honeycomb a swarm of bees had left. In the Old Testament Samson riddled, "Out of the eater came forth meat, and out of the strong came forth sweetness."

Of course no one could solve the riddle unless they knew what Samson had experienced.

Over the centuries, riddles became part of the traditions and ceremonies in many religions. One finds riddles in the Old Testament, the New Testament, the Koran, and the *Rig-Veda*. In parts of Turkey, a suitor who could not solve three riddles in a row was thought to be stupid.

Alvin Schwartz wrote, "Several thousand years ago people believed there was magic in riddles. If they answered riddles correctly, the gods would see to it that their crops would grow, or that a boy would grow to be a man, or that the spirit of a dead person would not haunt them" (Schwartz 1987).

Sometimes the life of a man or woman was at stake in riddling contests. In Norse mythology, Thor keeps the dwarf Alvis busy answering riddles until the sun rises and turns the dwarf into stone. Odin asks a giant a series of riddles, the last of which is unanswerable—and so the giant loses his head. Tolkien used riddles between Smaug and Frodo in his *Ring* books (Tolkien 1986). Another literary riddler was Lewis Carroll, who made up riddles for the young people he knew.

> Oedipus and the Sphinx, a creature with the head of a woman, the body of a lion, and the wings of an eagle, had a riddling contest. The Sphinx asked, "What goes on four legs in the morning, two legs at noon, and three legs in the evening?" Oedipus answered, "Man: as a baby [morning] he crawls, at noon he is on two legs, and as an old man [evening] he needs a cane."

One of the oldest riddles we know about is over six thousand years old. It was found in the city of Babylon carved in a stone tablet that was used in school. "What grows fat without eating?" Answer: "A rain cloud."

Many of the riddles can be found in ballads. The following folk riddle song is from the Kentucky mountains. An earlier version of this was found in an English manuscript dating from the fifteenth century.

The Riddle Song

I gave my love a cherry without a stone,
I gave my love a chicken without a bone,
I gave my love a ring that has no end,
I gave my love a baby with no cryin'.

How can there be a cherry without a stone?
How can there be a chicken without a bone?
How can there be a ring that has no end?
How can there be a baby with no cryin'?

A cherry, when it's blooming, it has no stone,
A chicken, when it's peeping, it has no bone,
A ring, when it's a-rolling, it has no end,
A baby, when it's sleeping, there's no cryin'.

Riddles Wisely Expounded

Another riddle ballad is found in Child's collection of English and Scottish ballads (Child 1965). There are several variants of the same riddle.

Child's Ballad

O what is higher than the trees?
    Gar lay the bent to the bonny broom
And what is deeper than the seas?
    And you may beguile a fair maid soon.

O what is whiter than the milk?
Or what is softer than the silk?

O what is sharper than the thorn?
O what is louder than the horn?

O what is longer than the way?
And what is colder than the clay?

O what is greener than the grass?
And what is worse than woman was?

O heaven's higher than the trees,
And hell is deeper than the seas.

And snow is whiter than the milk,
And love is softer than the silk.

O hunger's sharper than the thorn,
And thunder's louder than the horn.

O wind is longer than the way,
And death is colder than the clay.

O poison's greener than the grass,
And the Devil's worse than eer woman was.

One of Child's versions has this as the last verse:

> As sune as she the fiend did name,
> He flew awa in a blazing flame.

It would seem likely that the devil was using the riddle to duel for a person's soul. Of course, if people and gods were to use the riddles as contests, the devil would too; he always seems to be looking for ways to gather souls that are not wary. In this ballad, the last question is something of a trick. The young girl, however, is able to answer it and so innocence overcomes evil.

Grimm's Collections

In the stories collected by the brothers Grimm, there are several riddling tales.

A Riddling Tale

Three women were changed into flowers which grew in the field, but one of them was allowed to be in her own home at night. Once, when day was drawing near, and she was forced to go back to her companions in the field and become a flower again, she said to her husband, "If you will come this afternoon and gather me, I shall be set free and henceforth stay with you." And so he did.

Now the question is, how did her husband know her, for the flowers were exactly alike, without any difference?

Answer: Since she was at her home during the night and not in the field, no dew fell on her, as it did on the others, and by this her husband knew her.

The Riddle

A king's son once had a great desire to travel through the world, so he started off, taking no one with him but one trusty servant. One day he came to a great forest, and as evening drew on and he could find no shelter he could not think where to spend the night. All of a sudden he saw a girl going toward a little house. As he drew near, he saw that she was both young and pretty. He spoke to her, and said, "Dear child, could I spend the night in this house?"

"Oh yes," said the girl in a sad tone, "you can if you like, but I should not advise you to do so. Better not go in."

"Why not?" asked the King's son.

The girl sighed, and answered, "My stepmother deals in black magic, and she is not friendly to strangers."

The prince guessed easily that he had come to a witch's house, but it was now dark and he could go no farther. Moreover, he was not afraid, and he stepped in with his groom.

An old woman sat in an armchair near the fire. As they entered, she turned her red eyes on them. "Good evening," she muttered, pretending to be friendly. "Won't you sit down?"

She blew up the fire on which she was cooking something in a little pot. But her daughter had warned the travelers to be careful not to eat or drink anything, as the old woman's brews were likely to be dangerous.

They went to bed and slept soundly till morning. When they were ready to start, and the king's son had already mounted his horse, the old woman said, "Wait a minute, I must give you a stirrup cup." While she went to fetch it, the king's son rode off, and the groom, who had waited to tighten his saddle girths, was alone when the witch returned.

"Take that to your master," she said. But as she spoke the glass cracked and the poison spurted over the horse. It was so powerful the poor creature sank down dead. The servant ran after his master and told him what had happened, and then, not wishing to lose the saddle as well as the horse, he went back to fetch it. When he reached the spot, he saw that a raven had perched on the carcass and was pecking at it. "Who knows whether we shall get anything better to eat today!" said the man, and he shot the raven and carried it off.

Then they rode on all day through the forest without coming to the end. At nightfall they reached an inn. The servant made the landlord a present of the raven. Now, as it happened, this inn was the resort of a band of robbers, and the old witch, too, was in the habit of frequenting it. As soon as it was dark twelve thieves arrived, with the full intention of killing and robbing the strangers. However, they sat down first to table, where the landlord and the old witch joined them, and they all ate some broth in which the flesh of the raven had been boiled. They had hardly taken a couple of spoonfuls when they all fell down dead, for the poison had passed from the horse to the raven and so into the broth. There was no one left belonging to the house but the landlord's daughter, who was a good, well-meaning girl and had taken no part in all the evil doings.

She opened all the doors and showed the strangers the treasures the robbers had gathered together. The prince bade her keep them all for herself, as he wanted none of them, and so he rode on with his servant.

After traveling about for some time they reached a town where lived a lovely but arrogant princess. She had announced that anyone who asked her a riddle which she was unable to guess should be her husband, but should she guess it he must forfeit his head. She claimed three days in which to think over the riddles, but she was so clever that she invariably guessed them in much shorter time. Nine suitors had already lost their lives when the king's son arrived, and, dazzled by the princess's beauty, determined to risk his life. He came before her and propounded his riddle.

"What is this?" he asked. "One slew none and yet killed twelve."

She could not think what it was! She thought and thought and looked through all her books of riddles and puzzles. She found nothing to help her and could not guess. In fact, she was at her wits' end. As she could think of no way to guess the riddle, she ordered her maid to steal at night into the prince's bedroom and listen. She thought he might talk aloud in his dreams and so betray the secret. But the clever servant had taken his master's place, and when the maid came, he tore off the cloak she had wrapped about herself and chased her off.

On the second night the princess sent her lady-in-waiting, hoping she might succeed better. But the servant took away her mantle and chased her away also.

On the third night the king's son thought he really might feel safe, so he went to bed. But in the middle of the night the princess came herself, wrapped in a misty gray mantle, and sat down near him. When she thought he was fast asleep, she spoke to him, hoping he would answer in the midst of his dreams as many people do. But he was wide awake all the time and heard and understood everything very well.

Then she asked, "One slew none—what is that?" And he answered, "A raven which fed on the carcass of a poisoned horse."

She went on, "And yet killed twelve—what is that?" "Those are twelve robbers who ate the raven and died of it."

As soon as she knew the riddle she tried to slip away, but he held her mantle so tightly she was obliged to leave it behind.

Next morning the princess announced that she had guessed the riddle, and sent for the twelve judges, before whom she declared it. But the young man begged to be heard, saying, "She came by night to question me; otherwise she never could have guessed it."

The judges said, "Bring us some proof." So the servant brought out the three cloaks. When the judges saw the gray one, which the Princess was in the habit of wearing, they said, "Let it be embroidered with gold and silver. It shall be your wedding mantle."

Of course, the Grimms' brothers also collected the riddle story of Rumpelstiltskin. In that story, the queen's messenger overhears a comical little man reciting the verse:

Today do I bake, tomorrow I brew,
The day after that the Queen's child comes in;
And oh! I am glad that nobody knew
That the name I am called is Rumpelstiltskin!

Because of this verse, the Queen was able to answer the riddle as to the news of the little man and keep her child.

General Riddles

There are many riddles from other cultures. The first seven are from the Jewish folklore.

- Q. It's not a shirt—Yet it's sewed;
  It's not a tree—Yet it's full of leaves;
  It's not a person—Yet it talks sensibly.

  A. A book.

- Q. What is it? A deaf man has heard how a dumb man had said that a blind man had seen a running rabbit; that a lame man pursued it and that a naked man had put it in his pocket and brought it home?

  A. A lie.

- Q. One dreamed that he was on a ship at sea with his father and mother and that the ship had begun to sink. It was, however, possible to save himself and one other person only—either his father or mother—not both. What should he do?

  A. He should wake up.

- Q. Three merchants and three robbers had to cross a lake. However, only one rowboat was available and it could safely carry only two people at a time. How could they all manage to get across since one merchant was afraid to be left alone with two robbers?

  A. First of all two robbers crossed. One robber then brought the boat back and rowed across the third robber. Afterwards he returned once more and remained on shore. Then two merchants got into the boat and rowed across. One merchant in company with one robber returned with the boat. The robber got out of the boat. The merchant rowed across to the other merchant. After that a robber returned to fetch the last robber.

- Q. "What hangs on the wall, is green, and whistles?"

  A. "A herring."

  Q. "A herring?! Does a herring hang on a wall?"

  A. "Who stops you from hanging it?"

  Q. "Is a herring green?"

  A. "It could be painted green."

  Q. "But who ever heard of a herring that whistles?"

  A. "Nu, so it doesn't whistle."

- Pretty little girl, good little girl,
  I will ask you a clever riddle:
      What is higher than a house,
      What is swifter than a mouse?
  You foolish fellow, you simpleton,
  You have no sense in all your head;
      Smoke is higher than a house,
      The cat is swifter than a mouse.

- What kind of water is without sand,
  What kind of king is without a land?
  The water in the eye is without sand,
  The king of spades is without a land.

- Q. I have a little lady and every day I dance with her. What is she?

  A. A broom (Haitian).

- Q. It goes all over the world, but we cannot see it.

  A. The wind (Tibetan).

- Q. She eats all the best food and never gets fat.

  A. A saucepan (Tibetan).

- Q. It has two wings but cannot fly away.

  A. Scissors (Tibetan).

- Q. I am doing it, and you are doing it. Can you guess what it is?

  A. Breathing (Mayan).

- Q. Son, have you seen the green water holes in the rock? There are two of them, a cross is raised between them.

  A. They are a man's eyes (Mayan).

- Q. A riddle, a riddle, as I suppose,
     A hundred eyes, and never a nose.

  A. A potato (contemporary).

- Q. How many days of the week begin with "T"?

  A. Tuesday, Thursday, today, and tomorrow (contemporary).

- Q. How many seconds are in a year?

  A. Twelve—the second of January, the second of February, etc. (contemporary).

- Q. What did one strawberry say to the other strawberry?

  A. "If you weren't so fresh we wouldn't be in this jam" (contemporary).

Bibliography

Aardema, Verna. 1966. *More Tales from the Story Hat*. New York: Coward McCann.

Abrahams, Roger D., ed. 1985. *Afro-American Folktales: Stories from Black Traditions in the New World*. New York: Pantheon.

Abrahams, Roger D. 1980. *The Living from the Dead: Riddles Which Tell Stories*. Helsinki, Finland: Folklore Fellows Communications, #225.

Adams, Pam. 1973. *There Was an Old Lady*. New York: Grosset and Dunlap.

Adams, Robert G. 1973. *Introduction to Folklore*. Columbus, OH: Collegiate Press.

Adams, Samuel Hopkins, ed. 1927. *A Book of Clues for the Clever*. New York: Boni and Liveright.

Adler, Margot. 1986. *Drawing Down the Moon*. Boston: Beacon.

Aesop. 1968. *Aesop's Fables*. New York: Walck.

_____. 1964. *Five Centuries of Illustrated Fables*. New York: Metropolitan Museum of Art.

_____. 1962. *Fables from Aesop*. New York: Walck.

_____. 1947. *Aesop's Fables*. New York: Grosset and Dunlap.

_____. 1933. *Aesop's Fables*. New York: Viking.

Afanas'ev, Aleksandra. 1973. *Russian Fairy Tales*. New York: Pantheon.

Alegriu, Ricardo E. 1969. *Three Wishes: A Collection of Puerto Rican Folktales*. New York: Harcourt, Brace and World.

American Genealogical Research Institute Staff. 1975. *How to Trace Your Family Tree*. Garden City, NY: Doubleday.

American Heritage Dictionaries, eds. 1986. *Word Mysteries and Histories: From Quiche to Humble Pie*. Boston: Houghton Mifflin.

Angier, Bradford. 1974. *Field Guide to Edible Wild Plants*. Harrisburg, PA: Stackpole Books.

Arbuthnot, May Hill. 1961a. *The Arbuthnot Anthology of Children's Literature*. Chicago: Scott Foresman.

_____. 1961b. *Time for Fairy Tales Old and New*. Chicago: Follett.

Arceneaux, Tom E. 1984. "Learning and Lagniappe in Louisiana." *Childhood Education*, 54 (March): 238-41.

_____. 1980. "Elementary Cultural Journalism." In *National Workshop for Cultural Journalism: Workshop Report*, edited by S. Reynolds. Rabun Gap, GA: Foxfire Fund, Inc.

Arnott, Kathleen. 1971. *Animal Folk Tales around the World*. New York: Walck.

_____. 1967. *Tales of Temba: Traditional African Stories*. New York: Walck.

_____. 1963. *African Myths and Legends*. New York: Walck.

Arps, Louisa Ward, and Elinor Eppich Kingery. 1966. *High Country Names*. Denver, CO: The Colorado Mountain Club, Johnson Publishing Co. of Boulder.

Arrowsmith, Nancy, with George Morrse. 1977. *Field Guide to the Little People*. New York: Hill and Wang.

Asbjornsen, Peter Christen, and Jorgen Moe. 1960. *Norwegian Folk Tales*. New York: Viking.

Asian Cultural Center for UNESCO. 1975, 1976. *Folktales from Asia for Children Everywhere*. New York: Weatherhill.

Association for Childhood Education International. 1930. *Told under the Green Umbrella*. New York: Macmillan.

Aunt Sue's Budge of Puzzles. 1859. New York: T. W. Strong.

Ausubel, Nathan. 1948. *A Treasury of Jewish Folklore*. New York: Crown Publishers.

Babbitt, Ellen C. 1940. *Jataka Tales*. New York: Appleton-Century-Crofts.

Badger, Andrew. 1975. "Folklore, A Source for Composition." *College Composition and Communication* 26 (October): 285-88.

Baker, B. 1978. *Partners*. New York: Greenwillow.

_____. 1973. *At the Center of the World*. New York: Macmillan.

Bakhtin, M. M. 1981. *The Dialogic Imagination*. Austin, TX: University of Texas Press.

Ball, Rouse W. W. n.d. *Fun with String Figures*. New York: Dover.

Baring-Gould, William S., and Ceil Baring-Gould. 1962. *The Annotated Mother Goose*. New York: Bramhall House.

Baum, Willa K. 1971. *Oral History for the Local Historical Society*. Nashville, TN: American Association for State and Local History.

Baylor, Byrd. 1978. *The Way to Start a Day*. New York: Scribner's.

_____. 1976. *And It's Still Told That Way: Legends Told by Arizona Indian Children*. New York: Scribner's.

Becker, Carl. 1935. *Every Man His Own Historian*. New York: Crofts.

Bell, Corydon. 1955. *John Rattling Gourd of Big Cave: A Collection of Cherokee Indian Legends*. New York: Macmillan.

Bellows, Henry A. 1923. *The Poetic Edda*. New York: Biblo and Tannen.

Belting, N. M. 1961. *The Long-Tailed Bear and Other Indian Legends*. New York: Dial.

Berry, Erick. 1968. *The Magic Banana and Other Polynesian Tales*. New York: John Day.

Bierhorst, John, ed. 1976. *Black Rainbow: Legends of the Incas and Myths of Ancient Peru*. New York: Farrar, Straus and Giroux.

_____. 1970. *The Ring in the Prairie: A Shawnee Legend*. New York: Dial.

_____. 1969. *The Fire Plume: Legends of the American Indians*. New York: Dial.

Blamey, Marjorie. 1980. *Flowers of the Countryside*. New York: William Morrow and Co.

Bleecker, M. N. 1946. *Big Music or Twenty Merry Tales to Tell*. New York: Viking.

Bley, Edgar S. 1982. *The Best Singing Games for Children*. New York: Sterling.

_____. 1957. *The Best Singing Games for Children of All Ages*. New York: Sterling.

Blum, Ralph. 1982. *The Book of Runes: A Handbook for the Use of an Ancient Oracle, the Viking Runes*. New York: St. Martin's Press.

Bombaugh, C. C. 1961. *Oddities and Curiosities of Words and Literature*. New York: Dover.

Booss, Claire, ed. 1984. *Scandinavian Folk and Fairy Tales*. New York: Avenel.

_____, ed. 1944. *A Treasury of American Folklore*. New York: Avenel.

Borland, Hal. 1981. *A Countryman's Flowers*. New York: Alfred A. Knopf.

Botkin, B. A. 1983. *A Treasury of American Folklore*. New York: Bonanza Books.

_____. 1951. *A Treasury of Western Folklore*. New York: Crown Publishers.

_____. ed. 1944. *A Treasury of American Folklore*. New York: Crown Publishers.

_____. 1937. *The American Playparty Song, with a Collection of Oklahoma Texts and Tunes*. Omaha, NE: University of Nebraska.

Bowman, James Cloyd, and Margery Bianco. 1964. *Tales from a Finnish Tupa*. Chicago: Albert Whitman.

Brenner, Barbara. 1977. *Little One Inch*. New York: Coward, McCann and Geoghagen.

Brewer's Dictionary of Phrase and Fable. n.d. New York: Harper and Brothers.

Briggs, K. M. 1962. *Pale Hecate's Team*. London: Routledge and Kegan Paul.

Briggs, Katharine. 1979. *Abbey Lubbers, Banshees and Boggarts*. New York: Pantheon.

_____. 1978. *The Vanishing People: Fairy Lore and Legends*. New York: Pantheon.

_____. 1976. *An Encyclopedia of Fairies: Hobgoblins, Brownies, Bobies, and Other Supernatural Creatures*. New York: Pantheon.

_____. 1967. *The Fairies in English Tradition and Literature*. Chicago: University of Chicago Press.

_____. 1954. *The Personnel of Fairyland*. Cambridge, MA: Bentley.

Brodrick, Houghton A. 1972. *Animals in Archeology*. New York: Praeger.

Brown, Dee. 1979. *Tepee Tales of the American Indian*. New York: Holt, Rinehart and Winston.

Bruchac, J. 1975. *Turkey Brother and Other Tales: Iroquois Folk Stories*. Trumansburg, NY: The Crossing Press.

Brunvand, Jan Harold. 1981. *The Vanishing Hitchhiker: American Urban Legends and Their Meanings*. New York: W. W. Norton.

_____. 1978a. *The Study of American Folklore*. 2d ed. New York: W. W. Norton.

_____. 1978b. *The Study of American Folklore*. New York: W. W. Norton.

_____. 1976. *Folklore, A Study and Research Guide*. New York: St. Martin's Press.

_____. 1968. *The Study of American Folklore: An Introduction*. New York: W. W. Norton.

Bryan, Ashley. 1971. *The Ox of the Wonderful Horns and Other African Folktales*. New York: Atheneum.

Bryant, Sara Cone. 1907. *Epaminondas and His Auntie*. Boston: Houghton, Mifflin.

Budge, Sir E. A. Wallis. 1969. *Gods of the Egyptians*. 2 vols. New York: Dover.

Bulatkin, I. F. 1965. *Folk and Fairy Tales*. New York: Criterion.

Burland, Cottie. 1968. *North American Indian Mythology*. New York: Hamlyn Publishing Group.

Burton, William. 1962. *The Magic Drum: Tales from Central Africa*. New York: Criterion.

Busch, Phyllis S. 1977. *Wildflowers and the Stories behind Their Names*. New York: Charles Scribner's Sons.

Butler, Robert N. 1975. *Why Survive? Being Old in America*. New York: Harper and Row.

Calvino, Italo. 1980a. *Italian Folktales*. New York: Harcourt, Brace and Jovanovich.

———. 1980b. *Italian Folktales*. New York: Pantheon.

Campbell, B. G. 1976. *Humankind Emerging*. New York: Little Brown.

———. 1972. *Sexual Selection and the Descent of Man*. London: Heinemann.

Campbell, Joseph. 1988. *Historical Atlas of World Mythology. Volume 2. The Way of the Seeded Earth, Part 1: The Sacrifice*. New York: Harper and Row.

Cano, Robin E., ed. 1973. *Game Songs*. Boston: Houghton Mifflin.

Chafetz, H. 1964. *Thunderbird and Other Stories*. New York: Pantheon.

Chase, Richard, ed. 1972. *Old Songs and Singing Games*. New York: Dover.

———. 1967. *Singing Games and Playparty Games*. New York: Dover.

———. 1949. *Singing Games and Playparty Games*. New York: Dover.

Child, Francis James, ed. 1965. *The English and Scottish Popular Ballads*. 5 vols. New York: Dover.

Child Study Association of America. 1958. *Castles and Dragons: Read to Yourself Fairy Tales for Boys and Girls*. New York: Crowell.

Chrisman, Arthur Bowie. 1925. *Shen of the Sea*. New York: Dutton.

Christian, Paul. 1969. *The History and Practice of Magic*. New York: The Citadel.

Clarke, Kenneth W., and Mary W. Clarke. 1963. *Introducing Folklore*. New York: Holt, Rinehart and Winston.

Clutton-Brock Juliet. 1981. *Domesticated Animals in Early Times*. Austin, TX: University of Texas Press.

Coats, Alice M. 1956. *Flowers and Their Histories*. New York: McGraw-Hill.

Coffin, Tristram Potter. 1968. *Our Living Traditions: An Introduction to American Folklore*. New York: Basic Books.

Coffin, Tristram Potter, and Henning Cohen, eds. 1973. *Folklore from the Working Folk of America*. New York: Anchor Press.

Collins, Fletcher, Jr., ed. 1973. *Alamance Playparty Songs*. Norwood, PA: Norwood Editions.

Colum, P. 1966. *The Stone of Victory and Other Tales*. New York: McGraw-Hill.

Colwell, Eileen. 1974. *Round About and Long Ago: Tales from the English Countries*. Boston: Houghton Mifflin.

_____. 1968. *The Youngest Storybook: A Collection of Stories and Rhymes for the Youngest*. New York: Walck.

_____. 1937. *Legends of Hawaii*. New Haven, CT: Yale University Press.

Cothran, S. 1956. *The Magic Calabash: Folktales from America's Islands and Alaska*. New York: McKay.

_____. 1954. *With a Wig, with a Wag, and Other American Folktales*. New York: McKay.

Courlander, H. 1978. *The People of the Short Blue Corn and Legends of the Hopi Indians*. New York: Harcourt, Brace, Jovanovich.

_____. 1973. *Tales of Gods and Heroes*. Greenwich, CT: Fawcett.

_____. 1964. *The Piece of Fire and Other Haitian Tales*. New York: Harcourt.

_____. 1955. *Ride with the Sun: An Anthology of Folktales and Stories from the United Nations*. New York: Whittlesea House.

_____. 1950a. *The Fire on the Mountain and Other Ethiopian Tales*. New York: Holt.

_____. 1950b. *Kantchil's Lime Pit and Other Stories from Indonesia*. New York: Harcourt Brace.

Courlander, Harold, and Albert Kofi-Prempeh. 1957. *Hat-shaking Dance and Other Ashanti Tales from Ghana*. New York: Harcourt, Brace and World.

Courlander, Harold, and George Herzog. 1947. *The Cowtail Switch and Other West African Stories*. New York: Holt, Rinehart and Winston.

Cramblet, Wilbur H., and Luther W. Smith. 1953. *Christian Worship: A Hymnal*. Philadelphia, PA: Judson Press.

Crane, Walter. 1980. *Flowers from Shakespeare's Garden*. New York: Macmillan.

Credle, Ellis. 1957. *Tall Tales from the High Hills and Other Stories*. New York: Thomas Nelson and Sons.

Crompton, A. E. 1975. *The Winter Wife: An Abenaki Folktale*. Boston: Little Brown.

Crossley-Holland, Kevin. 1985. *Folktales of the British Isles*. New York: Pantheon.

_____. 1980. *The Norse Myths*. New York: Pantheon.

Cunningham, C. 1939. *The Talking Stone*. New York: Alfred A. Knopf.

Cunningham, James A., and John E. Klimas. 1974. *Wildflowers of Eastern America*. New York: Alfred A. Knopf.

Curry, J. L. 1965. *Down from the Lonely Mountain*. New York: Harcourt, Brace and World.

Curtis, E. S. 1978. *The Girl Who Married a Ghost and Other Tales from the North American Indian*. New York: Four Winds.

Curtis, Natalie, ed. 1987. *The Indians' Book: An Offering by the American Indians of Indian Lore, Musical, and Narrative, to Form a Record of Songs and Legends of Their Race*. New York: Bonanza Books.

Curtiss, Richard D., Gary L. Shumway, and Shirley E. Stephenson. 1973. *A Guide for Oral History Programs*. Fullerton, CA: California State University, Fullerton and the Southern California Local History Council, California.

Daly, Mary. 1973. *Beyond God the Father*. Boston: Beacon Press.

Dana, Mrs. William Starr. 1970. *How to Know the Wild Flowers*. New York: Holt, Rinehart and Winston.

Daniels, Cora Lynn, and C. M. Stevans. 1971. *Encyclopaedia of Superstitions and Folklore*, Vols. I, II, III. Detroit, MI: Gale.

Daniels, Guy. 1969. *Falcon under the Hat: Russian Fairy Tales and Merry Tales*. New York: Funk and Wagnalls.

Davidson, Levette J. 1951. *A Guide to American Folklore*. Denver, CO: Sage Books.

Davis, Cullom, Kathryn Back, and Kay MacLean. 1977. *Oral History from Tape to Type*. Chicago: American Library Association.

Davis, Russell, and Brent Ashabrenner. 1959. *The Lion's Whiskers: Tales of High Africa*. Boston: Little Brown.

Dawson, J. Frank. 1954. *Place Names in Colorado*. Denver, CO: Golden Bell Press.

deBray, Lys. 1978. *The Wild Garden*. New York: Mayflower Books.

Deering, Mary Jo, and Barbara Pomeroy. 1976. *Transcribing without Tears*. Washington, DC: Oral History Program, George Washington University.

Delsol, Paula. 1969. *Chinese Astrology*. New York: Warner.

Dembeck, Hermann. 1965. *Animals and Men*. Garden City, NY: Natural History Press.

Derrida, J. 1979. *Writing and Differences*. London: Routledge and Kegan Paul.

Deutsch, Babette, and Avrahm Yarmolinsky. 1963. *More Tales of Faraway Folk*. New York: Harper and Row.

_____. 1952. *Tales of Faraway Folk*. New York: Harper.

DeWit, D. 1979. *The Talking Stone: An Anthology of Native American Tales and Legends*. New York: Greenwillow.

Diendorfer, Robert G. 1980. *American's 101 Most High Falutin', Big Talkin', Knee Slappin' Gollywhoppers and Tall Tales: The Best of the Burlington Liars Club*. New York: Workman.

Dobbs, Rose. 1961. *More Once-Upon-A-Time*. New York: Random House.

Dobie, J. Frank, Mody Boatright, and Harry H. Ransom. 1965. *Coyote Wisdom*. Dallas, TX: SMU Press.

Dolch, Edward W., and Margaret P. Dolch. 1962. *Stories from Old Russia*. Champaign, IL: Garrard.

_____. 1956. *Pueblo Stories*. Champaign, IL: Garrard.

Dorliae, Peter G. 1970. *Animals Mourn for Da Leopard and Other West African Tales*. Indianapolis, IN: Bobbs-Merrill.

Dorson, Richard. 1964. "Introduction: Collecting Oral Folklore in the United States." In *Buying the Wind*. Chicago: University of Chicago Press.

_____, ed. 1972a. *African Folklore*. Bloomington, IN: Indiana University Press.

_____, ed. 1972b. *Folklore and Folklife: An Introduction*. Chicago: University of Chicago Press.

_____. 1972c. *Folklore: Selected Essays*. Bloomington, IN: Indiana University Press.

_____, ed. 1961. *Folklore Research around the World*. Indiana University Folklore Series No. 16. Bloomington, IN: Indiana University Press.

_____. 1959. *American Folklore*. Chicago: University of Chicago Press.

Downing, Charles. 1965. *Tales of the Hodja*. New York: Walck.

Downing, John, and Chekan Leong. 1982. *The Psychology of Reading*. New York: Macmillan.

Dudeney, Henry E. 1968. *300 Best Word Puzzles*. New York: Charles Scribner's Sons.

Duncan, Wilbur. 1975. *Wildflowers of the Southeastern United States*. Athens, GA: University of Georgia Press.

Dundes, Alan. 1969. "Folklore as a Mirror of Culture." *Elementary English*, 46 (April): 471-82.

_____. 1965. *The Study of Folklore*. Englewood Cliffs, NJ: Prentice-Hall.

Dunn, Donald H. 1981. "Personal Business." *Business Week*, no. 2701 (August 17): 114.

Durant, Mary. 1976. *Who Named the Daisy? Who Named the Rose?* New York: Dodd, Mead.

Eagleton, T. 1981. *Walter Benjamin or Toward a Revolutionary Criticism*. New York: Verso/Routledge, Chapman and Hall.

Edmonds, I. G. 1966. *Trickster Tales*. Philadelphia, PA: Lippincott.

Egan, Kieran. 1987. "_____" *Harvard Educational Review*, 57, 4 (November): 445-72.

Eichler, George R. 1977. *Colorado Place Names*. Boulder, CO: Johnson Publishing Co.

Elliott, Douglas B. 1976. *Roots*. Old Greenwich, CT: Chatham Press.

Emboden, William A. 1974. *Bizarre Plants*. New York: Macmillan.

Emrich, Duncan. 1972a. *Folklore on the American Land*. Boston: Little, Brown.

_____. 1972b. *The Hodgepodge Book*. New York: Four Winds Press.

Epstein, Ellen Robinson, and Rona Mendelson. 1978. *Record and Remember: Tracing Your Roots through Oral History*. New York: Simon and Schuster.

Erdoes, Richard, and Alfonso Ortiz. 1984. *American Indian Myths and Legends*. New York: Pantheon.

Evans, Joan. 1976. *Magical Jewels of the Middle Ages and the Renaissance*. New York: Dover Publications.

Fairies and Elves. 1984. Chicago: Time-Life Books.

Fairservis, Walter A., Jr. 1971. *Costumes of the East*. Riverside, CT: Catham Press.

Farrell, Edmund J. 1982. "Oral Histories as Living Literature." *English Journal* 71 (April): 87-92.

Field, E. 1973. *Eskimo Songs and Stories*. New York: Delacorte/St. Lawrence.

_____. 1929. *American Folk and Fairy Tales*. New York: Scribner's.

Fillmore, Parker. 1958. *The Shepherd's Nosegay: Stories from Finland and Czechoslovakia*. New York: Harcourt, Brace and World.

Firethunder, B. 1963. *Mother Meadowlark and Brother Snake*. New York: Holt, Rinehart and Winston.

Fisher, A. B. 1957. *Stories California Indians Told*. Berkeley, CA: Parnassus.

Fisher, John, ed. 1973. *The Magic of Lewis Carroll*. New York: Simon and Schuster.

Fluegelman, Andrew, ed. 1976. *The New Games Book*. Garden City, NY: Doubleday.

Foley, Bernice Williams. 1970. *Star Stories*. New York: McCall.

Fowler, Alastair. 1970. *Silent Poetry: Essays in Numerological Analysis*. New York: Barnes & Noble.

Frazer, Sir James George. 1981. *The Golden Bough, The Roots of Religion and Folklore*. New York: Avenel Books.

_____. 1955. *The Golden Bough*, vols. I & III. London, England: Macmillan.

_____. 1922. *The Golden Bough: A Study in Magic and Religion*, vol. I. New York: Collier Books.

Friend, Rev. Hilderic. 1889. *Flowers and Flower Lore*. New York: John B. Alden.

Frobenius, Leo, and Douglas C. Fox. 1966. *African Genesis*. New York: Benjamin Blom.

Frost, F. 1943. *Legends of the United Nations*. New York: Whittlesey House.

Gaer, Joseph. 1955. *The Fables of India*. Boston: Little, Brown.

Garner, Alan. 1969. *A Cavalcade of Goblins*. New York: Walck.

Gibbons, Euell. 1966. *Stalking the Healthful Herbs*. New York: David McKay.

Gillham, Charles E. 1955. *Medicine Men of Hooper Bay: More Tales from the Clapping Mountains of Alaska*. New York: Macmillan.

_____. 1943. *Beyond the Clapping Mountains: Eskimo Stories from Alaska*. New York: Macmillan.

Ginsburg, Mirra. 1973. *The Lazies: Tales of the People of Russia*. New York: Macmillan.

Glassie, Henry, ed. 1985. *Irish Folk Tales*. New York: Pantheon.

Goble, Paul. 1988. *Her Seven Brothers*. New York: Bradbury Press.

Goldstein, Kenneth. 1964. *A Guide for Field Workers in Folklore*. Hatboro, PA: Folklore Associates.

Gomme, Alice B., ed. 1967. *Children's Singing Games*. New York: Dover.

Gomme, Alice B., and Cecil J. Sharp. 1976. *Children's Singing Games*. New York: Arno Press.

Goss, Linda. 1984. "Storytelling Supplement." *Philadelphia Enquirer*, Newspaper in the Classroom Series (May 7): 2.

Green, Margaret. 1965. *The Big Book of Animal Fables*. New York: Watts.

Greenaway, Kate. 1978. *Language of Flowers*. New York: Gramercy Publishers.

Grimm, Jakob, and Wilhelm Karl Grimm. 1987. *Complete Fairy Tales of the Brothers Grimm*. New York: Bantam.

_____. 1945. *Grimm's Fairytales*. New York: Grossett and Dunlop.

Grimm, Jakob, Karl Rudwig, and Wilhelm Karl Grimm. 1973. *The Juniper Tree and Other Tales from Grimm*. New York: Farrar, Straus and Giroux.

Grimm's Complete Fairy Tales. n.d. Garden City, NY: Doubleday.

Gruenberg, S. M. 1955. *More Favorite Stories Old and New for Boys and Girls*. Garden City, NY: Doubleday.

Gupton, Oscar W., and Fred C. Swope. 1979. *Wildflowers of the Shenandoah Valley and Blue Ridge Mountains*. Charlottesville, VA: University Press of Virginia.

Guralnik, David B., ed. 1970. *Webster's New World Dictionary*. New York: World Publishing Co.

Haley, Alex. 1972. "My Furtherest-Back Person, The African." *New York Times Magazine* (July 16).

Haley, Gail E. 1970. *A Story, A Story: An African Tale*. New York: Atheneum.

Hall, Alan. 1976. *The Wild Food Trail Guide*. New York: Holt, Rinehart and Winston.

Hamlyn Publishing Group, Ltd. 1975. *Russian Fairy Tales*. London: Hamlyn.

Hardacer, Val. 1975. *Ginseng*. Northville, MI: Holland House Press.

Hardendorff, Jeanne B. 1969. *Just One More*. Philadelphia, PA: Lippincott.

_____. 1968. *The Frog's Saddle Horse and Other Tales*. Philadelphia, PA: Lippincott.

Hardy, B. 1968. "Towards a Poetic of Fiction: An Approach through Narrative." In *Novel: A Forum on Fiction*. Boston: Boston University Press.

Haring, Lee, and Ellen Foreman. 1975. "Folklore in the Freshman Writing Course." *College English* 40 (September): 13-22.

Harrington, E. B., ed. 1948. "The Tragedy of Macbeth." In *The Harbinger Shakespeare*. New York: Harcourt, Brace and World.

Harris, C. 1963. *Once Upon a Totem*. New York: Atheneum.

Harris, James A. 1978. "Speaking of History: Oral History in the Classroom." *Learning* 7 (October): 72-74.

Harris, Joel Chandler. 1955. *The Complete Tales of Uncle Remus*. Boston: Houghton Mifflin.

Harris, Marvin. 1974. *Cows, Pigs, Wars and Witches: The Riddles of Culture*. New York: Random House.

Haughton, Claire Shaver. 1978. *Green Immigrants*. New York: Harcourt Brace Jovanovich.

Haviland, V. 1979. *North American Legends*. New York: Collins.

Havlice, Patricia Pate. 1985. *Oral History: A Reference Guide and Annotated Bibliography*. Jefferson, NC: McFarland.

Hayes, Joe. 1983. *Coyote and....* Santa Fe, NM: Mariposa.

_____. 1966. *The Checker Playing Hound Dog*. Santa Fe, NM: Mariposa.

Hayes, W. D. 1957. *Indian Tales of the Desert People*. New York: McKay.

Heady, Eleanor B. 1973a. *Safire the Singer*. Chicago: Follett.

_____. 1973b. *Sage Smoke: Tales of the Shoshoni-Bannock Indians*. Chicago: Follett.

_____. 1970. *Tales of the Nimipoo: From the Land of the Nez Perce Indians*. New York: World.

_____. 1965. *Jambo Sungura: Tales from East Africa*. New York: Norton.

Henige, David. 1982. *Oral Historiography*. London: Longman.

Hill, Kay. 1970. *More Glooscap Stories: Legends of the Wabanaki Indians*. Toronto, Canada: Dodd, Mead.

_____. 1965. *Badger, the Mischief Maker*. New York: Dodd, Mead.

_____. 1963. *Glooscap and His Magic: Legends of the Wabanaki Indians*. Toronto, Canada: Dodd, Mead.

Hillman, J. 1975. *Loose Ends*. Dallas, TX: Springhill.

Hirsch, Ruth, and Miriam Lewinger. 1975. "Oral History: The Family Is the Curriculum." *Teacher* 92 (November): 60-62.

Hodges, M. 1972. *The Firebringer: A Paiute Indian Legend*. Boston: Little, Brown.

Hogrogian, Nonny. n.d. *The Thirteen Days of Yule*. New York: Thomas Y. Crowell.

Hoke, Helen. 1958. *Witches, Witches, Witches*. New York: Watts.

Hopper, Vincent Foster. 1969. *Medieval Number Symbolism*. New York: Cooper Square.

Howells, William. 1948. *The Heathens: Primitive Man and His Religion*. Garden City, NY: Doubleday.

Howland, Arthur C., ed. 1957. *Materials toward a History of Witchcraft*, vol. I. New York: Thomas Yoseloff.

Hulpach, V. 1965. *American Indian Tales and Legends*. New York: Hamlyn.

Hurlbut, Cornelius S., Jr. 1970. *Minerals and Man*. New York: Random House.

Hutchinson, Veronica S. 1927. *Candle-Light Stories*. New York: Minton Balch.

Hyde-Chambers, Fredrick, and Audrey Hyde-Chambers. 1981. *Tibetan Folk Tales*. Boulder, CO: Shambhala.

Hymes, Dell. 1982. "Toward Linguistic Competence." *Texas Working Papers in Sociolinguistic Papers No. 16.*

Indagine, Joannes de. 1531. "Chiromantia." In *Magic, Supernaturalism, and Religion*, edited by Kurt Seligman. New York: Grosset & Dunlap, 1948.

Inglis, Bessie D. 1951. *Wildflower Studies*. New York: Studio Publishers, Thomas Y. Crowell.

Insell, Deborah. 1975. "Foxfire in the City." *English Journal* 64 (September): 36-38.

Ito, Nanae. 1968. *Beautiful Wildflowers*. Kansas City, MO: Hallmark Cards.

Jablow, A., and C. Withers. 1969. *The Man in the Moon: Sky Tales from Many Lands*. New York: Holt, Rinehart and Winston.

Jacobi, Frederick, Jr. 1952. *Tales from Grimm and Andersen*. New York: Random House.

Jacobs, Joseph. 1968. *Celtic Fairy Tales*. New York: Dover.

_____. 1967a. *English Fairy Tales*. New York: Dover.

_____. 1967b. *More English Fairy Tales*. New York: Dover.

_____. 1950. *The Fables of Aesop*. New York: Macmillan.

Jagendorf, Moritz A. 1972. *Folk Stories of the South*. New York: Vanguard.

_____. 1957. *Noodlehead Stories from Around the World*. New York: Vanguard.

_____. 1949. *Upstate, Downstate, Folk Stories of the Middle Atlantic States*. New York: Vanguard.

_____. 1948. *New England Bean-Pot*. New York: Vanguard.

Jayne, Caroline Furniss. 1962. *String Figures and How to Make Them*. New York: Dover.

Jenkins, Sara, ed. 1977. *Past Present: Recording Life Stories of Older People*. Washington, DC: National Council on the Aging.

Johnson, Charles, ed. 1981. *Shao and His Fire*. St. Paul, MN: Macalester College.

Jones, Bessie, and Bess Lomax Hawes. 1972. *Step It Down: Games, Plays, Songs, and Stories from the Afro-American Heritage*. New York: Harper and Row.

Jones, H. 1974. *Coyote Tales*. New York: Holt, Rinehart and Winston.

_____. 1972. *Longhouse Winter: Iroquois Transformation Tales*. New York: Holt, Rinehart and Winston.

Jung, C. G. 1959. *The Archetype and the Collective Unconscious*. Vol. 4 of the *Collective Works of C. G. Jung*. New York and London/Princeton, NJ: Princeton University Press.

Jung, C. G., and W. Pauli. 1955. *The Interpretation of Nature and the Psyche*. New York: Pantheon.

Kaufman, Gerald L. 1940. *The Book of Modern Puzzles*. New York: Dover.

Kaula, Edna M. 1968. *African Village Folktales*. New York: World.

Kazemek, Francis E. 1985. "Stories of Our Lives: Interviews and Oral Histories for Language Development." *Journal of Reading* 78 (December): 211-18.

Keightley, Thomas. 1978. *The World Guide to Gnomes, Fairies, Elves, and Other Little People*. New York: Avenel.

———. 1968. *The Fairy Mythology*. New York: AMS Press.

Kelsey, Alice Geer. 1954. *Once the Mullah: Persian Folktales*. New York: McKay.

———. 1943. *Once the Hodja*. New York: McKay.

Kent, Jack. 1974. *More Fables of Aesop*. New York: Parents.

Kim, So-Un. 1955. *The Story Bag: A Collection of Korean Folktales*. Rutland, VT: Tuttle.

Kipling, Rudyard. 1941. *The Collected Works of Rudyard Kipling*. New York: AMS Press.

Kittridge, George L. 1972. *Witchcraft in Old and New England*. New York: Atheneum.

Knapp, Herbert, and Mary Knapp. 1976. *One Potato, Two Potato: The Secret Education of American Children*. New York: Norton.

Korel, Edward. 1964. *Listen and I'll Tell You*. Philadelphia, PA: Lippincott.

Kornbluh, Joyce, and Brady Mikusko, eds. 1964. *Working Womenroots: An Oral History Primer*. ILIR Oral History Project. Ann Arbor, MI: University of Michigan.

Kuntz, George Frederick. 1941. *The Curious Lore of Precious Stones*. New York: Dover.

Lampton, Christopher. 1988. *Stars and Planets*. New York: Doubleday.

Lang, Andrew. 1964. *50 Favorite Fairy Tales*. New York: Watts.

———. 1948. *The Rose Fairy Book*. New York: McKay.

———. 1927. *The Yellow Fairy Book*. New York: McKay.

———. 1901. *The Violet Fairy Book*. New York: Longmans Green.

———. 1889. *The Blue Fairy Book*. New York: Longmans.

Laubach, David. 1979. "Beyond Foxfire." *English Journal* 30 (May): 52-54.

Laufer, Berthold. 1917. "The Myths of P'An-Hu, the Bamboo King." *Journal of American Folklore* 30: 419-21.

Lea, Henry Charles, and Arthur C. Howland, eds. 1957. *Materials toward a History of Witchcraft*, Vols. I, II, III. New York: Thomas Yoseloff.

Leach, M. 1967. *How People Sang the Mountains Up: How and Why Stories*. New York: Viking.

_____. 1961. *Noodles, Nitwits and Numbskulls*. Cleveland, OH: World.

Leach, Maria, ed., and Jerome Fried, assoc. ed. 1984. *Funk and Wagnalls Standard Dictionary of Folklore, Mythology, and Legend*. New York: Harper and Row.

Leach, Maria, and Jerome Fried, eds. 1972. *The Standard Dictionary of Folklore, Mythology, and Legend*. New York: Harper and Row.

Leach, Maria, ed., and Jerome Fried, assoc. ed. 1949. *Funk and Wagnalls Standard Dictionary of Folklore, Mythology and Legend*. New York: Harper and Row.

Leacock, Eleanor Burke. 1981. *Myths of Male Dominance*. New York: Monthly Review Press.

Leakey, Richard, and Roger Lewin. 1979. *People of the Lake: Mankind and Its Beginnings*. New York: Avon.

Lee, Hector. 1970. "American Folklore in the Schools." *English Journal* (October): 994-99.

Lee, Jeanne M. 1982. *Legend of the Milky Way*. New York: Holt, Rinehart and Winston.

Leekley, T. B. 1965. *The World of Manabozho: Tales of the Chippewa Indians*. New York: Vanguard.

Leeks, Sybil. 1973. *Book of Herbs*. Nashville, TN: Thomas Nelson.

Legrand, Jacques. 1980. *Diamonds: Myth, Magic, and Reality*. New York: Crown Publishers.

Lehner, Ernest, and Johanna Lehner. 1960. *Folklore and Symbolism of Flowers, Plants and Trees*. New York: Tudor.

Leodhas, Nic Sorche. 1962. *Thistle and Thyme: Tales and Legends from Scotland*. New York: Holt, Rinehart and Winston.

Lerner, Carol. 1982. *A Biblical Garden*. New York: Morrow.

Levi-Strauss, Claude. 1969. *The Raw and the Cooked*. New York: Harper and Row.

_____. 1962. *Totemison*. New York: Mirlen.

Levy, G. Rachel. 1963. *Religious Conceptions of the Stone Age and Their Influence on European Thought*. New York: Harper and Row.

Levy-Bruhl, L. 1985. *How Natives Think*. Princeton, NJ: Princeton University Press.

Lexau, Joan M. 1969. *Crocodile and Hen*. New York: Harper.

Littledale, F. 1970. *Ghosts and Spirits of Many Lands*. Garden City, NY: Doubleday.

Livo, Norma J. 1984. "The Golden Spoon: Preserving Family History." *The National Storytelling Journal* 1 (Summer): 8-10.

_____. 1983. "Storytelling, An Art for All Ages." *Media and Methods* 10 (September): 24-26.

Livo, Norma J., and Sandra A. Rietz. 1987. *Storytelling Activities*. Littleton, CO: Libraries Unlimited.

_____. 1986. *Storytelling: Process and Practice*. Littleton, CO: Libraries Unlimited.

Lonnrot, Elias, comp. 1963. *The Kalevala*. Translated by Francis Peabody Magoun, Jr. Cambridge, MA: Harvard University Press.

Lord, Albert. 1960. *The Singer of Tales*. Cambridge, MA: Harvard University Press.

Lord, Albert B. 1964. *The Singer of Tales*. Cambridge, MA: Howard University Press.

Lowe, Patricia. 1970. *The Little Horse of Seven Colors and Other Portuguese Folktales*. New York: World.

Lowie, Robert A. 1970. *Primitive Religion*. New York: Liveright.

Lucas, Mrs. Edward, trans. 1979. *Sixty Fairy Tales of the Brothers Grimm*. New York: Weathervane.

Lum, Peter. 1948. *The Stars in Our Heaven*. New York: Pantheon.

MacDonald, M. R. 1982. *The Storyteller's Sourcebook: A Subject, Title and Motif Index to Folklore Collections for Children*. Detroit, MI: Neal Schuman, in association with Gale.

Macfarlan, Allan, ed. 1968/1985. *Handbook of American Indian Games*. New York: The Heritage Press/Dover.

Machart, Norman E. 1979. "Doing Oral History in the Elementary Grades." *Social Education* 43 (October): 470-80.

Macmillan, C. 1918. *Canadian Wonder Tales*. New York: Dodd.

Macrorie, Ken. 1980. *Searching Writing*. Rochelle Park, NJ: Hayden Book Co.

Maher, R. 1969. *The Blind Boy and Loon and Other Eskimo Myths*. New York: Day.

Makhlouf, Georgia. 1982. "Goha the Simple or the Wisdom of Folly." *The UNESCO Courier* (June): _____.

Manchee, Fred B. 1970. *Our Heritage of Flowers*. New York: Holt, Rinehart and Winston.

Manning-Sanders, Ruth. 1971a. *A Book of Charms and Changelings*. New York: Dutton.

_____. 1971b. *Gianni and the Ogre*. New York: Dutton.

_____. 1968a. *A Book of Mermaids*. New York: Dutton.

_____. 1968b. *The Glass Man and the Golden Bird: Hungarian Folk and Fairy Tales*. New York: Roy.

_____. 1962. *Red Indian Folk and Fairy Tales*. New York: Roy.

Mark, Alexandra. 1970. *Astrology for the Aquarian Age*. New York: Simon & Shuster.

Marriott, A. L. 1947. *Winter-telling Stories*. New York: Crowell.

Marriott, A. L., and C. K. Rachlin. 1968. *American Indian Mythology*. New York: Crowell.

Martin, Fran. 1975. *Raven-Who-Set-Things-Right: Indian Tales of the Northwest Coast*. New York: Harper and Row.

_____. 1951. *Nine Tales of Raven*. New York: Harper.

_____. 1950. *Nine Tales of Coyote*. New York: Harper.

Martin, Laura C. 1984. *Wildflower Folklore*. Charlotte, NC: The East Woods Press, Fast and McMillan Publishers, Inc.

Matson, E. N. 1972. *Legends of the Great Chiefs*. Nashville, TN: Nelson.

_____. 1968. *Longhouse Legends*. Camden, NJ: Nelson.

Mayo, Jeff. 1964. *Astrology*. London: The English University Press Ltd.

McCormack, Alan J. 1977. "Digging for Roots, A Learning Bonanza." *Learning* 6 (August/September): 58-66, 138, 144-45.

McDermott, B. B. 1975. *Sedna: An Eskimo Myth*. New York: Viking.

McDermott, Gerald. 1974. *Arrow to the Sun*. New York: Viking Press.

_____. 1972. *Anansi the Spider: A Tale from the Ashanti*. New York: Holt, Rinehart and Winston.

McDowell, John H. 1979. *Children's Riddling*. Bloomington, IN: Indiana University Press.

McMorland, A. n.d. *Children's Games from the British Tradition*. Washington, DC: Office of Museum Programs, Smithsonian Institution.

Mehaffy, George, and Thad Sitton. 1977. "Oral History: A Strategy That Works." *Social Education* 41 (May): 378-81.

Meltzer, Milton. 1984. *A Book about Names*. New York: Crowell.

Melzack, R. 1970. *Raven, Creator of the World*. Boston: Little, Brown.

_____. 1967. *The Day Tuk Became a Hunter, and Other Eskimo Stories*. New York: Dodd Mead.

Merriam, Eve. 1968. *Epaminondas*. Chicago: Follett.

Mobley, J. 1964. *Punia and the King of the Sharks: A Hawaiian Tale*. Chicago: Follett.

Monroe, Jean Guard, and Ray A. Williamson. 1987. *They Dance in the Sky*. Boston: Houghton Mifflin.

Monseau, Virginia, and William L. Knox. 1984. "Looking Back to the Future through Oral History." *English Journal* 73 (March): 49-51.

Montgomerie, Norah. 1964. *The Merry Little Fox and Other Animal Stories*. New York: Abelard-Schuman.

_____. 1961. *25 Fables*. New York: Abelard-Schuman.

Morris, William, and Mary Morris. 1962. *Dictionary of Word and Phrase Origins*. New York: Harper and Row.

Morton, Miriam, ed. 1967. "Simple Ivanushka." In *A Harvest of Russian Children's Literature*. Berkeley, CA: University of California Press.

Mullett, G. M. 1982. *Spider Woman Stories: Legends of the Hopi Indians*. Tucson, AZ: University of Arizona Press.

Nakosteen, Mehdi. 1974. *Mulla's Donkey and Other Friends*. Boulder, CO: University of Colorado Libraries.

Nancrede, Edith D., and Gertrude M. Smith. 1940. *Mother Goose Dances*. Chicago: H. T. Fitzsimons.

Natarella, Margaret A. 1979. "Getting Students Involved with Collecting Folklore." *Language Arts* 56, 2 (February): 156-58.

National Geographic Society. 1933. *The Book of Wildflowers*. Washington, DC: The National Geographic Society.

Neuenschwander, John A. 1976. *Oral History as a Teaching Approach*. Washington, DC: National Education Association.

Neumann, E. 1972. *The Great Mother: An Analysis of an Archetype*. New York: Princeton University Press.

Newell, E. W. 1970. *The Rescue of the Sun and Other Tales from the Far North*. Chicago: Albert Whitman.

Newell, William Wells. 1963. *Games and Songs of American Children*. New York: Dover.

Niehaus, Theodore. 1976. *Field Guide to North American Wildflowers*. New York: Alfred A. Knopf.

Notestein, Wallace. 1911/1965. *A History of Witchcraft in England from 1558 to 1718*. New York: Russell & Russell.

Olcott, William Tyler. 1911. *Star Lore of All Ages*. New York: Putnam.

Olson, Mary, and Barbara A. Hatcher. 1982. "Cultural Journalism: A Bridge to the Past." *Language Arts* 59, 1 (January): 46-50.

O'Neil, Paul. 1983. *Gemstones*. Alexandria, VA: Time-Life Books.

Ong, Walter J. 1982. *Orality and Literacy: The Technologizing of the Word*. New York: Methuen.

Opie, Iona, and Peter Opie. 1984. *Children's Games in Street and Playground*. New York: Oxford University Press.

_____. 1969. *Children's Games in Street and Playground*. London: Oxford University Press.

_____. 1959. *The Lore and Language of School Children*. London: Oxford University Press.

_____. 1955. *The Oxford Dictionary of Nursery Rhymes*. London: Oxford University Press.

_____. 1951. *The Oxford Dictionary of Nursery Rhymes*. London: Oxford University Press.

Oral History: What? Why? How? Guidelines for Oral History. 1975. ED 117 014. Washington, DC: ERIC Clearinghouse on Teacher Education; Harrisburg, PA: Pennsylvania State Department of Education.

Orlinsky, Harry M. 1970. *Studies in Biblical and Semitic Symbolism*. New York: KTAV Publishing House.

Page, Lou Williams. 1964. *A Dipper Full of Stars*. Chicago: Follett.

Palmer, Lawrence E. 1949. *Fieldbook of Natural History*. New York: McGraw-Hill.

Palmer, William R. 1957. *Why the North Star Stands Still*. Englewood Cliffs, NJ: Prentice-Hall.

Papashrily, George. 1946. *Yes and No Stories: A Book of Georgian Folk Tales*. New York: Harper.

Park, C. 1979. "Divination in Its Social Context." In *Magic, Witchcraft, and Curing*. Edited by John Middleton. Garden City, NY: Doubleday.

Parker, Arthur C. 1970. *Skunny Wunny: Seneca Indian Tales*. Chicago: Albert Whitman.

Parker, Derrek, and Julia Parker. 1971. *The Compleat Astrology*. New York: McGraw-Hill.

Paterson, John, and Katherine Paterson. 1986. *Consider the Lilies: Plants of the Bible*. New York: Thomas Y. Crowell.

Peabody, B. 1975. *The Winged Word*. Albany, NY: State University of New York Press.

Pearce, T. M. 1965. *New Mexico Place Names*. Albuquerque, NM: The University of New Mexico Press.

Pearl, Richard M. 1975. *Nature's Names for Colorado Communities*. Colorado Springs, CO: Earth Science Publishing Co.

Pellowski, Anne. 1987. *The Family Storytelling Handbook*. New York: Macmillan.

_____. 1984. *The Story Vine*. New York: Macmillan.

_____. 1980. *The Nine Crying Dolls*. New York: Philomel Books.

_____. 1977. *The World of Storytelling*. New York: Bowker.

Penney, G. J. 1953. *Tales of the Cheyennes*. New York: Houghton.

Perica, Esther. 1976. "SLJ/Practically Speaking." *School Library Journal* 22 (April): 49.

Perrottet, Oliver. 1987a. *Chinese Astrology: Interpreting the Revelations of the Celestial Messengers*. Wellingborough, Northamptonshire, England: Aquarian Press.

_____. 1987. *The Visual I Ching: A New Approach to the Ancient Chinese Oracle*. Topsfield, MA: Salem House.

Peters, Edward. 1978. *The Magician, the Witch and the Law*. Philadelphia, PA: University of Pennsylvania Press.

Peterson, Patricia. 1973. "The Foxfire Concept." *Media and Methods* 10 (November): 16-25.

Peterson, Roger Tory, and Margaret McKenny. 1968. *A Field Guide to Wildflowers of Northeastern and North Central North America*. Boston, MA: Houghton-Mifflin Co.

Picard, Barbara Leonie. 1958. *German Hero-Sagas and Folk Tales*. New York: Henry Z. Walck.

Piggot, Stuart. 1985. *The Druids*. New York: Thames and Hudson.

Platt, Rutherford. 1964. *This Green World*. New York: Dodd, Mead.

Powell, Claire. 1979. *The Meaning of Flowers: A Garland of Plant Lore and Symbolism from Popular Custom and Literature*. Boulder, CO: Shambhala.

Prieto, Mariana. 1973a. *Play It in Spanish: Spanish Games and Folksongs for Children*. New York: John Day.

_____. 1973b. *Spanish Games and Folk Songs for Children*. New York: John Day.

Pritchard, James B., ed. 1950. *Ancient Near East Texts Related to the Old Testaments*. Princeton, NJ: E. A. Speiser.

Radin, Paul. 1957. *Primitive Religion, Its Nature and Origin*. New York: Dover.

Raskin, Joseph, and Edith Raskin. 1971. *Tales Our Settlers Told*. New York: Lothrop, Lee and Shepard.

Rey, H. A. *The Stars*. 1970. Boston: Houghton Mifflin.

Reynolds, Barrie. 1963. *Magic, Divination and Witchcraft among the Barotse of Northern Rhodesia*. Berkeley, CA: University of California Press.

Reynolds, Sherrod. 1979. "Golden Hindesight, Homespun, Lagniappe, et al." *Teacher* 96 (March): 68-71.

Rickett, H. W. 1964. *The Odyssey Book of American Wildflowers*. New York: Golden Press.

Ridge, Alan D., ed. 1982. *Writing Local History*. (Publication No. 3.) Edmonton, Alberta, Canada: Historical Resources Division, Provincial Archives of Alberta.

Riordan, James. 1976. *Tales from Central Russia*. Harmondworth, Middlesex, England: Kestrel.

Ritchie, Jean. 1952. *The Swapping Song Book*. Fairhaven, NJ: Oxford University Press.

Robertson, Dorothy L. 1971. *Fairy Tales from the Philippines*. New York: Dodd.

Robinson, G., and D. Hill. 1976. *Coyote the Trickster: Legends of the North American Indians*. New York: Crane Russak.

Rockwell, Anne. 1975. *The Three Bears and Fifteen Other Stories*. New York: Thomas Y. Crowell.

_____. 1972. *The Dancing Stars*. New York: Crowell.

Rose, Anne. 1982. *Pot Full of Luck*. New York: Lothrop.

Rosen, Harold. 1986. "The Importance of Story." *Language Arts*, 63, 3 (March): 26-37.

_____. 1985. *Stories and Meanings*. Sheffield, England: National Association for the Teaching of English; and Portsmouth, NH: Heinemann.

Ross, Eulalie S. 1958. *The Buried Treasure and Other Picture Tales*. Philadelphia, PA: Lippincott.

Running, Corrine. 1949. *When Coyote Walked the Earth: Indian Tales of the Pacific Northwest*. New York: Holt.

Runot. 1944. *Kalevala*. Duluth, MN: Paivalehden Kirjapainossa.

Sakade, Florence. 1958. *Japanese Children's Favorite Stories*. Rutland, VT: Tuttle.

Sanacore, Joseph. 1981. "Creative Writing and Storytelling: A Bridge from High School to Preschool." Report from Phi Delta Kappa, 8th and Union, Bloomington, IN 47402. (9 pp.)

Sanecki, Kay N. 1974. *The Complete Book of Herbs*. New York: Macmillan.

Schaeffer, Elizabeth. 1972. *Dandelion, Pokeweed, and Goosefoot*. Reading, MA: Young Scott Books.

Scheer, G. P. 1968. *Cherokee Animal Tales*. New York: Holiday.

Schnacke, Dick. 1973. *American Folk Toys*. New York: Putnam.

Schram, Penninnah. 1987. *Jewish Stories One Generation Tells Another*. Northvale, NJ: Jason Aronson.

Schwartz, Alvin. 1987. *Unriddling*. New York: Harper and Row.

_____. 1975. *Whoppers: Tall Tales and Other Lies*. New York: Lippincott.

Seeger, Ruth Crawford. 1948. *American Folk Songs for Children*. Garden City, NY: Doubleday.

Seligmann, Kurt. 1948. *Magic, Supernaturalism and Religion*. New York: Grosset and Dunlap.

Selsam, Millicent B. 1986. *Mushrooms*. New York: Morrow Co.

Shadowitz, Albert, and Peter Walsh. 1976. *The Dark Side of Knowledge*. Reading, MA: Addison-Wesley.

Shannon, George. 1979. "Storytelling and the Schools." *English Journal* 68, 5 (May): 50-51.

Sheehan, E. 1970. *Folk and Fairy Tales from Around the World*. New York: Dodd.

Sherlock, Philip M. 1966. *West Indian Folk Tales*. New York: Walck.

_____. 1954. *Anansi the Spider Man: Jamaican Folk Tales*. New York: Crowell.

Shipley, Joseph T. 1962. *Word Games for Play and Power*. Englewood Cliffs, NJ: Prentice-Hall.

_____. 1960. *Playing with Words*. Englewood Cliffs, NJ: Prentice-Hall.

Shosteck, Robert. 1974. *Flowers and Plants*. New York: Quadrangle; The New York Times Book Co.

Shumway, Gary L., and William G. Hartley. 1973. *An Oral History Primer*. Box 11894, Salt Lake City, Utah 84111.

Siddique, Ashral, and Marilyn Lerch. 1961. *Toontoonie Pie and Other Tales from Pakistan*. Cleveland, OH: World.

Simon, Tony, ed. 1958. *Ripsnorters and Ribticklers: Tall Tales from United States Folklore*. New York: Scholastic.

Singer, Isaac Bashevis. 1966. *Zlateh the Goat*. New York: Harper and Row.

Sitton, Thad. 1979. "The Fire That Lit Up Learning." *Teacher* 96 (March): 65-67.

Sitton, Thad, George A. Nehaffy, and O. L. Davis, Jr. 1983. *Oral History: A Guide for Teachers (and Others)*. Austin, TX: University of Texas Press.

Skolnik, Peter L. 1974. *Jump Rope*. New York: Workman.

Smart, Ninian, and Richard D. Hecht, eds. 1982. *Sacred Texts of the World, a Universal Anthology*. New York: Crossroad.

Smith, Frank. 1988. *Understanding Reading: A Psycholinguistic Analysis of Reading and Learning to Read*. New York: Longman.

Snow, L. 1974. "Folk Medical Beliefs and Their Implications for Care of Patients." *Annals of Internal Medicine* 81: 82-96.

South, Malcolm, ed. 1987. *Mythical and Fabulous Creatures*. New York: Greenwood.

Spence, Lewis. 1985. *North American Indians*. New York: Avenel.

Sperry, Margaret. 1971. *Scandinavian Stories*. New York: Franklin Watts.

_____. 1952. *The Hen That Saved the World*. New York: Day.

Spicer, Dorothy G. 1964. *13 Monsters*. New York: Coward-McCann.

Stahl, Mark B. 1979. "Using Traditional Oral Stories in the English Classroom." *English Journal* 68, 7 (October): 33-36.

Stupka, Arthur. 1965. *Wildflowers in Color*. New York: Harper and Row.

Summers, Montague. 1956. *The History of Witchcraft and Demonology*. New Hyde Park, NY: University Books.

Taylor, Archer. 1951. *English Riddles from the Oral Tradition*. Berkeley, CA: University of California Press.

Thomas, Katherine Elwes. 1930. *The Real Personages of Mother Goose*. New York: Lothrop, Lee & Shepard.

Thompson, Paul. 1978. *The Voice of the Past: Oral History*. Oxford, England: Oxford University Press.

Thompson, Stith. 1977. *The Folktale*. Berkeley, CA: University of California Press.

_____. 1968. *One Hundred Favorite Folktales*. Bloomington, IN: Indiana University Press.

_____. 1955-1958. *The Motif Index of Folk-Literature*. Bloomington, IN: Indiana University Press.

Thompson, V. L. 1969a. *Hawaiian Legends of Tricksters and Riddlers*. New York: Holiday.

_____. 1969b. *Hawaiian Tales of Heroes and Champions*. New York: Holiday.

_____. 1966. *Hawaiian Myths of Earth, Sea, and Sky*. New York: Holiday.

Thorndike, Lynn. 1923. *A History of Magic and Experimental Science during the First Thirteen Centuries of Our Era*, vol. I. New York: Columbia University Press.

Toelken, Barre. 1979. *The Dynamics of Folklore*. Boston: Houghton Mifflin.

Tolkien, J. R. R. 1986. *The Fellowship of the Ring*. Westminster, MD: Random.

Toor, Francis. 1960. *The Golden Carnation and Other Stories Told in Italy*. New York: Praeger.

Tooze, Ruth. 1969. *The Wonderful Wooden Peacock Flying Machine and Other Tales of Ceylon*. New York: Day.

_____. 1968. *Three Tales of Turtle: Ancient Folktales from the Far East*. New York: Day.

Toye, W. 1969. *How Summer Came to Canada*. New York: Walck.

Tracy, Hugh. 1968. *The Lion on the Path and Other African Stories*. New York: Praeger.

Trevor-Roper, H. 1970. "The European Witch-Craze and Social Change." In *Witchcraft and Sorcery*. Edited by Max Marwick. Hammondsworth, England: Penguin Books.

Trout, Lawana. 1977. "The Student as Folklorist." *English Journal* 66 (May): 83-87.

Tyler, Royall, ed. 1987. *Japanese Tales*. New York: Pantheon.

Urbanek, Mae. 1974. *Wyoming Place Names*. Boulder, CO: Johnson Publishing Co.

Van Gennep, Arnold. 1960. *The Rites of Passage*. Chicago: University of Chicago Press.

Vansina, Jan. 1961. *Oral Tradition: A Study in Historical Methodology*. Translated by H. M. Wright. Chicago: Aldine.

van Straalen, Alice. 1968. *The Book of Holidays around the World*. New York: E. P. Dutton.

Vigfusson, Gudbrand, and F. York Powell. 1883. *Corpus Poeticum Boreale: The Poetry of the Old Northern Tongue*. Oxford, England: Clarendon Press.

Vinton, I. 1970. *The Folkways Omnibus of Children's Games*. Harrisburg, PA: Stackpole Books.

_____. 1898. *The Traditional Games of England, Scotland and Ireland*. London: Davis Nutt.

Vo Dinh. 1970. *The Toad Is the Emperor's Uncle: Animal Folktales from Vietnam*. Garden City, NY: Doubleday.

Voelker, Robert G. 1981. "How to Start a Family History." *Modern Maturity* 24 (August-September): 36-37.

Walker, Barbara G. 1988. *The Woman's Dictionary of Symbols and Sacred Objects*. San Francisco: Harper and Row.

_____. 1986. *The Woman's Encyclopedia of Myths and Secrets*. San Francisco: Harper and Row.

_____. 1983. *The Woman's Encyclopedia of Myths and Secrets*. San Francisco: Harper and Row.

Walker, Barbara K., and Warren P. Walker. 1961. *Nigerian Folk Tales*. New Brunswick, NJ: Rutgers.

Walters, Derek. 1987. *Chinese Astrology: Interpreting the Revelations of the Celestial Messengers*. Wellingborough, Northamptonshire, England: Aquarian Press.

Ward, Margarete. 1982. *Gong Hee Fot Choy*. Berkeley, CA: Celestial Arts.

Waters, Frank. 1963. *The Book of Hopi*. New York: Ballantine.

Weitzman, David. 1975. *My Backyard History Book*. Boston: Little, Brown.

Wells, Patricia Atkinson, and Patricia Hall. 1986. *Storytelling: A Folklorist's Perspective*. Homecoming '86. The Tennessee Arts Commission and Homecoming '86 Office of the State of Tennessee.

Weslager, C. A. 1973. *Magic Medicines of the Indians*. New York: New American Library.

Whistler, Nancy. 1979. *Oral History, Workshop Guide*. Denver, CO: Denver Public Library.

Whitney, Thomas. 1972. *In a Certain Kingdom: Twelve Russian Fairy Tales*. New York: Macmillan.

Wiggin, Kate D. 1954. *Tales of Laughter: A Third Fairy Book*. Garden City, NY: Doubleday.

Wiggin, Kate D., and Nora A. Smith. 1967. *The Fairy Ring*. Garden City, NY: Doubleday.

_____. 1936. *Tales of Wonder: A Fourth Fairy Book*. Garden City, NY: Doubleday.

Wigginton, Eliot. 1977. "The Foxfire Approach: It Can Work for You." *Media and Methods* 14 (November): 48-52.

_____. 1973. *Foxfire II*. New York: Anchor Press/Doubleday.

Williams, E. 1963. *Round the World Fairy Tales*. New York: Warne.

Williams, J. 1979. *The Surprising Things Maui Did*. New York: Four Winds.

Williams, Lynnda. 1982. "Storytelling, Oral Literature or ... Any Other Name Would Sound So Sweet." *English Journal* 71, 7 (November): 36-37.

Wilson, Barbara K. 1968. *Greek Fairy Tales*. Chicago: Follett.

Winn, Marie, ed. 1974. *The Fireside Book of Fun and Game Songs*. New York: Simon and Schuster.

_____. 1970. *What Shall We Do and Allee Galloo! — Play Songs and Singing Games for Young Children*. New York: Harper and Row.

Withers, Carl A. 1965. *I Saw a Rocket Walk a Mile*. New York: Holt.

Withers, Carl A., and Sula Benet. 1954. *The American Riddle Book*. New York: Abelard-Schuman.

Wood, Audrey, and Don Wood. 1987. *Heckedy Peg*. Niles, IL: Harcourt Brace Jovanovich.

Wood, Pamela. 1975. *You and Aunt Arie*. Washington, DC: Institutional Development and Economic Affairs Service, Inc. (IDEAS).

Wood, Ray, 1952. *Fun in American Folk Rhymes*. Philadelphia, PA: Lippincott.

Wyndham, Robert. 1971. *Tales People Tell in China*. New York: Messner.

Yellow Robe, R. 1979. *Tonweya and the Eagles and Other Lakota Indian Tales*. New York: Dial.

Zajdler, Zoe. 1959. *Polish Fairy Tales*. Chicago: Follett.

Zeitlin, Steven J., Amy J. Kotkin, and Holly Cutting Baker. 1982. *A Celebration of American Family Folklore*. New York: Pantheon.

Zemach, Margot. 1963. *The Three Sillies*. New York: Holt, Rinehart and Winston.

Zimmerman, William. 1982. *How to Tape Instant Oral Biographies*. New York: Guarionex.

Zipes, Jack. 1987. *The Complete Fairy Tales of the Brothers Grimm*. New York: Bantam.

Index